American Traditions in Watercolor

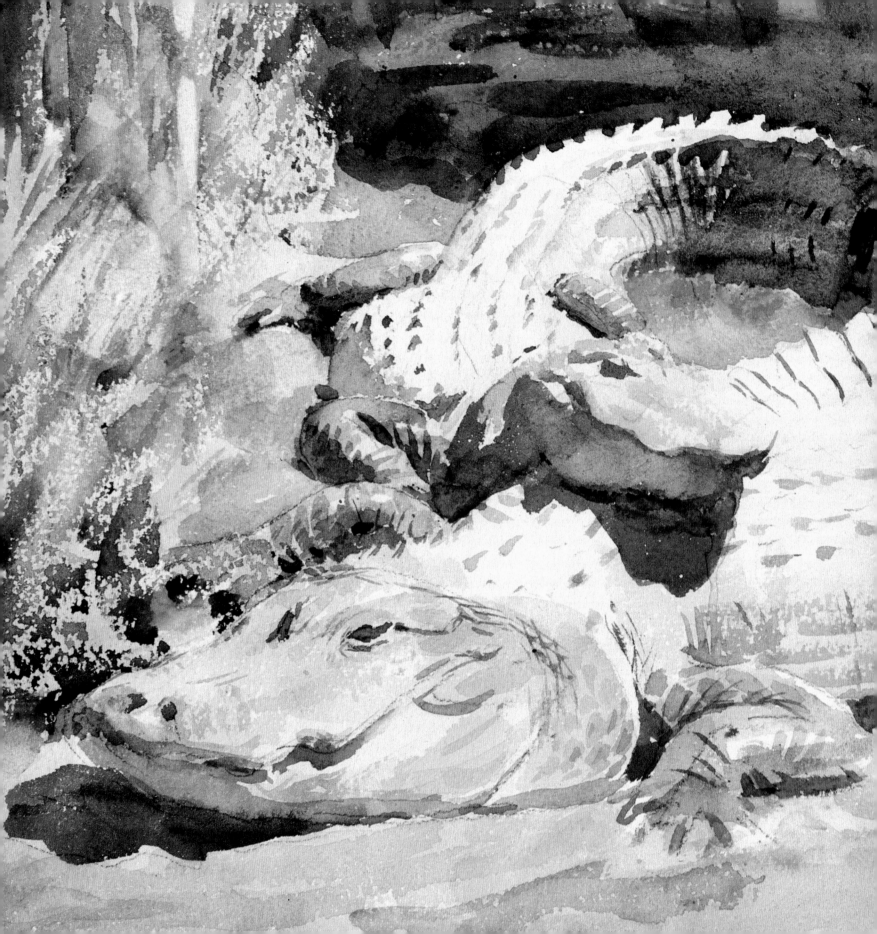

Edited by Susan E. Strickler

American Traditions in Watercolor

The Worcester Art Museum Collection

Worcester Art Museum
Abbeville Press Publishers New York

Manuscript editor: Janet G. Silver
Editor, Abbeville Press: Nancy Grubb
Designer: Florence Cassen Mayers
Production manager: Dana Cole

Front cover:
Winslow Homer, *Boys and Kitten*, 1873 (detail of
plate 59)

Back cover:
Carolyn Brady, *Last Red Tulips (Baltimore Spring 1984)*,
1984 (detail of plate 113)

Frontispiece:
John Singer Sargent, *Muddy Alligators*, 1917 (detail of
plate 82)

This book was published on the occasion of the exhibition *American Traditions in Watercolor: The Worcester Art
Museum Collection*, organized by Susan E. Strickler,
curator of American art, Worcester Art Museum. The
exhibition was on view at Worcester Art Museum,
Worcester, Massachusetts, March 8–May 10, 1987;
National Museum of American Art, Smithsonian Institution, Washington, D.C., September 17–November 22,
1987; and The Minneapolis Institute of Arts, Minneapolis,
Minnesota, December 13, 1987–February 14, 1988.

This book and the exhibition were made possible by
generous grants from Digital Equipment Corporation;
The Luce Fund for Scholarship in American Art, a program of the Henry Luce Foundation, Inc.; and the
National Endowment for the Arts.

Library of Congress Cataloging-in-Publication Data

Worcester Art Museum.
American traditions in watercolor.

Bibliography: p.
Includes index.
1. Watercolor painting, American—Catalogs.
2. Watercolor painting—19th century—United States—Catalogs.
3. Watercolor painting—20th century—United States—Catalogs.
4. Watercolor painting—Massachusetts—Worcester—Catalogs.
5. Worcester Art Museum—Catalogs.
I. Strickler, Susan E. II. Title.
ND1807.W67   1987   759.13′074′01443   86-14183
ISBN 0-89659-674-5
ISBN 0-89659-680-X (pbk.)

First edition

Contents

Preface

American Traditions in Watercolor is a celebration of American creativity, and Digital
Equipment Corporation is pleased to make
possible its showing in Worcester, Minneapolis, and Washington, D.C.

We believe strongly that corporate
support for the arts is both a privilege and
an obligation. All of us at Digital are
delighted to have this opportunity for partnership with our friends at the Worcester
Art Museum and to bring you this outstanding collection.

We hope you enjoy it.

Kenneth H. Olsen
President
Digital Equipment Corporation

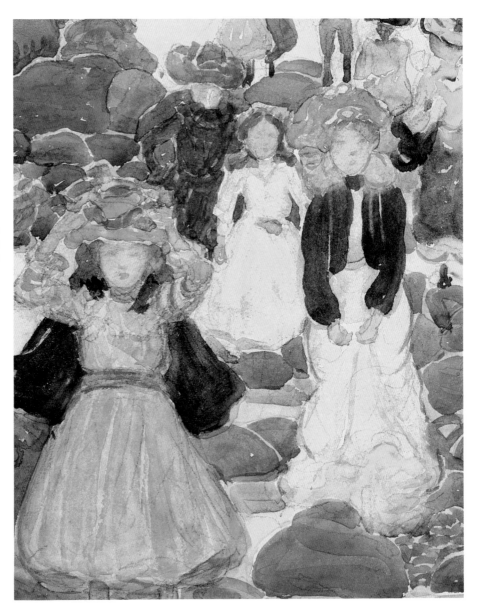

1
Maurice B. Prendergast
Low Tide, Beachmont, 1902–4
(detail of plate 89)

6

Foreword

This publication is the first to document the American watercolor collection of the Worcester Art Museum, and it is part of a continuing program to catalogue specific collections of exceptional importance. The traveling exhibition that coincides with the publication of this book supplements our effort to bring many of these watercolors to a national audience for the first time.

We are particularly grateful to Susan E. Strickler, curator of American art, who initiated this project and ably directed every aspect of organizing the exhibition and publishing the catalogue. Her devotion to this endeavor has been the key to its success.

Research for this catalogue began over four years ago, when the museum was awarded a generous grant from the Henry Luce Foundation. Without such crucial support, we could not have begun this extensive undertaking. We are also grateful to the National Endowment for the Arts, which provided additional funding through the Utilization of Museum Resources program.

The successful culmination of this entire effort could not have been realized without the generous support of our national corporate sponsor, Digital Equipment Corporation, which marks its thirtieth anniversary this year. Though now an international company, Digital, like so many of the masters of watercolor featured in this catalogue, has its roots in New England. Therefore, we are especially grateful to Digital, one of our leading corporate neighbors and an outstanding supporter of the arts, for enabling the museum to share with a wide audience its wonderful treasure of American watercolors.

James A. Welu
Director

Acknowledgments

This publication and the accompanying traveling exhibition could not have been achieved without the generosity of many organizations and individuals. I wish to extend a particular note of thanks to the Henry Luce Foundation, which over the past few years has made invaluable contributions to the study of our nation's culture through its Luce Fund for Scholarship in American Art. The National Endowment for the Arts also provided significant funding for this project through its Utilization of Museum Resources program.

Many individuals who have graciously contributed to the realization of this book and exhibition have our deep appreciation. As the director of the project, I would like to thank all the scholars who wrote the essays and entries that constitute this volume. The manuscript editor, Janet G. Silver, helped to sharpen many thoughts and provide cohesiveness among the writings of so many contributors; I am personally indebted to her for advice and support during the preparation of the manuscript. Norma Steinberg, project assistant, supervised much of the photography for this publication, compiled the checklist and bibliography, and saw to a myriad of details with unfailing good cheer. Roberta Gordon typed and retyped the entire text with remarkable precision and managed to untangle many a seemingly impenetrable manuscript page; Virginia Harding helped to expedite this process in the midst of a very demanding schedule. Ron White photographed the entire collection, providing the foundation for the high quality reproductions in this book. In addition to her fine essay comparing the techniques of Winslow Homer and John Singer Sargent, conservator Judith Walsh contributed invaluable information on artists' materials and techniques to me and many of the authors; she also treated a number of the watercolors in the collection. James A. Welu, formerly as chief curator and now director, has offered encouragement throughout the preparation of this project. I wish to add personal thanks to Tom L. Freudenheim, our past director, who was very supportive of my efforts during the early planning stages.

Other members of the staff who generously offered assistance are: Kathy Berg, Cynthia Bolshaw, and Peter Andrews, librarians; Sally R. Freitag, registrar; Sandra Petrie Hachey, coordinator of photographic services; Thomas Keaney, John Reynolds, and John Rossetti, preparators. Anne Gibson, director of publications, graciously offered counsel and assistance during the preparation of this book. The Andrew W. Mellon Foundation helped to fund staff salaries related to the planning and research of this book and the exhibition.

Many research facilities made their collections available, and on behalf of all the authors, I wish to express our appreciation to: The American Watercolor Society; Archives of American Art (especially Boston, New York, and Washington, D.C., offices); library of the Brandywine River Museum, Chadds Ford, Pennsylvania; New York Public Library; library of the Whitney Museum of American Art; and the Worcester Public Library. We would also like to acknowledge the assistance of: Kenneth Bendiner, University of Wisconsin; Suzanne Bergeron and Henrietta Tye, Bowdoin College Museum of Art, Brunswick, Maine; Craigen Weston Bowen, Center for Technical Studies, Fogg Art Museum, Harvard University; Georgia B. Bumgardner, American Antiquarian Society, Worcester; Margaret Burchenal and

Judy Hayward, Portland Museum of Art, Portland, Maine; Anne Corkadel; David Findley, formerly associate conservator, Worcester Art Museum; Abigail Booth Gerdts, National Academy of Design, New York; Dorothy Gleason, Worcester Historical Museum; Jenny Johnson, Map Room, Clark University, Worcester; Dan Burne Jones; Richard J. Koke; Florence Levins, Cropsey House, Hastings-on-Hudson, New York; Noreen O'Gara, Boston Public Library; Pam Read, Alice and Hamilton Fish Library, Garrison-on-Hudson, New York; Christine Ruggere, Van Pelt Library, University of Pennsylvania, Philadelphia; David Shayt, National Museum of American History, Smithsonian Institution, Washington, D.C.; and Catherine Stover.

We are delighted to bring highlights of this collection to audiences outside New England and wish to thank our colleagues in Washington, D.C., and Minneapolis who also host the exhibition, especially Charles C. Eldredge, director of the National Museum of American Art, Elizabeth Broun, chief curator, and Joann Moser, curator of graphic arts; and Alan Shestack, director of the Minneapolis Institute of Arts, and Mary Mancuso, exhibitions coordinator. Similarly, Abbeville Press has been a congenial partner in producing this publication: special thanks go to editor Nancy Grubb for her enthusiastic support and expert guidance, to Florence Cassen Mayers for the handsome design of this book, and to Dana Cole for her careful attention to every aspect of its production.

Finally, I welcome this opportunity to acknowledge the generous sponsorship of Digital Equipment Corporation, whose funding supported the national tour of the exhibition and assisted with the publication of this book. I am especially grateful to Nancy A. Dube, manager of corporate community relations, and Lewis T. Karabatsos, corporate community relations programs manager, for their initial enthusiasm for this project and their continued interest in our endeavor to share the riches of this splendid collection with you.

Susan E. Strickler
Curator of American Art

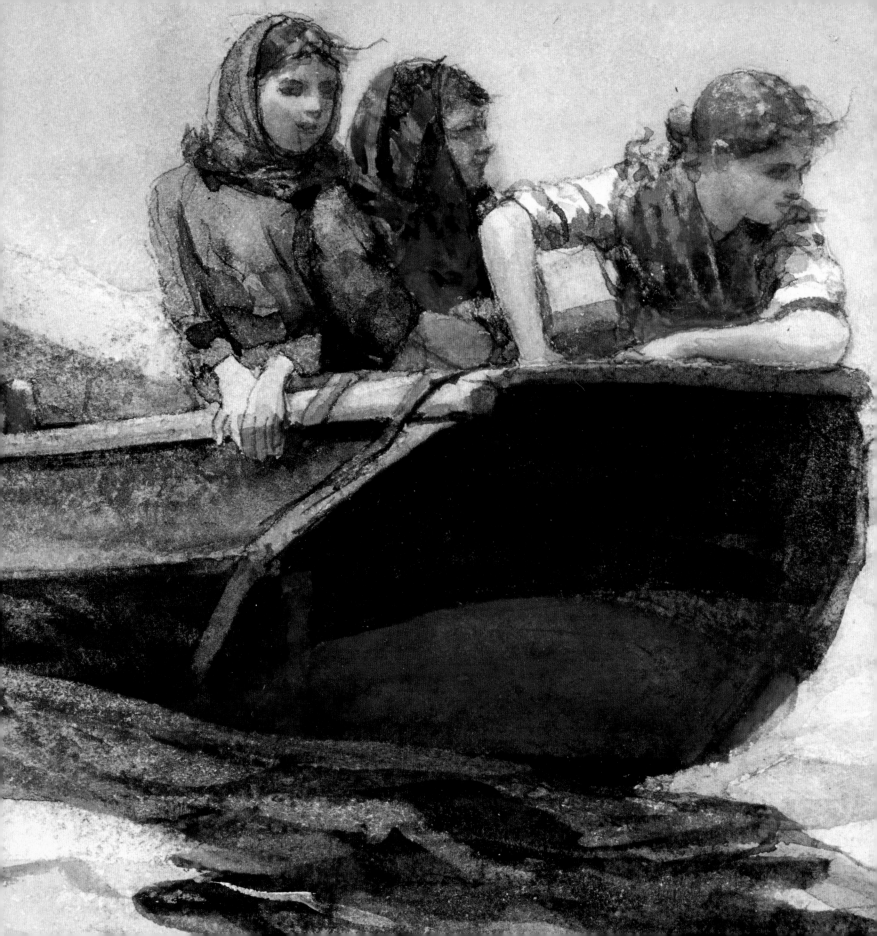

American Watercolors at Worcester

Susan E. Strickler

The Worcester Art Museum has one of the finest collections of American watercolors in public hands and certainly one of the foremost of any institution of comparable size. However, the museum has never professed to have a systematic approach to forming a comprehensive collection in this specific area. Indeed, its holdings, which are particularly rich in turn-of-the-century masters such as Winslow Homer, John Singer Sargent, Childe Hassam, John La Farge, and Maurice Prendergast, lack examples by such significant watercolorists of the twentieth century as Arthur Dove, John Marin, and Charles Demuth. The impetus for acquiring watercolors, especially during the 1910s, was the desire on the part of museum trustees and directors to build a representative collection of work in all media by recent American masters. Fortunately for us today, the early leaders of the Worcester Art Museum acknowledged watercolor to be a serious artistic medium, and they recognized the sheets by Homer and Sargent, in particular, to be powerful expressions of these artists' outstanding talents rather than merely self-indulgent exercises providing respite from their more important work in oil.

Founded in 1896 chiefly by a group of businessmen, the Worcester Art Museum was an ambitious and progressive enterprise for an industrial city at the turn of the century. It has grown today into one of New England's largest museums, with comprehensive collections covering fifty centuries of Western and Eastern art. In the early decades of this century, the museum became a leading acquisitor of watercolors and, in the case of Homer and Sargent, competed for works with larger institutions such as the Metropolitan Museum of Art, Boston's Museum of Fine Arts, and the Brooklyn Museum. The first major acquisition came in 1908 with the purchase of Homer's *Old Friends*, from E. L. Knoedler of the artist's gallery, M. Knoedler & Co., in New York (plate 3). Still a favorite with the museum's public, this Adirondacks scene was selected by one of the trustees, Mrs. Charlotte E. W. Buffington of Worcester. Upon her death in 1935, Mrs. Buffington bequeathed to the museum a group of watercolors and oils by Childe Hassam. The perspicacity of Mrs. Buffington's taste was remarked upon by the dealer, who wrote, "In my experience there are not many ladies who care for this broad manner, never-the-less, it is

2
Winslow Homer (1836–1910)
Crab Fishing, 1883
(detail of plate 62)

11

3

This group of works by Winslow Homer was arranged as a memorial to the artist at the *Eighth Annual Watercolor Exhibition*, the Pennsylvania Academy of the Fine Arts in 1910. *Old Friends*, lent by the Worcester Art Museum, is at the far left in the second tier. At the center of the top row is *The Turkey Buzzard*, which the museum would acquire seven years later.

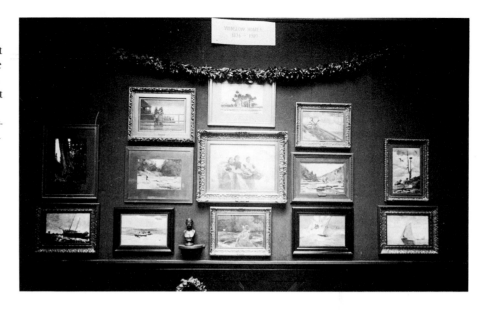

a good example and one which will prove to be a pleasure to look at."[1] Although today this dealer's comment may seem trite, if not a bit condescending, it does underscore the fact that many of Mrs. Buffington's generation had initially criticized Homer's watercolors as rough and unfinished, even trivial, in subject. However, in hindsight, this poignant composition by Homer provided an auspicious beginning and a high standard by which future acquisitions could be measured.

To a large extent, the subsequent purchases reflect the eye and intuition of the museum's first professional director, Philip J. Gentner (plate 4), whose nine-year tenure began in November 1908.[2] Trained at Harvard University in English literature, Gentner had lived abroad for several years and studied for a time at the American School of Classical Studies in Rome before his appointment as director. Although he came to Worcester with an expertise in medieval and Italian Renaissance art, he soon displayed a strong interest in contemporary American art, both through the purchases he recommended and the exhibitions he mounted. Gentner traveled frequently to see the work of living artists. Like the Corcoran Gallery of Art, the Carnegie Institute, and the Pennsylvania Academy of the Fine Arts, the Worcester Art Museum mounted annual exhibitions of recent American art, which were an integral part of its programming during its first fifteen years. Gentner seized upon these opportunities to bring good contemporary art to the Worcester public. Several of the artists whose watercolors were acquired during Gentner's directorship, including Homer, Hassam, Sargent, and Frank W. Benson, had been represented by oil paintings in the annuals, and thus their work was known to both the museum and its public.[3]

Among Gentner's greatest acquisitions in any field were the twelve Homer and eleven Sargent watercolors he purchased in 1911 and 1917,

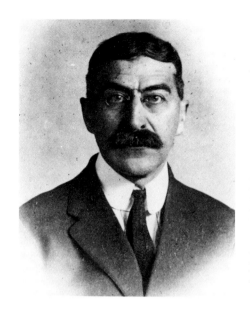

4

Philip J. Gentner during his tenure as director of the Worcester Art Museum.

respectively. Early in his directorship, Gentner revealed his enthusiasm for Homer's talents. Apparently he visited the artist at his Prout's Neck studio, where he saw a group of watercolors that Homer considered to be his best but had refused to sell. To the artist's dealer, Roland Knoedler, Gentner expressed his wish to exhibit and acquire the very best of Homer's work, for "I want every opportunity of impressing upon our trustees and the public here, that he is by all odds the greatest of our truly American painters."[4] The tone of urgency in Gentner's subsequent letters to Knoedler, following the artist's death in September 1910, suggests that he anticipated a rush in the art world for Homer's watercolors. His most serious competition would come from the museums in Boston, Brooklyn, and New York.

Gentner evidently negotiated an "agreement" with Knoedler in December 1910 that he would have first refusal of any significant Homers—watercolors or oils—that came through their gallery. Several times in early 1911 he tried through both Knoedler and the artist's brother, Charles Homer, to get hold of the watercolors in the Prout's Neck studio in the hope of selecting a group for acquisition.[5] First refusal had apparently already been promised to the Metropolitan Museum of Art, which purchased twelve in late 1910, following the Memorial Exhibition mounted there; however, Worcester was able to acquire three from the group.[6] Gentner's enthusiasm for Homer's work, however, was not satiated.

From December 1910 through May 1912 at least seventy-five watercolors were shipped to Worcester by Knoedler and Charles Homer for Gentner's consideration. "I personally am in favor of the purchase of all we can get at a reasonable price," Gentner wrote to Knoedler, "although some of my authorities are restive about the raised sum of the last batch. Kindly remember that Worcester is not closely in touch with the art-world and that I have great difficulty in making people understand why 'such things' should bring 'such prices.'"[7] The first Homers that Knoedler sent in late December 1910 were offered at $540 each; the next group, shipped in early January 1911, was priced at $675 each. By the end of January, Knoedler listed most of the watercolors in the range of $750 to $1,000 each (plate 5).

By February 1911 the twelve watercolors that Gentner had selected were approved for purchase, and these sheets still form the nucleus of the museum's holdings. The trustees were evidently satisfied with this group. Gentner's letter in January 1911 to trustee Helen Bigelow Merriman, wife of the museum's first president, hinted that his appreciation of Homer may not have been unreservedly supported by the board: "I am grateful to you and Dr. Merriman for favoring the purchase of the Homers at the very moment when the fates were turning against them."[8] 'Although many more watercolors were sent to Worcester for consideration, there was only one additional purchase in 1917, *The Turkey Buzzard*. As an example from Homer's last series of watercolors, this was a fitting conclusion to Gentner's endeavor.[9] Several important gifts have since filled out

13

5

Price list for thirty Homer watercolors offered to the Worcester Art Museum by E. L. Knoedler, January 27, 1911. From these thirty, the museum purchased four (numbers 12 [now titled *Sunset, Prout's Neck*], 16, 24, and 25).

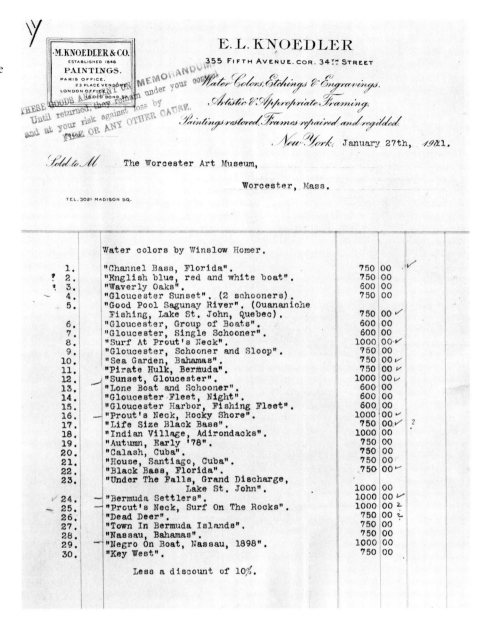

E. L. KNOEDLER

·M.KNOEDLER & CO.·
ESTABLISHED 1846
PAINTINGS.
PARIS OFFICE,
23 PLACE VENDÔME
LONDON OFFICE
15 OLD BOND STREET

355 FIFTH AVENUE. COR. 34TH STREET

Water Colors, Etchings & Engravings.

Artistic & Appropriate Framing.

Paintings restored, Frames repaired and regilded.

New York, January 27th, 1911.

Sold to M.   The Worcester Art Museum,

Worcester, Mass.

TEL. 3021 MADISON SQ.

	Water colors by Winslow Homer.		
1.	"Channel Bass, Florida".	750	00
? 2.	"English blue, red and white boat".	750	00
? 3.	"Waverly Oaks".	600	00
4.	"Gloucester Sunset". (2 schooners).	750	00
5.	"Good Pool Sagunay River". (Ouananiche Fishing, Lake St. John, Quebec).	750	00
6.	"Gloucester, Group of Boats".	600	00
7.	"Gloucester, Single Schooner".	600	00
8.	"Surf At Prout's Neck".	1000	00
9.	"Gloucester, Schooner and Sloop".	750	00
10.	"Sea Garden, Bahamas".	750	00
11.	"Pirate Hulk, Bermuda".	750	00
12.	"Sunset, Gloucester".	1000	00
13.	"Lone Boat and Schooner".	600	00
14.	"Gloucester Fleet, Night".	600	00
15.	"Gloucester Harbor, Fishing Fleet".	600	00
16.	"Prout's Neck, Rocky Shore".	1000	00
17.	"Life Size Black Bass".	750	00
18.	"Indian Village, Adirondacks".	1000	00
19.	"Autumn, Early '78".	750	00
20.	"Calash, Cuba".	750	00
21.	"House, Santiago, Cuba".	750	00
22.	"Black Bass, Florida".	750	00
23.	"Under The Falls, Grand Discharge, Lake St. John".	1000	00
24.	"Bermuda Settlers".	1000	00
25.	"Prout's Neck, Surf On The Rocks".	1000	00
26.	"Dead Deer".	750	00
27.	"Town In Bermuda Islands".	750	00
28.	"Nassau, Bahamas".	750	00
29.	"Negro On Boat, Nassau, 1898".	1000	00
30.	"Key West".	750	00
	Less a discount of 10%.		

the Homer watercolor collection, such as *The Swing*, from his early period at his brother's farm in West Townsend, Massachusetts; *Crab Fishing*, from his English years; and most recently *The Garden Gate, Bahamas*, documenting his trip to Nassau. These final acquisitions helped to form a survey of most periods and aspects of Homer's work in the medium.

Efforts to secure watercolors by John Singer Sargent began about 1913, and they were more protracted, despite the fact that Sargent's association with the city of Worcester predated the founding of the museum.[10] In the summer of 1890 Sargent had come to paint portraits of several prominent Worcester citizens, whose families would become closely asso-

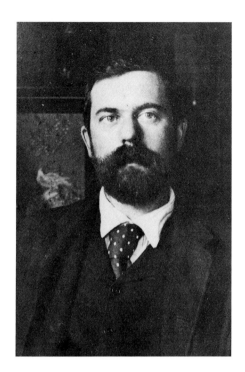

6
This photograph of John Singer Sargent was taken during one of his visits to Worcester in the summer of 1890 by Frederick Haven Pratt, the son of Frederick S. Pratt.

ciated with the museum during its early years (plate 6). One in particular was Frederick S. Pratt, an industrialist turned artist who became a museum trustee and served as acting director in 1908 and in 1917–18. Sargent had painted Pratt's daughter Katharine in 1890 and had also sketched with Pratt and offered him some instruction in painting. Thus, Pratt was the logical choice to contact the artist about the museum's desire to purchase some of his watercolors.

On June 13, 1913, Pratt visited Sargent in his London studio, at which time the artist promised Worcester first refusal of his next group of watercolors, after he had fulfilled the Metropolitan Museum of Art's request. By this time, Sargent's watercolors were in considerable demand. He gave increasingly more attention to his work in watercolor as his portrait and mural commissions weighed more heavily on him, and major museums began to acquire the ebullient, light-filled sketches that he often made on vacation. In 1909 the Brooklyn Museum acquired a group of eighty-three through the generosity of a patron; in 1912 the Museum of Fine Arts in Boston purchased forty-five; and in 1915 the Metropolitan bought eleven.

As a follow-up to Pratt's initial visit, Gentner met with Sargent in Florence the next summer. His report to Pratt, who had provided him with a letter of introduction, gives us a glimpse of Sargent's geniality and Gentner's assessment of his talents as a watercolorist:

> I have wanted very much to thank you for the favorable way in which Mr. Sargent received me and my proposals. I had two good interviews with him, and was a guest at luncheon of him and his delightful sister. I liked him immensely just as a wholesome, big-natured, wholly natural man, and he neither sought nor was bothered with tributes to his "genius." In short, I felt a lot better for having met him.
>
> He had come to the conclusion we were not interested in his water-colors. I soon persuaded him to the contrary, and he has promised to let us choose what we want, after the Metropolitan has gotten their group. This result alone is in my opinion worth my trip abroad. For he is a greater watercolor painter now than two years ago. I have seen certain of his recent works which make him the equal of Turner. Of course I was not fool enough to say so, for I think he dislikes set compliments. But he knew I admired them immensely.[11]

Sargent briefly visited Worcester and its new museum in June 1916 but offered no watercolors for consideration. In a letter to Pratt, Helen Bigelow Merriman may well have expressed more than just her own impatience, emphasizing that "the great point is to get him [Sargent] to promise us first choice, with the liberty to take as many as we can afford."[12] Pratt persisted and Sargent promised the museum a group of watercolors from his trip that summer to the Rockies. However, disappointment deepened when the "meagre results" that Sargent described in his letter to Pratt were dispersed elsewhere.[13] It was not until the following May, upon the artist's return from his three-month stay in Florida, that the museum was able to purchase a group of watercolors from Sargent: eleven sheets he had painted at Ormond Beach, near Daytona, and at James Deering's great villa, Vizcaya, in Miami. The four-year wait since Pratt had first approached Sargent, in 1913, was worthwhile: this group of Florida subjects shows Sargent at the height of his powers.

Equally remarkable was the low price of $2,750 for which Sargent sold this group of eleven sheets. That same year the museum had paid $2,200 for Homer's *The Turkey Buzzard*, and Gentner had acquired Childe Hassam's watercolor *Yonkers from the Palisades* for $450 in January 1917. In 1913 the museum had purchased two watercolors by Frank W. Benson for $250 each, at a time when he was relatively unknown for his work in this medium. In comparison, Sargent, who enjoyed an international reputation, offered his watercolors for a modest amount, especially in light of the demand for these works.[14] Indeed, the museum had paid the dealer, Knoedler, $25,000 for Sargent's imposing portrait of Lady Warwick and her son in 1913, an indication of the extraordinary prices his oils could bring even during his own lifetime.

The purposefulness with which Gentner sought American watercolors was not paralleled in the tenures of his successors Raymond Henniker-Heaton (1918–25), George W. Eggers (1926–30), or Francis Henry Taylor, who served twice as director (1931–40 and 1955–57). The most important addition to the watercolor collection during these years was Eggers's purchase of five Irish compositions by Rockwell Kent, whose recent works he had seen at two New York exhibitions organized by E. Weyhe and by Wildenstein & Company. Although Kent's reputation as a painter, illustrator, and designer was rapidly increasing, his work in watercolor had never been widely known. Carl Zigrosser, Kent's friend and then director of Weyhe Gallery, wrote Eggers that this was the first time a museum had purchased a representative group of Kent's watercolors.[15] Under Francis Henry Taylor's first term, Edward Hopper's striking *Yawl Riding a Swell* was acquired in 1935 from the museum's second biennial exhibition, having received the First Purchase Award. The second Hopper, *Cobb House*, came to the museum eight years later as a gift from the artist's patron Stephen C. Clarke.

Of comparable importance to Gentner's acquisitions of watercolors by Homer and Sargent was the purchase by director Charles H. Sawyer in 1941 of five watercolors that survey the prolific career of Maurice Prendergast. Previously director of the Addison Gallery of American Art at Phillips Academy in Andover, Massachusetts, Sawyer had long admired Prendergast's work and had come to know Maurice's brother, Charles, not long before he organized a retrospective at Andover of work by the Prendergast brothers in 1938. Sawyer is also credited with a wide range of purchases that include watercolors by Lyonel Feininger and Jacques

Lipchitz, both of whom had international reputations, and by the black artist Jacob Lawrence and the New England modernist Carl Nelson. Two important gifts during the 1940s helped to expand the breadth of the collection: a pair of landscapes by Arthur B. Davies from his patron Mrs. Cornelius N. Bliss and twenty-three watercolors and four pastels by the American expatriate Henry Bacon from the artist's widow, Mrs. Frederick L. Eldridge. The latter group, which constitutes the largest public collection of Bacon's work, came to the Worcester Art Museum because of the reputation and strength of its growing collection of watercolors.

Gifts have continued to be exceedingly important to the development of the museum's holdings. In the 1930s a gift was made of four works by La Farge that reflect the artist's travels and his talents as a designer. Three of these were given by Dr. Samuel B. Woodward of Worcester, who had exhibited two of them in the museum's *First Exhibition* in 1898.[16] Among the most varied and significant gifts in twentieth-century art have come from William H. and Saundra B. Lane, both of whom have had a longtime association with the museum as corporators and trustees. Pioneering and insightful collectors, the Lanes have added such seminal works as Charles Sheeler's *City Interior No. 2*; Mark Tobey's *Cycle of the Prophet*; and Morris Graves's *Moon Rising*. Other friends of the museum have recently helped to strengthen and update the watercolor collection with delightful discoveries in twentieth-century art, such as *Storage Tanks*, of 1931, by the Philadelphia modernist Earl Horter, the gift of David and Selma Medoff; Charles Burchfield's breezy landscape *June Wind*, of 1937, from the collection of Chapin and Mary Alexander Riley; *View of Dover, New Hampshire*, a 1976 work by the New England regionalist DeWitt Hardy, given by Dr. and Mrs. Robert A. Johnson; and the witty abstractions from the late 1970s and early 1980s by Boston artist Todd McKie, from the collections of Mr. and Mrs. Sidney Rose and Mr. and Mrs. B. A. King (plate 7). With funds provided by the National Endowment for the Arts, watercolors by three important contemporary artists—Carolyn Brady, Sol LeWitt, and William T. Wiley—were purchased in 1984 to reflect the diversity in today's revival of the medium. At the other end of the spectrum, the addition of landscape compositions by the English-born John William Hill, through purchase, and by the Hudson River School painter Jasper F. Cropsey, through a gift from the artist's great-granddaughter Mrs. John C. Newington, help to illustrate the progression of the watercolor movement as it developed in the nineteenth century. A lyrical view of Winchester, England, by John Ferguson Weir, a frequent visitor to Worcester County, is a gift from the artist's grandson the Reverend DeWolf Perry and his wife, along with three sparkling Spanish scenes by Weir's brother-in-law Truman Seymour. The strong tradition of giving continues through the generosity of an anonymous friend who has allowed us to include as a promised gift an important example by the major twentieth-century watercolorist Andrew Wyeth, who would otherwise not be represented in these pages.

Like the collection it documents, this catalogue does not attempt to cover the complete history of American watercolor. Rather, its primary purpose is to share with a wide audience an often hidden resource, which, because of its fragile nature, cannot be on permanent view. This publication not only provides us with a benchmark by which we can measure the growth of this evolving collection but it also stands as a testimony to those who helped to build these holdings. Most of all, this occasion allows us to recognize the achievements of the artists who contributed to this rich American tradition.

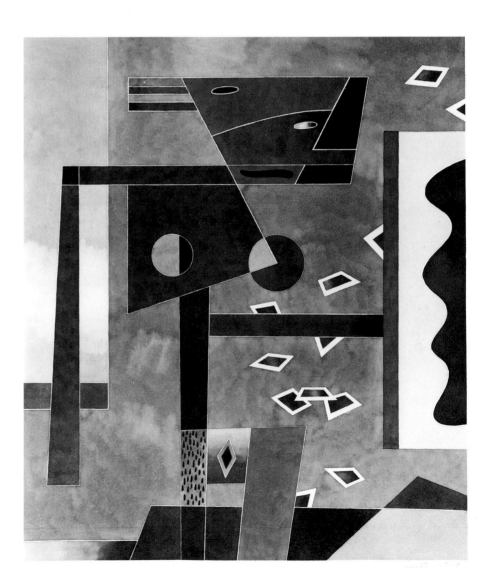

7
Todd McKie (b. 1944)
Slide Show, 1978
Watercolor on paper
24⅞ × 21⅛ in. (62.2 × 53.6 cm.)
Worcester Art Museum; Gift of Sidney Rose in memory of his mother, Mary D. Rose

1. William Pettee of M. Knoedler & Co. to Buffington, January 25, 1908, Worcester Art Museum files. Mrs. Buffington was a founding corporator and a trustee from 1904. She was particularly active on the Committee on the Museum (now Committee on the Collections), a group responsible for acquisitions.

2. A brief biography of Philip J. Gentner appears in the *Thirteenth Annual Report of the Worcester Art Museum* (1908), pp. 5–6.

3. Worcester's *First Exhibition* was held in 1898 and the annuals continued until 1912, when they were discontinued due to fiscal constraints. From the annuals held during the first four years of Gentner's tenure, the museum purchased Benson's *Girl Playing Solitaire* of 1909 in 1909; Hassam's *Breakfast Room, New York* of 1911 and Sargent's *Venetian Water Carriers*, c. 1880–82, in 1911.

4. Gentner to Knoedler, March 30, 1909, Worcester Art Museum files.

5. This unwritten agreement with Knoedler was probably made prior to December 1910, judging from the existing correspondence between Knoedler and Gentner in the Worcester Art Museum files. It applied to both oils and watercolors. In December 1911 Gentner felt that Knoedler had broken their promise through the sale to Henry Reinhardt of Homer's oil *Sunlight on the Coast*, which had been owned by the Philadelphia collector John G. Johnson.

Gentner had been interested in buying it, although Johnson had apparently declined to sell it previously. Reinhardt, a dealer himself, sold the oil to Mr. and Mrs. Edward Drummond Libbey, who gave it to the Toledo Museum of Art in 1912.

6. See Philippe de Montebello, "Director's Note," in *Winslow Homer at the Metropolitan Museum of Art* (New York: Metropolitan Museum of Art, 1982), p. 3. The three watercolors that Worcester purchased from this group were: *In a Florida Jungle; Coral Formation*; and *Fishing Boats, Key West*. See Helen A. Cooper, *Winslow Homer Watercolors* (Washington, D.C.: National Gallery of Art; New Haven, Conn.: Yale University Press, 1986), p. 241 n. 9.

7. Gentner to E. L. Knoedler, January 18, 1911, Worcester Art Museum files.

8. Gentner to Merriman, January 6, 1911, Gentner File, Worcester Art Museum Archives.

9. Gentner had considered several major oils by Homer for acquisition, but ironically, when Gentner was abroad in 1916, it was the trustees who made the final selection of *The Gale* for $27,500, a price Gentner described as "far too high," in a cable of April 18, 1916, Worcester Art Museum files.

10. For a detailed account of Sargent's association with Worcester and the museum, see my article "John Singer Sargent and Worcester," *Worcester Art Museum Journal* 6 (1982–83): 18–39.

11. Gentner to Pratt, July 8, 1914, Worcester Art Museum files.

12. Merriman to Pratt, June 8, 1916, Worcester Art Museum files.

13. Sargent to Pratt, November 18, 1916, Worcester Art Museum files.

14. Apparently Sargent did not offer Worcester a special price because the Brooklyn Museum's eighty-three watercolors were purchased for $20,000, or roughly $240 each.

An unfortunate episode in this chapter of the collection's history is that, in 1948, Worcester trustees voted to sell four of the Vizcaya watercolors to Chauncey McCormick of Chicago, who had married into the Deering family.

15. Zigrosser to Eggers, March 25, 1927, Worcester Art Museum files.

16. The two La Farge watercolors, then called *Geisha (Dancer and Musician)* and *Sacred Font* (see plates 55 and 56), were lent by Mrs. S. B. Woodward. *The First Exhibition* of the Worcester Art Museum included a section devoted to watercolors, composed, for the most part, of examples by many lesser talents. Among the Americans, La Farge, Ross Turner, and Dodge Macknight are the best known. The most noteworthy international talents represented were Dante Gabriel Rossetti, J. M. W. Turner, and John Ruskin (by his now-famous *Fragment of the Alps*, owned then by Harvard Professor Charles Eliot Norton).

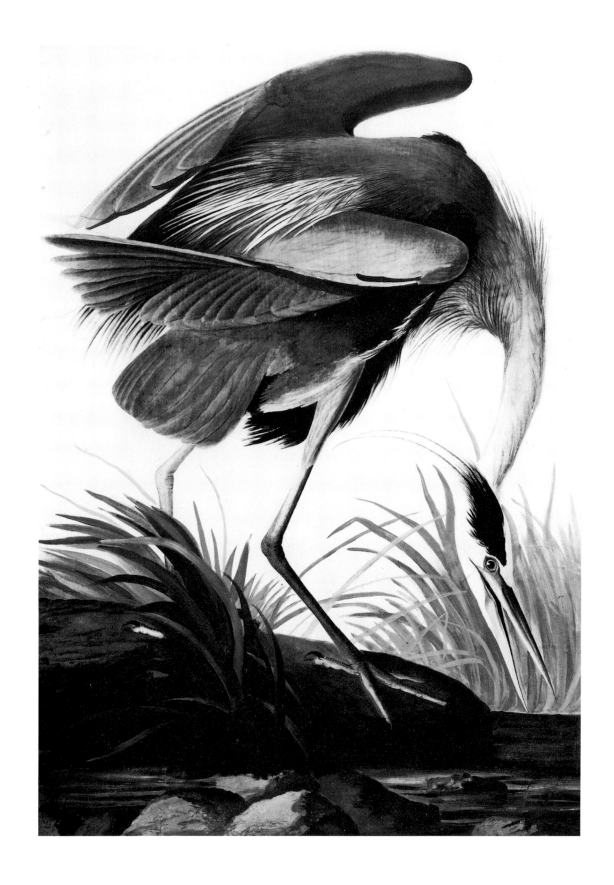

Donelson F. Hoopes

The Emergence of an American Medium

The history of watercolor painting in America parallels the broader progress of the nation's art. From its earliest manifestations and well into the nineteenth century, American watercolor painting shared with its sister arts a distinct debt to European precedent, especially the established tradition in England. In fact, for the first one hundred years most practitioners of the medium in America had been born abroad. It was not until the third quarter of the nineteenth century, when such masters as Winslow Homer turned seriously to watercolor to depict indigenous themes with unparalleled mastery, that critics began to refer to watercolor as "the American medium."

The use of watercolor in North America dates from the time of the earliest explorations of the New World in the sixteenth century, when artists traveled with explorers to document their discoveries for the benefit of civilized Europe. The first of these was Jacques Le Moyne de Morgues, who accompanied a French expedition to what is now Florida, Georgia, and the Carolinas in 1564. His idealized views of the landscape and its Indian inhabitants were engraved and published in Germany by Theodore de Bry, along with a narrative of the expedition by the artist. Le Moyne was succeeded by the Englishman John White, who visited Sir Walter Raleigh's colony on Roanoke Island in 1585. White's somewhat fanciful views of Virginia and its exotic aboriginals were also published by de Bry in 1590.

In the next century English, French, and Dutch artists continued this explorer-naturalist tradition, often providing important data for scientific study. One of the most accurate records of North American flora and fauna was painted by the English naturalist Mark Catesby, whose watercolors were published in London in 1731. This tradition continued through the eighteenth century and culminated in the work of John James Audubon. His supremely sensitive and realistic watercolor renderings of the birds and animals of North America, published in London in the 1820s and 1830s, remain to this day the most celebrated manifestation of this genre (plate 8).

As America began to expand its borders in the early nineteenth century, artists traveled westward, often with military expeditions or foreign adventurers. The most notable of these artists were the Swiss Karl

8
John James Audubon (1785–1857)
Great Blue Heron, 1822
Watercolor, pencil, pastel, and oil on paper
36 × 25⅜ in. (91.5 × 64.4 cm.)
The New-York Historical Society

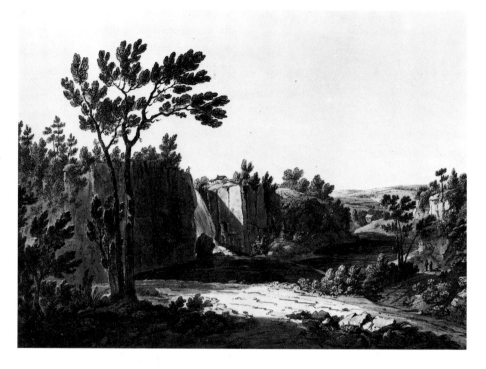

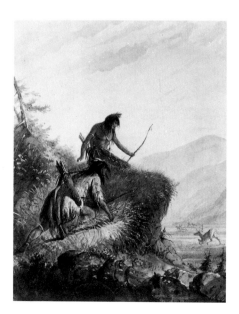

Bodmer and the Americans Alfred Jacob Miller, George Catlin, and Seth Eastman. They were among the first to record the life of the Plains Indians and their majestic environment, in watercolor sketches that were intended to be either engraved or worked up into more finished oils (plate 9).

About the same time, a succession of talented British watercolorists journeyed to the former colonies, and many of them settled there. Their picturesque views were frequently used to illustrate popular travelogues extolling America's natural beauty and often the historical significance of eastern locales. To Philadelphia came the London-trained William R. Birch, a painter of miniature portraits. His son Thomas Birch produced watercolors published by the family firm in 1800 as *Views of Philadelphia*. By 1816 the English aquatinter John Hill also had set up business in Philadelphia and was actively commissioning artists to produce watercolors for publication. His first major portfolio, *Picturesque Views of American Scenery* (1820), was engraved from the watercolors of the English-born landscape painter Joshua Shaw (plate 10) and published in 1820 by M. Carey and Son, Philadelphia. The Irishman William Guy Wall arrived in New York in 1818 and spent the next decade producing watercolor views of Hudson River scenery. Twenty of these formed the basis for the celebrated suite of aquatint engravings published by Hill in New York in various editions as *The Hudson River Portfolio* (1820–25). Thus, early in the nineteenth century, Americans were able to buy large, frequently hand-colored engravings celebrating their native scenery from resident publishers rather than exclusively from European sources. The widespread appreciation of illustrated publications likely laid the foundation for greater sophistication in the fine arts among the American public and prepared the way for the first truly indigenous group of painters, the Hudson River School.

The celebration of the American landscape that the Hudson River School proclaimed was led by Thomas Cole, who had emigrated from his native England in 1819. Within ten years of his arrival he had become the acknowledged leader of that school. His work was highly regarded abroad as well, and twelve of his paintings were reproduced in John Howard Hinton's *History and Topography of the United States*, published in London between 1830 and 1832. It is conjectural whether or not Cole's views of the American landscape spurred renewed interest in the subject abroad, but before the decade was out the British publisher George Virtue conceived what would become the period's definitive work on this theme. He assigned the project to the English watercolorist William Henry Bartlett, whose work became exceptionally important to the popularization of American landscape views in the first half of the nineteenth century. Beginning in 1836 Bartlett produced more than one hundred watercolor views that encompassed nearly every natural wonder and urban landmark between Niagara Falls and Washington, D.C. (plate 11). These watercolors appeared in a two-volume set entitled *American Scenery*, issued between 1839 and 1842, by George Virtue, London, with an accompanying text by Nathaniel Parker Willis. Theodore Stebbins sees this work as having established ''a basic iconography for the American Grand Tour—Bartlett's views became, almost by definition, *the* picturesque scenes of America.''[1]

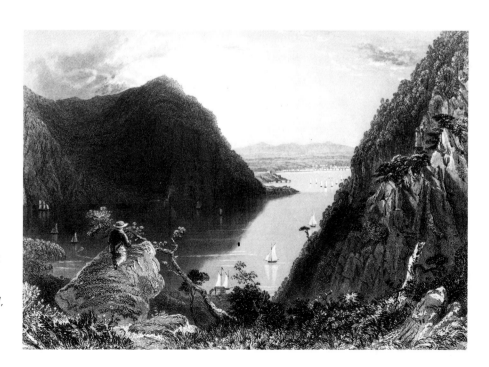

11
E. Benjamin, after William Henry Bartlett
(1809–1854)
Hudson Highlands
Engraving from *American Scenery; or, Land, Lake and River*, vol. I, 1840
Courtesy American Antiquarian Society, Worcester

Up to this time the American public and even American artists had only limited access to original watercolors, which were to be seen only in small numbers, principally at annual exhibitions of the academies in Boston, New York, and Philadelphia. The English artist George Harvey was one of the first to mount an exhibition entirely of watercolors, a group of some forty of his American scenes (plate 12) shown at the Boston Athenaeum in 1844, originally intended for publication as engravings—a project that was never realized. These watercolors, which Harvey called "atmospherical landscapes," were not cast in the standard picturesque mode nor in the loose, broadly applied wash method of predecessors such as William Guy Wall. Rather, Harvey employed a delicate stippling technique in the manner of a miniaturist to convey a colorful luminosity. This, together with their more informal compositions, gives Harvey's watercolors a convincing realism.

The standard of excellence set by English watercolorists in America contributed to the sudden flourishing of the medium after 1800. Its popularity with American painters was also encouraged by rapid developments in pigment chemistry. The introduction of less expensive synthetic colors in the early nineteenth century enabled the artist to employ a much wider range of hues without resorting to the traditional method of mixing primary and secondary colors, which inevitably diminished chromatic intensity. The artist was thus able to achieve effects of both delicacy and brilliance, taking greatest advantage of the luminous transparency that is watercolor's special virtue.

A parallel development was the growth of the colors-manufacturing industry in America. Formerly an expensive import, colors began to be

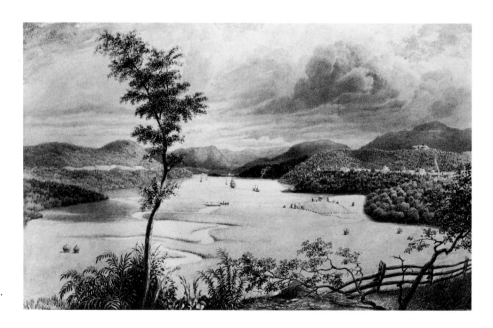

12
George Harvey (c. 1800–1878)
View of West Point from Constitution Island,
c. 1844
Watercolor on paper
10⅜ × 17⅛ in. (26.4 × 43.5 cm.)
Museum of Fine Arts, Boston; M. and M. Karolik Collection

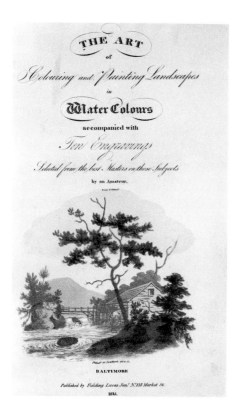

produced domestically as early as 1820 by the firm of G.W. Osborne of Philadelphia.[2] Watercolors were then prepared in the form of small dry cakes, or "pans," requiring the addition of water for use. With the invention of the collapsible metal tube in the 1840s, used for both oil and watercolors, the artist was able to keep liquified colors at hand almost indefinitely.[3] This was an enormous boon to the watercolor painter, for, unlike oil-based colors, which can be compounded easily from the basic raw materials, watercolors are especially difficult to prepare. By 1849 the London firm of Winsor & Newton was offering watercolors in such tubes; indeed, to this day their preparations are regarded as the best available.

In response to the growing general interest in the medium, books and pamphlets began to appear, providing the artist with specific instruction in watercolor technique. Not surprisingly, artists working in America first relied upon European manuals.[4] The first treatise on the use of watercolor published in America was *Elements of the Graphic Arts* by the Scotsman Archibald Robertson, which appeared in 1802.[5] Robertson and his brother Alexander had taught drawing and watercolor to ladies and gentlemen for over a decade in New York. Robertson's manual was supplanted by several other treatises aimed at both professional and amateur audiences. Among the most important was Fielding Lucas, Jr.'s *Art of Colouring and Painting Landscapes in Water Colours*, published in Baltimore in 1815, the first manual entirely devoted to the medium and one that clearly reflected the suitability of watercolor for landscape subjects (plate 13). In 1851 the American Art-Union *Bulletin* published an extended discussion entitled "The Art of Landscape Painting in Water Color," which presented to its largely lay readership information on materials and on techniques to achieve specific pictorial effects. Five years later, on the eve of the birth of the American watercolor movement, Henry Warren published a comprehensive book on the subject, aimed at the professional.[6] As general interest in the medium gained momentum in the 1860s, artists themselves took on the task of educating the public about collecting watercolors.[7]

By the first quarter of the nineteenth century a growing number of institutions in the nation were being established to train artists and foster an awareness of art on the part of the public. The Pennsylvania Academy of the Fine Arts was founded in 1806 in Philadelphia and was followed three years later by the American Academy of Fine Arts in New York. The National Academy of Design, which would host the first exhibition by an American watercolor association, was organized in 1826. These institutions were loosely modeled on European academies, notably the Royal Academy of Arts in London. In Britain the strong presence of a watercolor tradition since the mid-eighteenth century had contributed to the creation of specialized groups such as the Royal Society of Painters in Water-Colours. By the time a significant number of American artists turned their attention to watercolor in the mid-nineteenth century, they, too, recognized the need to form separate organizations. The exhibitions that

13
William Strickland (1788–1854). Engraved frontispiece from *The Art of Colouring and Painting Landscapes in Water Colours*
Courtesy American Antiquarian Society, Worcester

these organizations sponsored gave their work greater exposure among their fellow artists as well as the public at large.

In 1850 a group of thirty artists banded together in New York to form the Society for the Promotion of Painting in Water Colors.[8] A number of these painters were English-born, and it can be inferred that they furnished the impetus to organize formally in emulation of the British associations. The surviving records of the society tell of the first meeting, convened in the studio of John M. Falconer on Hudson Street in December 1850.[9] Born in Edinburgh, Scotland, Falconer had immigrated to the United States in the late 1830s and quickly formed friendships with some of the major artists in New York City, including Thomas Cole, William Sidney Mount, and Jasper F. Cropsey.[10] Falconer's studio served as the society's meeting place for the first year, and he became a pivotal figure in the group's activities, which included a school and sketching expeditions for members, such as one to Yonkers in 1853. The society's only exhibition, held at the National Academy of Design in April 1853, was open to nonmembers, which suggests the organization was hoping to increase its rolls. However, by the time of its annual meeting in December 1854, membership had dwindled to twenty-one, and the effectiveness of the group seems to have waned in its final year.

Out of this initial effort there emerged a new organization, the New York Water Color Society, led by Falconer, Cropsey, and John William Hill, son of the English aquatinter.[11] The inspiration for this regrouping was the 1853 New York World's Fair, where works of art were given a prominent place among exhibits of crafts and manufactures. The idea for the fair had evolved from the 1851 visit of a group of New York businessmen to the great Crystal Palace exhibition in London. The Americans determined to replicate not only the London exhibition's theme of internationalism but also the astonishing cast-iron and glass building by Sir Joseph Paxton in which it was held. The New York Crystal Palace, built on the present-day site of Bryant Park, offered some five acres of enclosed exhibition space—the largest structure in the city. The theme of the World's Fair was the "Exhibition of the Industry of All Nations," and before closing in 1854 it had attracted over one million visitors.[12] The New York Water Color Society mounted thirty-one pictures, mostly landscape views, in an alcove of the vast hall, and their presence was duly noted in the official catalogue.[13]

This modest venture of the New York Water Color Society was a significant event in the history of watercolor painting in this country. For the first time, works in watercolor had gained an honored place alongside the proud achievements of modern society's arts and technology. Few American artists had ever before exposed their work to such a wide and diverse audience. Yet, inexplicably, the New York Water Color Society presented no more exhibitions, and some of its members returned to the fold of the Society for the Promotion of Painting in Water Colors, which appears to have disbanded in September 1855. But the pioneering efforts of the New York Water Color Society to promote the medium through its school and exhibition blazed a trail that others would follow in the post–Civil War years.

Shortly after the demise of these two groups an important exhibition stimulated renewed interest and controversy regarding the watercolor medium. Mounted by a few enterprising Englishmen, *The American Exhibition of English Art*, as it was sometimes called in the press, opened at the National Academy of Design in October 1857 and traveled to the Pennsylvania Academy of the Fine Arts and the Boston Athenaeum the following year.[14] The exhibition brought nearly two hundred watercolors—and an equal number of oils—mostly by contemporary English painters, to audiences that had known their work chiefly through engravings. The range of artists was varied, perhaps dominated by the British Pre-Raphaelites, although their champion, John Ruskin, and earlier luminaries such as David Cox and J. M. W. Turner were also represented. American critics complained that literary and moralistic themes outweighed landscape subjects, but more important was the fact that the exhibition brought examples of current English watercolor technique to America.

The inclusion of John Ruskin's work in this exhibition was doubly significant. A fine painter in his own right, Ruskin was already famous in America as an art critic and theoretician. His *Modern Painters* and *Elements of Drawing*, readily available in America by the mid-1850s, were widely read by American artists, as were his contributions to American periodicals such as the *Crayon*, published between 1855 and 1861, and the *New Path*, which circulated during the Civil War years. Ruskin believed in art as an agent for the moral improvement of mankind and as a means of educating the public. His call for the exacting study of nature, combined with an aesthetic based on moralistic values, reinforced the transcendental philosophy inherent in American art at mid-century and deeply influenced American painters. In 1863 the Association for the Advancement of Truth in Art was founded.[15] The artists who joined the association—frequently called the American Pre-Raphaelites—included John William Hill, his son John Henry Hill, Thomas Farrer, Charles Herbert Moore, Henry R. Newman, and William Trost Richards. They selected watercolor as their primary medium and worked in elaborate, highly finished styles, favoring landscape, nature studies, and still life over the figural subjects with literary or moralistic themes preferred by their British counterparts. Throughout the 1860s and early 1870s the American Pre-Raphaelites exhibited regularly and were a vital force in the development of watercolor in America.

The decade of the 1860s, of course, was a great dividing point in American history. The end of the Civil War brought a newfound sense of national identity that also informed the country's cultural life. Institutions dedicated to the advancement of American creativity flourished in the postwar years, and cultural organizations in the major cities were revitalized. The National Academy of Design, in its majestic new neo-Gothic

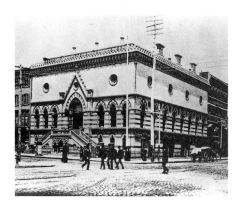

quarters at the corner of Twenty-third Street and Fourth Avenue (plate 14), reasserted its position as the premier art institution in New York. From the outset the academy had been a staunch supporter of the watercolor movement, frequently including watercolors and drawings in its annual exhibitions. In the fall of 1866, during its second season at its fashionable new location, the academy hosted a major watercolor exhibition. Organized under the patronage of the Artists' Fund Society, which had been established to assist needy artists and their families, the exhibition included more than 130 works by American and British artists; the Pre-Raphaelites were, not unexpectedly, in the majority among the Americans.

The academy's favorable disposition toward the watercolor movement offered encouragement to those artists who had suffered the demise of organizations such as the New York Water Color Society before the war. In December 1866 seven artists gathered in a studio in the old New York University building on Washington Square to form the American Society of Painters in Water Colors (which in 1877 became the American Water Color Society).[16] Within a year there were forty-two active and four honorary members. To cite here only those who are best remembered today, the membership included the first president, Samuel Colman, William Hart, Robert Swain Gifford, Charles Herbert Moore, John Whetten Ehninger, John George Brown, Seymour Joseph Guy, Emanuel Leutze, and Alexander Helwig Wyant, besides Falconer and Cropsey.[17] Fully one-third of the membership also enjoyed rank in the National Academy either as Associates or as senior Academicians, a fact that lent prestige to the new watercolor society. Two women were also members: Caroline Petigru Carson, a portrait and miniature painter, and Elizabeth Heaphy Murray, a landscape painter. Their admission to the fledgling society marked a break with custom, since artists' associations had heretofore been the domain of men.

When the American Society of Painters in Water Colors opened its inaugural exhibition at the National Academy on December 21, 1867, nearly three hundred works were on view, of which some one hundred were engravings. The majority of participants were nonmembers, including such younger artists as Winslow Homer, William Morris Hunt, and Louis Comfort Tiffany, as well as established painters such as the Hills. Also represented was John La Farge, who became the first candidate elected to membership at the annual meeting of the society in January 1868. For the next six seasons the society continued to hold its annual exhibitions at the National Academy as it grew steadily under the presidencies of William Hart and James Smillie.

For its Eighth Annual, in February 1875, the society opened its exhibition at the National Academy as usual; but, in an unprecedented move, it then sent most of the pictures to the Brooklyn Art Association's galleries for a second opening in March. The sheer size of the exhibition—550 pictures—may have induced euphoria in the ranks of the society's

14
The National Academy of Design, Twenty-third Street and Fourth Avenue, New York, after 1865

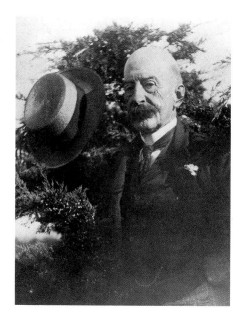

membership, and its officers no doubt wished to seize the opportunity for advancement of their cause. Brooklyn's participation in this event reflected a strengthening of interest in watercolor on the part of the gallery-going public, for the exhibitions of the society were becoming more varied in subject matter and style. For example, the 1875 exhibition included watercolors by two celebrities from abroad whose styles differed fundamentally: Edwin Austin Abbey, an illustrator and painter of literary and historical scenes, and the controversial expatriate James McNeill Whistler, whose ethereal, tonalist landscapes had already shocked Europe.

This exhibition also witnessed the emergence of Winslow Homer (plate 15) as a serious painter in watercolor, with ten pictures on view.[18] Homer had been an acclaimed artist for almost a decade, following the generous critical reception of his *Prisoners from the Front* (1866; Metropolitan Museum of Art) and his election to the National Academy as a full Academician. In the summer of 1873 he spent a highly productive few weeks in Gloucester, Massachusetts, working with watercolor (see plate 59). The next spring, in the Adirondacks, Homer gained his stride in the medium, producing the first of a stunning procession of images of rural life and landscape. Each succeeding year he increased the number of his submissions to the Water Color Society's annuals. In 1879, three years after his election to membership in the society, the Annual displayed twenty-nine of his watercolors, the largest group by any single artist.[19] His entries consisted mostly of scenes of rural life at Houghton Farm in Mountainville, New York, where he had spent several weeks the preceding spring. Reviewing the exhibition, the *Nation* lauded him: "Mr. Winslow Homer goes as far as anyone has ever done in demonstrating the value of water-colors as a serious means of expressing dignified artistic impressions."[20] Even in these early works there is a truthfulness and profundity in his depiction of rural America that, without sacrificing charm, imparts a conviction of realism and hints at his future greatness.

Astutely, Homer did not confine himself to the aegis of the American Water Color Society. In the interval between the society's Twelfth and Thirteenth Annuals he showed seventy-five Houghton Farm watercolors at the Matthews Gallery in New York and over one hundred of his Gloucester works at Doll and Richards Gallery in Boston. As the 1880s passed, Homer gravitated away from the American Water Color Society and toward these and other dealers in New York and Boston. He was beginning to enjoy a substantial portion of the exceptional fame that would be his by the turn of the century. Having earned the patronage of important private collectors and recognition in the form of prizes and honors at museum-sponsored international exhibitions, Homer eventually paid only cursory attention to the activities of the American Water Color Society. At the height of his career he manipulated the dealer-museum axis to great advantage. For example, his exhibition at the Carnegie International of 1897 was followed immediately by an opening at the Fifth Avenue gallery of his dealer, E. L. Knoedler.

15
Winslow Homer at Prout's Neck, 1908

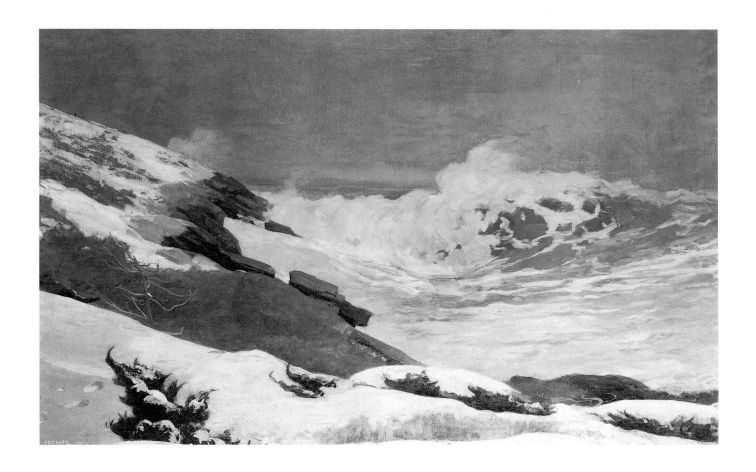

16
Winslow Homer (1836–1910)
Coast in Winter, 1892
Oil on canvas
23⅜ × 48⅜ in. (59.4 × 122.9 cm.)
Worcester Art Museum; Theodore T. and
Mary G. Ellis Collection

Homer's prodigious outpouring of watercolors in the last two decades of his life represents the very pinnacle of achievement in the medium by an American artist. Largely the product of vacations spent away from his Prout's Neck, Maine, studio, these watercolors express Homer's exultation in the light-struck climes of Bermuda, the Bahamas, and Florida (plates 64, 65, 71–76) and the more somber but equally delightful recesses of the Adirondacks and the Quebec woods (plates 66, 69, 70). His studio works, usually in oil (plate 16), convey a gravity of spirit far removed from the prevailing mood of joyousness that is so abundantly present in the brilliant light and color of his late watercolors. His unmatched technical virtuosity and profound vision of the simple world placed Homer at the forefront of the modern era of watercolor painting. His watercolors stand today as a major contribution to the history of American art.

Like Homer, American painters during the 1870s were beginning to shift away from Ruskinian notions of detail and "finish" and in search of greater stylistic diversity.[21] Perhaps because of its inherent spontaneity, watercolor was a logical choice of medium for American artists taking the first tentative steps away from the old descriptive mode toward a kind of

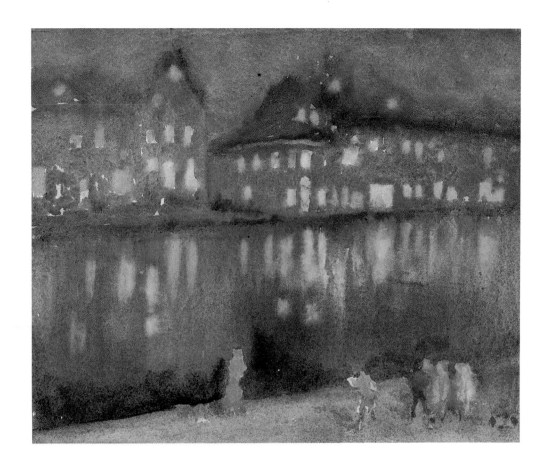

17
James McNeill Whistler (1834–1903)
Nocturne: Grand Canal, Amsterdam,
1883–84
Watercolor on paper
8⅞ × 11³⁄₁₆ in. (22.7 × 28.4 cm.)
Freer Gallery of Art, Smithsonian Institution, Washington, D.C.

proto-Impressionism. Characteristically, the public—and most critics—were slow to change their attitudes about what constituted acceptable finish in a work of art, particularly in pictures offered at formal exhibitions. Whistler, the London-based American expatriate, led the vanguard for Impressionism with pictures whose subjects were not naturalistically descriptive; rather, like music, they evoked moods—he even entitled his compositions ''nocturnes'' and ''symphonies'' (plate 17). To achieve such effects, as early as the late 1870s Whistler frequently employed a technique known as ''wet-into-wet,'' using paper with a water-saturated surface. Other artists, too, were using this method with greater frequency. To Ruskinian sensibilities the results appeared rather chaotic, and some critics were hostile to the innovation.[22]

While French practitioners of Impressionism made little use of watercolor, in America watercolor and the Impressionist idiom became securely identified by 1880, in a surge of creativity unmatched either in Britain or on the Continent.[23] Childe Hassam (plate 18), perhaps the quintessential American Impressionist, maintained parallel interests in oil painting and watercolor throughout his career. His late watercolors are charged with rich color combinations and energetic brushwork that often seem to acknowledge Expressionist influences as well. Hassam's summer visits to the Isles of Shoals, off the New Hampshire coast, after the turn of the century resulted in watercolors of great coloristic vibrancy, rivaling his work in oils (plate 19; see plate 94). Of the dissident Impressionist group, Ten American Painters, formed in 1897, the only colleague to share Hassam's devotion to watercolor was Frank W. Benson, whose brilliant handling of the medium provided inspiration for his contemporaries and a whole generation of aspiring watercolorists. Benson's innate sense of the medium's potential is best seen in his hunter and fishermen subjects (plate 96). Perhaps more than his oils, these watercolors remain resoundingly fresh to the eye.

Impressionism had broad appeal among American artists and also influenced conservative painters such as J. Francis Murphy, whose watercolors possess a great deal of Barbizon School charm but lack the force of genuinely original talent. George Inness produced a small group of innovative watercolor landscapes broadly executed in successive transparent washes, often in a limited tonal palette. Not intended for exhibition, these private works reflect the freedom signaled by the approach of Impressionism. La Farge, too, gradually shifted away from the linear, descriptive style that characterized his work when he first exhibited with the American Society of Painters in Water Colors in 1876. Arguably the most diverse talent of his day—he was an accomplished illustrator and designer as well as painter—La Farge employed watercolor in a variety of ways, from travel sketches to design renderings for stained-glass windows and mural projects (plate 57). Especially after his trips to Japan in 1886 and to the South Seas in 1890–91, he responded with great inventiveness to the aesthetics of Oriental art. His watercolors of landscape, figural, and still-life subjects reveal a freedom of handling and often a creative application of the medium that are in keeping with his place as a key figure in the Aesthetic Movement in American art.

In 1890 a number of artists separated from the American Water Color Society over the issue of the dominance of men in that organization, a circumstance that Hassam, among others, found unprogressive. The splinter group formed the New York Water Color Club and, because of his leadership in pressing for an organization that would be more open to women, elected Hassam president.[24] About half of the club's fifty-three members were women, and their first exhibition was held in March 1890 at the American Art Galleries on Madison Square. In spite of some initial critical animosity, the club flourished as a viable alternative to the rival American Water Color Society until 1921, when the two groups made their first move toward eventual unification.

Taken as a whole, the activity of watercolor organizations at this time can be seen as a function of the emerging self-identity of the American artist amid the clamor for attention of special-interest groups throughout the entire spectrum of society. Watercolor painters needed a stronger identity than was provided by simple membership in generalist

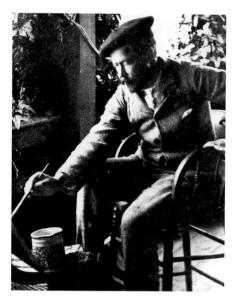

18
Childe Hassam painting a watercolor on the porch of Celia Thaxter's home on the Isles of Shoals, c. 1886.

19
Childe Hassam (1859–1935)
Sylph's Rock, Appledore, 1907
Oil on canvas
25 × 30 in. (63.5 × 76.2 cm.)
Worcester Art Museum; Gift of Charlotte
E. W. Buffington

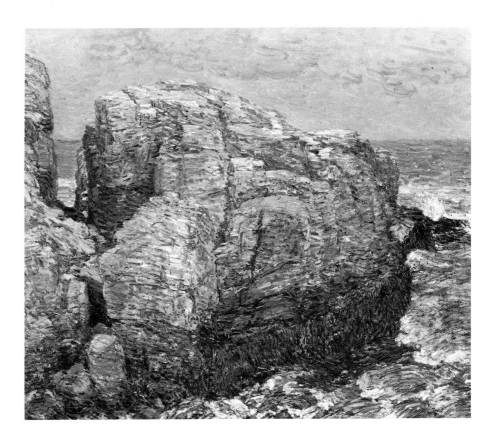

organizations such as the National Academy. Indeed, the American Water
Color Society initiated its first exclusive exhibition in 1877; and ten years
later Louis Comfort Tiffany went so far as to alter the galleries at the
National Academy temporarily in a pointed effort to distinguish the Water
Color Society's presentation from those of the host institution.[25] In like
manner, a number of American Impressionists who had been won over
to the pastel medium (largely through Whistler's influence) formed yet
another specialized group, the Society of Painters in Pastel, in 1881 or
1882.[26]

The American Water Color Society first began to hold its annual
exhibitions at locations other than the National Academy around 1895.
This change reflected the shift of the center of the New York art world
from Twenty-third Street to uptown. It also told of the growing schism
between progressive artists and the academy. The most significant event
of the period was the formation of the Ten American Painters in 1897,
with Hassam at its head.

In this period of transition and diversity, John Singer Sargent stands
as an independent figure, whose work in watercolor draws upon the
tenets of Impressionism but also presages the approach of modernism.
His innate abilities and remarkable eye place him beside the more taciturn
Homer as a talent of the greatest magnitude. As one of the triumvirate of

great expatriates of the nineteenth century—Whistler and Mary Cassatt are customarily cited as the other two—Sargent may appear to be only nominally American. Born in Europe of American parents, he lived there most of his life. His Parisian training and his orientation to English precedent in his principal career as a portrait painter seem to mark him as a European. But his attachment to his ancestral American roots was real, and unlike his friend Henry James, Sargent maintained his United States citizenship despite permanent residence abroad.

Sargent's explorations of the watercolor medium were merely tentative until about 1880, and the few earlier examples by him reveal little of the brio so characteristic of his work in oil at that time. This period also marked his growing interest in Impressionism, especially in his landscapes, which reflect the influence of his friend Claude Monet. Henry James, who introduced Sargent to American audiences in his reviews, was a fervent admirer of the young artist's work: "Wonderfully light and fine is the touch by which [this] painter evokes the small . . . realities."[27] But it was not until the turn of the century that Sargent made a concentrated effort in watercolor and began to develop his formidable command of the medium. It honed the sharp edge of his extraordinary visual acuity and became his favorite medium while he was on holiday in Italy and the Alps and on excursions to eastern Mediterranean lands.

Watercolor released Sargent from the constraints of "correct" pictorial formulas that he observed in his commissioned works. Since most of his watercolors were not intended for exhibition, he was able to free his impulse for seemingly spontaneous and often adventuresome creativity. As his fame grew, every available work came into demand by collectors, including the most casual watercolors that previously he had simply given away to friends. In February 1909 M. Knoedler & Company held an exhibition and sale in New York. Eighty-three examples, ranging in complexity from the briefest notation to fully developed papers, were immediately purchased by a patron for the Brooklyn Museum. During the first decade of the new century, when the American Water Color Society was in financial trouble and turning once more to nonmembers to fill its exhibitions, Sargent's New York and Boston dealers were being depleted of his work by avid collectors and museum directors.[28] In 1917, in an exhibition at the Carnegie Institute in Pittsburgh, his work shared gallery space with a selection of watercolors by the late Winslow Homer, then regarded as the greatest master of the medium that America had ever produced. The implication was clear: the mantle of greatness had been passed to Sargent. Even as his artistic reputation was being denigrated by critics hostile to his role as a society portrait painter, the watercolors, with their extraordinary vitality and freshness of vision, could not be faulted even by his detractors.

Just as Sargent's bravura style became the model for many academic portrait painters in the first decades of the twentieth century, so his watercolors found ardent admirers and, to some extent, imitators. Sargent's close connection with Boston, where he frequently exhibited at the Copley Society, offered the city's artistic community ample opportunity to study some of the best examples of his work firsthand. Benson, Edmund Tarbell, and to a lesser degree Joseph R. De Camp, all members of the Boston branch of the Ten American Painters group, admired Sargent's flashing brushwork. Dodge Macknight built his career as a watercolor painter essentially on Sargent's example, adding his own sometimes daring use of rather strident color to otherwise routine landscape compositions (plate 20).

In the decades bracketing the turn of the century the art establishment extended its reach westward. Chicago was the site of the World's Columbian Exposition in 1893, St. Louis hosted the Louisiana Purchase Exposition in 1904, and similar commemorative expositions were held in San Francisco and San Diego in 1915. Each of these boasted large "departments" of art, essentially offering surveys of contemporary American painting and sculpture. In this spirit, the American Water Color Society instituted its first "rotary exhibition" in 1905, with the bulk of its Thirty-eighth Annual traveling to St. Louis, Cincinnati, Detroit, Indianapolis, and Buffalo. This practice was continued until 1913, when the logistics grew too cumbersome for the society's volunteer staff, who turned the work over to the American Federation of Arts.[29]

Although the nation was experiencing an unprecedented and widespread cultural awakening during this period, New York continued to

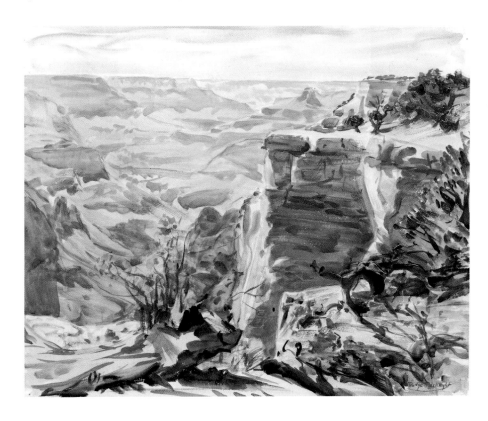

20
Dodge Macknight (1860–1950)
Grand Canyon of the Colorado (Looking West toward Havasupai Point), c. 1915
Watercolor over graphite on paper
17¾ × 22¼ in. (45 × 56.6 cm.)
Worcester Art Museum; Gift of Henry H. and Zoe Oliver Sherman

be the center for the emergence of new directions in art. In 1908 a group of dissident realist painters, "The Eight," challenged the genteel values of the art establishment with an exhibition that touched on themes of commonplace city life.[30] Of this group, Maurice B. Prendergast, George Luks, and Arthur B. Davies were accomplished watercolor painters. An artist of highly personal vision influenced by Post-Impressionism, Prendergast clearly demonstrated his preference for watercolor. He worked in an idiom of two-dimensional space, using bright, decorative color to create cityscapes and seaside resort scenes alive with human activity (plates 89–93). Luks abandoned the heavy, dark tonalities of his oil paintings in the vibrant watercolor views of woodland scenes that he painted on holiday. Davies, the most cerebral of the group, produced dreamy, ethereal landscapes using thin veils of wash color (plates 97A and 97B).

Recognition of the vital forces in contemporary French art had come in America as early as 1905, when the art dealer and photographer Alfred Stieglitz opened his gallery in New York. One of his earliest American protégés was John Marin, whose abstract watercolors helped to reinvigorate the use of the medium in the twentieth century. His vision acknowledged the principles of Cubism and Futurism while maintaining a hold on the associative imagery that was a common denominator of the early American modernists. Marin caught the spirit of New York's urban dynamism in watercolors charged with energetic color and line, while his landscapes of the Maine coast and New Mexico portray the natural environment in more lyrical terms but with no less an eye for its essential monumental structure (plate 21). Elements that characterized the work of the Fauve painters—distortion of forms and exuberant use of color—are part of the early watercolor work of Stuart Davis. In his mature work Davis generalized shapes and flattened color into geometric planes, producing a highly individual style of constructivist abstraction, which he often used for composition studies in watercolor and gouache. A deep feeling for natural forms and rhythms distinguishes the work of Arthur G. Dove, who toward the end of his long and prolific career concentrated on small, lyrical abstract watercolors. Georgia O'Keeffe developed an intuitively personal style that depended only slightly on the emerging modernist movement of the early twentieth century. The watercolors she made through the early 1920s, though based on landscape and still-life subject matter, are often taken to the point of pure abstraction, rendered in clear, simple color harmonies.

The modernist movement in American art began its ascendancy with the International Exhibition of Modern Art, the official title for what quickly became known as the Armory Show. It opened in New York in the winter of 1913 and immediately drew national attention in the press because of the dominance of avant-garde art on view. American artists who affiliated themselves with the modernists were represented alongside their European contemporaries. The majority of the nearly twelve

21
John Marin (1870–1953)
St. Paul's, Manhattan, 1914
Watercolor on paper
15⅞ × 18⅞ in. (40.3 × 47.9 cm.)
The Metropolitan Museum of Art, New
York; Alfred Stieglitz Collection

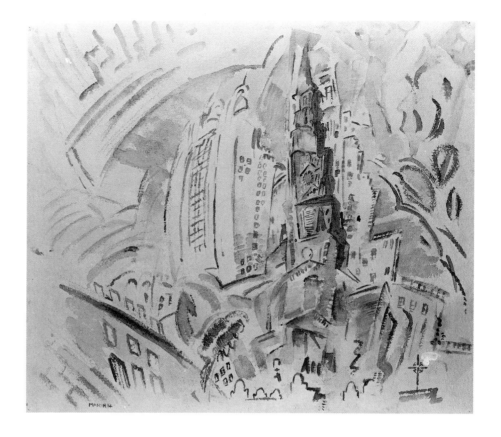

hundred entries were oil paintings and sculpture; of the American participants, only Davis and Marin chose to be represented exclusively by
watercolors.[31] No member of the American Water Color Society showed
work in this landmark exhibition; however, the society was by no means
inactive. At the same moment that the Armory Show was drawing huge
crowds to lower Lexington Avenue, the society was holding its Forty-
sixth Annual Exhibition at the prestigious M. Knoedler galleries on Fifth
Avenue and also drawing large numbers of visitors.[32]

Even while the birth of modernism was creating a tumult in American art circles, a steady output continued to flow from a largely unher-
alded conservative element of artists. If the nation's traditional watercolor
painters won for the medium "eventual celebration as a national idiom,"
they did so in spite of the revolution that was taking place.[33] The American
Water Color Society remained the principal apparatus for exhibiting the
work of these artists. Its Fiftieth Anniversary Exhibition in 1917 was
deluged by submissions: more than a thousand pictures had to be win-
nowed by two-thirds. This trend continued at the annuals through 1925,
when a limit was set on the number of submissions allowed each artist.

With the onset of the Great Depression, however, a serious decline in
participation and sales threatened the very existence of the society. By
1939 sentiment among members was running high for a merger with the

New York Water Color Club, which was not effected until 1941; even so, this union could muster only ninety-five members. Most of the names on the first joint roster have already retreated into obscurity. Yet there were some destined to become bright stars and to earn lasting fame, most notably Andrew Wyeth. As the most celebrated realist painter working today, Wyeth depicts his familiar rural Pennsylvania and Maine surroundings with a cool, precise detachment that conceals a strong underlying emotional response to the American landscape and its inhabitants (plate 111). While his youthful watercolors, particularly those of Maine subjects, acknowledge a debt to Homer in their vigorous handling of transparent wash, it is in the later dry-brush watercolors that Wyeth proclaims his mastery of the medium. More than any other living artist, he has become a source of inspiration for many younger painters who have chosen to follow a traditional approach to watercolor.

After the Depression the society's exhibitions came to be dominated by artists of the romantic-realist tradition, who favored a dry but impeccably correct skill. Notable among this group was Ogden M. Pleissner, a genial painter of picturesque, light-dappled European cityscapes (plate 22) as well as robust hunting scenes in a manner reminiscent of Benson. Another regular exhibitor, Millard Sheets, has become well known for his suave handling of the watercolor medium in subjects of the American West. The most eminent practitioner of the romantic-realist tradition in watercolor was Charles Burchfield. Largely a self-taught painter, he made haunting Depression-era watercolors of small-town America that are

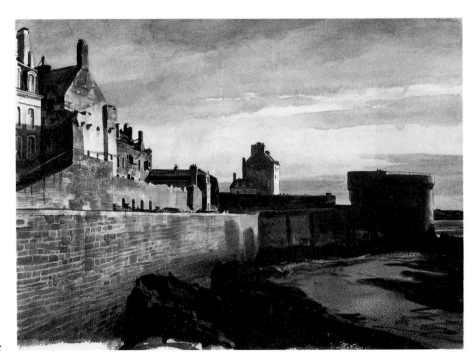

22
Ogden M. Pleissner (1905–1983)
The Ramparts, St. Malo, 1950
Watercolor over graphite on paper
19 × 27 in. (48.2 × 65.5 cm.)
Worcester Art Museum; Museum purchase

forceful evocations of the period. The lyricism of the later large watercolors for which he is best known reflects Burchfield's profound identification with the forces of the natural world (plate 107).

The declining fortunes of the American Water Color Society could be seen in the fact that some of the strongest talents of the day remained aloof from it. It is not surprising that Lyonel Feininger, whose main output was in watercolor, was content to work independently. He had been associated with the expressionist Blue Rider group in Berlin, and his astringent intellectualism was incompatible with the kind of romantic realism that dominated American art in the 1930s. Yet even those artists who preferred a more traditional realism did not feel compelled to join the society. In the case of Edward Hopper, his early success with watercolor was followed by the highest proficiency of execution and profundity of feeling. Some critics have found his subjects, such as the lonely Maine lighthouses, wanting in technical finesse; yet for all of their apparent indifference to painterly brushwork and a rich palette, Hopper's mature watercolors convey a disquieting simplicity and strength of design, which imbue them with a universal appeal (plates 103 and 104). More robust as a draftsman, Reginald Marsh reinvigorated the idiom of The Eight in his picturesque scenes of New York's low life, in which color is often subordinated to strong graphic description (plates 23, 109A, and 109B). Both these artists celebrated the American scene with a realism that even the staunchest conservative could understand and admire, while eschewing conformity to standards other than their own.

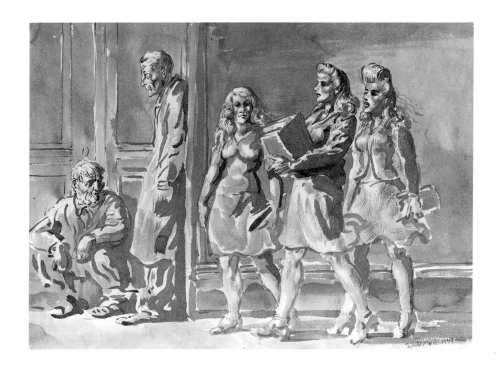

23
Reginald Marsh (1898–1954)
Street Scene, 1944
Watercolor on paper
13⅞ × 19⅞ in. (35.2 × 50.5 cm.)
Worcester Art Museum; Gift of Mr. and Mrs. Robert Warner

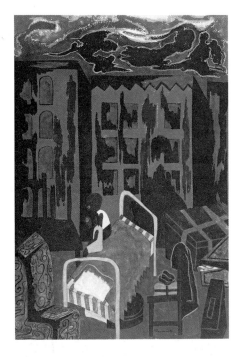

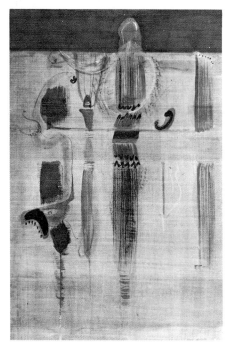

Other artists who were influenced by the aesthetics of early modernism continued to work independently. The watercolors of Charles Sheeler present a synthesis of realist imagery and a precise execution of underlying formal structure. Sheeler saw through the surface of the physical world to its essence, which became the real subject of his architectural and still-life pictures (plate 105). Concentrating mainly on still-life and figural subjects, Charles Demuth made brilliant and extensive use of transparent watercolor in a highly original style that combined elements of Expressionism, Cubism, and realism. A response to ethnic influence can be observed in the work of Jacob Lawrence, a black artist who paints primarily in watercolor and gouache. Lawrence composes his scenes of urban ghetto life in jagged patterns of broken, flat color reminiscent of the rhythms of jazz (plate 24). Mark Tobey and Morris Graves both matured in their art at a far remove from New York, in the Pacific Northwest, and their work is permeated by an interest in Oriental calligraphy and imagery (plates 106 and 110).

By 1950 the president of the American Water Color Society was urging its membership to regard the society as the "academy of American watercolor painting" and a scholar was appointed to chronicle its history from 1866.[34] Perhaps this was a fitting moment for the society to think about its past: certainly watercolor no longer needed to prove itself, and in the broader context American art had already demonstrated its special genius to the world. Yet in spite of active participation by its membership, the society's annuals seemed to exist in a kind of vacuum, serenely out of touch with current trends. Artists associated with the society characteristically remained committed to traditional representational art at a time when such values bore the brunt of critical scorn. As Clement Greenberg wrote in 1949, "The naturalistic art of our time is unredeemable, as it requires only taste to discover; and the sheer multitude of those who still practice it does not make it any more valid."[35]

The postwar New York art scene was witnessing the emergence of Abstract Expressionism. Younger artists were looking to a whole battery of new painting media and working on a scale undreamed of by conventional practitioners of watercolor. Mark Rothko, for example, experimented with surrealistic compositions in luminous watercolor and gouache (plate 25). These works are predecessors to his monumental, lyrical color rectangles of ambiguous space, but they also stand as fully independent works in his oeuvre. Similarly, the watercolors of Sam Francis anticipated his larger works in oil in their designs and in the way color is "dripped" onto surfaces. And Franz Kline produced a group of small, colored gestural works on typing paper, frequently combining watercolor with oil (plate 26).

Recent trends in American art, especially in the last ten years, indicate a reviving interest in watercolor. This is particularly apparent in the work of artists like Richard Estes, Robert Bechtle, and Ralph Goings, who have embraced Photo-realism, with its emphasis on the reflective surfaces

Opposite, top:
24
Jacob Lawrence (b. 1917)
They Live in Fire Traps, 1943
Gouache on paper
21½ × 14⅜ in. (54.7 × 36.6 cm.)
Worcester Art Museum; Museum purchase

Opposite, bottom:
25
Mark Rothko (1903–1970)
Vessels of Magic, 1946
Watercolor on paper
38¹⁵⁄₁₆ × 26 in. (98.8 × 66 cm.)
The Brooklyn Museum; Museum Collection Fund

26
Franz Kline (1910–1962)
Untitled, c. 1952
Watercolor and oil wash on typing paper
10⅞ × 8½ in. (27.7 × 21.6 cm.)
Worcester Art Museum; Gift of Mrs. Helen Sagoff Slosberg

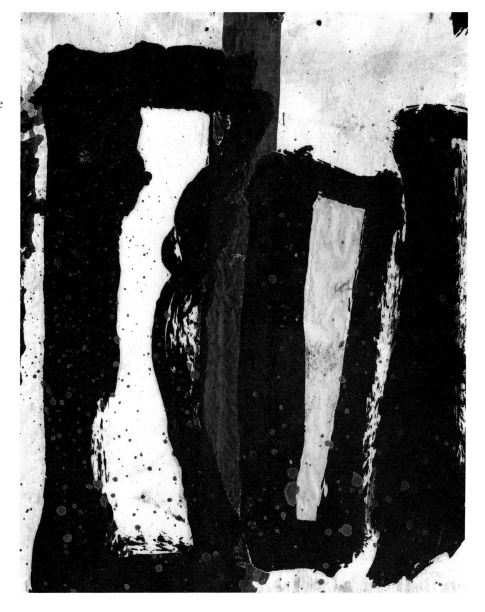

of city buildings and manmade objects.[36] In these artists' paintings watercolor imparts a translucency that is crucial to creating the illusion of reality. Other trends in postwar art, such as the Pop movement, have also seen watercolor used with notable success, for example, in the work of Jim Dine and Tom Wesselmann. Dine's extended watercolor series *Twenty Hearts* spins out seemingly endless variations on primary color notes. As realism has regained strength among our emerging group of young artists, watercolor is experiencing a profound renaissance in the carefully drawn work of Carolyn Brady (plate 113), Sondra Freckelton, DeWitt Hardy (plate 27), and John Stuart Ingle, or in the more painterly,

27
DeWitt Hardy (b. 1940)
View of Dover, New Hampshire, 1976
Watercolor over graphite on paper
21⅝ × 24⅞ in. (55 × 62.9 cm.)
Worcester Art Museum; Gift of Dr. and
Mrs. Robert A. Johnson

yet diverse, styles of Joseph Raffael and Susan Shatter, who have succeeded more established artists such as Philip Pearlstein and Neil Welliver. Some of these artists are establishing their reputations in watercolor and are now producing their most important works in the medium. Many work on a very large scale, partly in response to the monumental canvases executed by artists working in the various abstract movements of the 1950s and 1960s. As the final decades of the twentieth century draw to a close, watercolor may well continue to be regarded as "the American medium."

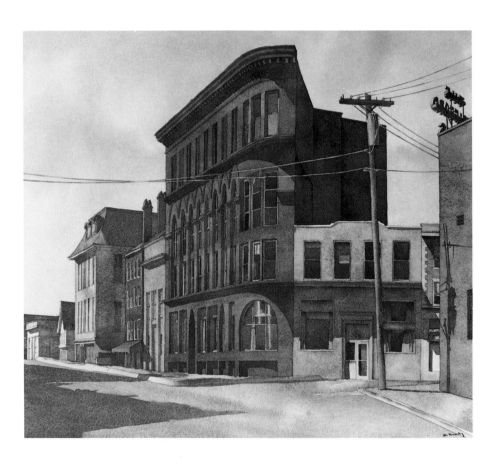

1. Theodore E. Stebbins, Jr., *American Master Drawings and Watercolors: A History of Works on Paper from Colonial Times to the Present* (New York: Harper & Row, 1976), p. 146.

2. See Albert Ten Eyck Gardner, *A History of Water Color Painting in America* (New York: Reinhold, 1966), p. 8.

3. See Richard J. Boyle, *American Impressionism* (Boston: New York Graphic Society, 1974), p. 27. The collapsible metal tube was invented by John G. Rand (1801–1873), an American living in London.

4. For example, in *Theory and Practice of Water-Colour*, published in London in 1840, the English writer George Barret offered useful advice about some common hazards, such as the use of gray undertones based on India ink and indigo, which fade—a practice that Barret saw as the source of criticism about the impermanence of watercolors. Another English author, John Burnet, in *Practical Essays on Various Branches of the Fine Arts*, published in London in 1848, stressed the importance of the medium's light-reflecting property and advised keeping as much of the paper visible as possible.

5. Archibald Robertson, *Elements of the Graphic Arts* (New York, 1802). See also the comprehensive bibliography on American manuals, Carl W. Drepperd, "American Drawing Books," *New York Public Library Bulletin* 49, no. 11 (November 1945): 795–812.

6. Henry Warren, *Painting in Water Color* (New York, 1856).

7. See A. F. Bellows, et al., eds., "Water Color Painting: Some Facts and Authorities in Relation to Its Durability" (New York, 1868).

8. My discussion concentrates on New York as the locus for the development of watercolor painting in America, for New York was, and continues to be, the center of the American art world. It should be remembered, however, that there were watercolor activities and institutions in other cities across the country during the period under review here.

9. "Constitution, By-Laws and Minutes, October 1850 to September 1855," Society for the Promotion of Painting in Water Colors, New York, New-York Historical Society.

10. For the most complete biography of Falconer, see Linda Ferber, "Our Mr. Falconer," in *Brooklyn before the Bridge: American Paintings from the Long Island Historical Society* (Brooklyn: Brooklyn Museum, 1982).

11. For a complete list of membership, see Stebbins, *American Master Drawings and Watercolors*, p. 148.

12. See Kenneth W. Luckhurst, *The Story of Exhibitions* (New York: Studio Publications, 1951), p. 221.

13. *Exhibition of the Industry of All Nations* (New York, 1853), p. 22.

14. For an in-depth discussion of this exhibition, see Susan P. Casteras, "The 1857–58 Exhibition of English Art in America and Critical Response to Pre-Raphaelitism," in Linda S. Ferber and William H. Gerdts, *The New Path: Ruskin and the American Pre-Raphaelites* (Brooklyn, N.Y.: Brooklyn Museum, 1985), pp. 109–31.

15. For a detailed discussion, see Kathleen Adair Foster, "The Pre-Raphaelite Medium: Ruskin, Turner, and American Watercolor," in Ferber and Gerdts, *The New Path*, pp. 79–107.

16. The seven were Samuel Colman, Gilbert Burling, A. L. Rawson, William Start, John M. Falconer, William Craig, and Alfred Fredericks.

17. "Minute Book" (1867), American Society of Painters in Water Colors, New York, Archives of American Art, Smithsonian Institution.

18. Clark S. Marlor, *A History of the Brooklyn Art Association* (New York: J. F. Carr, 1970), p. 50.

19. Gardner states that Homer insisted he was one of the founding members of the American Society of Painters in Water Colors in 1866, a claim not supported by the society's records (*History of Water Color Painting in America*, p. 15).

20. *Nation* 32 (February 3, 1881): 80.

21. For a full discussion, see Kathleen A. Foster, "Makers of the American Watercolor Movement, 1860–1890" (Ph.D. diss., Yale University, 1982), pp. 68–74.

22. Not everyone was hostile. The *Nation* praised the "graded tints [that] may be obtained of all the delicacy of an ethera." *Nation* 28 (February 6, 1879): 107.

23. See Foster, "Makers of the American Watercolor Movement," p. 4.

24. See Papers of the New York Water Color Club, Archives of American Art, Smithsonian Institution, microfilm file N68–10.

25. See Gardner, *History of Water Color Painting in America*, p. 14.

26. See Dianne H. Pilgrim, *American Impressionist and Realist Paintings and Drawings* (New York: Metropolitan Museum of Art, 1973), p. 11. Among its members were its first president, Robert F. Blum, John H. Twachtman, Childe Hassam, and William Merritt Chase.

27. Henry James, "John S. Sargent," *Harper's Magazine* 75 (October 1887): 689.

28. See Frank A. Gervasè, "A History of the American Water Color Society, 1866–1950," manuscript in the American Watercolor Society, New York, p. 52.

29. The American Federation of Arts was founded in 1909 in Washington, D.C.; incorporated in New York State in 1916.

30. Other associations were forming during these years, reflecting the new currents of modern art emanating from Europe. For example, the Society of Independent Artists was founded in New York in 1917 with the help of avant-garde Frenchmen Jacques Villon, Marcel Duchamp, and Francis Picabia.

31. See Milton Brown, *The Story of the Armory Show* (New York: Joseph H. Hirshhorn Foundation, 1963), pp. 230ff.

32. See Gervasè, "American Water Color Society," p. 47.

33. See Foster, "Makers of the American Watercolor Movement," p. 4.

34. See Gervasè, "American Water Color Society," p. 60.

35. Clement Greenberg, "New York Painters," *Magazine of Art* 42 (October 1949): 92.

36. For an in-depth survey of current trends in realism by watercolorists, see John Arthur, *Realist Drawings and Watercolors: Contemporary American Works on Paper* (Boston: New York Graphic Society, 1980).

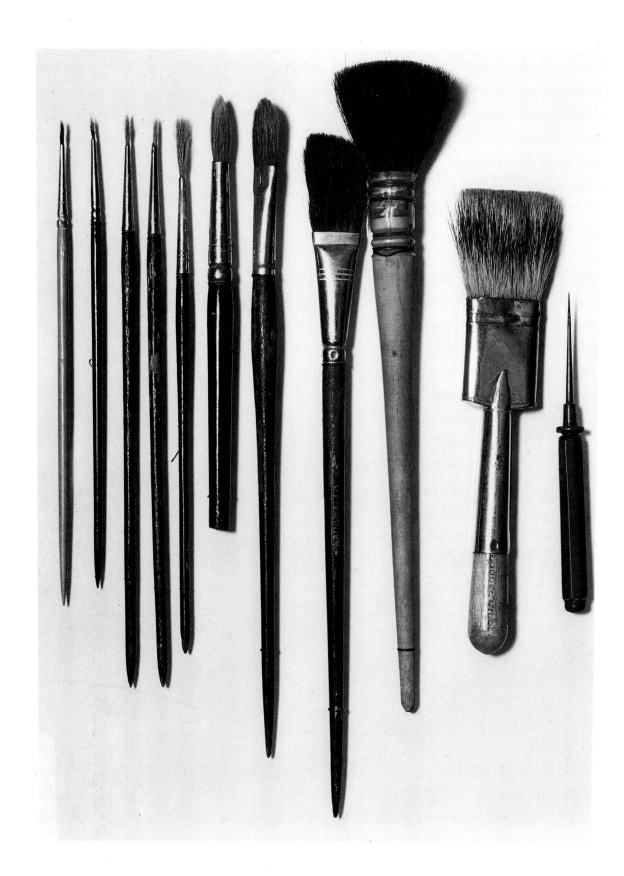

Judith C. Walsh

Observations on the Watercolor Techniques of Homer and Sargent

Watercolor is a very difficult medium to master. This difficulty is not readily apparent in the Worcester Art Museum's many watercolors because much of their beauty lies in their simplicity. Achieving this simplicity was surely not easy: the paper buckles when wet; the colors puddle and run into each other; fine washes laid on top of each other marry and become muddy; mistakes can't be painted out; underdrawing shows through the washes of color. Working outdoors made the task yet more arduous—especially when the watercolor manuals would nag, nag, nag the artist to create paintings that appeared spontaneous.[1] How did artists ever learn to control these paints, and how did they create works of such clear, delicate color?

Not much can be hidden in transparent watercolors, which makes them relatively easy to examine for technique.[2] Their transparency allows the viewer to see all the layers at once, and with a little imagination the artist's steps can be reconstructed. Areas of fresh paper are almost always visible. The graphite underdrawing is hardly hidden or disturbed by the first washes. Subsequent layers of paint can be identified by drying patterns. Surface scraping and composition changes can be spotted in raking, or oblique, light. By closely inspecting the watercolors by Winslow Homer and John Singer Sargent in the museum's collection we can learn how these two acknowledged masters of the medium created their watercolor paintings, applying their technical skills according to their differing temperaments and intentions.

Homer never ascribed to the idea that watercolors should look effortless. As he worked, he continually evaluated the results and apparently felt no qualms about altering his compositions at any point. Many times the changes he made were quite drastic and often remained obvious to the viewer. Indeed, one early critic characterized Homer's watercolor style as possessing a "sturdy disregard for elegance," a description that applied to both his subject matter and the surface of his paintings.[3] By the end of his career, however, Homer's watercolors were effortless not only in appearance but also in technique. After forty years of practice and experimentation, he was finally a "natural" watercolorist.

28
John Singer Sargent's watercolor brushes and scraper
Fogg Art Museum, Harvard University Art Museums, Cambridge, Massachusetts; Edward W. Forbes Collection of Artists' Materials

Sargent believed from the outset in giving the impression that his finished watercolors had been executed with ease. He sometimes made preliminary drawings, watercolor sketches, and repeated paintings of similar subjects, so that his final watercolor compositions would require few changes. For Sargent, maintaining the integrity of the surface was primary: rather than scraping the surface to allow the white of the paper to show through, he would "stop out" areas of paper to prevent it from absorbing the pigment and even change the consistency of the pigment itself to achieve certain effects. Having a rigorous academic training and a practiced eye, he was able to work swiftly and surely, with his designs well planned in advance. Rather than amending less successful efforts, he simply discarded them.[4]

Homer, on the other hand, rarely threw a watercolor away. In one of his daybook entries regarding ten pictures he was sending to his dealer, E. L. Knoedler, he wrote, "I am to get $200 ea. and all, good or bad, large or small."[5] This is not to say that Sargent took too much pride in the surface of his watercolors and Homer too little; rather, they had dissimilar *expectations* for the finished watercolor. Their paintings differed in part because their approaches to watercolor technique differed. While Sargent developed his technique early and varied it little, Homer's evolved as his career progressed.[6] His early paintings of the 1870s show a controlled and deliberate working method—appropriate for a self-taught artist who was active as an illustrator—but their obvious compositional changes and additions alert us to the artist's essentially experimental attitude. This willingness to change his technique finally made Homer a watercolor painter of the first rank.

Boys and Kitten (plate 59) of 1873 exemplifies Homer's early working method. First he laid out the composition in a graphite drawing, detailing the turned-up pants cuffs and even the boys' individual toes, and indicating shading on the kitten's face. Over the drawing, he applied transparent washes of color to block out figures, background, sky, and wall. These washes do not overlap, and areas of paper were left blank where Homer was to paint in the mother cat and kneeling boy. He graded the next washes to suggest textures and shadows in the foliage and architecture. Deep black touches and opaque gouache highlights were applied last, in washes both thin and quite thick, to make small changes, pick out details, and add interest to the foreground.

Homer began to sign the completed watercolor at the base of the wall, "H-O-M-E," then he stopped—apparently dissatisfied with the painting. Reappraising the composition, he painted in the ambiguous brown shading at lower right, which covered the end of the wall, the white and ocher gouache details on the beach, and his partial signature. The effect of the change was to balance the composition. Certainly, had he wanted to, a painter of Homer's talents could have hidden this alteration. He might have rewetted and blotted the opaque pigments or applied darker paint where these *pentimenti*, or changes, show through. But the

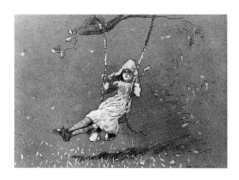

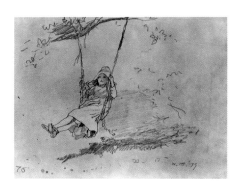

29
Winslow Homer (1836–1910)
Girl on Swing, 1879
Graphite and charcoal heightened with
white gouache on paper
8¼ × 12½ in. (21.6 × 31.7 cm.)
Museum of Fine Arts, Boston; Bequest of
the estate of Katherine Dexter McCormick

30
Winslow Homer
Girl on Swing, 1879
Graphite on paper
7¾ × 10¾ in. (19.7 × 27.3 cm.)
Private collection; courtesy Kennedy Gal-
leries, New York

artist was seeking an effect, and in his haste—and perhaps even delight—
he left his changes visible.

Homer soon abandoned his early use of opaque colors and gouache,
in keeping with the prevailing fashion of relying totally on transparent
watercolor.[7] His small painting *The Swing* (plate 60), dated 1879, shows
transparent washes carefully laid within the graphite outlines of the
preliminary drawing. The modulating tones of the washes give shape to
the figure, and only a few black outlines help define the final form. *The
Swing* represents a remarkable leap in technique. Where Homer had relied
on thick, dry paint to exercise control in *Boys and Kitten*, here he was
able to use overlapping transparent washes of color to achieve his desired
effects.

As an aid in developing this painting, Homer made at least two
drawings of the subject. One is in graphite on gray paper, worked up
with copious opaque white in the figure, with a few final touches of
charcoal (plate 29). It is similar in technique to the Worcester watercolor
Girl with Shell at Ear (plate 61). A second graphite drawing of the same
subject is extremely close to the composition and feeling of the watercolor,
which could, in fact, have been traced from it (plate 30).[8] Since the
design of the watercolor was worked out completely beforehand, and the
technique Homer used was considerably more difficult to control, *The
Swing* is not as spontaneous nor as complex in composition as the earlier
Boys and Kitten.

No one knows precisely why the forty-five-year-old Homer, having
had a successful career as an illustrator for *Harper's* and gaining repute as
a painter in both oil and watercolor, felt compelled in 1881 to move to
the remote fishing village of Tynemouth on the north coast of England.
Certainly the English school of painters had played a notable role in the
development of watercolor, but Tynemouth was in no way a hub of activity
in the medium. However, living there apparently provided Homer with a
chance to experiment with watercolor methods typically used by English
artists.[9] The English approach involved overlapping broad washes of
transparent color to build up a composition and then using contrasting
brushwork and a battery of "subtractive" techniques—scraping, sponging,
blotting, rewetting and lifting, and erasing—to remove pigment from the
sheet and thus create a variety of subtle effects.[10] Homer learned these
techniques quickly and later mastered them.

The loose, transparent painting method Homer adopted in Tynemouth
can be clearly seen in *Crab Fishing* (plate 62). In this one work, dated
1883, Homer used every English technique he had learned, including
every subtractive technique he would ever use in his watercolors. He first
drew the boat and figures in graphite, carefully delineating such details
as the girls' features and wisps of hair blowing in the wind. He then
colored the primary forms with dense washes. Homer altered the preliminary painting in several areas as the work progressed (plate 31). For
example, to change the perspective of the far side of the boat's hull, he

47

31
Winslow Homer
Crab Fishing, 1883
(detail of plate 62)
This detail shows Homer's use of the subtractive techniques of scraping, sponging,
blotting, rewetting and lifting, and erasing
previously laid washes.

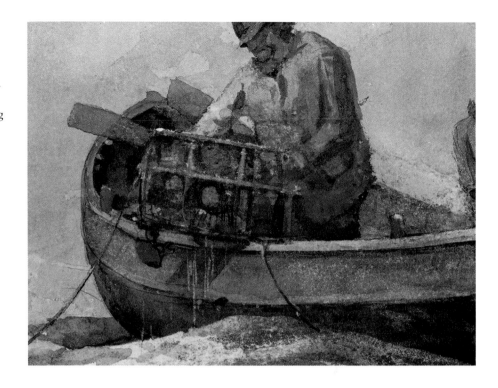

sponged, blotted, and scraped the pigment. To delineate the oar and trap,
blank paper had to be recovered from washes already laid in for the
boat, and a close look reveals where Homer scraped the sheet to remove
the paint film: the highlights and cross members of the trap are carved
into the surface of the paper. The swell under the small boat was sponged
and blotted several times to mottle the surface and create the effect of the
disturbance on the water made by pulling the trap. Seemingly simple
details, such as the fine drips of water falling from the trap, required
considerable manipulation of the medium. Homer first softened a bit of
the underlying blue wash by carefully applying water to the dried paint
film and then lifted it with a blotter. The addition of several dabs of
opaque white completed the highlighting throughout the composition.

All this reworking of the surface in the center of the sheet is surrounded by clear washes of color in the sea and sky, painted on water-
saturated paper in a technique called "wet-into-wet." Strokes of darker
gray-blues, added after the washes dried, articulate the crests of the waves
and layers of clouds. The hard edge between the darkest band of clouds
and the rest of the sky was reduced by rubbing with, perhaps, either "day
old bread" or an "India rubber," as contemporary manuals suggested.[11]

Homer used subtractive techniques with greater confidence in his
painting *In a Florida Jungle*, probably 1885-86 (plate 65), in which many
details were defined by rewetting and lifting existing paint layers.[12] To
create the lightest fronds of the palmettos, he applied clean water with
the tip of his brush to rewet the foliage areas (plate 32). He let the water

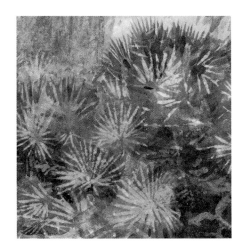

stand a few moments to soften the opaque green and brown, then blotted the area to reveal the washes or paper beneath.[13] Such precise, hard-edged lifting of watercolor requires the color to be worked up rich, that is, with lots of medium. The pigment of the foliage is quite thick and is also glazed with gamboge, an uncommonly transparent resinous yellow pigment, which gives it added richness.[14] To complete the palmettos, Homer painted dark green fronds over some of the uncovered areas and scraped some of the leaves for additional definition.

In an interview with the historian George William Sheldon in 1880, Homer endorsed the practice of painting outdoors: "I prefer every time a picture composed and painted outdoors. This making studies and then taking them home to use is only half right. You get composition, but you lose freshness; you miss the subtle and, to the artist, the finer characteristics of the scene itself."[15] Still, much of the work on a watercolor such as *In a Florida Jungle*, initially composed outdoors, must have been done in the studio. The delicate rewetting and blotting of the palm fronds, for instance, would require that the sheet lie flat and undisturbed as the water dissolved the washes.

Similarly, several major changes in this watercolor, such as the repositioning of the crocodile and spoonbill, were probably also carried out in the studio (plate 33). Originally, the crocodile was positioned on the

32

Winslow Homer
In a Florida Jungle, probably 1885–86
(detail of plate 65)
Homer rewetted and lifted previously laid washes to depict individual fronds of the palmettos in the same manner that he delineated the drips of water falling from the trap in *Crab Fishing* (plate 31).

33

Winslow Homer
In a Florida Jungle
(detail of plate 65)
To the right of the spoonbill are traces of the original placement of the crocodile, whose raised snout is barely visible among the palmettos.

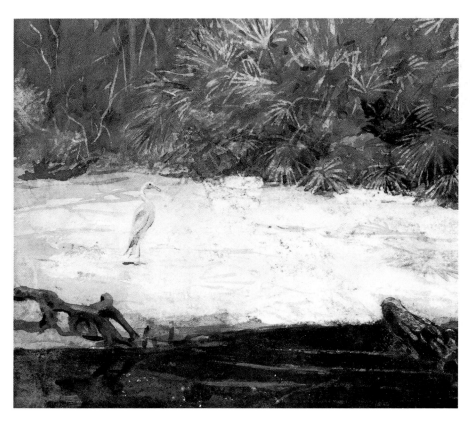

beach, sunning himself; traces of his raised snout are still visible in the foliage behind the beach. A faint silhouette of the spoonbill can be seen where it rested to the left of its present position. Later, Homer moved the crocodile into the murky swamp, with his pointed snout just emerging from the water, and placed the spoonbill at alert nearby. These changes gave the picture a new dramatic tension. As in his earlier works, Homer did not go to undue lengths to conceal these alterations from the viewer. The scraping and roughing of the sheet to remove the crocodile from the beach was done late, after the complicated painting of the jungle had been completed; the reconstruction of the leaves where the crocodile's head had previously obscured the jungle growth does not match the rest of the foliage in color or treatment.

Such final touches as highlighting particular areas with dabs of color to bring the composition together were no doubt also added in the studio. The bright blue highlights on the crocodile and the ripples of water around his head are the same pigment as the small blue shadow under the spoonbill. This blue links crocodile and bird in a subtle yet direct manner, in much the same way as the red touches in the darkest shadows of the jungle connect the spoonbill to the jungle and to the red tips of the turkey buzzards in the sky.

By 1895 or so Homer had gained a versatility and breadth of handling in the watercolor medium that far exceeded his earlier skill. He no longer relied on the use of gouache, nor did he seem to plan out his compositions in preliminary drawings. He had quickly adopted the English "wet" technique, as well as every device commonly used in manipulating watercolor. With his profound sense of color and composition, he created works of great complexity and beauty. Among these are the much-loved *Old Friends* (plate 66) and *The Light House, Nassau* (plate 72), which are as psychologically engaging as they are aesthetically pleasing.

Coral Formation (plate 74), painted in the Bahamas in 1901, testifies to Homer's new mastery of watercolor. The visual power of this work relies largely on the simplicity and directness of its composition. Homer achieved this impact in part by breaking up the potential monotony of the large areas of blue and blue-gray in the sea and sky.[16] Here he introduced rivers of water between dried or nearly dried washes of different blues to dissolve and redeposit the paint. These intricately painted wet passages, abutting the direct, dry-brush painting in the coral cliffs, balance the composition. At the center of the far left edge of the sheet can be seen Homer's thumb and palm prints in the first layer of washes on the background sea and rock formations. These impressions may have been made as he deftly rocked the sheet to spread the puddling water and pigment: on a sunny day in the tropics, how quickly, how surely he must have worked!

Homer's watercolors of earlier periods alone could have earned the artist his reputation in the medium. But in his last decade he developed a technical mastery and control unmatched by any other artist. The culmi-

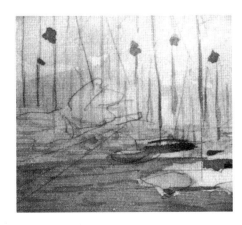

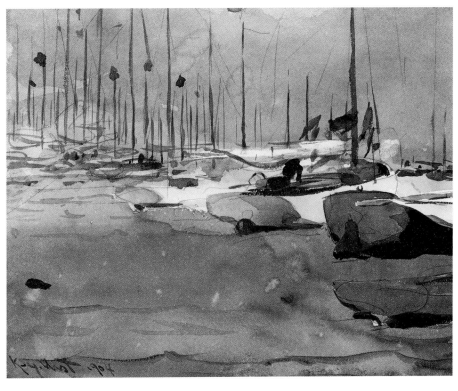

nation of Homer's genius as a watercolorist can be seen in *Fishing Boats,
Key West* (plate 75), dated 1904. This work is an unquestionable masterpiece of watercolor painting, in part because of the quality of Homer's
drawing and his subtle manipulation of washes. The scant preliminary
graphite sketch, which shows through the later washes, is quite loosely
drawn, giving only the barest indication of the composition (plate 34).
Fluid washes of gray-blues, applied wet-into-wet over a paler wash in the
sky and water, easily move around the white of the paper reserved for
the furled sails of the boats. Homer created the subtle gradations in the
gray wash at the upper right of the sky by dropping water on the drying
washes, causing them to merge and soften. At the bottom left corner of
this sheet, he backwashed, or rewetted, an entire area to suggest the
transient effect of a breeze across the water (plate 35). This section of the
work displays a finesse and control that cannot be overestimated.

Homer's mastery of his medium can be measured by just how haz-
ardous the introduction of water can be to a watercolor. Adding water
can move previously laid washes and blur carefully constructed effects or
create darker lines, often called tide lines, in broad areas of wash. Accidental spotting effects can be seen in the sky at the left of *Fishing Boats,
Key West*. Characteristically, Homer simply painted masts over the spots,
ignoring the error. However, at lower left he deliberately introduced water,
at tremendous risk. First he applied two blue washes, one brilliant blue
and the other gray-blue, representing the sea and the shadows of the

51

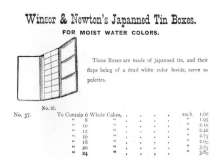

Winsor & Newton's Japanned Tin Boxes.

FOR MOIST WATER COLORS.

These Boxes are made of japanned tin, and their flaps being of a dead white color inside, serve as palettes.

No. 37.

No. 37.	To Contain 6 Whole Cakes,	.	.	.	.	.	each	1.60
"	8	"	.	.	.	.	"	1.95
"	10	"	.	.	.	.	"	2.10
"	12	"	.	.	.	.	"	2.40
"	16	"	.	.	.	.	"	2.75
"	18	"	.	.	.	.	"	2.90
"	20	"	.	.	.	.	"	3.25
"	24	"	.	.	.	.	"	3.80

boats. Before they had dried completely, he introduced a flood of clear water from the bottom left corner. He then rocked the sheet to manipulate the direction and spread of the water. As he tipped the sheet, the flood spread outward, carrying dissolved pigment at its tide line and mixing the washes in its wake. This untidy puddle approached the sterns of the sailboats, causing a slight bleeding of the reds in the central boat; then, as Homer rocked the sheet back, the flood retreated, and as it dried it deposited the carried pigment at its farthest reach. At this point, Homer daubed on *more* water in dots to indicate the first drops of rain in the storm. Maintaining perfect control, he magnificently produced the fleeting natural effects of wind and rain on water. It is a tribute to Homer's confidence with the medium that he attempted such delicate work and a credit to his genius that he succeeded. The artist Marsden Hartley, describing Homer's watercolors, may have been thinking of just this sort of painting when he proclaimed the artist "one of the few great masters the world has ever known."[17]

While the watercolors themselves reveal much about Homer's technique, relatively little is known about his actual working routine. His tools also tell us little, especially because they are commonplace for artists of his time. A few relics were found in his Prout's Neck studio in Maine at the time of his death in 1910, including some that relate to his work in watercolor: his daybook of 1902–3, some photographs, a couple of movable mannequins dressed as English fisherwomen, his watercolor boxes, and two of his brushes.[18]

36
Winsor & Newton's Japanned Tin Boxes
Wood engraving from Frost and Adams, *Priced and Illustrated Catalogue of Artists' Materials* (Boston, 1875)
Courtesy American Antiquarian Society, Worcester

37
Winslow Homer's watercolor box
Bowdoin College Museum of Art, Brunswick, Maine
The flap that bears Homer's signature is folded over the pans of pigments. Visible on the open wing are residues of mixed paints and some of his color notations.

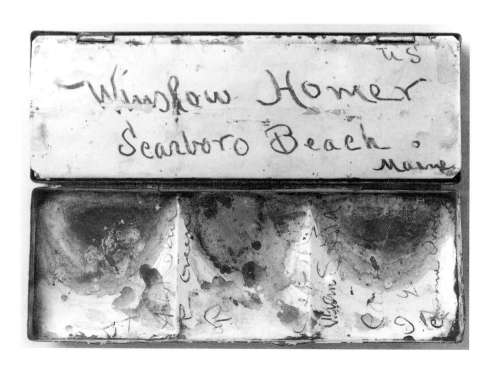

52

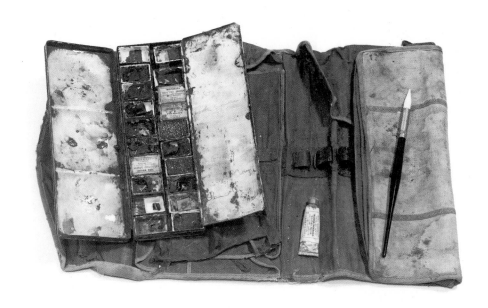

The two boxes are Winsor & Newton twenty-pan "Japanned black moist watercolor boxes" (plate 36) and bear Homer's signature and address in black waxy crayon on their inner flaps.[19] Both still bear his color notations next to the pans in the wings designed for color mixing (plates 37 and 38). The boxes contain full pans of moist watercolor in white ceramic cups, all bearing the Winsor & Newton logo on the bottom and some with printed labels identifying the pigments.[20]

One box was stored in a Winsor & Newton "folding Morocco pouch case," offered in their catalogues for "holding brushes or pencils." A porcelain-tipped burnishing tool, such as might be used to smooth down disturbed fibers of the sheet after scraping, was found within the case (plate 38).[21] The two Winsor & Newton watercolor brushes that Homer used are still remarkable for their fullness, flexibility, and beauty (plate 39). The brush hairs of "finest brown sable" were rolled into place by hand, their ends wrapped in magenta silk to cushion the hairs, then "tied with gold wire" before being set in the natural quill handles (plate 40). The brushes were named for the source of the quill: Homer's appear to be the small and large size "swan" brushes.[22] Their shafts, not perfectly round, are hollow and lightweight. The ends of the quill handles, stripped of their feathering, are blunt cut and quite sharp. The open ends of the quills were packed with a white material, possibly lead white, to counterbalance the head of the brush. Homer's brushes are all the more fascinating for the variety and amount of color caught at the sharp end of the quill. Perhaps this tool, ready to hand, was used in the vigorous

38
Winslow Homer's watercolor box with "folding Morocco pouch case" and porcelain-tipped burnisher
Portland Museum of Art, Portland, Maine; Gift of L. Robert Porteous, Jr., in honor of Bennett C. Porteous

53

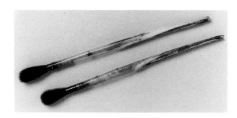

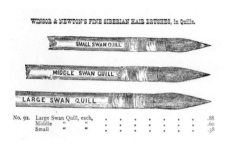

WINSOR & NEWTON'S FINE SIBERIAN HAIR BRUSHES, In Quills.

SMALL SWAN QUILL

MIDDLE SWAN QUILL

LARGE SWAN QUILL

No. 92. Large Swan Quill, each, ...88
        Middle "   "   .60
        Small   "   "   .38

39
Winslow Homer's sable watercolor brushes
Bowdoin College Museum of Art, Brunswick, Maine

40
Winsor & Newton's Fine Siberian Hairbrushes
Wood engraving from Frost and Adams,
*Priced and Illustrated Catalogue of Artists'
Materials* (Boston, 1875)
Courtesy American Antiquarian Society,
Worcester

scraping of his watercolors. None of Homer's penknives, scrapers, or sponges have ever been found, though certainly he must have owned these.

The success of subtractive watercolor techniques like the ones Homer used—scraping, gouging, lifting, and so on—depends a great deal on the resilience of the paper. Before he went to England, Homer used a variety of papers, some gray, brown, or green. After his trip he seemed to prefer heavier-weight watercolor papers, perhaps because they allowed him to apply his newly learned English techniques. His watercolors most often appear on a medium-weight, medium-toothed, off-white paper manufactured by J. Whatman, the leading manufacturer of watercolor paper at that time, recommended by almost every contemporary watercolor manual.[23]

Homer purchased his paper in blocks. An entry in his daybook for 1902 reads, "Monday 14th July ordered W.C. pan & blotting paper," and later that week he recorded his payment for a "watercolor block." These precut tablets of watercolor paper, bound on all four sides with glue and gauze, were available in several sizes.[24] Homer's watercolors are usually a fraction of an inch larger or several inches smaller than these standard dimensions. By wetting and stretching individual sheets prior to painting, the artist would inadvertently increase their dimensions by as much as one-half inch, a size they retained when freed from stretching. The size of the smaller sheets is explained by the fact that Homer no doubt trimmed the borders, discarding the portions he didn't like. Many of the Worcester sheets bear remnants of the block binding material along their edges, and a few have guiding pencil marks along unevenly cut edges. The uppermost sheet in a watercolor block must be removed carefully to prevent damage to the sheet below. *Rum Cay* (plate 71) shows the scar left by a tool when the previous sheet was removed. Irrigated by the scratch, the sheet took the color unevenly around the edges.

Winslow Homer was an intensely private man. In spite of the success he enjoyed during his lifetime, he left few interviews or reminiscences about his work. Close inspection of his works themselves may tell us more about the man than he would have liked. For close to forty years Homer persistently *worked* at developing his watercolor technique, accepting moments of inspiration as they came, unashamed of his struggles. Leaving one after another of his beautiful experiments behind, he finally became America's greatest watercolorist.

Like Homer, John Singer Sargent increasingly used watercolor for serious artistic expression as his career advanced. Having made his reputation and fortune as a portrait painter, he turned to watercolor in mid-career not only to record his travels but also as a respite from the pressures of his enormous success. In time, his watercolors, too, were in great demand, a demand he had trouble filling.[25]

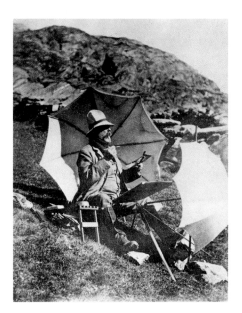

41
John Singer Sargent at Simplon Pass in the Tyrol, 1906–10

Unlike Homer, Sargent's development as a watercolorist cannot be followed by charting an increasingly complex technique. Sargent was a well-trained studio artist, having studied in Paris in the atelier of the popular French portrait painter Émile-Auguste Carolus-Duran. The French atelier system provided a group of students with a common studio, a program of painting exercises, and a regular weekly critique of their efforts by the painting master. In the atelier Sargent learned disciplined work habits and mastered a range of technical skills that allowed him to develop his prodigious talent and enter the mainstream of contemporary European art by the late 1880s. His work in watercolor, from about 1900 to his death in 1925, indicates that his mastery of the medium came early; we do not see the same stages of development that Homer experienced. In fact, one aspect of Sargent's work was his consistent use of a wide range of techniques in watercolor throughout his career. From the beginning he used both wet and dry methods, working with transparent watercolor or opaque gouache, with or without subtractive surface techniques. These approaches he used singularly or in combination in any particular watercolor to create a variety of effects.

Sargent's working method was described with admiration by Adrian Stokes, a fellow member of the Royal Watercolour Society and his companion in the Tyrol during summer holidays in 1911 and 1914. Stokes reports that Sargent would rise each morning and leave the house by 8:30, whatever the weather, in the company of his "heavy laden" Italian manservant, Nicola. He would proceed to a previously scouted spot and settle in.[26] A photograph of Sargent on such an excursion shows him seated on a stool, holding brushes and watercolor pan aloft, before a tripod easel that holds his watercolor block at a low angle (plate 41). A small collapsible camping table is wedged into the hillside next to him, bearing wash water, rags, and other implements. Sargent's booted feet (with tall gaiters to protect his pants on these alpine treks) rest on boulders, and around his head are large white umbrellas to protect him from wind and sun. One observer said the setup gave him the aspect of "a newly hatched chicken, surrounded by broken eggshells."[27] Thus seated, Sargent was ready for work. Stokes recorded his companion's approach:

> Fine and correct drawing was the foundation on which all his work was built: while natural taste, combined with long practice in composition, seemed to make it easy for him to place his subjects on paper in a telling way. . . . The rapidity and directness with which he worked was amazing. . . . His hand seemed to move with the same agility as when playing the keys of a piano. That is a minor matter; what was really marvelous was the rightness of every touch. . . . All was rendered or suggested with utmost fidelity. On a few occasions when I saw him begin a drawing, he simply opened a block and began to paint straight away.[28]

In contrast to Stokes's description of the artist's careful drawing and use of a dry sheet, Sargent's early biographer, Evan Charteris, observed

42
John Singer Sargent (1856–1925)
Venice, about 1902
(detail of plate 81)
The speckled effect in the dark areas resulted from the bursting of tiny air bubbles trapped in the hollows of the dry paper.

that the artist also used another, but still rapid, method: "His general habit was to make the lightest indications in pencil to fix the relative position of objects, and then, after wetting the paper, to paint with a great rapidity."[29]

With his technical vocabulary polished by training and practice, Sargent's approach to watercolor might have appeared almost intuitive and his execution amazingly swift. However, close scrutiny of individual works reveals dexterous manipulation of the medium. The swiftness and ease of execution that the artist developed was not a matter of mere pretension on his part; rather, it was an important part of his aesthetic sensibility.[30] Sargent praised the watercolors of his friend Hercules Brabazon, in which he saw "immediate sensations flower again with a swiftness that makes one, for a time, forget there was a medium."[31] He characterized his own watercolors as "snapshots," perhaps indicating his desire to capture a fleeting effect of light or atmosphere, which may have seemed, to a portrait painter, to be the "flashes of personality" in a particular landscape.[32]

The earliest watercolor by Sargent in the collection of the Worcester Art Museum is *Venice* (plate 81), from about 1902. It is a fine example of the effects Sargent achieved by painting over either wet or dry areas of the sheet. Some strokes, such as those indicating the gondolas at the left, were made with a heavily loaded brush dragged across dry paper. The tiny white "holidays" in the dark paint were caused by the bursting of

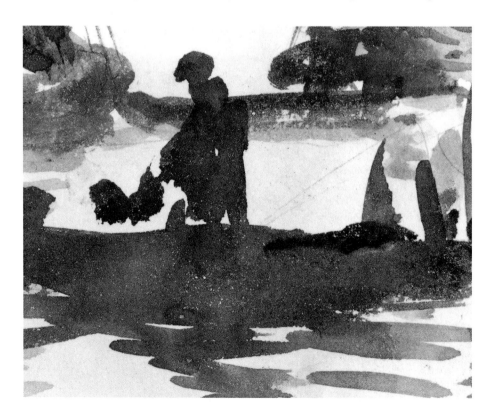

Below:
43
John Singer Sargent
Fish Weirs, 1922
Watercolor over graphite on paper
13½ × 21 in. (34.3 × 53.2 cm.)
Worcester Art Museum; Gift of Mr. and
Mrs. Richard C. Storey in memory of Richard C. Storey, Jr.

Right:
44
John Singer Sargent
Derelicts, 1917
(detail of plate 86)
The textured areas in the foliage show
where Sargent applied resist.

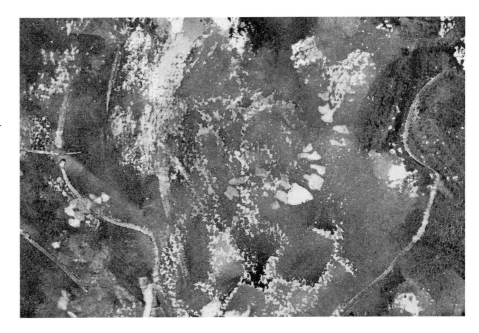

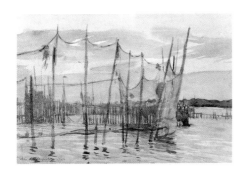

air bubbles trapped in the hollows of the dry paper's texture (plate 42). Later, with a similarly loaded brush, Sargent laid pigment on a wetted portion of the sheet, leaving the bleeding lines of purple-gray at the roof of the palazzo and clear blue in the canal. This particular wash technique quickly provided soft-focus impressions of brilliant light and reflection. Both these effects can be seen in Sargent's later works—for example, the bursting bubbles in the sky of *Boats at Anchor* (plate 88) of 1917 and the soft, bleeding lines in *Fish Weirs* (plate 43) from 1922.

Seven of the watercolors by Sargent in the Worcester Art Museum collection were painted in Florida during the winter of 1917, and they provide excellent examples of the range of Sargent's technical skills. Here are found many of the techniques Sargent often used: variations in wet-and-dry washing, the combination of opaque and transparent paints, calculated reserving of the existing color or the blank paper from later washes, and adulteration of the paint by additives, as well as all the subtractive methods also used by Homer.

Especially interesting in these works are the two methods Sargent used to preserve the white of the sheet. One technique was the use of resist—a colorless wax stick, a crayon, or perhaps a knife-sharpened candle—applied to the sheet to protect the paper and existing washes from later painting. Sargent applied resist in *Derelicts* (plate 86) to achieve the flickering effects of sunlight on the foliage above the submerged boat. The soft wax that caught in the valleys of the paper's twill repelled water-based washes and created a rough texture (plate 44). Sargent further enhanced the effect by scraping the surface with both a blunt instrument and a small knife, then covering the newly revealed whites with peach and yellow washes.

For *Shady Paths, Vizcaya* (plate 84), the artist used an alternative method of reserving the whites of the paper. Here he applied a frisket, a liquid blocking agent that is brushed on the sheet in localized areas. After washes of color are laid across the area, the frisket is removed with a solvent or by rubbing. In an early manual on watercolor technique, George Barnard suggested using a frisket of egg whites, which could be removed by rubbing with mild abrasives like bread crumbs or an eraser.[33] Later manuals suggested a mix of wax and lead white, which could be removed with turpentine.[34] Although natural rubber was apparently not recommended in the literature, it was available at this time and might have been used as a frisket. Today, rubber cement or masking tape are commonly used for this purpose, and "frisket paper," with a pressure-sensitive adhesive backing, is also available.

In *Shady Paths, Vizcaya*, the brilliant white sunlight effects on the statue at the right foreground were created in the traditional way: Sargent painted around the form he had delineated in his underdrawing. For the statue at the left, however, he protected areas of the paper by applying a frisket. A frisket must be placed deliberately, in anticipation of the work's final design. Sargent's precise underdrawing, visible today under infrared reflectography, allowed exact placement of the frisket to protect the shape of the statue subsequently defined by dark washes (plate 45).

The type of frisket Sargent used cannot be identified, but certainly it was removed by rubbing rather than by a solvent: below and around the left statue's breast are the unmistakable marks of abrasion caused by rubbing. The hard, even drying pattern of the wash and the sharp-edged void in the painterly scrubbing effects in the underbrush behind the statue indicate use of a frisket. Sargent also employed his wax-resist technique in this painting to represent the rays of sunshine cutting through the dense foliage of the trees. The wax can still be seen on the surface of the watercolor, at the right of the largest statue's head.

By using resist and frisket, Sargent modified the way his paper accepted watercolor, adapting it to his own needs. He also modified the paint itself in some cases, to give it more body. Gum megilp, a translucent viscous material derived from gum tragacanth, was recommended in the literature as an additive. It was preferred above other additives because it preserved the transparency of the watercolor and imparted no gloss.[35] Sargent modified his paint, perhaps with gum megilp, for *Derelicts*. Here the darkest green foliage bears the unmistakable pattern of brush strokes, in which the dark and light ridges of paint suggest the density of the growth and the penetrating sunlight. Their presence indicates the use of gum megilp since watercolor alone does not allow this texture, and gouache, which can be worked into brush marks, is far more opaque. Paint mixed with gum megilp covers the whiteness of the paper completely but does not obscure the sheet's texture.

Sargent brought to his watercolors a cooler vision than did Homer. The competence he gained from his studio training and his willingness to

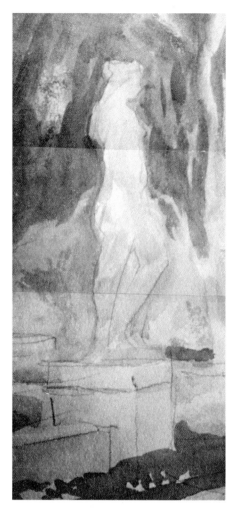

45
John Singer Sargent
Shady Paths, Vizcaya, 1917
(detail of plate 84)
This composite photograph taken under infrared light shows the graphite underdrawing that Sargent used as a guide in laying down the frisket.

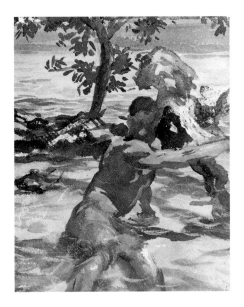

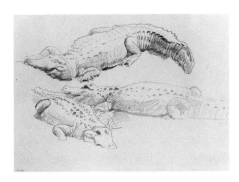

experiment with materials like resist, frisket, and gum megilp allowed him to achieve spectacular and highly original effects in his watercolor paintings. As his great-nephew and biographer Richard Ormond wrote, "It cannot be said Sargent was indifferent to the subjects he selected to paint, but they are primarily vehicles for statements about colour and light, even paint itself." He was "more concerned with what took place on the surface of his painting than in the reality of the scene before him."[36]

For sheer delight in a surface, *The Bathers* (plate 85) would be hard to match. In this gouache and watercolor painting Sargent employed a free technique, using a wetted sheet and painting with gestural strokes in transparent colors and opaque white. As in some of his earlier Tyrolean and Bedouin compositions, he applied watercolor paint in high impasto (plate 46), directly from the tube, and glazed over it with transparent color, here to indicate waves and foliage, in other pictures to add some detail, such as a small flower in the woods, or to model a subject's face. The high impasto in paintings of this type is more typical of oil paintings than watercolors.

Sargent's depiction of the most exotic subject in his Florida series—sunning alligators—reveals a more studied approach than usual. Particularly unexpected are the several drawings and watercolor studies that eventually culminated in *Muddy Alligators* (plate 82). Four of Sargent's many pencil study sheets of the subject are in Worcester's collection (plate 47). Since these poses were later amended in the watercolors, these drawings are not preliminary sketches of the typical sort. Rather than trying to work out a composition in advance, Sargent seems to have used these sketches to discover the technical approach that would best render the reptiles' unique appearance. In the drawings he used patterned jottings—crosshatching and inverted V's—to indicate the texture of the alligators' skin and the series of ridges down their backs and tails. These same patterns can be seen in the underdrawing and brushwork of the watercolors.

After making several drawings of the reptiles, Sargent made at least two preliminary watercolors of alligators, which, like the drawings, are not compositional but rather technical studies. Beginning with a simple wash drawing (plate 48), he developed a meticulous technique for painting alligators found in *Crocodiles* (*sic*) (Metropolitan Museum of Art) and then fully developed it in the great *Muddy Alligators*.[37]

A close examination of just one alligator in *Muddy Alligators*, the small one facing the viewer at the lower right, reveals Sargent's careful calculations and his light touch in scraping, blotting, and rewetting and lifting. The initial pencil underdrawing of the reptile was filled in with overlapping washes of blues. When dry, the tail, temporarily protected by a frisket, was washed in brown, as were the shadows and the outlines of the eyes and mouth. The sharply focused, bright white teeth of the alligator were scratched into his jaw with a sharp tool while the brown

46
John Singer Sargent
The Bathers, 1917
(detail of plate 85)
The white opaque highlights in the water and to either side of the bather's head are examples of Sargent's use of high impasto.

47
John Singer Sargent
Three Alligators, 1917
Graphite on paper
7 × 10 in. (17.8 × 25.4 cm.)
Worcester Art Museum; Gift of Mrs. Francis Ormond and Miss Emily Sargent

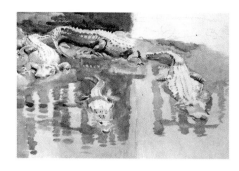

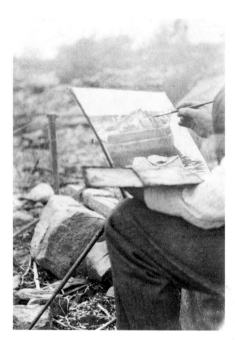

pigment was still wet. Ridges of pigment pushed aside by the deep strokes can be seen around the teeth. All along the left side of the alligator, under the tail and at the shoulder, Sargent indicated highlights and textures by broadly scraping into the dried washes with a flat implement. On the alligator's right rear leg the artist used a sharper point to crosshatch the distinctive pattern of the animal's skin.[38] Crosshatching at the back of the alligator's neck was made by rewetting the dried wash and blotting. All this Sargent worked into an area only 3½ by 5½ inches!

The blue-gray belly of the adjacent alligator has a unique fibrous pattern, which Sargent created by quickly tamping the wet paint with cotton. In raking light, stray hairs of cotton wool can be seen embedded in the paint. The smoother, but still textured, skin of the reptile covers an area no bigger than a quarter, and the blotting technique Sargent used to describe it is evident nowhere else in this picture. Sargent used this, as he did all his techniques, locally and in such subtle combinations that we must search to find them. In spite of his professed spontaneity, he constructed this picture carefully; this is no "snapshot."

As in the case of Homer, it is not certain how much work Sargent might have done later in his studio. All of the Florida watercolors in the Worcester collection bear two tiny holes in the upper portion of the sheet. Sargent may have pinned up these sheets for any number of reasons after they were dry, but since these paintings did not languish in his studio, one can guess that he displayed them briefly to see if he wanted to make any final touches before releasing them to the purchaser.[39]

Not only did Sargent use his full repertoire of technical skills throughout his career as a watercolorist, he also consistently used the same paper. Just as he chose specific papers for pencil drawings, charcoal portraits, and drapery and figure studies, his love of surface and surface effects in watercolors led to his choice of a heavyweight off-white, twill-textured paper, manufactured by J. Whatman.[40] The paper is definitely two-sided; the more textured side has a pronounced twill pattern, which Sargent often exploited. For example, in the watercolor *Boats at Anchor* the blue washes in the sky have "granulated" in the pattern of the paper twill.[41] The brighter blue washes, applied over the dried paper, show a distinctive pattern caused by bursting air bubbles caught in the twill diagonals. Dragging thick or drier paint over the surface provided additional dramatic effects, such as the brilliantly articulated fishnets in *Fish Weirs* (plate 43), in which the weave of the nets was created by painting only the peaks of the twill texture.

To achieve many of these effects, Sargent, like Homer, used relatively ordinary tools of the trade. Two photographs, one taken in the Austrian Tyrol about 1906–10 (plate 41) and the other in Maine about 1922 (plate 49), show him holding a tin folding box of moist watercolor and clutching a group of brushes. Sargent once said, "I find 'box color' very useful, and I use a great many brushes, keeping my fist full when I work."[42]

50

50
John Singer Sargent's moist colors in tubes
Fogg Art Museum, Harvard University Art Museums, Cambridge, Massachusetts; Edward W. Forbes Collection of Artists' Materials

A collection of Sargent's painting equipment, including ten watercolor brushes and fifteen tubes of watercolor paint, was found in his studio at the time of his death.[43] The extant brushes would certainly constitute a "fistful" and are varied enough to provide the widest range of effects for a watercolorist (plate 28). The large, full, round brush, called a "mop," would hold quantities of water and pigment sufficient to lay down an even wash of constant color in the early stages of work. The flat, square-tipped "sky" brush would allow control of broad or thin lines of wash for variations in tonality, especially useful at the horizon line. The small brushes would have been used for painting details or for careful rewetting and lifting. Sargent's brushes are from various manufacturers and appear to have been heavily used. The bristles are worn and out of position—some look as if they should have been discarded. The fifteen tube colors (listed in Appendix I), all bearing manufacturers' labels and color names, give us a good idea of Sargent's palette (plate 50). It is interesting to note that while many of these colors are American, some are English. Perhaps as he traveled Sargent came to prefer one maker's color over another, or perhaps he simply purchased available colors as he needed them.

The individuality and genius of Sargent's watercolor technique can be found in his unique resolution of the conflicting desires for an "invisible hand" and complexity in his compositions. He applied his enviable facility in color, brushwork, and technique to the problem, using every possible device to adapt the watercolor medium to his vision. If his paper was liable to accept too much of the wash, he stopped out the paper; if the paint was too thin for certain brush techniques, he changed the texture of the paint. He used the basic components of watercolor painting as his tools, deliberately customizing them to his needs. Sargent's subtle and elegant manipulations of the medium required patience and meticulous planning—an approach that contrasts sharply with Homer's tendency to make vigorous ad hoc changes in his watercolors. Homer, less concerned with finish and more patient with the challenges the medium presented, eventually learned to exploit its self-activating qualities to achieve his own vision.

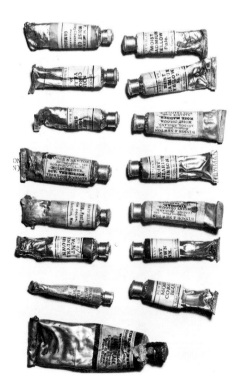

The close examination of a gifted artist's painting in order to discover his technique tells us something very intimate about him and allows us to experience vicariously the pleasure of watching him work. We also learn respect for the artist's skills, especially in the case of watercolor: although experience in the medium brings facility, not even Winslow Homer or John Singer Sargent made watercolors easily. But while knowledge of a great artist's technical skills gives important insight into his work, we should nonetheless remember that technique alone does not constitute genius. In the words of Adrian Stokes, it is always ". . . the Nature of the man rather than that of his methods or materials, that lifts his work so high."[44]

1. See, for example, George Barnard, *The Theory and Practise of Landscape Painting in Water-colours* (London: Hamilton & Adams, 1858), which provides a fine example of the usual admonition: "An appearance of dexterity and ease is attractive in every art; and none more than in watercolour painting. The labour with which the effect is attained is hidden; and the general effect, that which strikes the eye of everyone, as a passing glance at nature would, is represented" (p. 120).

2. The history of watercolor materials, including pigments, papers, binders, and paraphernalia, has been well covered elsewhere and will not be discussed here. For information on these topics, see Marjorie B. Cohn, *Wash and Gouache: A Study of the Development of the Materials of Watercolor* (Cambridge, Mass.: Fogg Art Museum, Harvard University, Center for Conservation and Technical Studies; and Foundation of the American Institute for Conservation, 1977), an indispensable survey on the history of the medium. Martin Hardie's three-volume opus, *Water-colour Painting in Britain* (London: B. T. Batsford; New York: Barnes & Noble, 1966–68), contains valuable historical and technical information, especially vol. 1, pp. 9–45.

3. "Fine Art," *Nation* 814 (February 3, 1881): 80–81.

4. Evan Charteris reports: "Mrs. James said to him, 'How delightful it must be to know that everytime you work you will bring back something fine.' Sargent replied: 'But I hardly EVER do! Once in a great, *great* while' " (*John Sargent* [1927; New York: Benjamin Blom, 1972], p. 225). In 1916 Sargent went to the Rocky Mountains and sent a letter of apology to the trustees of the Worcester Art Museum, who were eagerly waiting to purchase watercolors from the trip: "I am afraid you will be very dissatisfied with me for the meagre results of my Rocky Mountain campaign. . . . I only did two or three watercolors" (Sargent to Frederick S. Pratt, November 18, 1916, Worcester Art Museum files). These words from Sargent contradict reports that watercolors lay around his studio "in great bundles" (Richard Ormond, *John Singer Sargent: Paintings, Drawings, Watercolors* [New York: Harper & Row, 1970], p. 68). It would seem he made many watercolors but considered only a small number good enough for museum collections.

5. From Homer's daybook of 1902–3, Homer Memorabilia Collection, Bowdoin College Museum of Art, Brunswick, Maine; unpaginated.

6. For a convincing argument and details about dating Homer watercolors by technique, see Hereward Lester Cooke, "The Development of Winslow Homer's Water-Color Technique," *Art Quarterly* 24 (Summer 1961): 169–94.

7. Transparent watercolor was certainly gaining popularity at this time, in reaction to Pre-Raphaelite technique, which relied on chinese white as body color to make watercolors approximate oil paintings. Contemporary watercolor manuals disparage the combination of opaque and transparent colors, and artists' works reflect the change in attitude. In 1881 a reviewer of the annual New York Water Color Society show remarked, "Judging from the present aspect of the Academy, the demand for 'Chinese White' this year must have been inconsiderable compared with former seasons" (*Nation* 814 [February 3, 1881]: 80).

8. There is no evidence that this watercolor was traced; however, a painting from the same year, in the same style, *Two Boys Rowing* (Museum of Fine Arts, Boston), has faint blue outlines around the central group, which were strengthened with graphite prior to watercolor washing. Unique to this sheet, the blue lines could be from carbon paper, copy pencil, or another method of transfer.

9. Marjorie Cohn suggests that Homer's friend John La Farge may have first introduced him to many English techniques, since their studios were in the same building during the 1870s (*Wash and Gouache*, p. 80 n. 12).

10. For a complete survey of the history of English watercolors, practitioners, and their techniques, see Hardie, *Water-colour Painting in Britain*.

11. Barnard, *Landscape Painting in Water-colours*, pp. 120, 122.

12. Hardie discusses the genesis of this technique and concludes, "It seems probable Turner deserves the credit for development of a process which he constantly employed" (*Water-colour Painting in Britain*, vol. 1, p. 36).

13. The intricate lifting process, seen in this and only a couple of other watercolors by Homer, has been described by Hereward Cooke as having been accomplished by the use of frisket; see "Homer's Water-Color Technique," p. 184. Vestiges of washes, which would not appear if a frisket had been used, are visible in the palmetto fronds of *In a Florida Jungle* and *Thornhill Bar* (1886; Museum of Fine Arts, Boston), another work that Cooke cites, and thus dispute his claim. Similar blotting of re-wetted washes is evident in many of Homer's watercolors, for example in isolated details that I described in *Crab Fishing*. Although stunning in their extravagant use of the lifting technique, *In a Florida Jungle* and *Thornhill Bar* do not give any further reason to assume the effect was achieved by the use of a frisket. Moreover, what we know of Homer's direct approach to watercolor makes his use of a blocking agent, which requires premeditation and calculation, highly unlikely.

14. Gamboge was often used to glaze dark areas of watercolor to increase saturation. Its use here is confirmed by the unfortunate presence of yellow staining on the reverse of the sheet, corresponding to the foliage areas, which was leached from the painting during a solvent treatment in the 1950s. (The amount and pattern of staining on the reverse and the remaining green on the front of the sheet imply gamboge's use as a glaze rather than as a component in a mixture such as hooker's green.)

15. Homer, in Lloyd Goodrich, *Winslow Homer* (New York: Whitney Museum of American Art, 1973), p. 28.

16. A faint purple wash in the sky, now faded, added to the distinction between the blues. The fading of watercolor pigments is especially distressing since pigments fade at different rates and to different degrees, altering the color balance of a picture; the effect is different from, say, a black and white photograph of a color subject. Few of Homer's watercolors have escaped the damage of light, which is cumulative and nonreversible. Several of his most cherished pigments are particularly susceptible to fading, such as the deep, cool pinks of crimson lake, which fade to orange-beige, or indigo, which loses its warmth to become gray.
    As early as 1888 Dr. Russell and Captain Abney published their research in London on "The Action of Light on

Colors." Their *Blue Book* was the first of a series of investigations by scientists culminating in the development of a "permanent palette," that is, a list of colors less adversely affected by light. In 1892 the colormen Winsor & Newton made the remarkable decision to publish information on the manufacture and permanence of their materials. Unfortunately, Homer did not change his palette based on this new data. See Cohn, *Wash and Gouache*, pp. 61–64, with much additional information in the footnotes; see also current Winsor & Newton catalogues for a reprint of their disclosure statements of 1892.

17. Hartley, in Albert Eugene Gallatin, *American Water-colourists* (New York: E. P. Dutton, 1922), p. 8.

18. All this material, excepting one watercolor box, belongs to the Homer Memorabilia Collection, Bowdoin College Museum of Art, Brunswick, Maine. That box, with its "folding Morocco pouch case" and a porcelain-tipped burnisher, belongs to the Portland Museum of Art, Portland, Maine. The Worcester Art Museum also owns a box camera said to have belonged to Homer.

19. "Moist color," first introduced in the 1830s, incorporated glycerine in the previously available "hard cakes," making them easier to work into washes. The colors, which are not actually moist to the touch but slightly sticky, predate the truly moist "tube colors" by about fifteen years. See Cohn, *Wash and Gouache*, pp. 54–55.

20. See Appendix II for a palette concordance that lists Homer's pigments.

21. This exact tool is described by Hardie as having been used by "the old water-colour painters" (*Water-colour Painting in Britain*, vol. 1, p. 37).

22. Descriptions found in the Winsor & Newton product catalogue of 1869, bound with Thomas Hatton, *Hints for Sketching in Watercolor from Nature*, 10th ed. (London, 1869).

23. Whatman Mills produced several different papers specifically for watercolor painting, of varying thickness and surface texture. Homer was partial to a medium-thick paper of moderate texture, although some of his watercolors are executed on very heavy paper of rough texture. Not many of Homer's sheets bear watermarks, but those that do are J. Whatman's. Henrietta Benson Homer, the artist's mother, also occasionally used Whatman papers for her botanical studies. Two of her watercolors, *Peach Bough* (n.d.) and *Morning Glory* (n.d.), both in the collection at Bowdoin College, are painted on heavyweight twill papers watermarked "J Whatman 1877." For a complete discussion of watercolor papers and the history of Whatman papers and watermarks, see Cohn, *Wash and Gouache*, pp. 16–23.

Homer was not as consistent in his choice of papers for other works. In a letter to Philip Gentner, the director of the Worcester Art Museum, Homer's brother Charles described ". . . what Winslow used to use when in a hurry. I have sketches of great beauty on shirt box covers and back of portfolios" (September 11, 1911, Worcester Art Museum files).

24. Traditional paper sizes, in inches, are:

16th Imperial	5 × 7
Quarto Imperial	10 × 14
Demy	20 × 15½
Medium	22 × 17½
Royal	24 × 19
Imperial	30 × 22
Double Elephant	40 × 26¾
Antiquarian	53 × 31

Only the smaller sheets were available in blocks, the larger sheets being purchased in single-sheet lots.

25. For an interesting account of the Worcester Art Museum's three-year effort to secure a group of Sargent watercolors, see Susan E. Strickler, "John Singer Sargent and Worcester," *Worcester Art Museum Journal* 6 (1982–83): 30–33.

26. Adrian Stokes, "John Singer Sargent, R. A., R. W. S.," *Old Water-Colour Society Club, Third Annual Volume*, ed. Randall Davies, F.S.A. (London: Chiswick Press, 1926), pp. 51–60.

27. M. Birnbaum, in Ormond, *John Singer Sargent*, p. 68.

28. Stokes, *Third Annual*, p. 60.

29. Charteris, *John Sargent*, p. 224.

30. Adrian Stokes, Sargent's friend and fellow watercolorist, wrote, "Obviously he liked his work to be smartly done. He was acquainted with every device, but I am sure he *never* left a touch that looked clever unless it expressed what it was intended to convey" (*Third Annual*, p. 60).

31. Sargent, in Martin Hardie, *Famous Watercolour Painters* (New York: Wm. Edwin Rudge, 1930), p. 4.

32. Sargent remarked, in reference to selling his watercolors, that he did not know "what to ask for a mere snapshot, especially if it does not happen to be a miraculously happy one" (in Hardie, *Water-colour Painting in Britain*, vol. 3, p. 159).

33. Barnard, *Landscape Painting in Watercolours*, p. 60.

34. Francis Nicholson invented a "stopping out process" utilizing a formulation of "whitened beeswax in oil of turpentine to which may be added as much flake white [white lead] as will give sufficient body," which was presented to and published by the Society for the Encouragement of the Arts in *Transactions*, 1799. Nicholson later published the information in his own watercolor manual of 1820. See Hardie, *Water-colour Painting in Britain*, vol. 1, p. 36.

35. "Gum TRAGACANTH. Both glutinous and dull watercolor megilp is made from this. By its introduction the colours may be applied pulpily, after the manner of Oil Painting, as it prevents their flowing. Trees are sometimes treated by the addition of a very small quantity of this gum to the colours, and when this is judiciously managed, the effect is exceedingly good and transparent. Rice water will answer the like purpose" (Aaron Penley, *The English School of Painting in Water-Colours* [London: Leighton Bros., 1872], p. 13). Rice water was not used by Sargent in this case, as the green pigment mixture gives a negative chemical test for starch.

36. Ormond, *John Singer Sargent*, p. 69.

37. The author is indebted to Marjorie Shelley, paper conservator at the Metropolitan Museum of Art, who graciously shared her impression of the technique used by Sargent in the watercolor *Crocodiles* (acc. no. 50.130.63). In my opinion, this work really depicts alligators rather than crocodiles.

38. This work might have been done with the wooden-handled, harpoon-shaped tool found among Sargent's materials, now in the collections of the Fogg Art Museum (see plate 28).

39. The sheets were undoubtedly pinned up when dried: several of the pinholes show channels created by the pin's shaft as it was pressed through the sheets, which bear unsmudged watercolor.

40. The papers Sargent chose for each type of drawing were "correct" choices, being specifically designed by their manufacturers for charcoal or pencil, for instance. Two particular idiosyncrasies of Sargent's use of paper are worth noting: he typically used full sheets of expensive paper and rarely, if ever, used the reverse; and he seems not to have used his charcoal sketch paper for watercolors or pencil drawings, or used those papers for different purposes. He must have had great stores of paper on hand, which he used in liberal quantities but specifically by technique. From these observations, even if it was not already known to be the case, it might be surmised that Sargent was wealthy and academically trained.

41. Certain pigments that have the property of settling in water can be applied in a broad wash and then manipulated by rocking the sheet, causing the pigment particles to fall in the valleys of the paper, leaving the higher points bright. For example, cerulean blue, cobalt (and in mixtures with other pigments), and emerald green do granulate; prussian blue and vermilion do not. See L. Richmond and J. Littlejohn, *The Technique of Watercolor Painting* (New York: Pitman Publishing, 1939).

42. Sargent, in Ormond, *John Singer Sargent*, p. 70.

43. Collected by Edward Forbes for the Fogg Art Museum.

44. Stokes, *Third Annual*, p. 60.

Appendix I
John Singer Sargent's Watercolor Palette*

The fifteen tubes of moist watercolor found in Sargent's studio after his death all bear manufacturers' labels identifying the colors.
Alizarin carmine (Newman)
Brown pink (Newman)
Burnt sienna (Newman)
Cadmium yellow pale (Newman)
Cadmium yellow #2 (Newman)
Chrome yellow (Newman)
Cobalt blue (Newman)
Gamboge (Weber)
Lamp black (Winsor & Newton)
Rose madder (Winsor & Newton)
Ultramarine (Schminke)
Vandyke brown (Newman)
Scarlet vermilion (Winsor & Newton)
Deep vermilion (Hatfield)
Viridian (Winsor & Newton)

*From Marjorie B. Cohn, *Wash and Gouache: A Study of the Development of the Materials of Watercolor* (Cambridge, Mass.: Fogg Art Museum, Harvard University, Center for Conservation and Technical Studies; and Foundation of the American Institute for Conservation, 1977), p. 66.

Appendix II
Winslow Homer's Watercolor Palette

Two watercolor boxes that belonged to Homer, now in the collections of Bowdoin College Museum of Art, Brunswick, Maine, and the Portland Museum of Art, Portland, Maine, were examined for information to help identify the pigments they still contain. Each is a twenty-pan, Japanned-black moist watercolor box made by Winsor & Newton.

Thirty-nine of the possible forty pans are still extant: each is made of white ceramic, with the words "Winsor & Newton, London" impressed on the bottom. Three of the pans, all in the Portland box, retain their original foil and paper wrappers (plate 38). Eight other pans still bear small printed labels identifying the pigments, and several could be named based on Homer's notations in black waxy pencil that withstood his color mixing on the wings of the boxes (plates 37 and 38). Furthermore, each pan in the Bowdoin box had been analyzed by Richard Newman, Craigen Weston, and Eugene Farrell at the Center for Technical Studies at the Fogg Art Museum, Cambridge, Massachusetts, using sophisticated chemical analysis (see "Analysis of Watercolor Pigments in a Box Owned by Winslow Homer," *Journal of the American Institute of Conservation* 19 [1980]: 103–4).

Many of the colors appear in both boxes, and some colors appear twice or more in one box, since they were offered in more than one shade by the manufacturer. For instance, hooker's green is found in both boxes, and in the Portland box both shades #1 and #2 are found. But, to further complicate analysis, a color called prussian green is also noted by Homer to be in both boxes. In the late nineteenth century, prussian green was a mixture of prussian blue and gamboge, the exact components of the traditional hooker's green. Chemically, these three pigments would appear identical, although they would certainly look different on the page. Similarly, each box contains three pans of vermilion.

Twenty different colors, which fill thirty-three of the thirty-nine pans, have been identified from all the sources noted above. They are listed here in alphabetical order. The listing is incomplete, however, since the Portland box has never been analyzed, and some of Homer's notes resist even creative interpretation.

Pigments in Homer's Two Extant Moist Watercolor Boxes

* = pan still wrapped in foil from Winsor & Newton factory

1 = information from printed label still attached to pan of pigment

2 = deciphered notation in Homer's hand from wings of watercolor box

3 = chemical analysis of pigments from Bowdoin College watercolor box (Newman, Weston, and Farrell, "Analysis of Watercolor Pigments"; authors' qualifiers on identification in parenthesis)

1. Identified as "cochineal lake made in the presence of copper, causing the deep purple color instead of the normal red" in a conversation with Wendall Upchurch, Technical Advisor, Winsor & Newton, Inc., 555 Winsor Drive, Secaucus, N.J. 07094.

2. Upchurch identified this as a mixture of prussian blue and gamboge during the late nineteenth century. The color is still available from Winsor & Newton, although it is not made the same way today.

Pigment Name (Homer's Notation)	Source of Identification	Owner of Watercolor Box
Antwerp blue (Antw Blue)	2, 3 (prussian blue with extender)	BCMA
Aureolin (Aureolin)	2	PMA
Bone black	3 (or ivory black)	BCMA
Burnt sienna (B Sien __)	3	BCMA
	2	PMA
Burnt umber	3 (a brown earth)	BCMA
Cadmium yellow (Cad __)	2, 3	BCMA
Chinese white (tube)	1	PMA
Chrome orange (Chrome Orange)	2, 3	BCMA
(C Orange)	2	PMA
Crimson lake (C Lake)	1	PMA
	2, 3 (red lake: alizarin and carminic acid)	BCMA
Green earth	3 (with prussian blue contaminant)	BCMA
Hooker's green	3	BCMA
Hooker's green, both #1 and #2 (Hook green)	1, 2	PMA
Indian purple[1] (Indian Purple)	1, 2	PMA
Indian red (I Red)	1*	PMA
	2, 3 (or red ocher)	BCMA
Indian yellow (I Yel)	2, 3	BCMA
Prussian green[2] (P Green)	1	PMA
	2	BCMA
Payne's grey (Pay __Grey)	2	BCMA
(P __Grey)	2	PMA
Scarlet lake (SCA _l Lake)	2	PMA
Sepia (Sepia)	2	BCMA
Vandyke brown (V __B __)	1, 2, 3 (or cologne earth, two pans)	BCMA
Vermilion (Scarl V _)	1* (two pans), 2 (another pan)	PMA
(Ver __)	2, 3 (three pans)	BCMA
Warm sepia (Warm Sepia)	1, 2, 3 (possibly)	BCMA

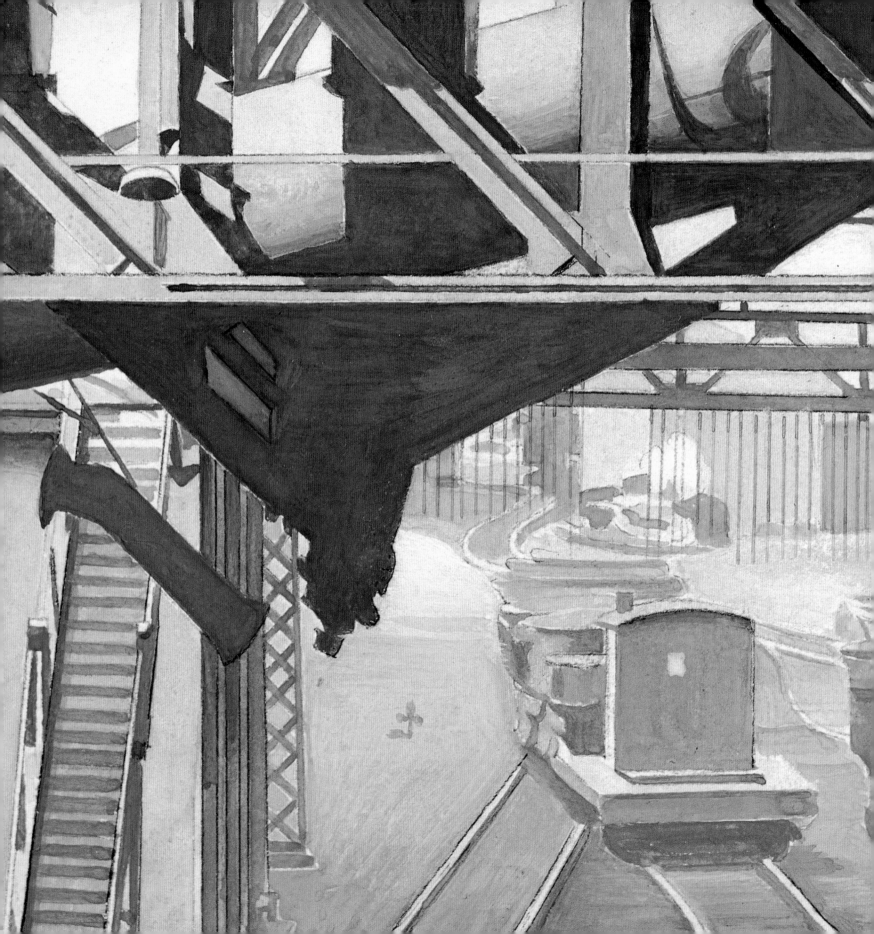

Highlights from the Collection

52A and 52B
Edward Savage (1761–1817)
Falls of the Passaic at Patterson, **1806**
Jefferson's Rock, **probably 1807**

A native of Worcester County, Massachusetts, Edward Savage might be best characterized as an artist-engraver-entrepreneur, a man with some artistic talent who also had an eye for the monetary potential of his creative endeavors. Although today remembered chiefly for his painted and engraved portraits of George Washington and his family, Savage was also proprietor of his own museum, whose collection ranged from portraits of statesmen to specimens of natural curiosities. His early artistic training remains a mystery, but he seems to have sharpened his skills first in Boston in the mid-1780s, copying portraits by John Singleton Copley, and then during a three-year visit to London from 1791 to 1794, where he saw current portrait styles and engraving techniques.

These two wash drawings belong to a relatively little-known group of some thirty grisaille views that document two scenic tours Savage made of the eastern United States in 1806 and 1807.[1] *Falls of the Passaic* is the earliest drawing of the 1806 expedition that took him from Paterson, New Jersey, on July 29, up the Hudson to the Mohawk River, then westward across New York State to Genesee Falls, and ultimately to Niagara Falls, where he arrived in September.[2] In a cursive and notational manner, Savage accurately portrayed the scene from its most familiar vantage point, which reveals only a glimpse of the narrow falls deep in the ravine and features the distinctive squared-off rocks and ledges. Even in his own day, Savage was deemed a better painter than draftsman or engraver, and the unsophisticated style and naive rendering of space and form in this drawing, as in many of his others, confirm that characterization.[3]

Although undated, *Jefferson's Rock* fits into the itinerary of Savage's more extensive circuit, which began at the head of Chesapeake Bay in July 1807 and took him to Connecticut, Rhode Island, Massachusetts, and Vermont in August, down the Hudson River, along the Delaware, across southern Pennsylvania in November, and finally to Jefferson's Rock, a craggy promontory near the confluence of the Potomac and Shenandoah rivers (now called Harper's Ferry), just north of the Blue Ridge Mountains.[4] The site was named for Thomas Jefferson, who described it as "one of the most stupendous scenes in nature" in his *Notes on the State of Virginia,* published in 1787 and often quoted at length in subsequent travel literature. The two tiny figures who survey the panorama from the rock in Savage's composition connote the sublime feelings the site had elicited from Jefferson.

Up to this time, landscape had not been a dominant subject in Savage's oeuvre, and the scenic routes that he traveled suggest he had more than just casual sketching trips in mind. In a letter of June 17, 1799, he wrote to President Washington, whom he had first painted in 1789, about a new printmaking process called "aquatint," adding, "I intend as soon as time will permit to execute a set of large prints of the most striking and beautifull views in America in that stile of Engraving as it is best calculated for Landskip and a very expeditious method of working."[5] Savage's views, rendered quickly in simple gray washes over faint graphite underdrawing, seem well suited to translation into black and white aquatints, as this etching process allowed the printmaker to articulate broad areas of tonal gradations with considerable subtlety. Unfortunately, no record of any aquatints or engravings of these views by Savage has yet been discovered.

Undoubtedly Savage recognized the financial gain such a project could realize. Since the mid-eighteenth century, Europeans and Americans had been fascinated by the natural wonders of North America, which had been recorded in literature and published engravings by the time of Savage's trips. Passaic Falls, the Hudson River, and particularly Niagara Falls were well-known sites, visited with increasing frequency by tourists and artists. In the 1820s there was a proliferation of popular illustrated publications that described many of the same locations Savage had visited, and these works found a receptive audience among the American public well into the third quarter of the century.[6] In his most active period as an engraver and publisher, during the 1790s, Savage had enjoyed commercial success with his portraits of American statesmen, and a decade later he probably had similar ambitions for this enterprise, which for unknown reasons was never realized.　*SES*

1. The attribution of these two views to Savage is based on similarities of style, handwriting, and paper to signed works from the 1806 and 1807 trips. Nineteen other views of Savage's 1807 trip were recently acquired by the Worcester Art Museum; see illustrated checklist. Seven graphite drawings executed in a distinctly different style in the museum's collection document a third trip that Savage made to the province of Quebec in 1809.

2. In addition to Worcester's example, there are twelve views from the 1806 trip, all of which are in the collection of the Rush Rhees Library, University of Rochester, and four of which are signed. For a checklist, see Louisa Dresser, "Edward Savage, Painter, 1761–1817," *Art in America* 40, no. 4 (Autumn 1952): 209–11.

3. Harold E. Dickson, *John Wesley Jarvis: American Painter 1780–1840* (New York: New-York Historical Society, 1949), p. 43.

4. I am grateful to Pamela Read of the Alice and Hamilton Fish Library in Garrison, New York, for helping to locate Jefferson's Rock.

5. Savage, in Charles Henry Hart, *Edward Savage, Painter and Engraver* (Boston: Massachusetts Historical Society, 1905), p. 12.

6. Among the best known of these books is Nathaniel P. Willis, *American Scenery; or, Land, Lake and River* (London: George Virtue, 1840), illustrated by William Henry Bartlett. This was helpful in identifying Jefferson's Rock.

Provenance
(Dealers and auction sales appear in parentheses in the provenance entries.)
Falls of the Passaic at Patterson and *Jefferson's Rock* (Augustus E. Peck, Worcester, c. 1890); Henry Phelps, Worcester; Edwin S. Phelps, Dorchester, Mass., until c. 1920; Edward F. Coffin, Worcester; museum purchase, 1934

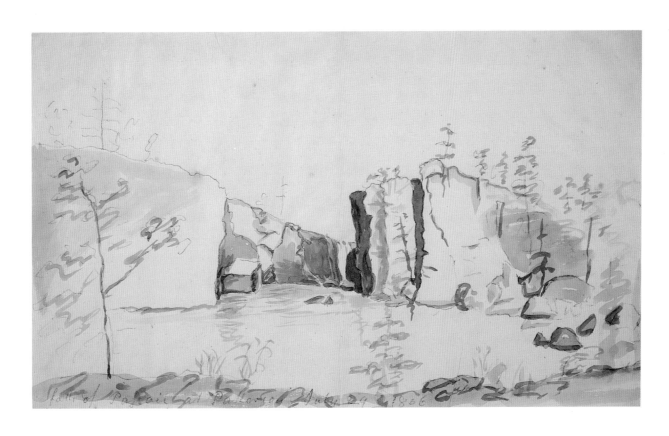

Falls of Passaic at Paterson Aug 29 1856

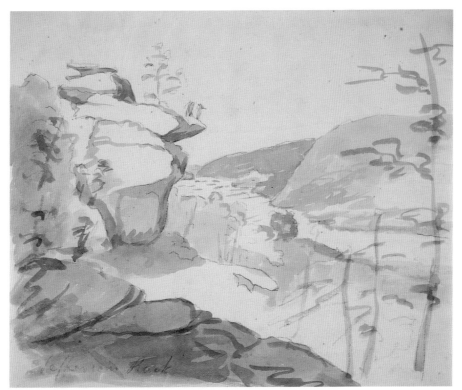

53
John William Hill (1812–1879)
Mountain River, 1868

John William Hill was an important figure in the emergence of watercolor as a serious medium for artistic expression in mid-nineteenth-century America. He was the oldest member of the American Pre-Raphaelites, a small, radical group that banded together officially in 1863, modeling itself after the English Pre-Raphaelite Brotherhood of 1848. Its credo, "The earnest loving study of God's nature," was founded on the writings of the great British aesthetician John Ruskin.[1]

Like most of his American Pre-Raphaelite colleagues, Hill chose watercolor as the primary medium for all his subjects: landscapes, nature studies, and still lifes. His penchant for watercolor and landscape was undoubtedly stimulated by his apprenticeship to his father, the landscape aquatinter John Hill, and by his work as a topographical artist in the 1830s and 1840s, and it was subsequently reinforced by his introduction in the mid-1850s to Ruskin's enormously influential books *Modern Painters* and *Elements of Drawing.* Hill's early landscapes were rendered in the traditional English manner of broad washes of a single tone applied over a graphite sketch, which also typified almost all watercolors produced in America up to the mid-1850s. However, the fastidious technique of *Mountain River* reflects the dramatic stylistic conversion that Hill—and all of the American Pre-Raphaelites—experienced following their introduction to Ruskin's principles and their increasing familiarity with the minutely rendered nature studies of such English Pre-Raphaelites as William Holman Hunt and John Everett Millais, who were championed by Ruskin.

In his characteristic manner, Hill lightly blocked out the different elements of this composition in very pale washes. He then applied darker hues in single, stipple-like brush strokes laid down one next to the other or in a crosshatch pattern to articulate the foliage, the rushing water, and even the mottled sky. The boulders, however, were drawn primarily with transparent washes. The limited palette is typical of Hill's roughly complementary colors of yellow-green and violet, brownish-orange and blue, which heighten the vibrancy of the scene. Following Ruskin's advice, Hill worked on white paper, instead of cream or gray, to enhance the luminosity of his pigments, and he used only spare touches of opaque gouache to suggest the froth of the turbulent water and to delineate the slender birch tree in the background. By giving equal attention to the rendering of foreground and distant detail, Hill also abandoned traditional atmospheric perspective; as a result, the atmosphere has an added clarity and crispness. As fellow Pre-Raphaelite Charles Herbert Moore recollected, in such works Hill "endeavored to attain more brilliancy and luminousness; to express something of the true blue of the sky, the light of summer clouds . . . the golden greens of sun-lighted foliage, and the blues and purples of the distant hills."[2]

Although the site of *Mountain River* has yet to be positively identified, it does meet Ruskin's demand that the artist study familiar subjects, such as neighboring rivers and streams, that can be enjoyed and understood by everyone.[3] Hill found the Catskills and Adirondacks north of his Nyack, New York, home especially rich sketching grounds. This scene is not a grand panorama such as those often favored by the earlier Hudson River School. Rather, Hill depicts a contemplative, intimate setting that one might happen upon during a hike in the woods, a tone reinforced by the almost unnoticed passage of the horses and carriage on the bridge. Following the Pre-Raphaelite mandate, Hill undoubtedly executed this scene on the spot. He was said to have worked outdoors for ten hours at a stretch, which is not surprising, considering the fussy brush strokes he used to build up his composition.[4] The small awkward passages along the left edge of the riverbed may indicate the difficulties Hill faced in using this particular technique outdoors.

The impact of the American Pre-Raphaelites was relatively short-lived, and the movement was defunct by the early 1870s, though Hill and his son John Henry carried on the tradition long beyond that. The group was criticized for the severity of its realism and the limitations of its technique and for what was considered a lack of the poetic sensibility that constituted a "true" painting. Certain critics, however, felt Hill progressed beyond mere faithful transcription of nature, and indeed the tiny, faceless figure provides more than just a note of contrasting color to this composition. Diminutive in scale, he becomes a romantic emblem of man's humble place in the universe and of the virtues of contemplating the abundant natural riches God has placed before us. *SES*

1. For the most comprehensive study of the American Pre-Raphaelites, see Linda S. Ferber and William H. Gerdts, *The New Path: Ruskin and the American Pre-Raphaelites* (Brooklyn, N.Y.: Brooklyn Museum, 1985). In 1863 John William Hill was elected the first president of the Association for the Advancement of Truth in Art, the official name of the American Pre-Raphaelite group.

2. Charles Herbert Moore, "An Artist's Memorial," in John Henry Hill, ed., *John William Hill: An Artist's Memorial* (New York: privately printed, 1888), p. 6.

3. The Hill expert Richard J. Koke has tentatively identified the site as Luzerne Bridge across the Sacandaga River at Luzerne (once called Hadley), New York, based upon a strikingly similar arched stone bridge that spanned the falls at least by 1866, when it was illustrated in B. J. Lossing, *The Hudson from the Wilderness to the Sea* (New York: Virtue and Yorston, 1866), p. 62. Both John William and John Henry Hill painted in this region in the 1867–69 period, as indicated by their numerous dated views of the Catskills and lower Adirondacks. The date of this work has been variously misread as 1852 or 1858. Under microscopic examination, the date clearly reads 1868.

4. Edward Cary, "Some American Pre-Raphaelites: A Reminiscence," *Script* 2, no. 1 (October 1906): 5.

Provenance
(Robert W. Skinner, Inc., Bolton, Mass., sale 724, Jan. 2, 1981, no. 138, listed as *White River*); (Jeffrey Brown, Boston); (Rifkin-Young Fine Arts, Bronx, N.Y.); museum purchase, Loring Holmes Dodd Fund, 1985

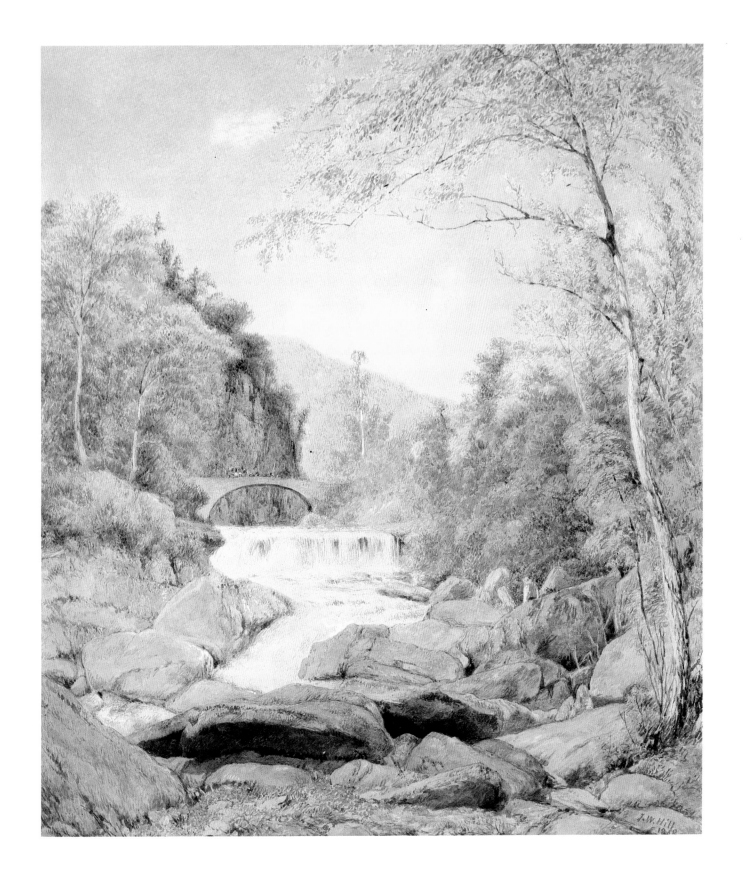

71

Jasper F. Cropsey (1823–1900)
On the Susquehanna River, 1889

Of all the major Hudson River School painters, Jasper Cropsey worked most actively in watercolor, especially during the last two decades of his life. This view of a bucolic stretch along the Susquehanna River, rendered in broad transparent washes over a graphite sketch, draws on the evocative potential of the landscape, rather than focusing solely on purely topographical description. In technique and style this work indicates the lingering influence that the mainstream of nineteenth-century English landscape watercolor painting had on Cropsey at a time when the monumental naturalism of Homer and bravura Impressionism of Sargent signaled sweeping changes in the American watercolor movement.

Cropsey's conservatism was instilled early.[1] As an aspiring young artist he had undoubtedly studied the numerous drawing manuals published during the early nineteenth century, whose instruction in watercolor reflected the English approach. He received his first instruction in the medium about 1840, from an obscure English painter named Edward Maury, during his apprenticeship in a New York architect's office. Cropsey's interest may also have been reinforced by the watercolors of several English-born artists, such as William Guy Wall and George Harvey, whose picturesque views of American scenery were exhibited at the National Academy of Design.

But Cropsey's most significant exposure to the English watercolor movement came during his second visit abroad, when he settled in London from 1856 to 1863. There he came to know John Ruskin, who favored the use of watercolor in making direct studies from nature, and he also saw the brilliant washes of J.M.W. Turner, the nature studies of John Constable, and picturesque views by less innovative contemporary British watercolorists.[2] These various influences are all reflected in *On the Susquehanna River*.

The quiet villages and low-lying farmland along the Susquehanna, which meanders through New York and Pennsylvania, had provided inspiration for artists, writers, and travelers since the mid-eighteenth century.[3] The region sounded a tranquil, pastoral note in contrast to the rugged, sometimes wild terrain of the Catskills, Adirondacks, or White Mountains preferred by other artists associated with the Hudson River School. Cropsey visited the Starrucca Valley in 1852 and 1853 and the Wyoming Valley in 1864. Essentially a painter of peace and harmony, he continued to depict Susquehanna subjects, mostly in oil, well into the 1890s, largely from his earlier drawings. The gently asymmetrical composition of this watercolor, with a vista across open foreground meadows, looking toward a glimpse of water in the distant middle ground and a relatively low horizon, is one that Cropsey often used from the early 1860s; it appears in a more panoramic variation in his best-known oil painting of this area, *Valley of the Wyoming* (1865; Metropolitan Museum of Art).

The colorful palette of this watercolor reflects Cropsey's decided preference for autumnal subjects, although the hues here are more restrained and naturalistic than in some of his late oils, which by the 1870s frequently include touches of bright orange and pink in the foliage. The luminosity of the reflective, calm river and the radiant glow from the sun in this work find parallels in many of Cropsey's oils from the late 1860s and 1870s and in the landscape paintings by his colleagues Sanford R. Gifford and John F. Kensett.

The most striking feature of the landscape is the cloud-laden sky, which not only enhances the pictorial effect but also governs the emotive powers of the scene. The rendering of the clouds, which are subtly built up by a series of transparent washes of rose and gray, seems to articulate the philosophy Cropsey had expounded in his influential essay of 1855, "Up Among the Clouds." He compared the fantasy and poeticism of the fair-weather cirrus and cumulus clouds with the moody drama of "the nimbus, the region of the rain-cloud, [which] is perhaps in its grandest moods more impressive than all other cloud regions."[4] Cropsey explained, "It is this class of sky, owing to its nearness, and stronger grade of color, and the more powerful impressions it is capable of producing, that is susceptible of the highest and noblest results in art." In this meadowland scene, the artist has captured a subtle shift in nature's moods: from behind "the light portions of a brickish red" cloud, the emerging (or retreating) sun reflects on the shimmering water below, while "in its dark and gloomy parts" the nimbus "has a heavy, inky and black look" that casts a murky veil over the river at the right. In both his prose and his painting Cropsey conjoined the poetic and scientific, the evocative and the empirical. These qualities were not lost on Cropsey's patron Arthur Edwards, who, upon buying a Susquehanna view in watercolor in 1889, wrote to the artist: "I envy your ability and opportunity to lift, soften, instruct and bless so many people. The pencil and brush preach and teach as well as does the tongue."[5]

SES

1. The best source on Cropsey's watercolors is the exhibition catalogue by Carrie Rebora, *Jasper F. Cropsey Watercolors* (New York: National Academy of Design, 1985).

2. See William S. Talbot, *Jasper F. Cropsey, 1823–1900* (New York: Garland Publishing, 1977), pp. 120–21.

3. See Roger Stein, *Susquehanna: Images of the Settled Landscape* (Binghamton, N.Y.: Robinson Center for the Arts and Sciences, 1981).

4. Cropsey, "Up Among the Clouds," *Crayon* 2, no. 6 (August 8, 1855): 79.

5. Edwards to Cropsey, February 16, 1889, Newington-Cropsey Foundation; in Rebora, *Cropsey Watercolors*, p. 21. Edwards, editor of the Northwestern Christian Advocate, wrote that he had just purchased the watercolor at the Twenty-second Annual Exhibition of the American Water Color Society in New York (no. 692); it is possible that Edwards's watercolor is the one now owned by Worcester.

Provenance
(Richard Weimar, Darien, Conn.); Mrs. John C. Newington; gift of Mrs. John C. Newington, 1985

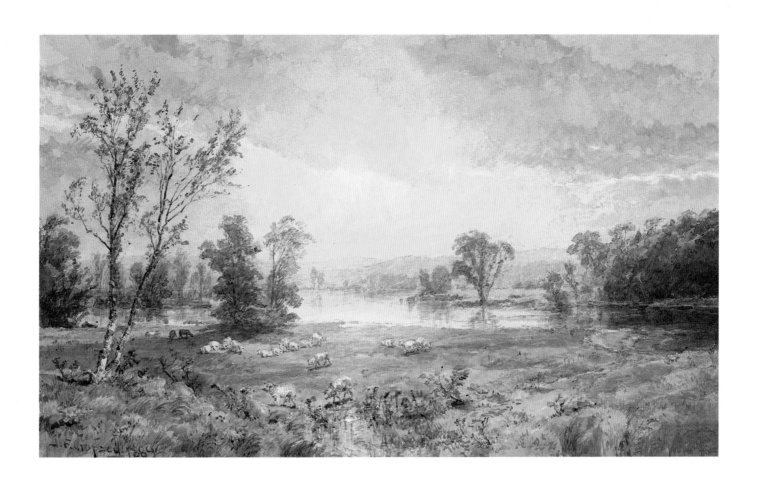

55
John La Farge (1835–1910)
Sacred Font, Iyémitsu Temple, Nikko, **1886**

From the beginning of his long career John La Farge demonstrated his mastery of the watercolor medium. Although he had no formal training, his grandfather, a miniaturist, apparently gave him lessons at home as a child. His father wanted him to pursue a career in law, but after graduating from college in 1855, La Farge made a Grand Tour of Europe that swayed him to art. In 1856 he visited Paris, where he admired the works of the nineteenth-century French Romantics, especially Eugène Delacroix and Théodore Chassériau. At this time he also traveled to England and viewed old master paintings, English Romantic art, and Pre-Raphaelite art at the Manchester Art Treasures Exhibition. These experiences influenced him throughout his career, providing pictorial and technical models for his work in illustration, easel painting, murals, and stained glass. After his tour, in 1859, La Farge moved to Newport, Rhode Island, to study with William Morris Hunt. In addition to working in the studio, he began to draw and paint directly from nature, rapidly developing skillful techniques for the depiction of landscape and still life.

In 1886 La Farge's friend the historian and writer Henry Adams invited the artist to tour Japan. La Farge readily accepted, enticed by exotic notions of Eastern culture. Arriving in Yokohama on July 3, 1886, he was immediately struck by Japan's beauty: "We are coming in; it is like the picture books. Anything I can add will only be a

filling in of detail."[1] La Farge sketched continually during the next nine months, capturing every aspect of his travels. These sketches served as the basis for numerous other compositions, including illustrations for narratives published both in periodicals and as a masterfully crafted book, *An Artist's Letters from Japan.* In these writings La Farge described at length his visits to the famous Iyéyasu and Iyémitsu shrines on the holy mountain of Nikko, during which he produced numerous drawings and watercolor studies of the temples, the surrounding landscapes, and the people he encountered in his daily ambles.

Sacred Font, Iyémitsu Temple, Nikko, is typical of sketches in which La Farge sought to capture a rapid impression of nature from which a more elaborate, finished work of art might later be produced. He was less concerned with recording details than with rendering generalized outlines and lighting effects through broad washes of color. A similar watercolor study of the sacred font was published as an illustration to La Farge's travel writings. In accompaniment the artist noted: "As we turn to the highest court of the left and ascend slowly steep, high steps to a gorgeous red gate above our heads, whose base we cannot see, the great cedars of the opposite side are the real monuments, and the little water-tank . . . seems nothing but a little altar at the foot of the mountain forest."[2]

La Farge's travel watercolors recall French and English Romantic painting of the 1830s, particularly that of Delacroix and J.M.W. Turner, who also produced sketches of picturesque sites for publication in travel books. Like his European counter-

parts, La Farge subscribed to many of the conventions of travel illustration that were well established at the time. Figures, landscape, and architecture were factually recorded, without dramatizing the subject through narrative elements or exaggerated light and color; the view was captured with an eye for picturesque composition, but without falsification. When La Farge's exotic pictures toured the country during the late 1890s, he called the exhibition *Records of Travel;* in every sense, *Sacred Font* is precisely that.[3]   *JLY*

1. John La Farge, *An Artist's Letters from Japan* (New York: Century, 1897), p. 1.

2. Ibid., pp. 88–89. The illustration in the book does not include the figures on either side in the Worcester watercolor nor many of the architectural details. In all likelihood, La Farge executed this variant work during the 1890s specifically for reproduction, utilizing the Worcester image as his source.

3. This particular watercolor was shown at all the stops of the exhibition *Paintings, Studies, Sketches and Drawing, Mostly Records of Travel 1886 and 1890–91 by John La Farge* (New York, Cleveland, and Chicago), including the reduced version held at the Paris Salon of 1895; the work was also included in other exhibitions of travel works in New York and Boston during the early 1890s.

Provenance
(Probably Doll and Richards, Boston); Dr. Samuel B. Woodward, Worcester, c. 1900; gift of Dr. Samuel B. Woodward, 1939

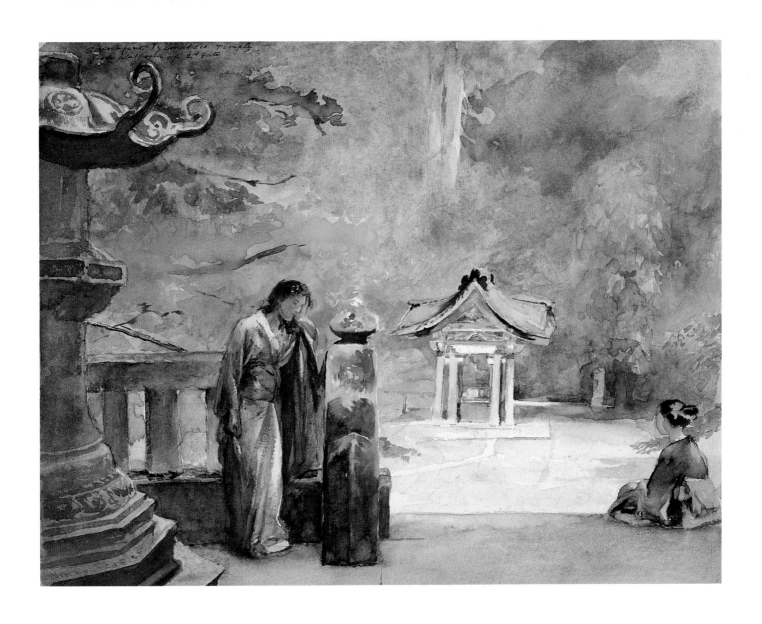

75

56
John La Farge (1835–1910)
Musicians in Ceremonial Costume, **1887**

During his trip to Japan in 1886 La Farge was impressed by the harmonious simplicity of daily life there. Like other nineteenth-century Western travelers, he viewed the Japanese as uncorrupted by the evils of modern technology and civilization. He intently studied Japanese "types," including peasants, priests, athletes, and geishas. La Farge described the geishas in his *Artist's Letters from Japan:*[1] "[They are] one of the institutions of Japan. . . . They cultivate singing and dancing, and often poetry, and all accomplishments and most of the exquisite politeness of their country. They are the ideals of the elegant side of woman. To them is entrusted the entertainment of guests and the solace of idle hours."

Musicians in Ceremonial Costume depicts two geishas La Farge hired to pose "at the same price and no more than I should have paid them had I called them in to entertain me and my guests with singing and dancing." In contrast to more casual studies, this gives the impression of being a studio work, for the figures appear posed as they gaze out at the viewer. La Farge spent considerable time on the picture, recalling that the models demonstrated "all the impatience of girls who, knowing what it was all about, still could not put up with the slow ways of European work, when their own artists would have been as agile and rapid and sketchy as themselves."

While the composition abounds in striking details, such as the carefully studied fan, screen, and native dresses, the overall presentation seems awkward, reflecting La Farge's career-long weakness as a figure painter. In general his rendering of figures seems most natural when left unfinished, as in the *Sacred Font* watercolor (plate 55).

This and similar studies reveal the interest in physiognomy and ethnology that characterized La Farge's late years. During a tour of the South Pacific in 1890 and 1891 the artist portrayed Hawaiian, Samoan, Tahitian, and Fijian natives with similar quasi-scientific accuracy.[2] Throughout the last two decades of his life, the Japanese and South Sea sketches served La Farge not only as the basis for travel writings but also as the inspiration for numerous major canvases, decorative works, and exhibitions that propounded the virtues of exotic lands and their inhabitants. This desire to edify and instruct motivated all of La Farge's serious art work but became particularly pronounced in later years. *JLY*

1. John La Farge, *An Artist's Letters from Japan* (New York: Century, 1897), p. 190 (quotations that follow are from the same source).

2. La Farge's trip to the South Seas was also prompted by his friend Henry Adams. A detailed chronicle of their journey is provided in my Ph.D. dissertation, "The Role of Landscape in the Art of John La Farge" (University of Chicago, 1981).

Provenance
The artist; (American Art Association, New York, *Sale of Art Property of John La Farge,* March 31, 1911, cat. no. 550, listed as *Study of Geisha Girls*); George Woodward; Dr. Samuel B. Woodward, Worcester; gift of Dr. Samuel B. Woodward, 1939

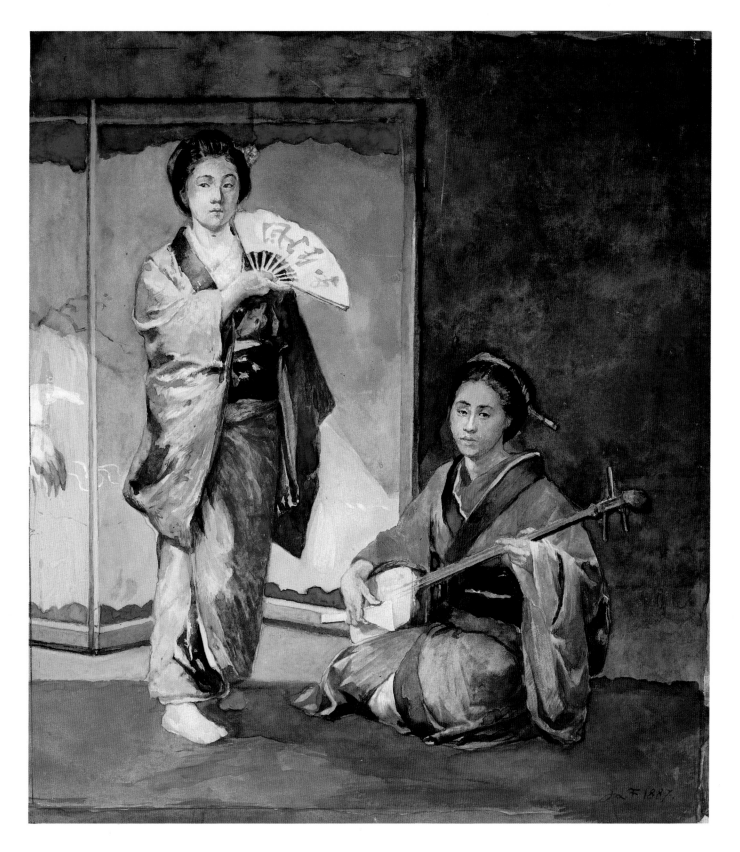

57
John La Farge (1835–1910)
The Three Marys: Study for the South-worth Window, Church of the Ascension, New York, **1889**

For La Farge, watercolor painting was intimately linked to the processes of study, experimentation, and design. In conjunction with drawing in pencil and crayon, he utilized watercolor in planning most of his serious large easel paintings, murals, illustrations, and stained-glass windows. Often these watercolors marked the end of La Farge's actual execution of his designs and were transferred to paint or glass in large scale by assistants under his direction. Watercolor provided the ideal means for developing glass designs because it approximated the translucency and vibrant colors of glass in a medium that could be handled quickly and flexibly.

During the 1870s La Farge became renowned as a designer of stained-glass windows and invented a new type of richly colored, thickly textured glass known as "opalescent" glass.[1] This watercolor is his principal study for the Southworth Memorial Window, commissioned in 1889 for the Church of the Ascension in New York City.[2] Prior to this commission La Farge had produced many renderings of the three Marys visiting Christ's tomb on the morning of the Resurrection. The majority of these were related to a now-destroyed altarpiece he designed in 1877 for St. Thomas Church in New York.[3] In designing the Southworth Window, La Farge referred back to the St. Thomas mural, although he altered poses and gestures in order to strengthen the emotional expressiveness of the scene and to adapt forms to the shape of the window.

Like many of La Farge's late glass designs, this scene—from Luke, chapter 24—is presented in a suggestive manner, delicately juxtaposing the natural and the supernatural. The three Marys arriving at the tomb of Christ are greeted with the miraculous news of his Resurrection by angels, who on the ground seem startlingly real and in the air seem to materialize magically. The scene is bathed in realistic light, yet it also contains indistinct and evocative passages that appear to lead to an ethereal realm. The way the figures draw away from the center of the picture creates a dramatic tension as well as a convenient space for the division of the composition into left and right window spandrels. The figures are delineated in a curvilinear and expressive manner reminiscent of the decorative works of Edward Burne-Jones, whom La Farge had visited in 1873, and other British Pre-Raphaelites.[4]

This watercolor is executed on smooth, translucent tracing paper in thin, transparent washes, which attain the bejeweled effect of stained glass. La Farge's assistants obviously relied heavily on it during the execution of the window, as evidenced by pencil markings that note the placement of spandrels and cross-supports.   *JLY*

1. La Farge's development of opalescent stained glass is documented in H. Barbara Weinberg, *The Decorative Work of John La Farge* (New York: Garland Publishing, 1977).

2. A preparatory drawing for the female figures inscribed "For Marys in Ch. Ascension window" is in the Princeton University Art Museum.

3. La Farge's decorative production related to this project is thoroughly documented in Weinberg, *Decorative Work*, pp. 146–67. The three Marys formed one of several major groupings within this mural dedicated to episodes of the Resurrection.

4. La Farge had traveled to England in 1873 to accompany the exhibition of some of his major works mounted by Durand-Ruel in London. He visited Burne-Jones in early 1873: see Cecilia Waern, *John La Farge, Artist and Writer* (London: Seeley, 1896), p. 29.

Provenance
The artist; (Doll and Richards, Boston, 1892); Mrs. Isaac Fenno, Roxbury, Mass., 1892; Felix A. Gendrot (second husband of Mrs. Fenno), Roxbury; gift of Felix A. Gendrot, 1935

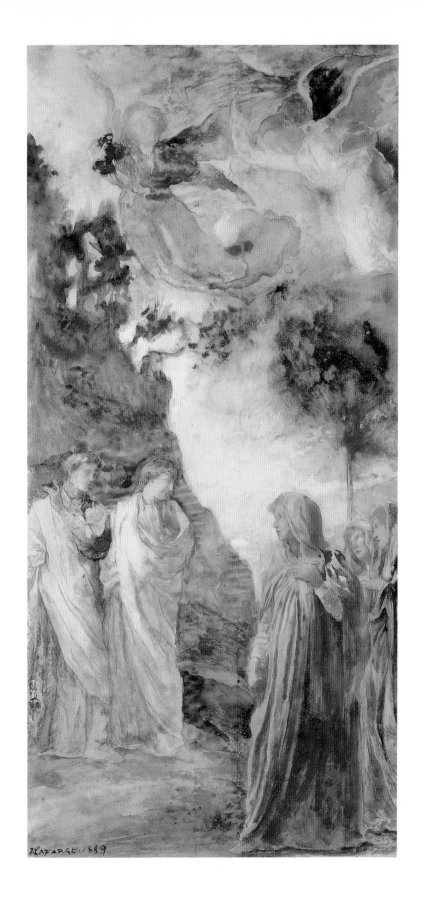

LAFARGE · 1889

58
John La Farge (1835–1910)
The Last Sight of Tahiti: Trade Winds,
1891

Throughout the nineteenth century the South Pacific conjured up visions of classical antiquity intertwined with "noble savagery." During the 1840s Herman Melville's novels popularized the idea that the South Pacific was peopled by innocent, classically beautiful races; utopian reports from scientists, adventurers, and casual travelers reaffirmed such beliefs. In 1890, stimulated by these notions, La Farge accepted an invitation from Henry Adams to journey to the South Seas.[1] Departing from New York in August, La Farge and Adams crossed the United States by train and embarked from San Francisco for Hawaii, one of four stops on their year-and-a-half-long tour. Although they soon realized that Hawaii's native culture had already been corrupted by the intrusion of American industrialism, the subsequent stops on their South Sea tour—Samoa, Tahiti, Fiji—fulfilled their expectations of idyllic lands and civilizations.

La Farge was enthralled by the picturesqueness of the landscapes and the exoticism of the people. He sketched incessantly, much as he had done in Japan five years earlier. The works he produced, from quick drawings to highly detailed landscapes and figures in watercolor and oil, provided a basis for many later canvases.[2] *The Last Sight of Tahiti: Trade Winds* typifies La Farge's rapid watercolor studies, executed in a fleeting moment of inspiration. Intended to preserve outlines and effects of lighting for later elaboration, the picture is simple in composition and, like a journal entry, summarizes the essentials about a given moment. In this case, the picture documents the final departure of La Farge and Adams from Tahiti on June 4, 1891, aboard the USS *Richmond*.

The picture is particularly interesting in terms of technique. Pencil underdrawing shows through the thin washes of clouds; blue and green washes block out large masses without detailing forms. The picturesque Aorai Mountain, rising in the background, is presented as a flat, reddish-purple mass. La Farge utilized the perimeter of the paper to the right of the image for testing colors, specifically to mix the hues of the bold yellow highlights that appear in the foreground expanses of the waves. As in the *Sacred Font* (plate 55), these techniques for studying directly from nature indicate La Farge's knowledge of Romantic watercolor painting and his familiarity with conventions of travel sketching.   *JLY*

1. A detailed chronicle of the journey is provided in my Ph.D. dissertation, "The Role of Landscape in the Art of John La Farge" (University of Chicago, 1981).

2. The most elaborate easel painting is an epic landscape extolling South Sea life, *After-Glow, Tautira River, Tahiti* (National Gallery of Art, Washington, D.C.). This picture was based on several on-the-spot sketches, a photograph, and at least one major intermediate watercolor. I discuss this and other examples in "Landscape in the Art of John La Farge," pp. 394–402.

Provenance
The artist, 1891–96; (Doll and Richards, Boston, 1896); Dr. Samuel B. Woodward, Worcester, 1896–1939; gift of Dr. Samuel B. Woodward, 1939

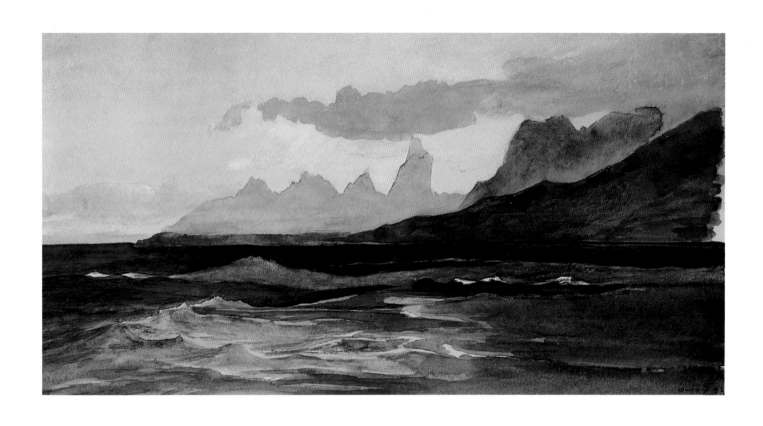

59
Winslow Homer (1836–1910)
Boys and Kitten, 1873

Winslow Homer's watercolors are acknowledged to be among the greatest achievements in American art. Created largely during working vacations first at the New England seaside and later in the Adirondacks, Quebec, the Bahamas, Bermuda, and Florida, when Homer was free from the anxiety of what he considered more serious work in oil, these works are unsurpassed for their directness, luminosity, and economy of means. The fluid brushwork and saturated color of the mature works in particular have influenced much subsequent American watercolor painting. By 1873 the thirty-seven-year-old artist was at a critical point in his career. The early promise of outstanding success as a painter, following the sensation created in 1866 by his canvas *Prisoners from the Front* (Metropolitan Museum of Art), had not materialized, and he derived little sense of achievement from his work as an illustrator for *Harper's Weekly* and other publications. In part he may have been inspired by the much-discussed international watercolor exhibition in New York in early 1873, which established the legitimacy of watercolor beyond question.

Although undated, *Boys and Kitten* is undoubtedly one of the large group of watercolors that Homer executed at Gloucester, Massachusetts, during the summer of 1873, when he first applied himself seriously to the medium in which he would become preeminent.[1] The Gloucester watercolors established what would be, with few exceptions, his lifelong pattern in the medium: concentrating for a period of time, usually one summer, on a single type of subject, suggested by a particular locale. At Gloucester, Homer expanded on a

theme he had touched on only occasionally in his paintings, that of rural childhood. In more than two dozen small works, he depicted the activities of the local children as they played in dories and along the wharves. The newness of watercolor to him as a medium for serious expression may have suggested the need for a fresh subject as well; at the same time, he was adopting a subject that was already popular in literature.

Until 1873 Homer's watercolors were linked stylistically to his work as an illustrator and might more accurately be described as wash drawings heightened with white or touches of colors. At Gloucester his watercolor technique suddenly took a giant leap forward. His dozens of watercolors of local children are small in size but have the originality of observation and vigor of design that characterize the majority of his works. Homer was still working as an illustrator, and his preoccupation with the needs of the engraver underscores these watercolors in their flat, single washes, sharp sense of pattern, precise outlines, and interest in light and shadow. Compared to the brushwork of many of his contemporaries, who favored a more finished watercolor style, Homer's is relatively free.

Boys and Kitten shows a young boy seated on a wall, cradling a kitten, while two other small boys and a large black cat look on. The firm compositional structure of simplified forms gives to this small sheet a striking clarity and presence. Homer achieved the sharp delineation between the lights and darks by freely applying generous amounts of white gouache to the boys' trousers and shirts and to dabs and lines that articulate the foreground, the wall on which the boys sit, and the pickets of the fence in the background. In other areas the

artist used gouache to lighten the color, as in the green leaves of the shrub in the middle distance. Opaque color—easier to control than transparent washes—played a prominent role in many of Homer's watercolors of this period. In *Boys and Kitten* he applies it in the manner of oil painting by building up forms from dark to light as he was accustomed to doing, rather than working from light to dark to achieve a transparent effect.

Homer received his first reviews as a watercolorist for the Gloucester works. Critics thought them original but also eccentric because of their lack of traditional finish. Some reviewers were especially bothered by the commonplace subject matter of works like *Boys and Kitten.* Henry James detested the "little barefoot urchins" and chastized Homer for not caring for "the distinction between beauty and ugliness. . . . He has chosen the least pictorial features of the least pictorial range of scenery and civilization; he has treated them as if they *were* pictorial, as if they were every inch as good as Capri and Tangiers." James nonetheless conceded that "to reward his audacity, [Homer] has incontestably succeeded."[2]   *HAC*

1. All the Homer entries in this catalogue are based upon research I conducted for *Winslow Homer Watercolors* (Washington, D.C.: National Gallery of Art; New Haven, Conn.: Yale University Press, 1986), which accompanied a major traveling exhibition.

2. Henry James, "On Some Pictures Lately Exhibited," *Galaxy* 20 (July 1875): 90, 93, 94.

Provenance
Estate of the artist; (William Macbeth, New York); museum purchase, 1911

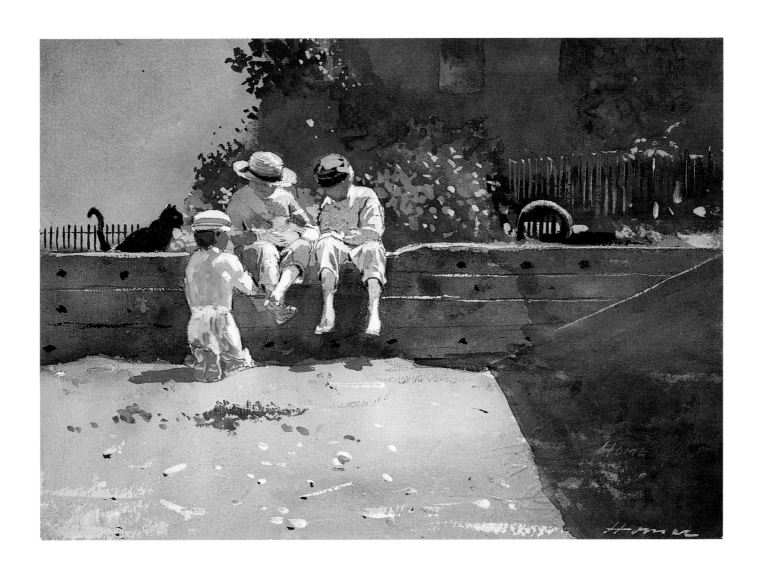

60
Winslow Homer (1836–1910)
The Swing, **probably 1879**

During the 1870s Homer usually left New York City for summer vacations in the country. In the summer of 1879 he visited the family farm of his brother Charles's wife, Mattie, at West Townsend, Massachusetts. This stay resulted in a series of *plein air* watercolors of rural subjects, of men and boys plowing and little girls picking apples or berries, lying in the grass, or playing on swings.

Like the large series of watercolors Homer had executed the previous summer at Houghton Farm in Mountainville, New York, his works from the summer of 1879 capture a sense of unpremeditated execution. Small in size and composed directly on the sheet over the most summary and faint graphite sketch, they are characterized by energetic drawing and delicate colored washes, to which gouache was often added. *The Swing*, one of several studies of this subject, was rendered with careful brush work, the figure of the girl reinforced and articulated by point-of-brush over graphite drawing. Her lavender-pink dress and white stockings and cap sound a note of fresh color against the tender, watery greens of the landscape. The strong design made by the centralized vertical ropes hanging from the sheet-wide horizontal branch both controls and contrasts with the fluid painting style.

Only a few years before, Homer had been harshly criticized for the unfinished sketchiness of his watercolors. Now, more contemporary reviews praised works such as *The Swing* for their fresh originality and what was described as an "American" directness. Also, by 1879 an important development in critical taste had occurred: many American critics and painters associated the looseness of handling and lack of traditional finish of Homer's watercolors with the same qualities in works by the new group of French painters known as "Impressionists." Homer, however, was lauded for being a purely American Impressionist, "entirely homemade and to American soil, indigenous. . . . Impressionist in the true and broad sense, but not as limited by the exact forms of procedures used by certain artists in France," which included the use of saturated hues, broken brush strokes and widespread use of complementary contrast of color.[1] Nevertheless, Homer's perceived connection to the avant-garde—and thus to the wider art world—made his work more acceptable to critics.

HAC

1. *New York Times*, February 1, 1879.

Provenance
The artist; James F. Sutton, New York; Dr. Edward J. Davin; (American Art Association, Anderson Galleries, New York, sale no. 4227, January 23, 1936, cat. no. 5); (Babcock Galleries, New York, 1936); (Robert C. Vose Galleries, Boston, 1936); Dr. and Mrs. Loring Holmes Dodd, Worcester, 1936–68; Mrs. Howard W. Preston, Cranston, R.I., 1968–69; gift of Mrs. Howard W. Preston in memory of Dr. and Mrs. Loring Holmes Dodd, 1969

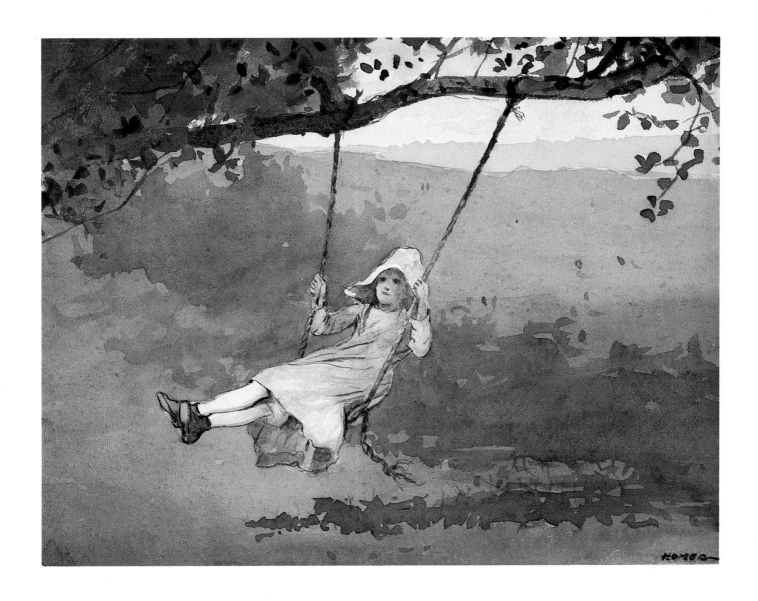

61
Winslow Homer (1836–1910)
Girl with Shell at Ear, 1880

Girl with Shell at Ear is one of a small series of drawings of a young woman Homer made during the summer of 1880, probably at Ten Pound Island, off Gloucester, Massachusetts.[1] Executed outdoors and rendered in white gouache and charcoal over graphite on gray paper, these sheets have a directness and vivacity that set them apart from the more labored depictions of the same young woman that the artist produced in his studio.

Drawings such as *Girl with Shell at Ear* were meant as finished works of art. Homer's confident draftsmanship and his knowing use of the materials are evident in the short, quick chalk strokes, hard and soft, which are charged with a life of their own. Homer used this technique in a variety of ways: with parallel hatching, as in the bodice, or with shading, as in the skirt; to firmly contour the form in some places, in others, to suggest tone. The gouache is applied freely to describe light, atmosphere, and a range of textures.

Finished charcoal and white gouache drawings were an important part of Homer's artistic expression until shortly after he returned from England in 1882. After that time his sketches were usually preliminary studies for etchings, watercolors, and oil paintings.   *HAC*

1. For example, *Young Girl with a Basket, Seated* (1880; Cooper-Hewitt Museum, Smithsonian Institution, New York).

Provenance
Gift of the artist to Grenville H. Norcross, 1907; bequest of Grenville H. Norcross, 1937

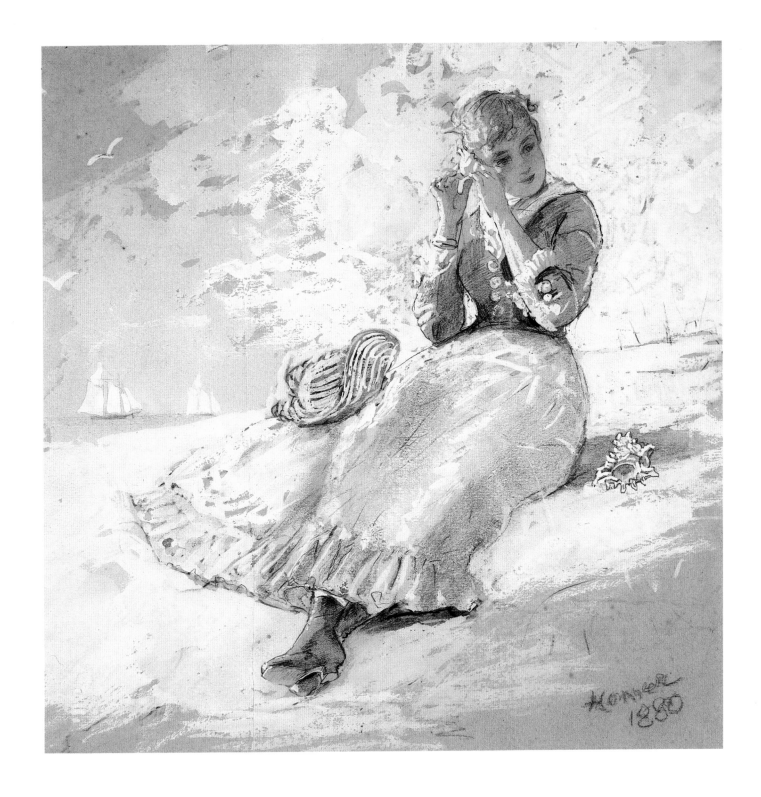

62
Winslow Homer (1836–1910)
Crab Fishing, **1883**

Although by 1881 Homer had achieved some recognition as a watercolorist, he decided to travel to England to increase his mastery of the medium and to find new subjects. There, in an artistic atmosphere that valued the serious use of watercolor, he could study firsthand the pictorial effects achieved by such techniques as layering, scraping, and masking of washes. The huge popularity in England of sea genre paintings and of the somber scenes of fishermen and fisherwomen by nineteenth-century Hague School artists such as Jozef Israels probably influenced Homer's choice of a similar subject matter and artistic treatment. At the same time, depicting the daily lives of those who earned a living by the sea presented the opportunity to reach deeper levels of meaning in his art. In England, Homer adapted his nostalgic sense of childhood and rural life to subjects of timeless struggle.

Crab Fishing belongs to a group of highly finished watercolors of fisherfolk subjects. Probably begun in 1881 or 1882, during Homer's twenty-month stay in the picturesque Northumbrian fishing village of Cullercoats on the North Sea, it was completed in New York early in 1883, shortly after his return to America. This watercolor is an ambitious work. Set in late afternoon, it shows three young women and a fisherman hauling crab pots into a coble, the traditional fishing craft of Northumbria.[1] The women, in particular, are carefully drawn and owe considerable allegiance to contemporary Victorian figure painting. In contrast to their finish is the misty atmosphere, the lack of a discernible horizon, and the choppy sea. Restraining his natural sketching style and fresh palette, for his works in this series Homer turned to tradi-

tional watercolor techniques and more subdued colors. Using a tonalist scheme of grayed pinks and greens, he relied on layered and sponged washes to create the silvery sky and sea, leaving reserves of the paper to achieve the gleaming reflections on the surface of the water.

The Cullercoats watercolors were greeted with much acclaim by reviewers who saw them exhibited in New York and Boston. Critics praised the dignity, strength, and grandeur of these paintings, calling them "serious works of 'high art' in spite of their peasant subjects and their watercolor medium."[2] The wide acceptance of the Cullercoats group ensured Homer's reputation as a watercolorist. He went on to adapt both the subject and style of the Cullercoats watercolors to oil, producing such masterful canvases as *The Life Line* (1884; Philadelphia Museum of Art). *HAC*

1. Similar groups of figures in cobles appear in *Returning Fishing Boats* (1883; Fogg Art Museum, Harvard University), and *An Afterglow* (1883; Museum of Fine Arts, Boston).

2. Mariana Griswold Van Rensselaer, "An American Artist in England," *Century Magazine* 27 (November 1883): 19. The Cullercoats watercolors were exhibited at the American Water Color Society in New York and at Doll and Richards and J. Eastman Chase Gallery in Boston.

Provenance
(Doll and Richards, Boston, 1883); Miss L. Norcross, 1883; Grenville H. Norcross, Boston, by 1911; bequest of Grenville H. Norcross, 1937

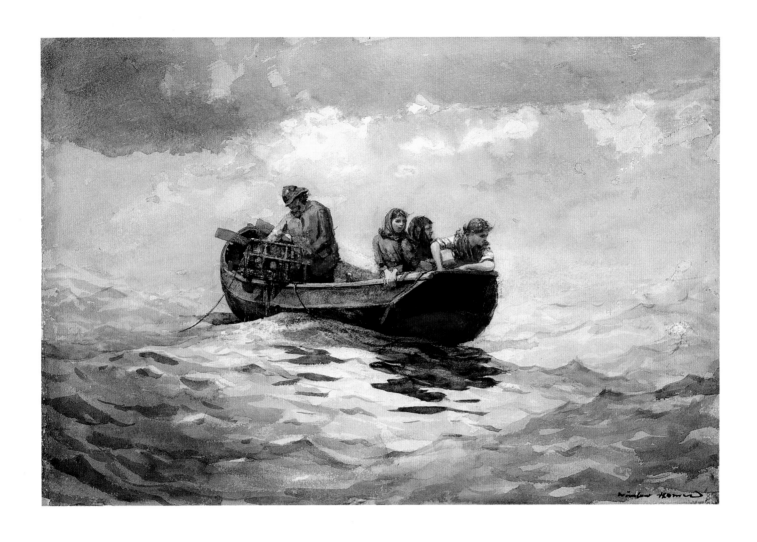

63
Winslow Homer (1836–1910)
Prout's Neck, Rocky Shore, 1883

Shortly after he returned from his stay of almost two years in the English village of Cullercoats, Homer decided to make Prout's Neck, Maine, his permanent home. His experience in England had forever changed the direction of his life and art. Prout's Neck offered him the solitude he now cherished and direct contact with the kind of wild and elemental nature he had come to care for. The rocky peninsula jutting into the Atlantic, its gray cliffs rising out of the water, and the surf breaking spectacularly against huge rocks gave the setting a majestic and dramatic power. Homer settled in a house and studio that commanded a breathtaking view of the coast.

In more than a dozen watercolors, of which *Prout's Neck, Rocky Shore* is typical, Homer tried to capture the massive power of the waves, the speed and spray of the breakers, and the impact of tons of water crashing against the great rocks. These watercolors were Homer's first attempts at pure seascape. Characterized by a diagonal format that divides the picture into two principal sections, with the rocks massed darkly into the lower part, these seascapes anticipate Homer's later marine subjects in oil. He relied on a restricted palette of somber grays and green-blues for the water, purple-grays (now somewhat faded) for the sky, and tones of raw and burnt umber for the rocks. The artist brought to *Prout's Neck, Rocky Shore* all the technical skills he had mastered in England: flooding wet paint into wet; scraping the paper (for example, in the highlights of the foam in the center foreground); layering the washes; lifting the wet paint from the surface (as in the rock at the far left); and sponging to achieve tone and texture.

For the most part, however, the Prout's Neck watercolors are not entirely successful; Homer himself was reportedly dissatisfied with the group.[1] The palette lacks depth, and the rocks do not seem massive and unyielding nor the waves relentless. In a sense, the inherent delicacy of the medium is at odds with the overwhelming power of the subject.   *HAC*

1. Philip C. Beam, *Winslow Homer at Prout's Neck* (Boston: Little, Brown, 1966), p. 86.

Provenance
Estate of the artist; (E. L. Knoedler, New York); museum purchase, 1911

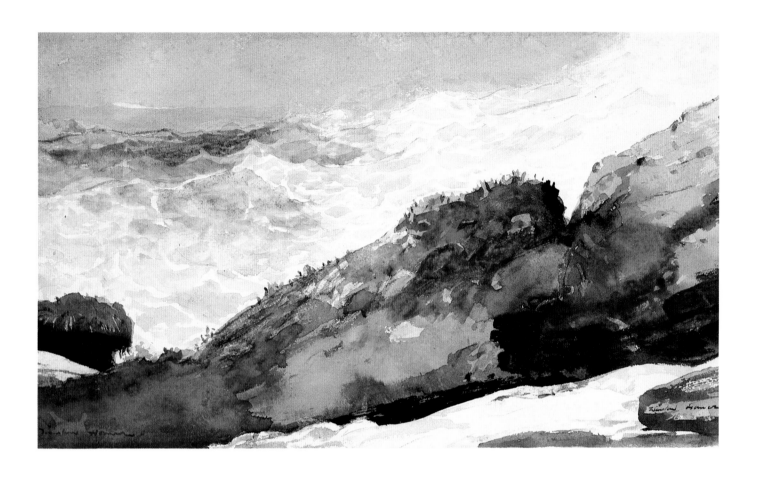

64
Winslow Homer (1836–1910)
The Garden Gate, Bahamas, **1885**

In 1884 *Century Magazine* commissioned Homer to illustrate an article it was planning on the Bahamas.[1] By that time the islands had become a popular tourist resort much praised for their beautiful setting and temperate climate. Accompanied by his father, Homer arrived in Nassau in December 1884, where he remained until mid-February.[2] During his two-month stay he created close to thirty watercolors, taking for his principal subject the tropical landscape and the activities of the local black population.

The Caribbean light and lush tropical color had an immediate impact on Homer's technique. The watercolors he produced during this visit employ a brighter palette, greater exploitation of the white paper, and an increased suggestiveness, fluidity, and freedom of brushwork. *The Garden Gate, Bahamas* shows two black women carrying fruit-laden baskets on their heads, the tropical fruit and plants virtually silhouetted against the characteristic Bahamian coral walls with their distinctive pyramid-shaped capitals.[3] The women convey a quiet dignity reminiscent of Homer's paintings of black women in Virginia a decade earlier. With less sponging, scraping, and lifting of the paint from the surface to create lighter areas than in his English watercolors of a few years earlier, Homer gave the Bahamas watercolors a direct, seemingly unpremeditated quality. However, the contemporary public was perplexed by these works. To an audience that had recently praised Homer for the beauty of line and finish of the Cullercoats watercolors (see *Crab Fishing,*

plate 62), the unfamiliar subjects, sketchy brushwork, and brighter palette of the Bahamas works came as a not entirely pleasant surprise. Whereas half of the Cullercoats watercolors were immediately sold, few of the Bahamas works were purchased at the time. *HAC*

1. The article appeared more than two years later. See William Church, "A Midwinter Resort," *Century Magazine* 33, no. 4 (February 1887): 499–506. Nine illustrations by Homer are included.

2. Homer was not the first well-known American artist to visit the Bahamas. Thomas Moran visited in the late 1870s, and during the 1870s and 1880s Albert Bierstadt periodically visited Nassau, where his wife, who suffered from chronic consumption, regularly wintered.

3. Based upon Homer's palette and a smudge of pigment on the reverse of the sheet, the coral wall appears to have faded significantly from a purple-red to a faint orange.

Provenance
(Doll and Richards, Boston, 1886); father of Miss Miriam Shaw; bequest of Miss Miriam Shaw, Harvard, Mass., 1983

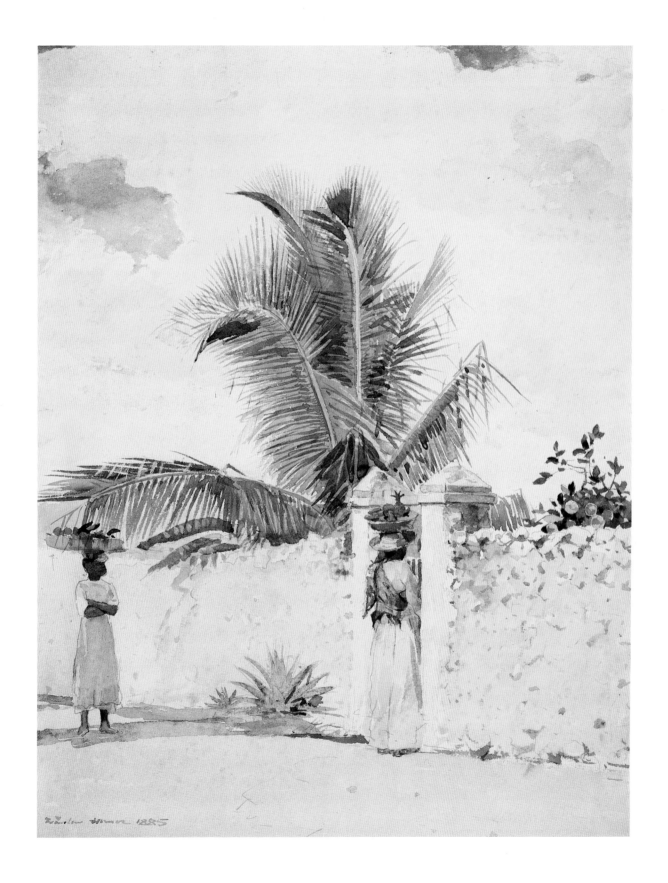

93

65

Winslow Homer (1836–1910)
In a Florida Jungle, **probably 1885–86**

Beginning in the winter of 1885–86, Homer visited Florida at least seven times over the next twenty-four years. These were primarily fishing trips, and only three—in 1885–86 to Tampa and Key West, in 1890 to Enterprise, and in 1903–4 to Key West and Homosassa—resulted in watercolors. Based on thematic and stylistic similarities to dated examples from the first trip, *In a Florida Jungle* can be dated to the winter of 1885–86.[1]

Although Tampa was known for its excellent fishing, and Homer was there for the sport, none of the watercolors from this trip depicts a fishing subject. Instead, the artist focused on images of exotic birds, alligators, live oaks, coconut palms, and palmetto jungles thickly hung with Spanish moss. For *In a Florida Jungle*, Homer used a wide variety of watercolor techniques that impart a rich visual texture to the two-dimensional surface. Layers of gray wash suggest the moss-hung trees in the distance, and scraping was used to create the white clouds and sand beach in the foreground. Similarly layered washes in a range of greens, from yellow to blue, set the foundation for the palmetto fronds, which are rendered through both positive and negative shapes (created by the lifting of paint), achieved by a complex process of scraping and rewashing.[2] In places, as in the deep browns and brilliant blues in the foreground water, Homer brushed color onto the exposed paper where pigment had been removed.

In a Florida Jungle subtly foreshadows the mortal themes Homer would treat more fully in later years, especially the poignant moment in which a creature is poised between life and death. In the center foreground an alligator juts its snout out of the still, brackish water. Its eyes seem to be fixed on the apparently unaware roseate spoonbill that stands on the white sand beach. From a distance we witness the last moments of the innocent bird's life. In the years following, Homer repeatedly depicted scenes like this one, in which, as part of nature's cycle, an unsuspecting creature is about to die.   *HAC*

1. Other examples from this same trip are *At Tampa* (1885; Canajoharie Public Library and Museum, Canajoharie, New York) and *Thornhill Bar* (1886; Museum of Fine Arts, Boston).

2. For an in-depth discussion of Homer's technique in this work, see the essay by Judith Walsh in this book.

Provenance
Estate of the artist; (M. Knoedler & Co., New York); museum purchase, 1911

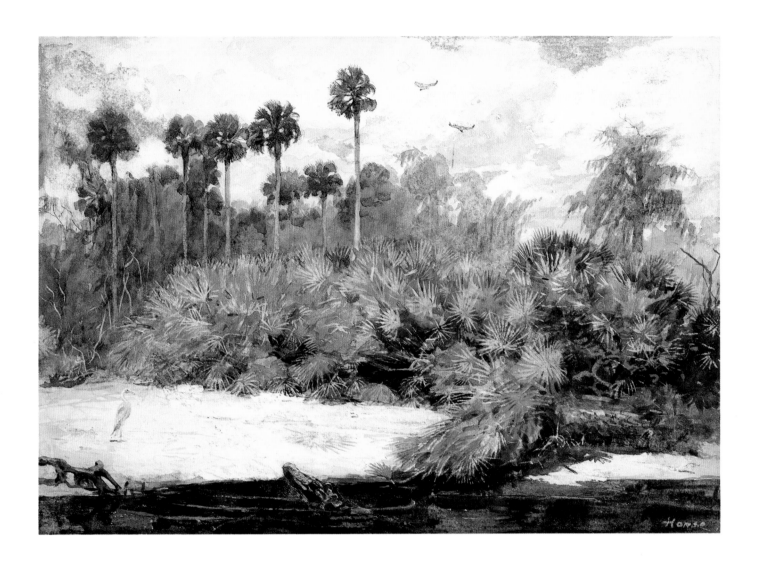

66
Winslow Homer (1836–1910)
Old Friends, 1894

The group of watercolors of the North Woods in the Adirondacks that Homer produced over a decade, from 1889 to 1900, are among the master achievements of his career. Painted during sporting vacations at the North Woods Club, a private hunting and fishing preserve near Minerva, in Essex County, New York, these works reveal a more intimate side of the artist's emotionally reserved, intensely private nature.

Homer's profound love for the Adirondack wilderness is nowhere more evident than in *Old Friends*. Like the other sheets in this group of watercolors, it deals with the death of the North Woods at the hands of the lumbering industry. Although not intended to depict a specific progression, the group can be arranged, beginning with *Old Friends*, to form a narrative sequence on the destruction of the forests.[1] In *Old Friends* a gray-bearded woodsman—a favored subject in Homer's Adirondacks watercolors— looks up at the huge tree that towers above him, his gentle touch betraying a depth of feeling for these majestic presences, which had been an integral part of his existence.[2] It is also a gesture of farewell, for the destruction of the wilderness signaled the end of a way of life.

The power of *Old Friends* is in part a function of the dramatically vertical composition, in which the great tree is silhouetted against a white sky. Contrasting with the sky, where the textured surface of the scraped paper shows through, thin brush strokes of black-brown render the branches with an almost Oriental simplicity. Throughout the sheet, Homer used color to express emotion. He underscored the kinship between the old man and the ancient tree by rendering both in the same rich grays and siennas. The dappled light and centuries-old quiet of the deep woods is evoked through layers of luminous transparent greens, blues, and gold. At the foot of the tree is the suggestion of piles of fallen leaves. Slashes of crimson in the deep gash in the bark and daubed onto the ground— as if the great tree itself were bleeding— convey a sense of ripeness and autumnal melancholy. Here, as in many of the Adirondacks watercolors, there is a coincidence of outward stillness and intense emotional poignancy.   *HAC*

1. Among other watercolors that can be considered part of this narrative are *The Woodcutter* (1891; private collection); *Hudson River* (1892; Museum of Fine Arts, Boston); *Hudson River—Logging* (probably 1892; Corcoran Gallery of Art, Washington, D.C.); and *The Pioneer* (1900; Metropolitan Museum of Art).

2. In the Adirondacks watercolors, Homer repeatedly shows two woodsmen, separately and together: a young man and an older man with a beard. The old man is said to have been based on either Orson "Mountain" Phelps, Rufus Wallace, or Harvey Holt, one of three well-known guides in the Keene Valley, all of whom were interchangeable as types. See Philip C. Beam, *Winslow Homer at Prout's Neck* (Boston: Little, Brown, 1966), pp. 102–3.

Provenance
The artist; (E. L. Knoedler, New York); museum purchase, 1908

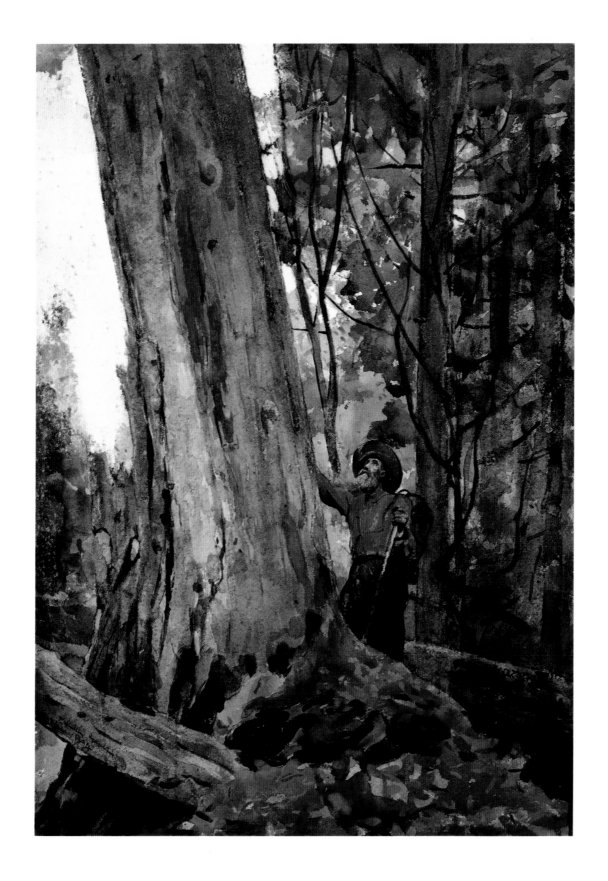

67
Winslow Homer (1836–1910)
Sunset, Prout's Neck, **1895**

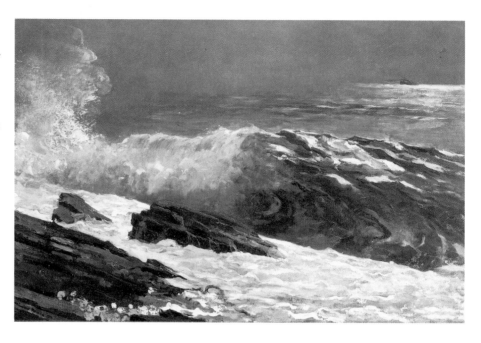

The image of breakers crashing against huge rocks had fascinated Homer from the time he had moved to Prout's Neck, Maine, in 1883. He produced a series of watercolors of the subject that year and subsequently portrayed it in oil in the 1890 *Sunlight on the Coast* (plate 67a). This was followed by another watercolor series and a number of marine paintings in oil in 1894. In 1895 he turned again to watercolor for the subject. *Sunset, Prout's Neck* is one of a series of watercolors he executed then.

Homer studied the waves from every aspect and under many conditions of weather and light. In this painting, broad gestural strokes of saturated royal blue and blue-grays convey with forceful simplicity the rolling motion of the huge wave as it moves toward the shore. The reflection of the setting sun in the foreground sea is caught in pale crimson washes. Paint-loaded strokes of blue-black and brown define the massive rocks at the right, and reserved and scraped paper suggests the white foam. Gray clouds move across the sulphurous sky (unfortunately now faded somewhat from its originally more intense tones of purple-gray). Two sailboats darkly silhouetted on the fiery horizon give a human presence and scale to the sky-wide sea and underscore the precariousness and vulnerability of man within the vast ambivalence of nature.   *HAC*

1. The watercolor was previously titled *Sunset, Gloucester,* based upon an inscription on the reverse of the sheet. The inscription is not in Homer's hand, and there is no evidence that Homer visited Gloucester in 1895.

Provenance
Estate of the artist; (E. L. Knoedler, New York); museum purchase, 1911

67a
Winslow Homer
Sunlight on the Coast, 1890
Oil on canvas
30¼ × 48½ in. (76.9 × 123.3 cm.)
Toledo Museum of Art; Gift of Mr. and Mrs. Edward Drummond Libbey

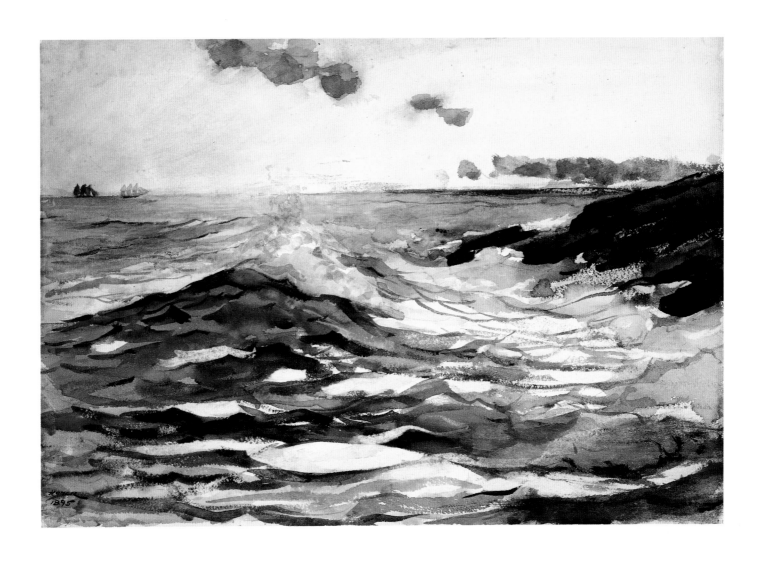

68

Winslow Homer (1836–1910)
Prout's Neck, Surf on Rocks, 1895

Prout's Neck, Surf on Rocks is another of the many studies that Homer made of the waves along the Maine coast. The view is probably looking across Saco Bay to Pine Point and Old Orchard beaches in the distance, under a sky illuminated by a glowing sunset. A streak of purple-red, washed into pale yellows and grays and animated with broad slashes of black, renders the foreground waves crashing against the rocks. The sinuously curving spume, whose outlines on the paper are faintly marked in graphite, rises up in an almost humanoid form. The suggestion of a human form in imminent danger of dissolution endows the composition with an emotional power that transcends the specifics of the scene itself. Throughout, the brushwork is gestural, even agitated, imparting to the two-dimensional surface a force and intensity that suggest the sense of nature's power.

It seems that the transparent and delicate watercolor medium was not forceful enough to convey fully the weight and grandeur of the breakers, elements that characterized Homer's great seascape oils of the 1890s. The broken, complex surface of *Prout's Neck, Surf on Rocks,* with its waves churning between the rocks and its plume of spray, may have served as the study for the later oil *West Point, Prout's Neck* (plate 68a). HAC

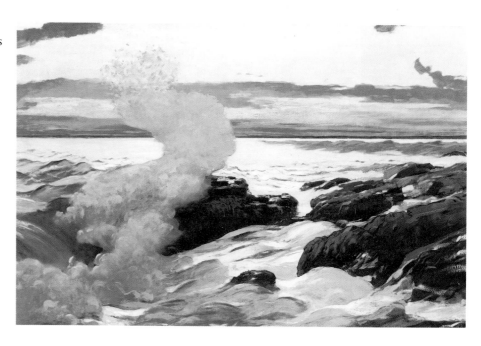

68a
Winslow Homer
West Point, Prout's Neck, 1900
Oil on canvas
30 1/16 × 48 1/8 in. (76.4 × 122.2 cm.)
Sterling and Francine Clark Art Institute, Williamstown, Massachusetts

Provenance
Estate of the artist; (E. L. Knoedler, New York); museum purchase, 1911

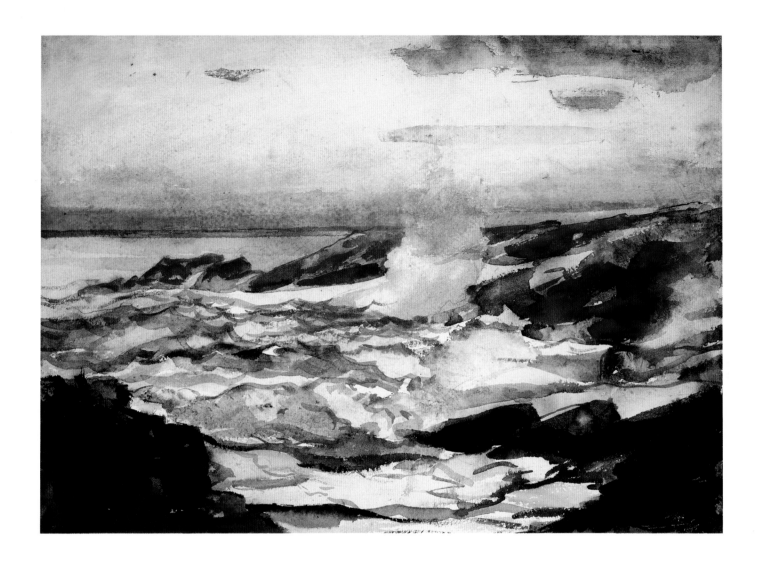

69
Winslow Homer (1836–1910)
Grand Discharge, Lake St. John, probably 1897

Homer first visited Quebec province in the spring of 1893, and over the next decade he vacationed there a number of times. He wrote that "the place suits me as if made for me by a kind of providence."[1] He chose to stay in the region about one hundred miles north of Quebec City, along the Saguenay River near its headwaters at Lake St. John, an area famed for the ouananiche, a landlocked salmon. As he did on his vacations in the Adirondacks, during his visits to Quebec, Homer often combined fishing and art. Watercolors exist from his Canadian visits of 1895, 1897, and 1902.

The turbulent Saguenay River, called by some the "River of Death," became the principal subject of most of Homer's Quebec watercolors. In some sheets he focused on images of fishermen trying to land the feisty salmon in the swirling waters. In others, among them *Grand Discharge, Lake St. John*, the water itself is the subject, especially the spectacular rapids where the lake discharges into the river.

The technique in *Grand Discharge, Lake St. John* is rapid, broad, and expressive. The direct and energetic execution are a response to the dynamic setting. Bold brush strokes within a firm design convey the swirling of the water. The river's unique purple-gray and yellow-rust colors, the result of the water's strong iron content, are depicted in saturated washes of ochers, gray-blues, and grays. Deep gray-blues and blacks render the densely wooded background hills, while reserved and scraped paper suggests the billowing foam. "Something of the vigor and vitality of the cold air of these northern latitudes has entered into the artist's brush" wrote one critic upon seeing the Quebec watercolors; "Mr. Homer's watercolors are permeated with outdoor feeling and with the atmosphere of the region."[2] Homer himself considered the Quebec watercolors to be among his best works.   *HAC*

1. Homer to Charles S. Homer, Jr., February 23, probably 1896, Homer Collection, Bowdoin College Museum of Art, Brunswick, Maine; in Philip C. Beam, *Winslow Homer at Prout's Neck* (Boston: Little, Brown, 1966), p. 127.

2. *New York Times*, April 9, 1898, p. 242.

Provenance
Estate of the artist; (E. L. Knoedler, New York); museum purchase, 1911

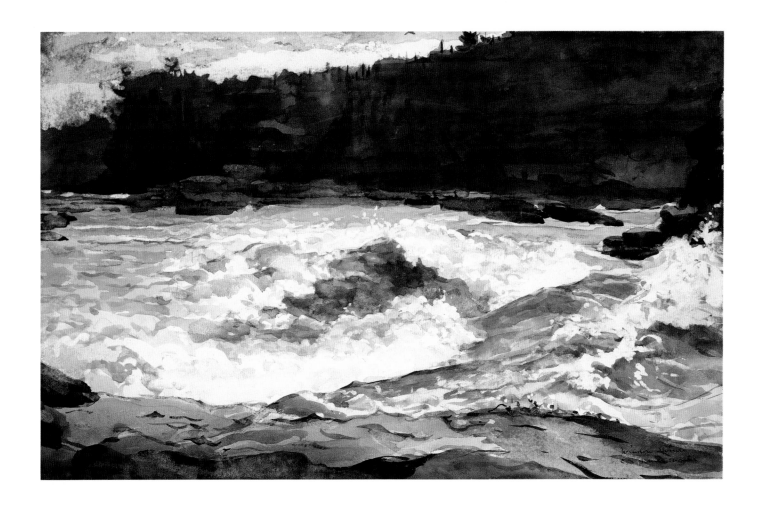

70

Winslow Homer (1836–1910)
Saguenay River, Lower Rapids, **1897**

''Mr. Homer paints the rapids as if he had breasted them and had got their strength into his brush.''[1] This comment by one critic aptly describes the sense of grandeur and thrilling excitement conveyed in *Saguenay River, Lower Rapids*, which depicts a group of canoers fishing in the seemingly impassable rapids at Grand Discharge, at the mouth of the Saguenay River. Against a background of deep woods conceived in washes of saturated blues and grays, sweeping strokes of liquid pigment—bright blues and grays, slashes of black, and layers of yellow ocher—render the color of the Saguenay's distinctive iron-rich water, while the white of the scraped paper suggests the foaming rapids. In the middle distance, carried along on the swirling currents, are three canoes. In each craft one of the figures is, in all likelihood, a native guide; the trip down the river over the rapids in frail birch-bark canoes was safely made only with the skillful assistance of French Canadian or Indian canoemen. The contrast of tiny figures and wide expanse of surging water reiterates a recurring theme in Homer's late watercolors, namely the fragility of the human presence in the face of nature's power.   *HAC*

1. *New York Daily Tribune,* April 10, 1898, p. 6.

Provenance
Estate of the artist; (E. L. Knoedler, New York); museum purchase, 1911

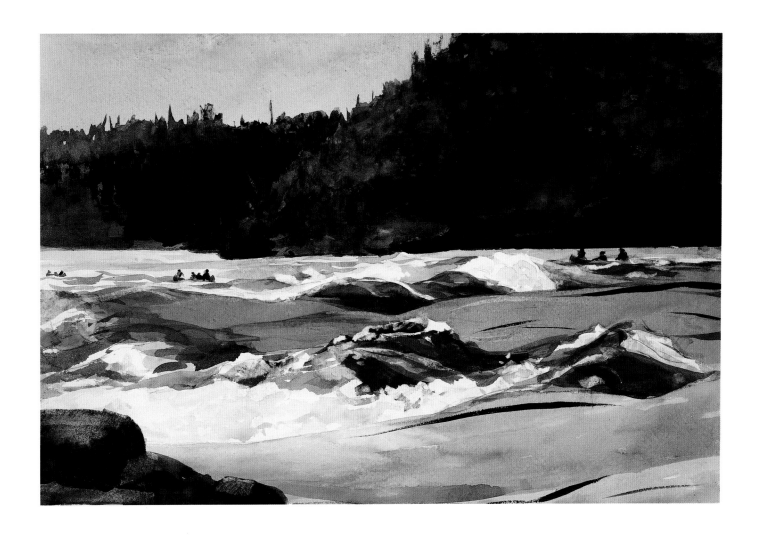

71
Winslow Homer (1836–1910)
Rum Cay, **1898–99**

Although undated, *Rum Cay* is undoubtedly from Homer's second visit to the Bahamas, in the winter of 1898–99. It is one of a series of watercolors in which the artist portrayed the black man as a magnificently formed being, intimately in harmony with nature. In the fourteen years since his first visit to Nassau, in the winter of 1884–85, the theme of man's relationship to nature had played an increasingly significant role in Homer's work. During the same period, his sense of design and his watercolor technique had also matured, so that in these late works he was able to achieve maximum visual impact through strong color and uncluttered compositional structure.

Homer's original title for the watercolor was *Turtle Cay*, which he inscribed beside the tiny sketch in his daybook entry of July 5, 1902 (plate 73a).[1] The location of the scene therefore may be Green Turtle Cay, a long stretch of beach famous for its turtles, which lies offshore north of Nassau. Turtles were hunted for their valuable shells, which were exported, and for their meat, which was a staple of the local diet. Found among the rocky little outer islands and cays of the Bahamas, they were usually captured on the beach by natives who quickly turned them over and bound their flippers.

Rum Cay is a powerful image, memorable above all for the stark clarity of its conception. A gleaming young man, grandly dark against an azure sky and deeper blue-green sea, chases a huge turtle cross the white sand beach. In contrast to the broadly painted landscape and sky, Homer gave careful attention to the man and the turtle. Outlining the forms in graphite before applying the washes, he reinforced them afterward by drawing with the point of his brush.

Homer underscored the interdependence of man and beast through the use of echoed gestures and shapes. For example, a similar pattern appears on the reptile's shell and in the man's pectoral muscles, and the positions of the man's limbs are reiterated in a more primitive form in the turtle's flippers. But while the turtle appears trapped—an impression reinforced compositionally by the strongly defined horizontal band of sand he sits on—the running man is more ambiguously situated. Towering above the landscape, under the high sun of midday, he is caught in motion, like an athlete on a frieze, at once free and trapped in his place. Homer's depiction speaks of the irony of man's relationship to nature, which at once grants him freedom and imposes limitations.   *HAC*

1. No. 6 in the daybook, Homer Collection, Bowdoin College Museum of Art, Brunswick, Maine.

Provenance
Estate of the artist; (M. Knoedler & Co., New York); museum purchase, 1911

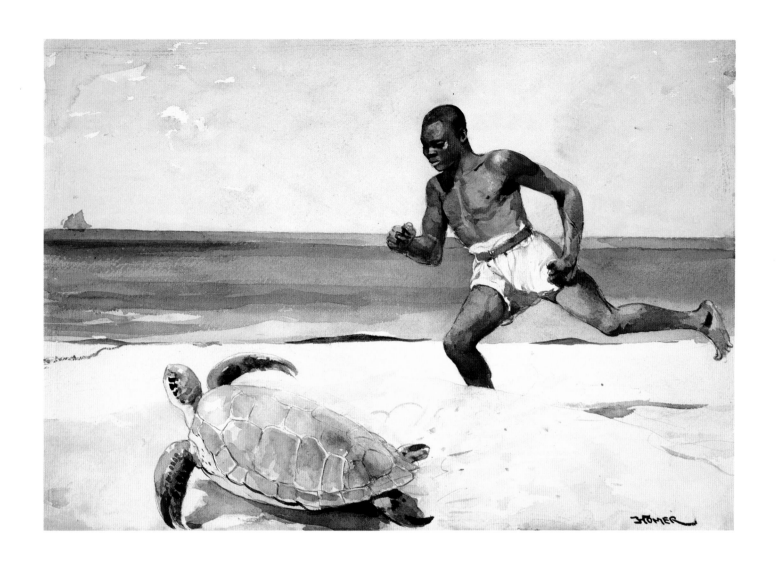

72
Winslow Homer (1836–1910)
The Light House, Nassau, **1899**

"I think [the] Bahamas the best place I have ever found," said Homer to his old friend the Boston lithographer Louis Prang.[1] The freedom bestowed upon the artist by a vacation in a lush tropical environment is apparent in this watercolor dating from his second visit to the Bahamas, during the winter of 1898–99.

In a half-submerged open boat filled with red-tinged conch shells, a bare-torsoed young black man waves to a group of figures, also in a boat, in the direction of the distant shore. At the right, next to the red flag, is Nassau's white coral lighthouse, built in 1816 on the southern tip of Hog Island to protect the port and to house a powder magazine. Despite the steep waves, rendered in broad, form-defining brush strokes, the figure of the man is relaxed, giving no sense of impending danger. Rather, by concealing the man's legs and arranging his body so that the boat suggests an enormous tail or fin, Homer gave the overall contour of man and boat the form of a huge aquatic creature, thereby emphasizing the impression of the man's closeness to nature.

Homer's masterly control of the watercolor medium is apparent throughout this sheet. Brilliant saturated color is laid down freely but confidently, with liquid strokes over little or no graphite. The broadly washed gray sky, with its scudding white clouds, opens to reveal patches of bright blue. The effect of the white Caribbean light is conveyed in the man's gleaming bronze skin and the glittering blue water. In such late tropical sheets, Homer's watercolor technique reached its most confident maturity.   *HAC*

1. Homer, in Lloyd Goodrich, *Winslow Homer* (New York: Macmillan, 1945), p. 193.

Provenance
Estate of the artist; (E. L. Knoedler, New York); museum purchase, 1911

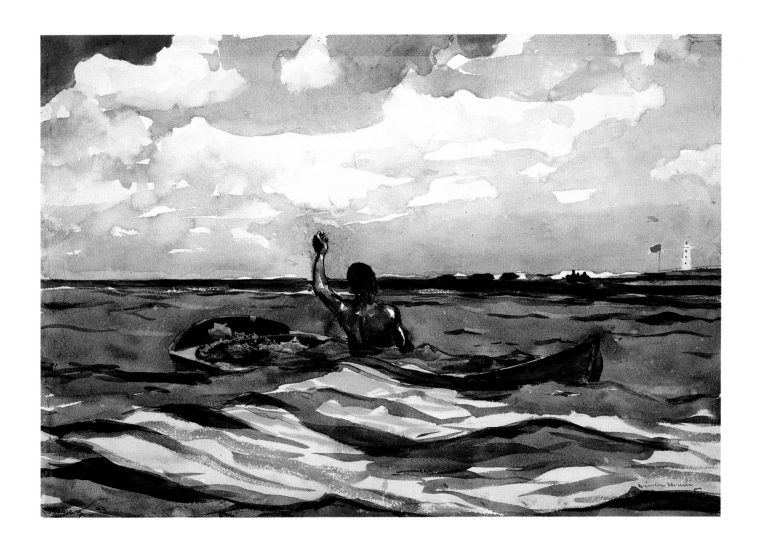

73
Winslow Homer (1836–1910)
Bermuda Settlers, 1901

At the turn of the century Bermuda's popularity as a winter resort for Americans was growing. Its reputation was enhanced by occasional articles in such periodicals as *Harper's* that praised the temperate climate and the setting unspoiled by modern life. Homer first visited Bermuda in the winter of 1899–1900. The special beauty of this coral island cluster apparently charmed the New Englander, for he returned the following year, when he painted this watercolor.

In his daybook entry of July 5, 1902, for a group of watercolors sent to Knoedler's, his New York dealer, Homer entitled his sketch of this watercolor *Bermuda Pigs* (plate 73a).[1] In the watercolor itself he shows five gray-black razorback hogs, one of which gazes steadily out at the viewer. The subject reflects Homer's occasional indulgence of his feeling for fun, a tone enhanced by the freedom and ease with which he handled the medium. The warm, natural atmosphere of the scene, as if the viewer simply happened upon these wild pigs in a cedar grove, is imparted through fresh, saturated colors and spontaneous brushwork. A variety of yellow-greens on the ground suggest the play of sunlight on the grassy clearing, while strokes of deeper greens describe the bushy outcroppings on the rocky terrain. Two dabs of bright red on a high branch, meant to suggest birds, add an exotic note. Girded by an azure sea in the left distance and lighter blue water in the foreground, the whole scene evokes the sense of an innocent, untouched natural world.   *HAC*

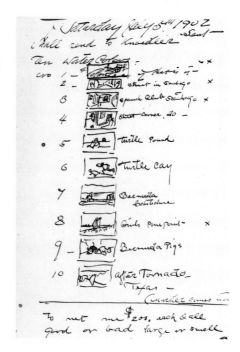

73a
Winslow Homer's daybook entry of July 5, 1902, with sketch of *Rum Cay* (plate 71) and *Bermuda Settlers*
Bowdoin College Museum of Art, Brunswick, Maine

1. No. 9 in the daybook, Homer Collection, Bowdoin College, Museum of Art, Brunswick, Maine.

Provenance
Estate of the artist; (E. L. Knoedler, New York); museum purchase, 1911

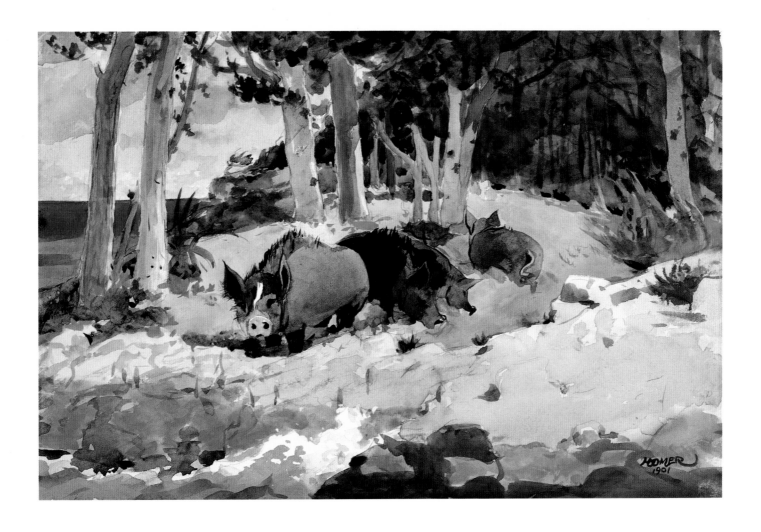

74
Winslow Homer (1836–1910)
Coral Formation, 1901

Coral Formation was painted during Homer's second visit to Bermuda. It depicts one of the curious stratified formations worn into fantastic shapes by the action of the water along the Bermuda coast. This particular formation appears to be a site on the westernmost part of the island opposite the Royal Bermuda Dockyard, which at the time was a British naval garrison, close to Homer's boardinghouse at Scaur Hill. At the left, on top of the broad rock, stand two red-coated soldiers, who point across the inlet to one of Bermuda's garrisons, seen outlined against the distant sky.[1]

The military played a significant role in Bermuda life. The crown colony's strategic location made it an important center for the storage of arms in the event of a war against the United States. The British government also used Bermuda as a detention area for Boer prisoners of war from 1900 to 1902. That these military figures appear at a distance in Homer's painting may in part be the result of legislation forbidding the close-up sketching or photographing of fortified posts. However, close-up views of other local figures are absent as well in Homer's Bermuda watercolors. When he did include people, they are small and seem incidental to the scene, serving only to give scale to the composition. Bermuda apparently did not present the artist with the thematic and pictorial possibilities of encounters between man and nature

that he found in the Bahamas. Whereas in the Bahamas watercolors the black population is repeatedly the principal subject, the Bermuda watercolors focus for the most part on the coral island's natural splendors—dazzling light, brilliant color, and beautiful vistas.

Rendered in saturated hues of azure, royal blue, golden yellow, and deep gray, *Coral Formation* perfectly captures the dazzling effect of sunlight striking the soft white coral sandstone. Homer's ability to exploit the accidental effect that results at the point where two soaking washes touch is evident in the area of the inland water, where he allowed the deep blue washes to dry in such a way as to suggest the crystal clarity of the deep water and light gleaming off its surface. The purity of the reserved white paper and the ease of the brushwork in fluid layered washes combine to create a work of striking luminosity.   *HAC*

1. Homer included similar military figures in at least two other Bermuda watercolors: *Rocky Shore, Bermuda* (1900; Museum of Fine Arts, Boston) and *Natural Bridge* (probably 1901; Metropolitan Museum of Art).

Provenance
Estate of the artist; (E. L. Knoedler, New York); museum purchase, 1911

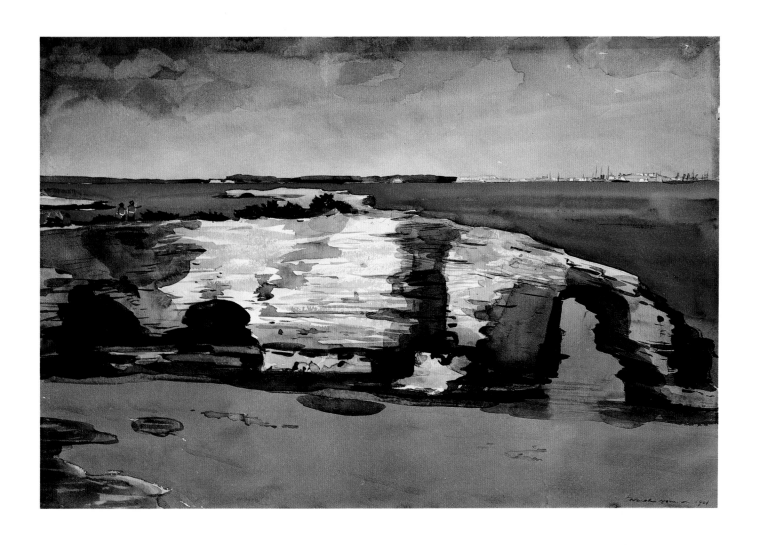

113

75
Winslow Homer (1836–1910)
Fishing Boats, Key West, 1904

This is one of at least nine watercolors of
sloops that Homer executed during his stay
at the island town of Key West during his
visit to Florida from December 1903 to
early January 1904. In *Fishing Boats, Key
West* the artist concentrated on capturing
the atmosphere of a brooding storm. It is
among his most luminous works, conceived
in broad washes of rich grays and blues of
purest transparency for the sea and sky,
and floodings of crimson, browns, and
rusts for the boats. Homer used a small
amount of scraping and left parts of the
white paper untouched to form a diagonal
swath through the center of the composition, as if the boats have been struck by
the flash of light that precedes the storm.
He drew the masts with the point of his
brush to create an abstract pattern of parallel vertical lines, while graphite underdrawing loosely defines the boats. Homer
used these graphite notations independently
from the wash, and they have a lively,
playful quality that gives a freshness and
vivacity to the rendering. Homer's control
of watery pigment is evident in the foreground, where he manipulated washes of
different blues to create the effect of murky,
stirring waters before the onset of a storm.

HAC

Provenance
Estate of the artist; (E. L. Knoedler, New York); museum
purchase, 1911

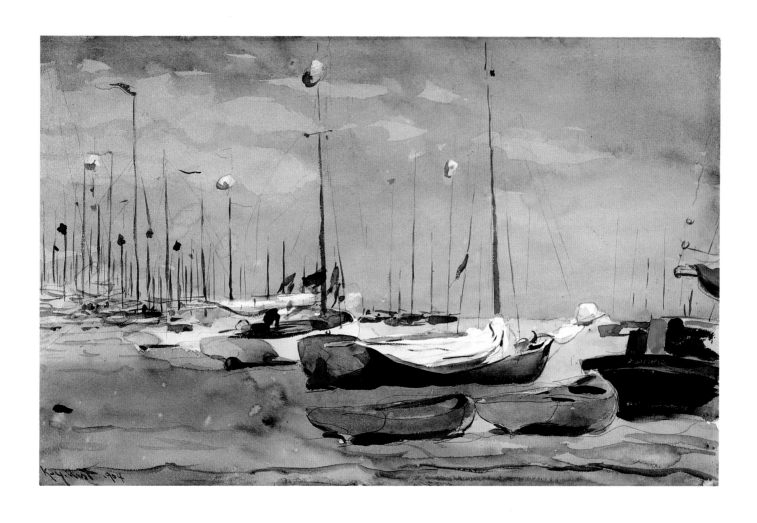

76
Winslow Homer (1836–1910)
The Turkey Buzzard, 1904

Following his visit to Key West (see *Fishing Boats, Key West*, plate 75), in December 1903, Homer moved north in early January 1904 to Homosassa, a small town on the river of the same name, about four miles from the Gulf of Mexico in an area that was renowned as a fisherman's paradise. The eleven or twelve watercolors from this visit constitute the last series he would ever paint. *The Turkey Buzzard*, like the other Homosassa watercolors, presents the scene from the vantage point of a fisherman on the river.[1] The composition and the rendering have an almost Oriental simplicity and abstraction. The colors—rich blues, greens, and ochers applied in strong contrasts of light and shadow—are washed wet onto dry and wet into wet. Calligraphic brushwork describes the foreground grasses, while the men in the boat at the right are suggested by mere dabs of black. The gray-washed palm trees are reflected in the foreground water through scraping. At the left a little family of five birds enlivens the limpid blue water, while their red-beaked counterpart soars in the pale azure sky. Under a sky of softly moving clouds, the whole scene is pervaded with a sense of tropical lushness and quiet.

Watercolor played a critical role in Homer's artistic development. Throughout more than three decades of work in this medium, he captured new subjects, experimented with color, and explored the effects of light and atmosphere. The apparent ease of his technique disguised the deliberateness of his method and the extraordinary control he had over the liquid pigment. Except for a watercolor of 1905 (*Diamond Shoal*; IBM Corporation), the Homosassa works mark Homer's final efforts in the medium. His watercolor achievement remains unparalleled and it exercised a wide and liberating influence on much subsequent American watercolor painting.   *HAC*

1. Related Homosassa watercolors in public collections are in the Brooklyn Museum; National Gallery of Art, Washington, D.C.; and Fogg Art Museum, Harvard University.

Provenance
The artist; Dr. Alexander C. Humphreys, 1906–17; (American Art Association, New York, *Catalogue of the…Collection…Formed…by Dr. Alexander C. Humphreys*, February 15, 1917, cat. no. 129); (R. C. & N. M. Vose, Boston, 1917); museum purchase, 1917

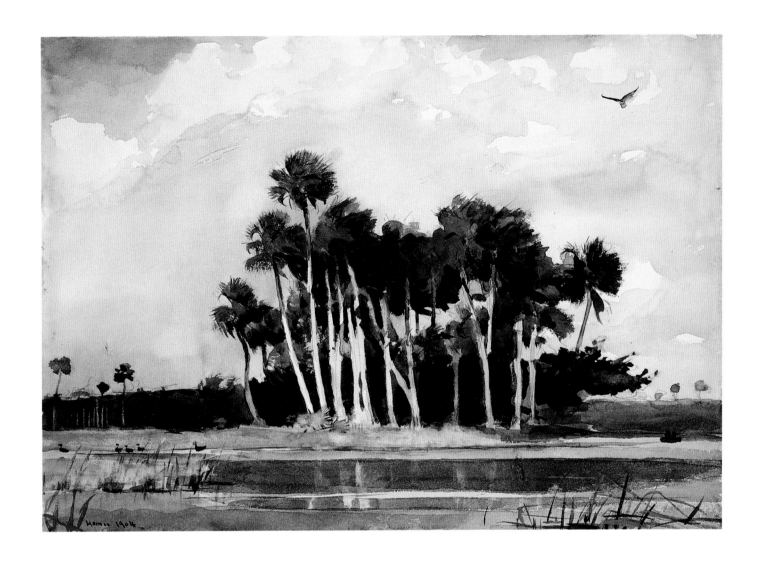

117

77
Henry Bacon (1839–1912)
Queen Arsinoë in the Form of Isis Presenting the Wand of Everlasting Life to Ptolemy, **about 1900**

Henry Bacon had two careers as an artist. He began as an expatriate genre and figure painter in Paris, where he exhibited in the Salon almost yearly from 1867 to 1896. In 1897, when the artist was fifty-eight, he and his second wife, Louisa Lee Bacon, started to travel extensively in Egypt, Greece, Sicily, Ceylon, and Italy. In about 1904 they moved from Paris to London and began to winter regularly in Egypt, a popular resort for the wealthy as well as for artists, writers, and archaeologists. Like many nineteenth-century academic artists, Bacon found new inspiration in Egypt, which motivated him to explore more fully the pictorial effects of light, atmosphere, and color. His belief that these could be rendered "more faithfully in watercolors" led him to turn from his long career as an oil painter of anecdotal genre works of detail and finish and to focus on watercolor as his primary medium at the turn of the century.[1] Egypt and its antiquities, landscape, and people were favorite subjects until his death in Cairo in 1912.[2]

During the winter of 1899–1900 Bacon and his wife spent several weeks on the Nile at Shellal, a port near Aswan. They moored their rented houseboat near Philae, "the pearl of Egypt," a sacred island reputed to be the burial place of Osiris.[3] Its temples, dedicated to Isis and Osiris, dated from the Ptolemaic period but would soon be submerged by the new dam at Aswan, begun in 1898.

In her book *Our Houseboat on the Nile,* Mrs. Bacon described the contrasts of the island. She found "the solemnity of the place . . . is lost by day by reason of the numberless excursionists who come by donkey and by train from Assouan" and by the noise of workmen blasting rock down the river at the dam construction. But peacefulness returned in the evening when the "new Ramadan moon . . . sheds its lustre into every nook of the long porticoes, galleries, courts, and chambers of the temples, lights even the wall decorations of the goddess Isis."[4]

In this watercolor Bacon records a painted wall carving in the staircase room of a temple dedicated to Isis. Queen Arsinoë, in the form and costume of the goddess Isis, presents a staff to Ptolemy II Philadelphos with her left hand, while in her right she clasps an ankh, the emblem of life. A label on the back of Bacon's painting states that the date of the bas-relief, "according to [Sir John Gardener] Wilkinson, was 286 to 247 B.C.," and that the "colours are destined to immediate destruction from the dampness arising from the backing up of water at the new dam."[5]

Affected by the beauty of the colors on the walls at Philae, Bacon strove to replicate them. Using pale washes with little body color, he created both an air of mystery and a sensuous feel for the beauty of the original color. In the wall behind the queen, veillike washes of transparent watercolor are layered one on top of the other, often allowing the early pencil notations to show through. These washes give even interior scenes such as this a translucent quality that seems to reflect light as well as to absorb it.

Bacon's depiction of a dimly lit interior bas-relief is an unusual subject in his oeuvre, and it is unlike the works of other watercolorists who portrayed Egypt's antiquities and landscape, such as the well-known English archaeologist-watercolorist Howard Carter, who discovered the tomb of Tutankhamen in 1922, and the American Joseph Lindon Smith. Where both these artists employed a heightened realism to achieve a *trompe l'oeil* precision, Bacon was chiefly interested in the manipulation of color and light to enhance mood.   *SCJ*

1. A. J. Philpott, "Bacon Water Colors Shown in Boston," *Boston Globe,* November 16, 1912.

2. An unpublished list of known Bacon watercolors compiled by the author includes eighty-five watercolors: fifty-six of Egyptian scenes; five of Etretat, France; eight of Venice; eight of the Acropolis, Athens; four of England; and four miscellaneous scenes.

3. Lee Bacon, *Our Houseboat on the Nile* (Boston: Houghton Mifflin, 1902), p. 275.

4. Ibid., pp. 283, 275.

5. See Worcester Art Museum files. The handwritten label is from the backing of the watercolor's original frame. The approximate dates of King Ptolemy II's reign are 286 to 247 B.C. I am grateful to Emma Swan Hall, New York Institute of Fine Arts, for her assistance with information on Egyptian archaeology throughout these entries.

Provenance
The artist; Louisa Lee Andrews Bacon (Mrs. Henry Bacon, later Mrs. Frederick L. Eldridge), Ardsley-on-Hudson, N.Y.; gift of Mrs. Frederick L. Eldridge, 1943

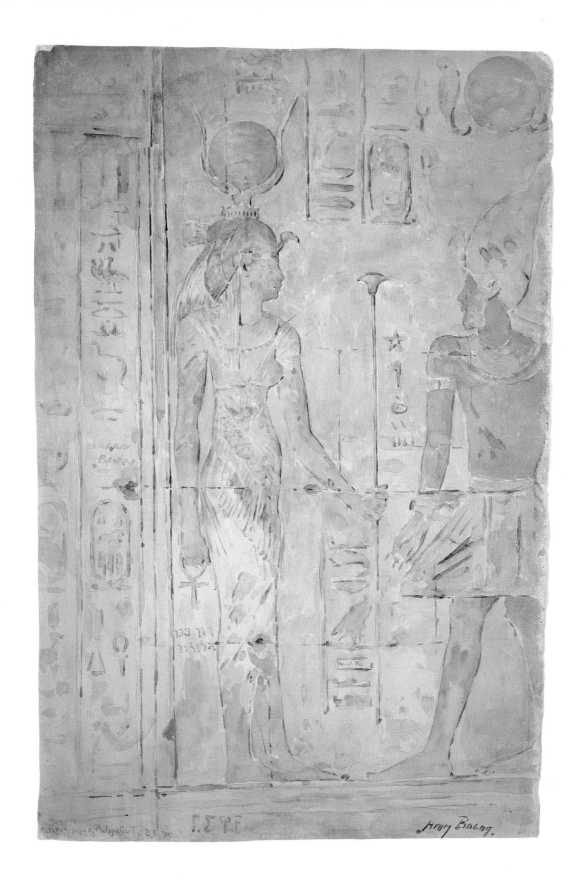

78
Henry Bacon (1839–1912)
The Colossi of Thebes, **1904**

Since Napoleon's Egyptian campaign in 1798, monuments of ancient Egypt such as the Colossi of Thebes had become familiar to Westerners through historical accounts and travel literature as well as the depictions of traveler-artists, perhaps most notably the nineteenth-century Salon painter and Orientalist, Jean-Léon Gérôme.[1] Located on the west bank of the Nile opposite the ancient city of Thebes, the seated stone figures of the Colossi, each nearly fifty-two feet high, originally guarded the tomb of Amenhotep III, one of the great New Kingdom rulers, who lived from about 1403 to 1365 B.C.

Like other Orientalist painters drawn to the exotic ambience of the Near East and North Africa, Bacon was interested not only in archaeological subject matter but also in capturing the effects of desert light at different times of the day.[2] In this southeastern view of the Colossi, both statues face directly into the morning sun. The obliquely angled, close-up perspective of the scene dramatically crops the closest Colossus, emphasizing its enormous legs and marred surfaces, while the northern Colossus appears in full-length.

In this watercolor Bacon abandoned the smooth forms and refined finish of his earlier figural paintings. Instead, he has simulated the roughness and variation of the weathered sandstone and of the tilled land by freely manipulating the medium. The newly plowed earth and the vegetation are defined first by loosely layered washes of light browns, gray-greens, and yellow-greens. Broken brush strokes of darker browns and black suggest furrows, and a final darker brown delineates the cracks and articulates the torsos of the statues. This last overlay of line is not continuous but dotted, and its "lost and found" edge heightens the sense of realism and textural detail.

Bacon was charmed by the picturesque, preindustrial ways he encountered in Egypt, and he often depicted Egyptian agricultural life in his watercolors. Here the Egyptian farmer, or "fellah," plowing with his camel and ox between the statues not only emphasizes the enormous scale of the Colossi but also reminds the viewer of the enduring nature of these archaeological monuments, in contrast to the transience of man.   *SCJ*

1. Maryanne Stevens, ed., *The Orientalists: Delacroix to Matisse* (Washington, D.C.: National Gallery of Art, 1984), p. 139. Gérôme painted *The Plain of Thebes, Upper Egypt* (1857; Musée des Beaux-Arts, Nantes), depicting the Colossi of Thebes.

2. See Stevens, "Western Art and Its Encounter with the Islamic World, 1798–1914," *The Orientalists;* p. 20.

Provenance
The artist; Louisa Lee Andrews Bacon (Mrs. Henry Bacon, later Mrs. Frederick L. Eldridge), Ardsley-on-Hudson, N.Y.; gift of Mrs. Frederick L. Eldridge, 1943

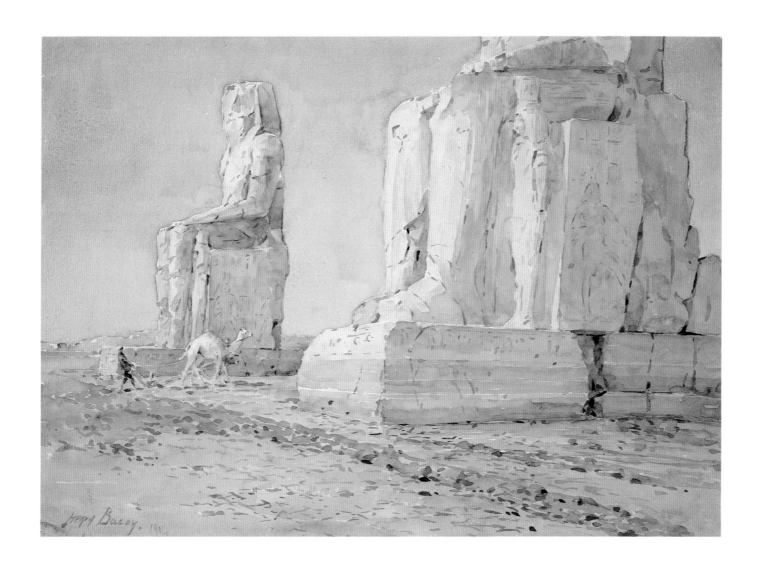

79
Henry Bacon (1839–1912)
Street in Cairo, 1905

Street in Cairo represents a change in Bacon's style after the turn of the century. In the 1880s Bacon had written ambivalently of one young Parisian painter's sketches as "mere *pochades*,—impressions of form and color, very effective, but unsatisfactory except to artists; they are devoid of detail, yet delicious in tone, serving as memoranda or suggestions to the memory of the artist, who, if he possesses a peculiar talent, is able to reproduce in picture the original effect with greater detail."[1] While some of Bacon's own watercolors of the 1880s and 1890s are more tightly drawn and detailed in finish, in keeping with his academic training, by 1905 his style had loosened considerably, as this Cairo street scene reflects.

It is difficult to pinpoint the exact influences that led to the change in Bacon's style. His move to England, where there was an established tradition in the medium, certainly provided him with greater opportunities to see exhibitions and works by other watercolor artists. One British artist whose work may have influenced Bacon is Arthur Melville, an Impressionist, who was fascinated with "the heat and glamour of the East" and "the movement of motley crowds in white-walled courts and mysterious bazaars."[2] Another influence was possibly Bacon's friend John Singer Sargent, who was living in London. Sargent had twice visited Egypt and the Holy Land looking for material for his murals at the Boston Public Library and often sketched in watercolor.[3]

In Bacon's lifetime, Cairo, though still ruled by an Egyptian *khedive*, or viceroy, was essentially governed by the British. The city was divided into the New Quarter, with broad avenues shaded by trees near well-kept houses and gardens, and the Old Quarter, the medieval part of the city, with narrow, winding lanes and Saracenic ar-chitecture, whose beauty lay largely in the latticed, upper-story balconies called *mouchrabiyehs*.

Street in Cairo depicts the Old Quarter and its streets dotted with vendors offering their wares. This watercolor was done in a rapid but skillful sketch style that enhances the immediacy of the scene. A minimal series of strokes and drops of color in the right foreground creates the barest impression of a squatting man. Broad washes and staccato lines summarily articulate the buildings on either side of the street. Using impressions of form and color, Bacon conveyed the intense sensation of Oriental illumination. The painting is divided almost in half by a dramatic contrast of light and shadow. The result is a scene that captures both the hot, blanching sunlight, relieved by dark shadows, and the "gray tint" that "the dust imparts to everything" in the city.[4]   *SCJ*

1. Henry Bacon, *Parisian Art and Artists* (Boston: James R. Osgood, 1883), pp. 22, 14, 95.

2. Martin Hardie, *Water-colour Painting in Britain. Vol. 3: The Victorian Period* (London: B. T. Batsford; New York: Barnes & Noble, 1966–68), pp. 199–202.

3. The full extent of Bacon's friendship with Sargent remains unknown. However, Bacon owned four oil sketches by Sargent. Two of the four, *Brittany Boatman* (1875; unlocated) and *Cook's Boy* (1875; private collection), are inscribed "To my friend Bacon." I am grateful to Odile Duff of Coe Kerr Gallery for bringing these to my attention. The two others were *The Artist's Mother Aboard Ship* (1875; private collection) and an oil sketch in black and white, *Rehearsal of the Pasdeloup Orchestra at the Cirque d'Hiver* (Museum of Fine Arts, Boston), which Sargent gave to Bacon, who used it as an illustration in his 1880–81 *Scribner's Monthly* series called "Glimpses of Parisian Art" and his 1883 book *Parisian Art and Artists*.

4. Charles D. Warner, *My Winter on the Nile among the Mummies and the Moslems* (Hartford, Conn.: American Publishing, 1876), p. 36.

Provenance
The artist; Louisa Lee Andrews Bacon (Mrs. Henry Bacon, later Mrs. Frederick L. Eldridge), Ardsley-on-Hudson, N.Y.; gift of Mrs. Frederick L. Eldridge, 1943

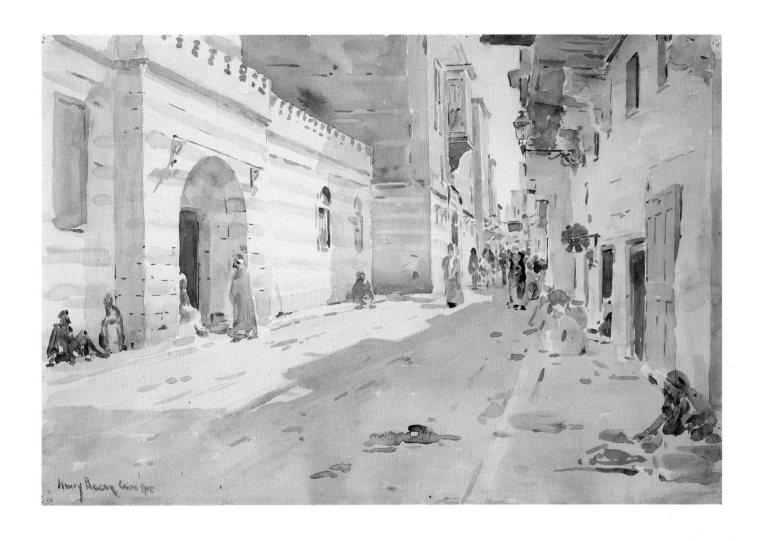

80
Henry Bacon (1839–1912)
Bedouin Camp Fires, **about 1911**

Bacon spent the last fifteen years of his career "in a whirl of activity, of work and new impressions."[1] His travels in Egypt were guided by a search for the historical, the visual, and the spiritual. Fearful of the intrusion of the modern age in the form of the Cape to Cairo Railroad, he spent part of every year accompanying Bedouin tribes in an effort to record a way of life that would soon disappear. A newspaper obituary noted that "every year he spent many weeks with the caravans of the desert, often being the only Christian among several hundred Arabs."[2] His wife described a similar scene in her reminiscences:

> A caravan of a dozen camels under the charge of several men mounted on donkeys passes slowly along. . . . They pass close to us, but never look to the right or left, do not even pass the time of day or give us a blessing, which is more to the point than the time of day in a country where time is reckoned in dynasties. It is such a picturesque procession that the temptation is to hold them up long enough to make a sketch, for with our crew armed with sticks and staves, the picture would indeed have Oriental flavor. These are the things that will pass away forever with the Cape to Cairo Railroad; no camels, no guards, no dervishes, but iron monsters driving ahead. Time will be gained, but how many other things lost![3]

Bedouin Camp Fires, painted probably just a year before Bacon's death, captures a fragment of contemporary nomadic life during an enormous pilgrimage of six to seven thousand Bedouins, traveling in families and in large or small parties. A few of the groups have set up their "evening bivouac . . . on their way back from a yearly pilgrimage to 'Abou Shreer,' a desert shrine in the Hill country near the Red Sea."[4]

Carefully rendered, this work reveals a variety of techniques that Bacon used to achieve a romantic and exotic image. To create the effect of smoke—a motif that helps to unify the composition with its gentle curve—Bacon rubbed off color with a sponge or cloth. His excellent draftsmanship, a product of his academic training, is revealed in the carefully studied still life of two jugs at the right of the main campfire. Similarly, Bacon's polished and realistic characterization of the figures—the graceful woman and black-robed figures—recalls the work of Orientalists such as Gérôme.   *SCJ*

1. *Catalogue of a Memorial Exhibition of Water Colors of Egypt, Greece, France, Italy, and England, by Henry Bacon* (Washington, D.C.: National Gallery of Art, 1931), p. 3.

2. "Henry Bacon, American Artist," *Boston Evening Transcript,* March 14, 1912, obituaries. See also Artists Clippings Files, Boston Public Library, Art Department.

3. Lee Bacon, *Our Houseboat on the Nile* (Boston: Houghton Mifflin, 1902), pp. 86–87.

4. *Memorial Exhibition of Water Colors,* p. 4. Another watercolor, *Bedouins on Annual Pilgrimage to the Desert Shrine of "Abou Shrier,"* was probably done on this same pilgrimage and is also in the Worcester Art Museum's collection of twenty-three watercolors and four pastels by Bacon.

Provenance
The artist; Louisa Lee Andrews Bacon (Mrs. Henry Bacon, later Mrs. Frederick L. Eldridge), Ardsley-on-Hudson, N.Y.; gift of Mrs. Frederick L. Eldridge, 1943

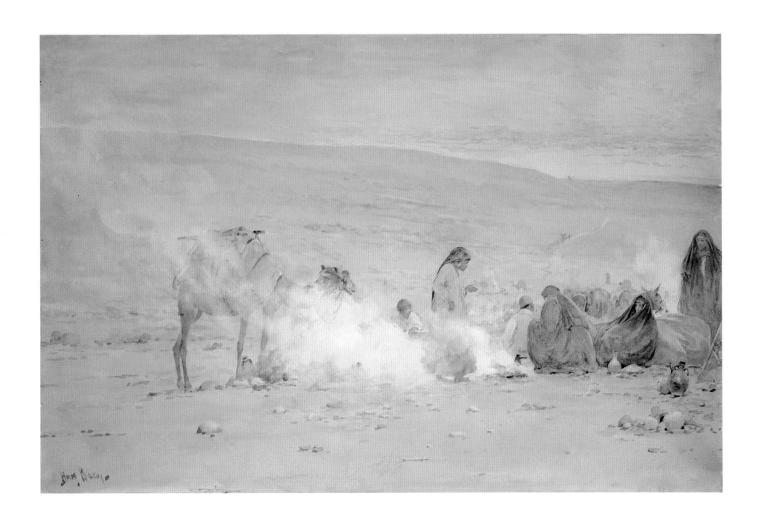

81
John Singer Sargent (1856–1925)
Venice, about 1902

John Singer Sargent has long been recognized as one of the world's great masters of watercolor. Until the early years of this century he was known chiefly for his portraits and figure studies in oil, although he produced watercolors throughout much of his career. In childhood he may have been encouraged by his mother, who, like so many Victorian women of the upper class, made a hobby of sketching in watercolor. His first proficient works in the medium are sketches of picturesque scenes he encountered on family travels in Europe during his adolescence in the late 1860s. His final works date from 1924, just a year before his death, when, for example, he painted fine watercolors aboard the yacht of the eminent Bostonian Herbert Sears.[1] It was in the years 1902 to 1918, however, when Sargent was the premier Edwardian portraitist, that he produced most of his watercolors. These works represent the fullest and most individual expression of the Impressionist style, which he first explored in the 1880s. Their informality and beauty testify to the pleasure Sargent found away from the business of his London studio during late-summer holidays with relatives and friends. Starting in 1903 he exhibited these watercolors in London virtually every year until his death, showing regularly with the Royal Society of Watercolour Painters from 1904.

Of all the places in which Sargent painted in watercolor—Europe, the Middle East, North Africa, and North America— Venice was his special muse. He worked there on many occasions, the most documented periods being the years 1880 to 1882 and 1902 to 1913. During his 1880s visits, inspired by Velázquez and his modernist interpreter Manet, Sargent produced mostly somber oils of working-class inhabitants; in contrast, the more numerous, overtly holiday visits after the turn of the century resulted in brightly colored, dashingly executed watercolors. Focusing on the city's architectural monuments rather than its inhabitants, these scenes offer the viewer unexpected impressions of the corners of buildings and casual glances down side canals. The compositions often include the prow of the gondola from which Sargent sketched. Like many artists, he was inspired by Venetian light, both the exhilarating brilliant sunshine and the enveloping, mysterious haze that represent the extremes of the city's changing moods. Such nuances of light and color, heightened and enlivened by the reflective surface of the canals, offered an endless aesthetic challenge to the bravura Impressionist style Sargent employed for his watercolors.

Venice captures the essential luminosity of the city. On this particular day the atmosphere was limpid and gentle. The artist's extensive use of thin washes of pale colors on moistened paper perfectly communicates the mood. In an effort to evoke the breathtaking and expansive vistas so frequently encountered on the Grand Canal, Sargent structured the composition around daring and oddly cropped transitions, emphasizing the contrast between the foreground and the distant horizon. The viewer's eye is drawn across the sketchy steps, through a middle-ground screen of small boats and a building, to a huge steamer and a distant shore. Classic landmarks also make slightly unconventional appearances: the steps belong to the Baroque Santa Maria della Salute, one of the glories of the Venetian skyline, here wittily demoted to a mere foreground device; and the Customs House is seen with its tower obscured and its statue of Fortune on a golden orb cropped at the top.

Stylistically, *Venice* differs from Sargent's earliest professional watercolors, made around 1880. The mannered and relatively tight execution of these earlier works is reminiscent of paintings by his contemporaries Giovanni Boldini and Mariano Fortuny.[2] Although *Venice* is undated, its freer, more Impressionistic style suggests that it probably belongs to Sargent's largest group of Venetian watercolors, made between 1902 and 1913. These works, few of which were dated by the artist, display a variety of techniques, sizes, and even papers.[3] A tentative date of 1902 for *Venice* can be proposed on the basis of similarities of style, composition, palette, and size with two other watercolors: *The Grand Canal, Venice* (undated; Fogg Art Museum, Harvard University) and *Side Canal, Venice* (1902; Ormond Family Collection).[4]   *TJF*

1. An 1869 view of the Matterhorn is illustrated facing page 12 in Evan Charteris, *John Sargent* (New York: Charles Scribner's Sons, 1927). The 1924 watercolor *Herbert Sears on His Yacht "Constellation"* is illustrated in David McKibbin, *Sargent's Boston* (Boston: Museum of Fine Arts, 1956), p. 60.

2. On a rare occasion at the beginning of his career, Sargent exhibited two Venetian watercolors at the Paris Salon in 1881, both entitled *Vue de Venise*, which possibly are the pair now owned by the Corcoran Gallery of Art, Washington, D.C. Although the same size as *Venice*, they lack its daring with wet washes and fluent composition. See Edward J. Nygren, *John Singer Sargent: Drawings from the Corcoran Gallery of Art* (Washington, D.C.: Smithsonian Institution Traveling Exhibition Service, 1983), pp. 53–54.

3. Scholarly analysis of this kind of evidence has not been attempted in order to ascribe more accurate dates. For example, Margaretta M. Lovell, in *Venice, the American View, 1860–1920* (San Francisco: Fine Arts Museums of San Francisco, 1984), dated Worcester's *Venice* 1903–12 (pp. 115–16), giving no evidence to support her date.

4. These three works are close in their treatment of water reflections and silhouetted elements; their compositions, with strong diagonal masses thrusting in from the right; and their palettes (particularly the avoidance of impastoed opaque pigments). That Sargent produced a significant body of watercolors in 1902 is documented in a letter from Ralph Curtis to Isabella Stewart Gardner: "[Sargent] has been three weeks [at the Palazzo Barbaro, Venice] doing delicious acquarelles . . ." (October 17, 1902, Isabella Stewart Gardner Museum, Boston). All three works were inscribed and given as gifts by the artist: the Worcester picture to American painter Julius Rolshoven; the Fogg picture to French pianist Léon Delafosse; and the Ormond Family picture to Sargent's sister Violet Ormond. More information about Sargent's friendships with Rolshoven and Delafosse might help date these watercolors. Rolshoven was an expatriate artist, who could have befriended Sargent in Venice, Paris, or London by 1881. Sargent painted Delafosse's portrait in Paris in 1893, and might have given him the watercolor now in the Fogg Art Museum at that time. Sargent was in Venice in 1892, 1898, and 1899, although no Venetian watercolors have been documented to this decade. (The author is grateful to Stanley Olson for information about the 1892 visit and to Richard Ormond for his advice on dating Worcester's *Venice*.)

Provenance
Julius Rolshoven; (Grand Central Art Galleries, New York); Dr. Loring H. Dodd, Worcester; Mr. and Mrs. Stuart Riley, Jr., Cranston, R.I.; gift of Mr. and Mrs. Stuart Riley, Jr., 1974

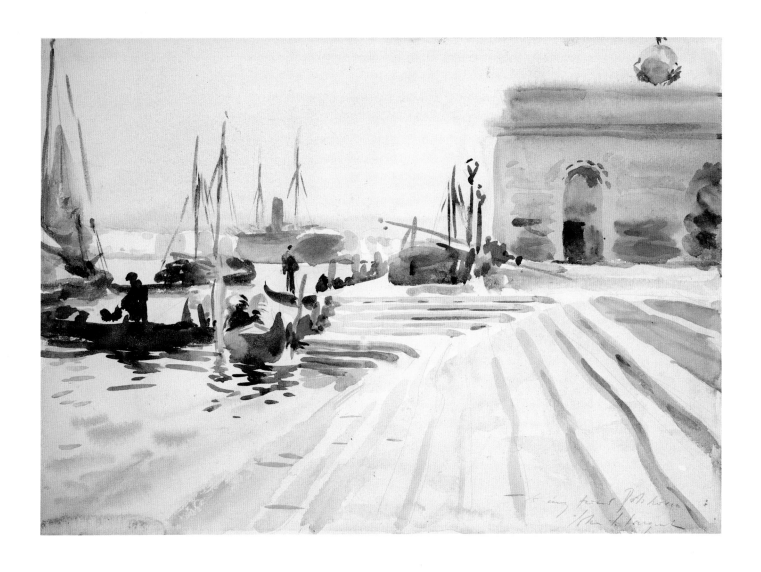

82
John Singer Sargent (1856–1925)
Muddy Alligators, 1917

In February 1917 Sargent traveled to Ormond Beach on the northeastern coast of Florida, near Daytona, to paint the portrait of seventy-eight-year-old John D. Rockefeller at his winter home, The Casements. By 1910 Sargent had effectively stopped painting oil portraits on commission, but he made a few exceptions: for friends, for a Red Cross charity during World War I, and, in the Rockefellers' case, for a remuneration of $15,000 for two portraits, the highest fee he charged. A resident of London since 1886, Sargent had returned to the United States in 1916 to complete a commission for mural decorations for the Boston Public Library.[1] The Rockefellers had been pursuing him to paint their patriarch, and when he eventually agreed to accept the commission in Florida, he no doubt anticipated some sort of winter holiday as a break from his hectic Boston schedule.[2] Completing the first of two portraits of Rockefeller in about three weeks, he traveled to Miami to visit his old friends Mr. and Mrs. Charles Deering; his Florida sojourn eventually lasted almost three months.

It has been thought that all Sargent's Florida watercolors were painted in the Miami area; however, the artist's letters seem to place *Muddy Alligators* and *The Pool* (plate 83) at Ormond Beach. His correspondence indicates that he was somewhat bothered by the heat, by the short sittings Rockefeller provided, and by pangs of guilt for not being at work in Boston. Painting watercolors provided some solace and distraction. On March 11 he wrote to his Boston friend Thomas Fox, "I have been sketching a good deal about here but palmettos and alligators [*sic*] don't make very interesting pictures."[3]

Despite that deprecating comment, the alligators inspired a watercolor that is a tour de force. The work has commanded the public's fascination since it was first exhibited in 1917. In the context of his portraits of fashionable Anglo-American society and his sketches of the resorts they frequented, such an undistinguished subject as alligators sprawling in mud seems an aberration, perhaps the result of boredom in Ormond Beach. However, Sargent's lively curiosity was always seeking out new subjects, and these unusual beasts must have intrigued him. Moreover, representing the light color of their mud-caked skin on white paper in watercolor presented a challenge to his skill and ingenuity. Sargent had taken up this challenge in earlier watercolors with such subjects as a line of bed linen drying in the sun and a part of a massive white Baroque building.[4] The alligators were another stimulus to record the play of light and shadow on white forms with intriguing configurations. Apparently wanting to clarify his purpose, in a rare move he specifically requested that the Worcester Art Museum retitle the work *Muddy Alligators*, rather than simply *Alligators*, perhaps so that the public would understand why he had intentionally rendered these dark-skinned creatures white.

The picture shows a torpid group of alligators on a beach in a close-perspective view. Though seemingly random, the composition has a careful diagonal arrangement that leads the viewer from the left foreground vegetation through the curving mass of bodies. As if to invigorate the lazy repose of the central group, the artist included a more evil-looking young creature slithering into the blue-shadowed foreground. In its open jaws, Sargent scratched tiny gleaming highlights to indicate sharp teeth.

Four related pencil drawings and two unfinished watercolors probably preceded *Muddy Alligators*.[5] Although Sargent used no direct quotations from these preparatory sketches, they served to familiarize him with the creatures and with the effects of light and texture that apparently fascinated him. He began *Muddy Alligators* with a cursory pencil sketch of the major forms. A series of striated wet washes was laid down with a full brush in single strokes to create the rows of tree trunks, looking almost like massive pickets, and their reflections were reiterated in the foreground using a drier brush. Sargent articulated the lumpy, scaled surfaces of the sun-baked muddy skins with a minimum of small blue and lavender notations against the white of the paper. The larger blue shadows cast by the alligators' heads and tails and the nearby trees help give greater definition to their undulating forms. The white-on-white effect of their bodies combines with a palette of bold, brilliant purples to magnificently capture the sun-drenched effects of tropical light.　　　*TJF*

1. Sargent was in Boston by April 9, 1916. He spent the summer in the Canadian Rockies and completed the Boston Public Library murals in December. He subsequently commenced a new commission for a decorative scheme for the rotunda of the Museum of Fine Arts, Boston, whose new building on Huntington Avenue had opened in November 1909.

2. Sargent painted the two oils of John D. Rockefeller in 1917; the second was executed at the family's Pocantico estate near Tarrytown, New York. He declined invitations to paint other family members.

3. Sargent to Fox, March 11, 1917, from Hotel Ormond, Ormond Beach, Boston Athenaeum. On February 26 he had asked Fox to send express some blocks of watercolor paper "measuring about 15¾ inches by 21."

4. The washing-line picture is *La Biancheria* (c. 1910; Museum of Fine Arts, Boston). An example of a white architectural detail is *The Salute, Venice* (c. 1903–13; Yale University Art Gallery). Other examples of watercolors of white animals include *Bus Horses in Jerusalem* (1905; Isabella Stewart Gardner Museum, Boston) and *Oxen in Repose* (1906–10; Ormond Family Collection).

5. The Worcester Art Museum owns all four drawings of alligators; see plate 47 for an illustration of one. One watercolor is at the Metropolitan Museum of Art, the other in the Ormond Family collection (plate 48). These six works belonged to the artist's estate and had not been exhibited by him.

Provenance
The artist; museum purchase, Sustaining Membership Fund, 1917

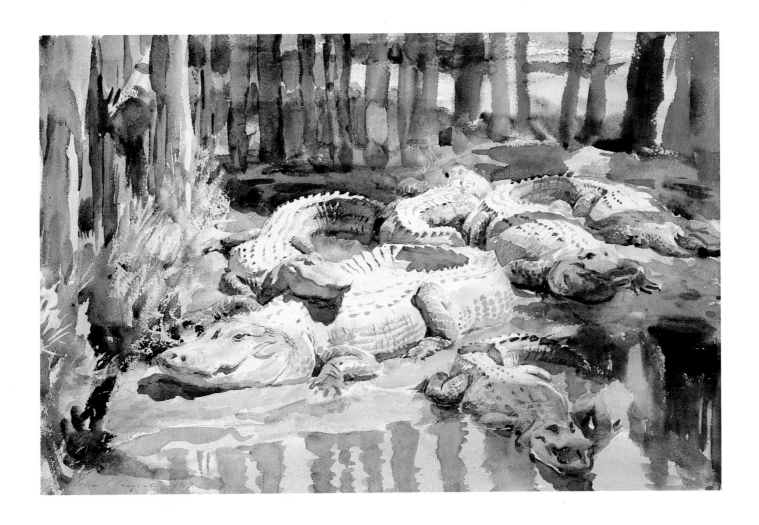

83
John Singer Sargent (1856–1925)
The Pool, 1917

Throughout his career Sargent relished the challenge of sketching the random disorder of landscape scenes that captured his fancy during his travels. One of his special talents was the ability to convey in a quick, impressionistic style the general clutter of a setting such as this jungle pool and, at the same time, to articulate very precisely the spatial relationships of the entangled vegetation.

The Pool has a powerful abstract quality, but the artist seems to have made no exaggerations to attain this effect. In truth, Sargent chose a remarkably commonplace Florida scene: it is the way he perceived and painted it that is extraordinary, not the subject itself. We are struck immediately by the convoluted, intricate forms of the palmettos, which dominate the composition with an explosive energy. When viewed from a distance, the palmettos stand out in obvious relief from the middle-ground tree trunks, and the intense blue sky glimpsed through the thicket gives the illusion of great depth.

The pool itself is somber and mysterious, its dark green and brown surface enriched by notes of blue in the reflections of the sky and a warm dark red passage, possibly the play of sunlight on the still, murky water. The artist evidently found this bower exotic for the variety of colors and textures it presented, including the pallid, shriveled palmettos and the colorful, scaling bark of the tree trunks. The overall impression is one of teeming tropical fecundity.

What is astonishing to most viewers is how Sargent could paint something so complex while giving it the look of having been executed so effortlessly. Sargent enthusiasts have always applauded the spiritedness of his watercolors and have perhaps unwittingly created the popular misconception that he could paint a work like *The Pool* with little effort. One critic who saw many of these Florida works on exhibition at the Copley Gallery in Boston in 1917 encouraged this notion:

> One realizes that the artist enjoyed ''doing'' these watercolors, so joyous, free and spontaneous are they in execution. There is the hand of the master in them all. One can not blame the painter for wishing to take these little excursions in watercolor to relieve his mind, if nothing more—after such ''heavy'' performances as his mural decorations for the Boston Public Library. (Our great capitalists go trout fishing occasionally.)[1]

Like so many of Sargent's seemingly casual works in watercolor and oil, *The Pool* was created with far more painstaking work than might be imagined. It epitomizes the technical discipline and power of concentration needed to create a great watercolor. Close study shows that the application of different washes of green for the plants was guided by some light pencil underdrawing, and the clarity of the design was maintained during the complex layering and juxtaposing of washes by using masking or blocking agents.

The artist made at least five related watercolors. Like the sketches related to *Muddy Alligators*, these are not as fully developed as the Worcester watercolor. None can be called a preparatory study, and it seems that they represent something of a warming-up exercise. The fact that none of these preliminary works was exhibited or sold during his lifetime adds support to the idea that Sargent considered *The Pool* the masterwork of the group.[2]   *TJF*

1. Geo. Washington [''Boston'' pseud.], *American Art News* 15 (June 16, 1917): 4.

2. All five related watercolors passed through the artist's estate to his sisters, Emily Sargent and Violet Ormond. Mrs. Ormond gave two to the Metropolitan Museum of Art in 1950 (*Palmettos* and *Landscape with Palms*). Two more remain in the Ormond family. The fifth is illustrated in *Loan Exhibition: Selections from the Drawings of David Daniels* (Cambridge, Mass.: Fogg Art Museum, Harvard University, 1968), cat. no. 71. The latter work is titled *Palm Thick, Vizcaya*, but evidence suggests that this group was painted at Ormond Beach; see plate 82.

Provenance
The artist; museum purchase, Sustaining Membership Fund, 1917

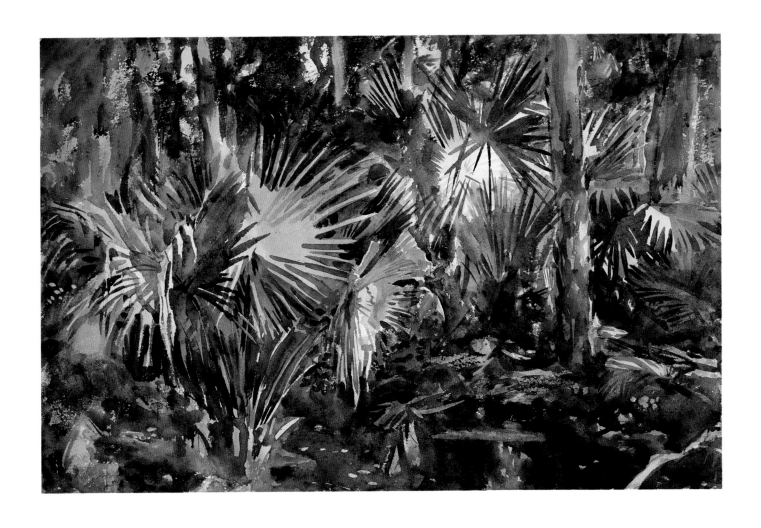

131

84
John Singer Sargent (1856–1925)
Shady Paths, Vizcaya, 1917

When he left the Rockefeller home at Ormond Beach on March 20, Sargent journeyed south to Brickell Point, Miami, where he was the guest of his old friend Charles Deering. Charles and his half-brother James Deering had derived their fortunes from the family harvester-manufacturing industry and were accustomed to spending their winters in Florida rather than Chicago, where the business was based. It happened that James Deering was nearing completion of his residential estate in south Miami, an enormous Italianate palazzo and garden he called Vizcaya. Work had begun in 1914, and in the intervening three years a specially constructed railroad transported to the 180-acre site all that was needed to create the great limestone villa and the terraced gardens with fountains, statues, and grottos. Constructed around an open courtyard, the villa's thirty-odd rooms were filled with antique European furnishings and accessories.[1] Sargent was amazed to find himself in a private paradise, as if he had been magically transported to his beloved Venice. The restful beauty of Vizcaya was a welcome relief, and he took advantage of this vacation from professional responsibilities

to indulge himself in sketching Vizcaya's grounds in watercolor. After three weeks on the estate, Sargent wrote to a friend in Boston, "[Vizcaya] is a mine of sketching. It is like a grand Venetian villa in the Brenta with colonnades and loggias and porticos and steps down to the water. And dark gardens and statues just like Frascati."[2]

Shady Paths depicts an oval terrace just beyond the north gateway of the villa's forecourt.[3] The statues are seventeenth- and eighteenth-century Italian marbles, and their formal setting was inspired by such Italian sites as the Boboli Gardens in Florence. The artist had previously painted similar combinations of sculpture and trees dappled with sun in those gardens and in estates outside Lucca, Florence, and Rome.

Shady Paths has the aura of deserted space haunted by graceful statues of mythological figures; it depicts a haven of old world culture. That the war in Europe remained on Sargent's mind is evident in his letters from Florida, but that the gardens

at Vizcaya offered solace and hope is here abundantly clear. Sargent re-created for the viewer the joyous sense of suddenly coming upon this charming spot during a walk on the paths through the dense jungle thickets that surrounded the villa and terraced gardens. The Mediterranean character of the hot blue sky and dramatic shade belie the more tropical and enclosed atmosphere of the actual site. At the moment when Sargent made this watercolor, sunlight was falling in greater amounts on the tree trunk and statue in the right foreground. As the eye circles deeper into the pictorial space from the left, the shadow becomes stronger and more engulfing on each successive statue. It is conceivable that Sargent returned on other days to complete this work, since this precise and exquisite lighting effect must have been short-lived.   *TJF*

1. The best discussion of Vizcaya in the context of other American palaces of the period is James T. Maher, *The Twilight of Splendor* (Boston: Little, Brown, 1975). See also Marcus Binney, "Villa Vizcaya, Florida," parts 1 and 2, *Country Life* 167 (January 10 and 17, 1980): 71–74.

2. Sargent to Thomas Fox, April 10, 1917, from Brickell Point, Miami, Boston Athenaeum.

3. Although the palazzo was essentially complete in the spring of 1917, its formal gardens were still being worked on. In fact, they have changed several times because of devastating hurricanes. The statues Sargent painted are no longer on these low plinths but can be found on terrace walks that flank the formal garden south of the villa.

Provenance
The artist; museum purchase, Sustaining Membership Fund, 1917

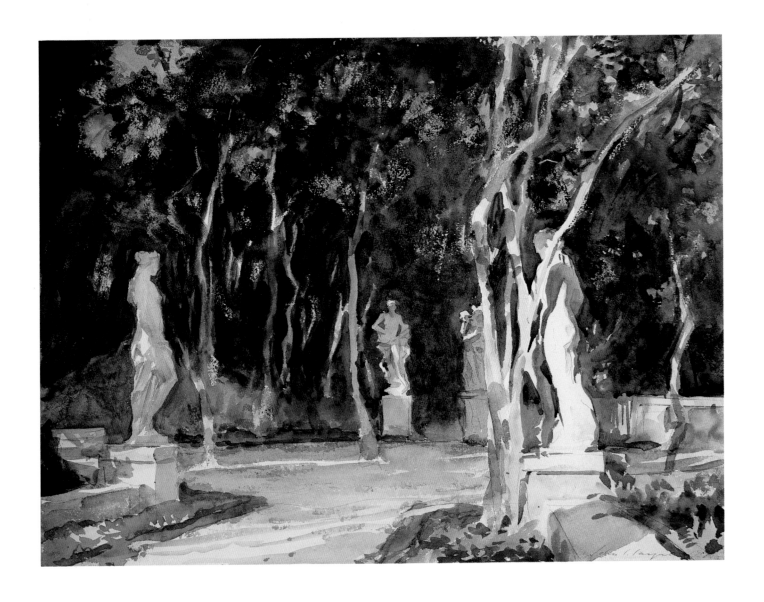

85
John Singer Sargent (1856–1925)
The Bathers, 1917

During his stay at Vizcaya, Sargent made watercolor sketches not only of the estate's formal gardens; he also explored the outskirts of Deering's property, where the lush tropical landscape had been left intact. Although *The Bathers* includes a glimpse of the stately architecture of Vizcaya in the distant background, Sargent's primary concern is the scintillating sandy beach, where three young black men, probably laborers on Deering's estate, relax beneath an intimate arbor. The location of this picture was a small beach southeast of Vizcaya, not far from Deering's boathouse (plate 85a), now demolished. Characteristically, Sargent rendered the view before him with utmost fidelity. The stone bridge seen at the center of the horizon leads from the terrace to a yacht landing. To the left of the bridge is the great white stone barge that rises from the water in front of the east façade of the mansion. The barge functioned as a sea wall, protecting the house from the tides of Biscayne Bay, and also served as an enormous pedestal for an extraordinary assemblage of Baroque-style obelisks, urns, and statues.[1]

Seeing *The Bathers* on exhibition in Boston just weeks after it was painted, art critic William Howe Downes wrote that it was

> a subject that would have greatly interested Winslow Homer. . . . Three nude negroes bathe in a shallow cove, beyond which we see a bay or lagoon shimmering in the sunlight. The suggestive method, as distinguished from the literal or realistic, is wonderfully well exemplified in this highly characteristic work.
>
> One feels vividly the heat of the day and the delightful sensation of relief and refreshment that these bathers are experiencing as they loll in the shallow pool, partly shaded by the surrounding trees. It is like a true momentary impression of something seen, and seen by eyes of a marvelous perception, instantaneous as a snapshot, but with nothing of the mechanical element.[2]

In mentioning Homer, Downes had in mind that artist's watercolor views of Caribbean natives and scenery, such as *Rum Cay* (plate 71). The comparison between Homer and Sargent is instructive: in treating similar subject matter, the artists revealed completely different sensibilities and artistic concerns. Homer's depiction of a man's pursuit of a desperately scurrying turtle exemplifies his principal theme of the heroic struggle of life and death, and his animated, graphic composition elicits the passion of the chase. Sargent is not concerned with narrative and treats the people before him merely as figures in a landscape. They are not portrayed in any formal sense; in fact, their faces lack defined features. However, an attitude of quiet sensuousness is communicated by the perceptive rendering of the nude men's relaxed and natural poses. Using the "suggestive method" Downes described, Sargent conveys the warmth and brilliance of the tropical atmosphere, whose mood also encompasses the figures on the beach.

The figure in the right foreground, who turns to confront the viewer, demonstrates the spectacular bravura of Sargent's fully impressionistic technique. At a distance, the figure assumes a striking solidity and presence; but close inspection reveals it to be a complex of dashing, painterly gestures. Washes of brown, orange, and deep violet were overlaid with bold effects, such as the scratched-out white highlight on the nose, the thin opaque highlight on the knee, and the dark blue outline for the shadowed edge of the torso.

As with *Muddy Alligators* and *The Pool*, there is a group of related watercolors that seems to lead up to this more complex statement. Each uses only a single figure and is considerably more sketchy than *The Bathers*.[3]   *TJF*

1. Alexander Stirling Calder designed much of the sculpture for the stone barge, which is the subject of two Sargent watercolors: *At Miami, Florida* (1917; National Gallery of Victoria, Melbourne) and *Landing, Miami* (1917; private collection). The barge also appears still under construction at the edge of *The Basin, Vizcaya* (1917; formerly Worcester Art Museum, now private collection).

2. William Howe Downes, "Another Sargent Show: Watercolors Painted Recently in Florida exhibited for Benefit of Red Cross," *Boston Evening Transcript*, June 7, 1917, p. 11. Downes observed that *The Bathers* reminded him of "powerful watercolors" Winslow Homer made in the Bahamas, specifically the examples in the Metropolitan Museum of Art.

3. Four watercolors of black male nudes in the artist's estate were given to the Metropolitan Museum of Art in 1950 by Violet Ormond. Three of them deal only with figure and setting (*Bather in Florida; Figure on Beach, Florida;* and *Figure and Pool*); however, *Figure and Trees, Florida* delineates the face and offers insight into the subject's character.

Provenance
The artist; museum purchase, Sustaining Membership Fund, 1917

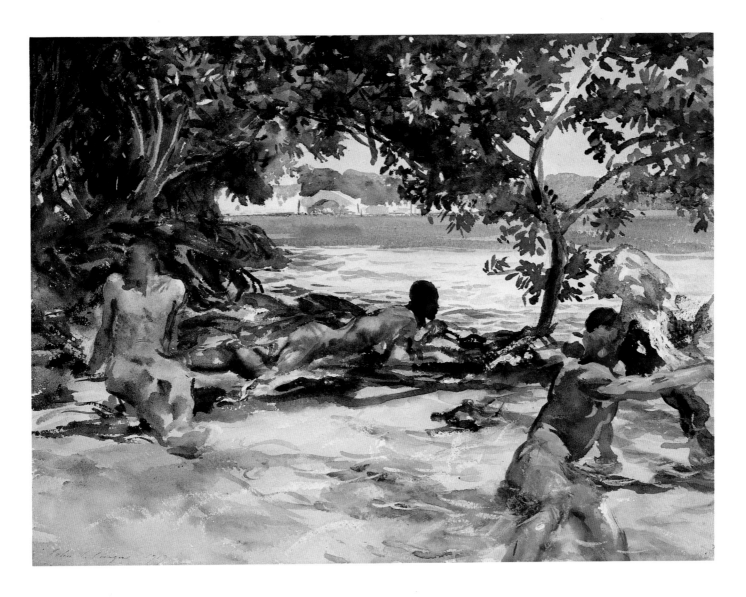

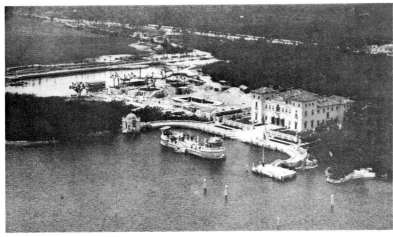

85a
View of the villa Vizcaya and the gardens under
construction, from *Harper's Bazaar,* July 1917

135

86
John Singer Sargent (1856–1925)
Derelicts, 1917

During his three-month stay in Florida, Sargent had the chance to explore the waterways near Miami, particularly the working zones for the unfinished landscaping of the Vizcaya estate, and also around the Keys during an extensive fishing trip to the Gulf of Mexico.[1] The artist probably came across many water-logged ships during these excursions, although the exact location of *Derelicts* remains unknown. This sketch is exceptional in Sargent's watercolor oeuvre: while the scene is not an unusual one, it evokes powerful and poetic feelings of decline and abandonment. Rarely did Sargent invest his watercolors with such emotional content, and one can only speculate on why this scene so affected him. It is clear from his Florida correspondence that the war in Europe was much on his mind. To a London friend, he wrote: "In a small way down here in Florida one feels that war is an actuality. Everybody is giving up their yachts and launches. [Deering's houseboat] is to be handed over to the government at once. We have been warned off from the neighborhood of viaducts for fear we were Germans laying mines—and in a certain place had to have a couple of soldiers on board to see that we were really fishing for tarpon."[2] Sargent betrayed his underlying fears in describing Vizcaya: "It combines Venice and Frascati and Aranjuez and all that one is likely never to see again. Hence this linger-longering."[3]

It is possible, then, that *Derelicts* echoes the artist's concern for Europe, for its imagery is that of collapse and decay: the light-colored remains of a fallen tree and a swamped boat fairly glow against the dark greens of the water and the jungle. Sargent chose a viewpoint that juxtaposes the seemingly anguished, upward-reaching branch of the tree with the pathetically collapsed boat. That the visually arresting juxtaposition of fallen tree and ruined boat would appeal to Sargent's artistic concerns is not surprising. As Adrian Stokes once noted,

> Sargent's watercolors . . . usually record, with the utmost directness, something that had excited his admiration, or appealed to his artistic intelligence. That may have been the clearly defined and exquisite edge of some rare object; or the way in which a dark thing, when opposed to vivid light, is invaded by it and loses local color; or the change that seems to occur in the color of things along the edge where they meet.[4]

The qualities of edge, form, and chromatic effect that Stokes noted are all present in *Derelicts*. They are particularly apparent in the dead branch edged with blue shadows that stands before the shambles of the abandoned boats, a dramatic, skeletonlike presence. *Derelicts* is both moving and evocative, as well as a superbly crafted watercolor.
                                              TJF

1. The party on the cruise, which took about ten days (probably April 11–21), seems to have included only Sargent and the Deering brothers aboard the eighty-foot steam yacht *Nepenthe*.

2. Sargent to Mrs. Charles Hunter, April 21, 1917, Archives of American Art, Microfilm Roll D 169.

3. Sargent to his cousin Mary Newbold Patterson Hale, in Hale's 1927 essay, "The Sargent I Knew." For a reprint see Carter Ratcliff, *John Singer Sargent* (New York: Abbeville Press, 1982), pp. 235–38.

4. Adrian Stokes, "John Singer Sargent, R.A., R.W.S.," in *Old Water-Colour Society Club Third Annual Volume*, ed. Randall Davies, F.S.A. (London: Chiswick Press, 1926), p. 60.

Provenance
The artist; museum purchase, Sustaining Membership Fund, 1917

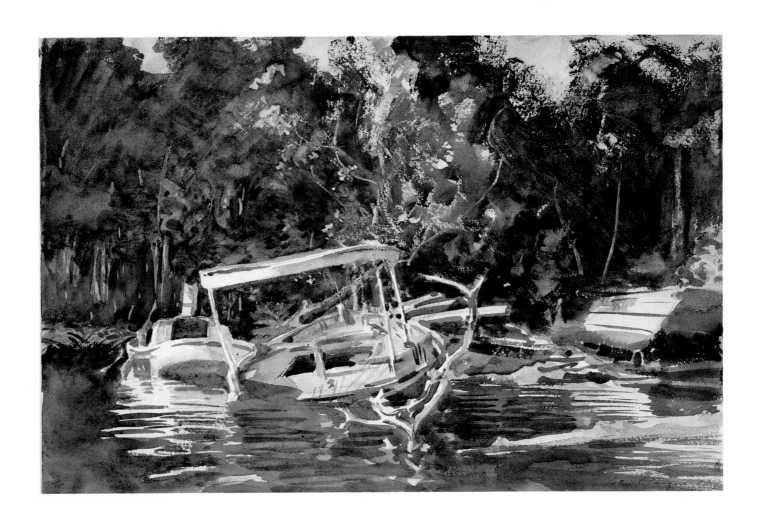

87
John Singer Sargent (1856–1925)
Palms, 1917

Today palm trees have become such a commonplace emblem of commercial tropical resorts that they seem banal; viewing Sargent's watercolor of these stately trees reinvests them with a sense of their striking grandeur. The contrast between their colorful, shaggy tops—large spheres of rustling, wafting foliage—and tall, spindly trunks was perhaps the impression the artist was most eager to communicate. The elevated field of vision he chose allows the tops of the foreground palms to loom high above the horizon against an expanse of blue sky.

Most striking in this watercolor is the nearness and immediacy of the image. This intimate view from within the grove is quite different from the more traditional landscape view of palm trees in Homer's *Turkey Buzzard* (plate 76), where the viewer is distanced from the subject by a great deal of space. Sargent's perspective is unusual: he willfully intersects his foreground plane at the right of center with a tree trunk whose base and foliage are cropped by the sheet in a photographic manner. Without that forceful vertical dividing line, the image would look flat and undistinguished; its presence energizes the pictorial space occupied by all the trunks. The foreground trunk dividing the composition reveals the artist's careful scrutiny of the interplay of light and color. At the bottom the trunk receives direct sunlight and is very pale orange-yellow; at the center, catching the shadow of another tree's crown, it is lavender; at the top, in full sun again, it takes on a pink cast.

This kind of visual analysis, free from the nineteenth-century narrative concerns that Homer exalted, indicates an underlying abstract structure and attests to Sargent's interest in the formal qualities of the image.

In the 1910s Sargent, famous for his portraits, was considered by the new generation of modernists to be an establishment painter. In more recent years the modern aspects of some of his works have become more apparent.[1] His use of bold color effects, such as the strident oranges and blues in *Palms*, indicates a sensibility that cannot be considered staid or conventional. And a daring experimentation with technique combined with the exploration of compositions having an inherent abstract quality make the watercolors his most astonishing, lively, and somehow timeless pictures.

Sargent made about thirty-six watercolors in Florida in 1917, responding to an unusually broad range of subjects, from jungle scenes to the loggias, terraces, and formal gardens of Vizcaya. Early in June that year, shortly after Sargent's return to the North, many of these new watercolors were exhibited at the Copley Gallery in Boston. The Worcester Art Museum was given first pick and purchased eleven examples.[2]   *TJF*

1. A landmark in this new perception of Sargent was Fairfield Porter's essay "Sargent: An American Problem," *Art News* 54 (January 1956): 28–31 and 64. Porter published a photograph magnifying a detail from a 1911 watercolor and wrote, ". . . a scratched background in a Sargent watercolor relates to certain American abstract paintings more closely than do Cézanne, Picasso or even Monet."

2. The Worcester Art Museum now owns seven of the original eleven watercolors purchased in 1917. When James Deering died a bachelor in 1925, he left Vizcaya to his nephews and nieces. Charles Deering's two daughters, Marion Deering McCormick and Barbara Deering Danielson, bought out all other interests. They sold two tracts of land and in 1952 sold the remainder for one million dollars to Dade County to establish the present Vizcaya museum. Mr. and Mrs. Chauncey McCormick first approached the Worcester Art Museum about purchasing some of the Sargent watercolors in 1941, through the Art Institute of Chicago, where McCormick was vice president (and president by 1944). In 1948 they acquired the four watercolors from Worcester that depict the villa. For illustrations of all eleven watercolors, see *Bulletin of the Worcester Art Museum* 8 (January 1918): 61–85.

Provenance
The artist; museum purchase, Sustaining Membership Fund, 1917

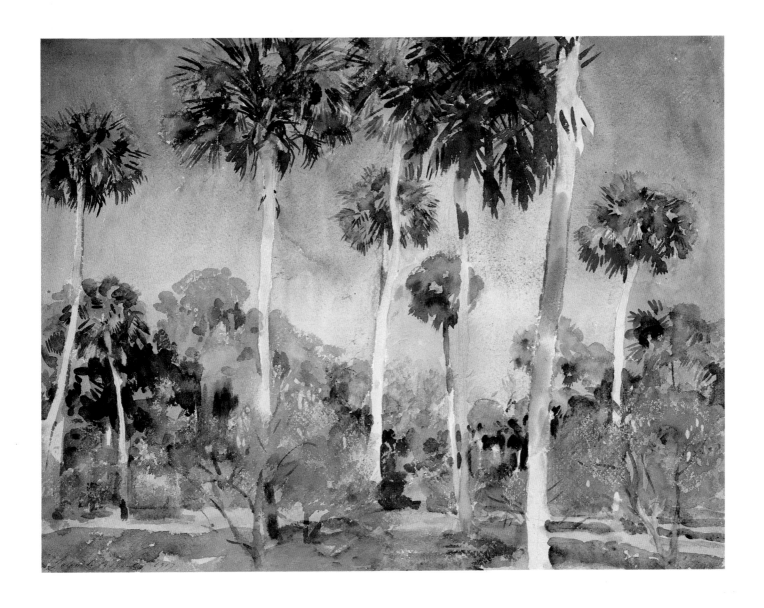

88
John Singer Sargent (1856–1925)
Boats at Anchor, 1917

Boats at Anchor is an excellent example of the unusual and intriguing arrangements that Sargent discovered in harbors. Several of his contemporaries, including James McNeill Whistler and Claude Monet, made casual depictions of ordinary vessels, but none developed Sargent's special interest in the close-up, almost water-level point of view. It is possible that he learned to favor this perspective while painting from gondolas in Venice. Usually working in a small boat moored alongside larger vessels, he painted watercolors with the same basic elements as *Boats at Anchor* in Venice, Palestine, Majorca, and Maine. The location of this work is the Miami River, probably looking east.[1]

Again it was a luminous effect that attracted Sargent to subjects such as this, with the light here bouncing off the water onto the hulls and the fragmented reflections on the gently rippled surface of the water. As with *Muddy Alligators* (plate 82), the challenge of suggesting shadows and highlights on a white subject painted on white paper appealed to him. In this instance, small portions of paper were left without pigment, although most of the different "whites" of the hull of the large vessel were created with very thin transparent washes, expertly manipulated.

The three boats that are the focus of the composition make a pleasing recession from left to right, their reflections reinforcing the diagonal axis of the composition. The open vista on the right carefully balanced the blurred white detail of another boat glimpsed at the bottom left. The informal, workaday feel established by the low vantage point from another boat is enhanced by the hatted figure ambling across the bridge.

The very ordinariness of his subject in *Boats at Anchor* seems to confirm that Sargent's primary objective was not to find exceptional subject matter but to paint a scene exactly as he saw it. His watercolors often convey the pleasure he took in executing a work in a bold, efficient way. In a sense, it hardly mattered whether he painted boats, alligators, or palmettos; his true subject was the process of painting itself.   *TJF*

1. Today the site is part of downtown Miami, near the Miami Avenue bridge. The continuous truss bridge (which no longer exists) was known in 1917 as the Avenue D bridge. A related 1917 oil painting, *Charles Deering at Brickell Point* (private collection), shows Sargent's host seated outdoors near a coconut grove with a similar view of the Miami River. For an illustration, see *Art News* 35 (September 18, 1937): 12. The author is grateful to David Hertzberg and Rebecca A. Smith for their help in researching the location of *Boats at Anchor*.

Provenance
The artist; museum purchase, Sustaining Membership Fund, 1917

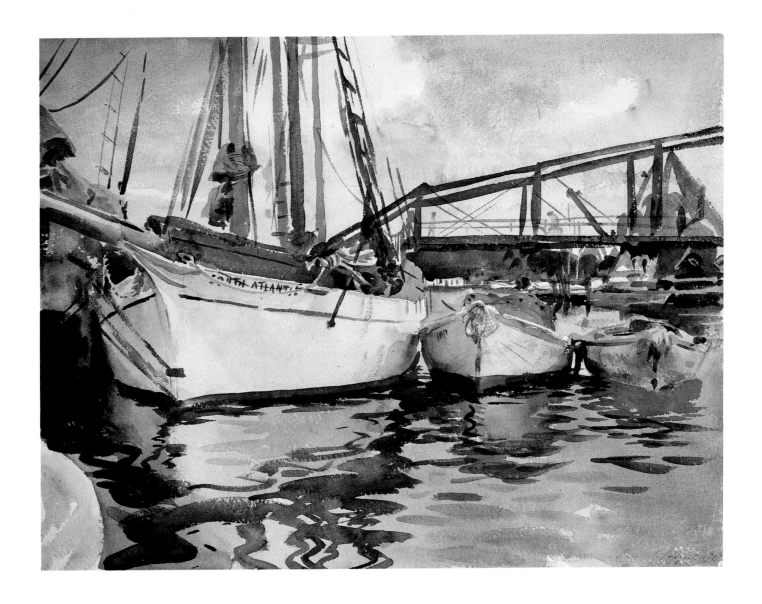

89
Maurice B. Prendergast (1858–1924)
Low Tide, Beachmont, probably 1902–4

Scenes of beaches and seaside parks formed the core of Maurice Prendergast's oeuvre for the more than thirty years of his professional career.[1] He reached artistic maturity in the 1890s, at a time when many other American artists were experimenting with Impressionist interpretations of coastal resorts, and after 1900 he viewed his favorite subject through a kaleidoscope of modern styles. From 1900 to 1915 Prendergast restlessly applied lessons learned from the French artists Paul Cézanne and Henri Matisse and from the American Arthur B. Davies, as well as other influential contemporaries, to produce paintings marked by various aspects of realism, Post-Impressionism, and Symbolism. The explorations of these years eventually led to the motionless, color-filled fantasy world that characterized the work of his final years.

Trained as a letterer and showcard painter, Prendergast became skillful with water-based paints. Although he began to use oils as early as 1891, when he first left Boston to study at the Académie Julian in Paris, watercolor remained his primary and most successful medium until after 1900. When he returned to Boston in 1894, he established his reputation by exhibiting mostly watercolors of the Breton and Massachusetts coasts.

Prendergast found great visual and tactile pleasure in the seaside, perhaps, in part, because he was growing deaf. Writing to his friend and fellow artist Esther Williams about his visits to the L Street beach in Boston, he rejoiced: "To take off one's clothes and lay full stretched on the sand exposed to the wind and the sun is the finest sensation I know. All ages and classes seem to come here . . . it is open free to all."[2] The combination of personal pleasure and community spirit that he enjoyed there permeates works such as *Low Tide, Beachmont.*[3] Unlike earlier painters of the American coast, Prendergast presented nature shaped by human experience: he painted public and well-populated beaches such as

Beachmont's and the neighboring Revere Beach just north of Boston. The latter was one of the most highly developed day resorts on the East Coast at this time, boasting an amusement park, Wonderland, with its Lightning Roller Coaster.

Low Tide, Beachmont represents a curious phase in Prendergast's interpretation of the coast. While it exemplifies his view of the seaside as a place for human interaction, it presents a new relationship between figure and setting. In comparison to earlier works, the figures are larger, more individual in details of face and costume, and more dominant because of their frontal poses and foreground location. In earlier works such as *Low Tide, Nantasket* (c. 1897; private collection), the figures were downplayed so that they would harmonize with the setting; detail was burned out by sunlight and wind, and figures were dispersed along a series of diagonals to suggest recession into space. In *Low Tide, Beachmont,* however, the sedate individuals are carefully posed in a layered arrangement, and although the boats and reflections are naturalistic, the figures seem impervious to wind and weather. Prendergast's deliberate rejection of his earlier naturalistic style may parallel his rejection of photography, which had influenced many aspects of his earlier beach scenes. In liberating painting from photographic naturalism, Prendergast may have looked to a number of sources that were admired by advanced artists in his circle: folk art, French Post-Impressionists such as Cézanne, Georges Seurat, and Vincent van Gogh, and non-Western "primitives" of all kinds.[4]

The distinctive style of *Low Tide, Beachmont* is seen in several closely related works, including *Beachmont* (New Britain Museum of American Art, New Britain, Connecticut) and *Low Tide* (Huntington

Library and Art Collections, San Marino, California) as well as a number of other seaside watercolors that show wharves in awkward perspective and backgrounds crowded with sailboats. This same style can be seen in Prendergast's most important oil painting from this era, *Salem Willows*[5] (Terra Museum of American Art, Chicago), which makes it likely that the watercolors in this style are from the same period, about 1902–4.[6] In these years Prendergast was enjoying the success of a number of exhibitions across the United States and generally favorable critical reception. He had become acquainted with Robert Henri and other future members of The Eight, and in addition to his annual sketching trips to coastal areas of Massachusetts and Maine, he began to spend part of each year working in New York. Prendergast's stylistic experimentation in this period may be linked to his association with the most forward-thinking young artists of his day.

NMM

1. The research and conclusions presented in the entries for plates 89–93 are the result of a team effort involving all members of the Prendergast Project at the Williams College Museum of Art, Williamstown, Massachusetts. The year of Prendergast's birth was previously uncertain. Recently discovered baptismal records and a family bible indicate he was born in 1858.

2. Prendergast to Williams, May 14, 1905, Archives of American Art, Smithsonian Institution, Washington, D.C.

3. Beachmont seems to have been consistently misspelled "Beechmont" by Maurice Prendergast and his brother, Charles, in titling their works. The correct spelling is used here for clarity.

4. Prendergast's generation classified as "primitive" an international array of styles: Byzantine, Egyptian, and Persian, as well as native American art.

5. See Prendergast to Esther Williams, October 31, 1905, Archives of American Art, Smithsonian Institution, Washington, D.C. This bill of sale states that *Salem Willows* (also called *The Promenade, Salem Harbor*) was painted in 1904.

6. There are two dates inscribed in the lower right of the watercolor: "1897" is to the right of the signature, and a blotted number, which may also be read as "1897," is below. The two dates and the signature were painted in slightly different colors, indicating that they were added at three different times and making the dates unreliable as documentary evidence.

Provenance
Charles Prendergast; museum purchase, 1941

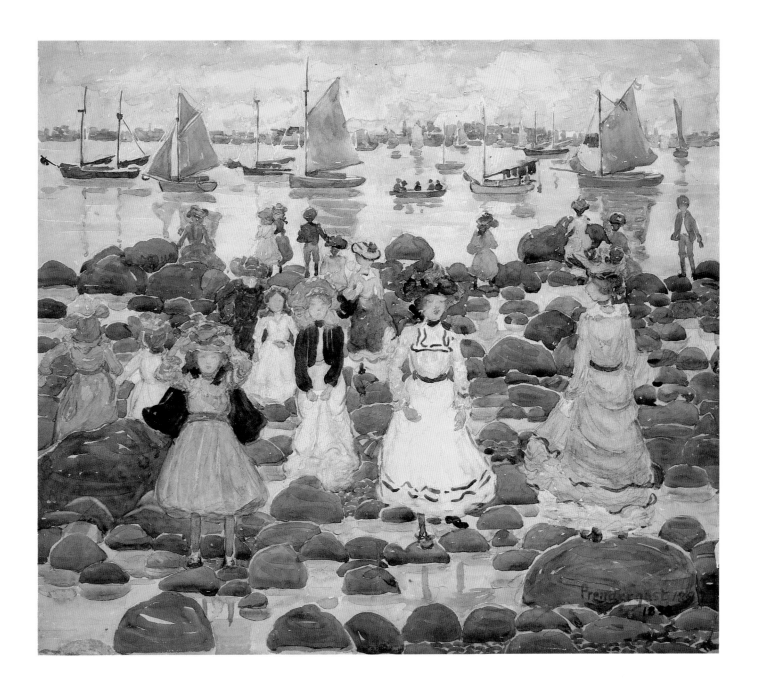

143

90
Maurice B. Prendergast (1858–1924)
Across the Harbor, Salem, about 1905–7

Across the Harbor, Salem is one of Prendergast's rare snow scenes. Views of the city in winter were not uncommon in the oeuvre of his Impressionist and Ash Can colleagues, but painting a seaside park—the quintessential summer subject—in the snow had a certain novelty. The season doesn't chill the typically sociable nature of Prendergast's subject; on the contrary, it calls attention to the fashionably dressed figures by providing a light background for their dark shapes and royal blue outlines. Prendergast abandoned here the stiff frontality seen in *Low Tide, Beachmont* in favor of figures that convey a more lively sense of movement: the curves of their bustles, boas, and large feathered hats not only follow current fashion but also exaggerate poses and gestures. In this use of costume Prendergast may have been influenced by Charles Condor, a British artist he had met in Paris during the early 1890s, who specialized in rococo groupings of women, often painted on fans.

Across the Harbor, Salem is a simpler version of the closely related watercolor *April Snow, Salem* (Museum of Modern Art, New York)[1] and a similar winter scene of Boston, *Park Street Church* (private collection). Beginning in 1901 Prendergast exhibited numerous works painted in and around Salem, Massachusetts. This venerable American seaport held a special attraction for him in the form of its new amusement park, Salem Willows, at the tip of the promontory forming Salem's harbor. Like the popular Wonderland at Revere Beach, Salem Willows catered to Boston day-trippers who could take either the electric railway or a pleasure steamer out to the park. Prendergast's marked prefer-

ence for Salem after 1900 may have been due to its combination of special features—sideshows, rides, swimming beaches, and grassy lawns—which provided him with a variety of settings and situations to study. Even in the snow, the park drew pleasure-seekers into picturesque tableaux.

The figures and the palette of *Across the Harbor, Salem* recall the watercolors Prendergast painted during the first weeks in his 1907 trip to Paris, including *Notre Dame, Paris* (see plate 91). Although the figures are larger and darker in *Across the Harbor, Salem*, they have the same elaborate costumes and gray-blue coloring of Prendergast's Paris watercolors, suggesting that they were painted just before that trip. In this work, as in many of his other watercolors from the period, Prendergast scraped into areas of dark color—especially the skirts of the three figures on the right—presumably to lighten them by exposing the paper. This and additions such as the bright blue outlining over dried washes anticipate the active layering, excising, and painting over of Prendergast's later years.

NMM

1. The simplest version of this subject is the pencil drawing on the verso of *Across the Harbor, Salem*, which includes only the figures of the woman on the left and the child behind her, with the small figures and the harbor in the distance.

Provenance
Charles Prendergast; (C. W. Kraushaar Art Galleries, New York); museum purchase, 1941

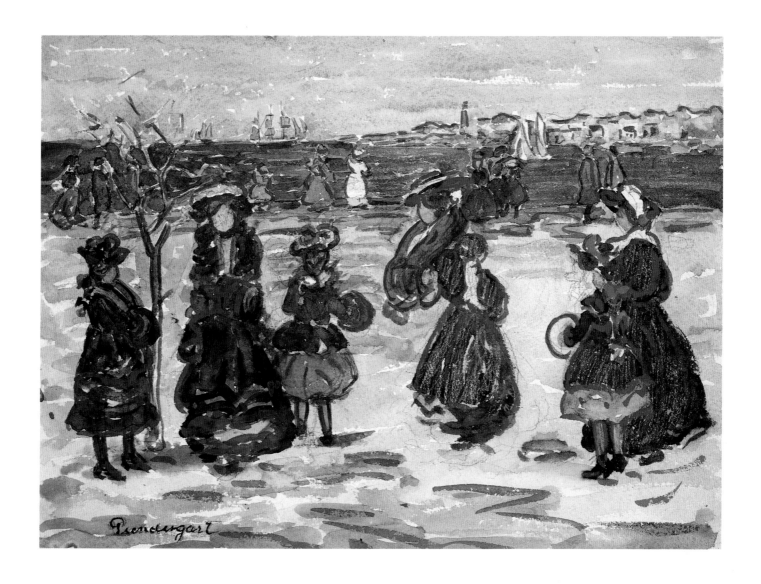

145

91
Maurice B. Prendergast (1858–1924)
Notre Dame, Paris, 1907

When Prendergast went to France in 1907, he landed at Le Havre, hoping to work for a while nearby; but he was disappointed in the painting conditions on the coast and after a few days decided to go immediately to Paris. Although still beset by rainy weather, he was inspired by both the art and the scenery he found there. To his brother, Charles, a framemaker and artist, he wrote: "I have just seen the Champs de Mars exhibition and it was worth travelling 100,000 miles to see. [It] made me feel like an artist once again. . . . You ought to see the Luxembourg garden, now it is in full swing, the band playing and the children romping about. I see pictures in every direction. . . ."[1]

While it is tempting to focus on Prendergast's response to the radical styles on view in Paris that year, pictures like *Notre Dame, Paris* must be seen as equally important results of this pivotal trip. Prendergast had already painted unsurpassed scenes of city life in his extremely successful series of views of Venice and other Italian cities (1898–99) and his subsequent series on New York and Boston (1901–2). He approached these cities as a typical tourist, painting the famous buildings and picturesque rivers and parks with great fidelity and even inscribing the name of the site on the front of the painting next to his signature and date. Since he had not yet fully developed his skill in painting city views while a student in Paris in 1891–94, Prendergast may have wanted to start a Paris series with *Notre Dame, Paris.* Several other watercolors belong to this group, including *The Balloon* (Addison Gallery of American Art, Andover, Massachusetts) and the *Band Concert* (Mead Art Museum, Amherst College, Amherst, Massachusetts), but they do not form as consistent a series as the earlier Venice, New York, or Boston views, or the later Venice group of 1911–12.

After the stylistic change evident in *Low Tide, Beachmont* and *Across the Harbor, Salem* (plates 89, 90), in which the figures dominate, Prendergast reverted to his earlier, more traditional structure, with figures forming just a small part of a larger, more naturalistic composition. The famous Gothic cathedral is the focus of attention, seen from a typical tourist's point of view in a panoramic sweep from the bridge in the foreground. The blue and red costumes of the French soldiers can be found in most of Prendergast's paintings from this trip, a device many foreign artists used to identify the French locale.

Prendergast had been working with the blue-gray palette of *Notre Dame, Paris* for a number of years, and it provides the context of the artist's double-edged response to the colors he saw in the Paris exhibitions. While he noted the wild hues of the Fauves and would later experiment with non-naturalistic colors at St. Mâlo, what impressed him at first were paintings that achieved "a beautiful quality of grey."[2] Thus, although Prendergast went to France seeking "a new impulse,"[3] at the same time he was gratified to find confirmation of directions he had already followed.

NMM

1. Prendergast to Charles Prendergast, May 1907, Prendergast Project, Williams College Museum of Art, Williamstown, Massachusetts.

2. Ibid.

3. Prendergast to Esther Williams, October 10, 1907, Archives of American Art, Smithsonian Institution, Washington, D.C.

Provenance
Charles Prendergast; museum purchase, 1941

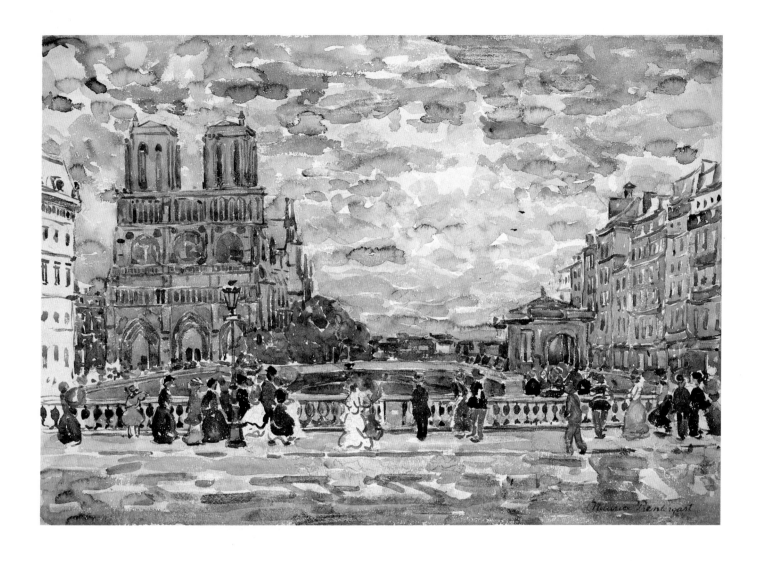

92
Maurice B. Prendergast (1858–1924)
Venice, **probably 1911**

In mid-August 1911 Prendergast returned to Venice, where he joined his brother, Charles, and spent several weeks "taking in all the sights."[1] The memory of his first Italian trip, in 1898 and early 1899, clearly had haunted Prendergast, and he had longed to return to the city whose exotic architecture and festive crowds had inspired dozens of his watercolors. His watercolor technique had become less descriptive in the intervening years, and his perceptions of Venice had changed: now it was symbolized for him by the rebuilt Campanile di San Marco. To Esther Williams he described it as "still sourrounded [sic] in some parts by scalffolding [sic] and what I see of it looks awfully new."[2] He added that he planned to stay in Venice another two months "and have another wack [sic] at the canals," whose bridges with decorative railings particularly held his attention on this trip.

Prendergast began *Venice*,[3] which shows the Ponte Calcina on the Fondamenta delle Zattere, in late December 1911 and finished it either there or upon his return to Boston early in 1912. Just after his brother's departure for home in mid-October, Prendergast fell ill, and he underwent emergency surgery and an extended convalescence at the Cosmopolitan Hospital in the Giudecca. From his "warm and sunny corner room next door to the Calcine,"[4] he had a felicitous view along the

Zattere, one of the most pleasant vistas in Venice, commanding an open and exhilarating stretch of the Giudecca Canal with the distinctive dome of Andrea Palladio's Il Redentore beyond. The city, empty of summer tourists and with its colors in winter "richer and deeper,"[5] held a particular charm for Prendergast. Perhaps depressed by his illness, he expressed his artistic discouragement to Esther Williams: "My sketching experience this time has been disastrous. . . . With all its beauty I am never going to do my best work here."[6] Nevertheless, he produced a handful of fresh and exuberant watercolors in Venice, each modern in outlook and technique.

Prendergast painted this bridge five times,[7] in part because of its beauty and in part because it was convenient. He tired easily and "chilled quickly during his recuperation,"[8] and so he may have been confined to painting variations on the Ponte Calcina viewed from his room or from the little terrace below it. In *Venice* he filled his foreground with the Rio San Vio canal, and the bridge and its decorative railing weighted the composition to the right. To the left, a walled garden is guarded by carved stone figures, overhung with lush foliage. *Venice* displays the watercolor technique that Prendergast had developed in response to the modernist paintings he had seen in Paris four years earlier. Fluid, calligraphic lines define the figures, and the water and bricks are executed in rapid strokes. His style did not require detailed finish; some figures are just outlined, and one boat lacks a gondolier.

On the verso of this watercolor is a faint pencil drawing of another view of

Venice, unusually panoramic for Prendergast. On the right is the Ponte della Paglia, looking toward the column of St. Theodore and Sansovino's library, and to the left is a view across the bay to Santa Maria della Salute. Instead of completing this ambitious and complex view of the city's most characteristic sites, Prendergast turned over the paper to paint the view from his window as he regained his health during the last weeks he spent in Venice. *CC*

1. Prendergast to Esther Williams, September 15, 1911, Archives of American Art, Smithsonian Institution, Washington, D.C.

2. Ibid.

3. Inscribed "Venice" by the artist on the verso and misdated, possibly by another hand, to 1909, this watercolor acquired its present title in 1941 upon purchase by the Worcester Art Museum from William Macbeth, Inc. See the letter from Robert G. McIntyre to Benjamin H. Stone, July 1, 1941, Worcester Art Museum files.

4. Prendergast to Charles Prendergast, December 14, 1911, Prendergast Project, Williams College, Williamstown, Massachusetts. Prendergast refers to this pensione as the Casa Festari; today it is called the Seguso.

5. Ibid.

6. Prendergast to Esther Williams, December 18, 1911, Archives of American Art, Smithsonian Institution, Washington, D.C.

7. The others are *Venice, The Zattere, Bridge at Venice,* and *Ponte S. Vio,* all in private collections.

8. Prendergast to Charles Prendergast, December 23, 1911, Prendergast Project, Williams College Museum of Art, Williamstown, Massachusetts.

Provenance
Charles Prendergast; Lizzie P. Bliss; (William Macbeth, Inc., New York); museum purchase, 1941

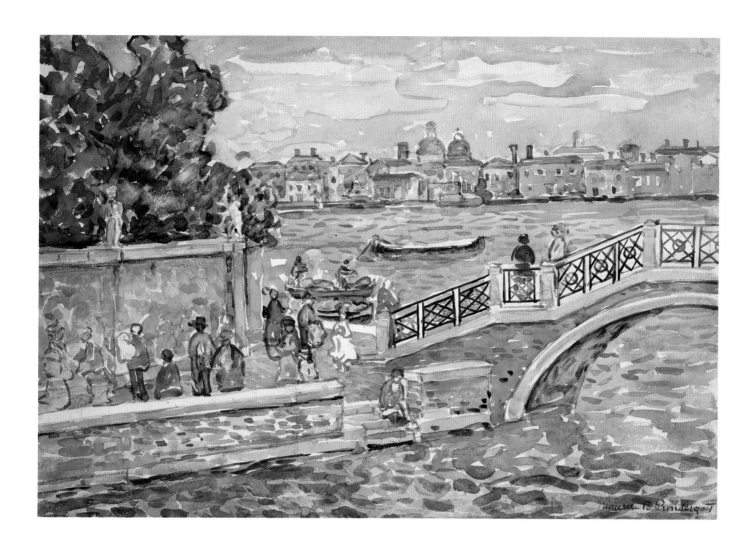

93
Maurice B. Prendergast (1858–1924)
Gloucester Park, about 1916

In 1914, following the Armory Show and his subsequent move with Charles from Boston to New York, Prendergast became involved in a decorative mural project with Arthur B. Davies and Walt Kuhn. These murals (two by Prendergast and one each by Davies and Kuhn) were purely speculative undertakings: they had no unifying program, no intended site, and no patron.[1] The artists were motivated purely by their desire to create a major public statement in a modern style.

Gloucester Park is related to Prendergast's two murals, *Picnic* and *Promenade,* and especially to a watercolor sketch for *Picnic.*[2] The picnic theme of both murals and of *Gloucester Park* had recurred in Prendergast's work since his 1901 Central Park series, which often included groups of picnicking children. In the murals he monumentalized the outdoor dining party, transforming a casual event into a timeless scene, while maintaining a balance between naturalism and stylization. Prendergast derived the poses of his central group from Edouard Manet's *Le Déjeuner sur l'herbe* (1863; Musée d'Orsay, Paris).[3] He tamed his reference to Manet's masterpiece—the nude female surrounded by clothed men in a Parisian park had caused a scandal—by clothing all the figures and thereby concealing the historical reference in an otherwise naturalistic seaside scene.

The seaside park comprises a series of undulating knolls. The figures are organized in small groups—the picnickers, the people on two of the benches, and the women strolling in from the right—and arranged in a composition similar to that of *Picnic* (plate 93a). The lone man looking across the inlet at the center of *Gloucester Park* is a common motif in Prendergast's

paintings, and the figure striding in from the left is the same as one found in the right background of *Picnic.*

The intensity of the colors is characteristic of Prendergast's palette during these years, and he carefully distributed primary and secondary colors, along with modest amounts of black and gray, across the paper. Particularly striking are the orange legs, indecorously bared to the knees, of one of the women seated at left. Prendergast also used the whiteness of exposed paper as a design element or as scattered highlights. To stress the horizontality and the panoramic qualities of his image, he left unpainted about two inches of paper above and below the composition; this feature relates the watercolor even more obviously to the murals.

Despite the reference to Manet, this watercolor is natural and refreshing, reminiscent of the summers Prendergast spent along the New England shore after his move to New York. During this last decade of his career he painted increasingly in oil; yet he never abandoned watercolor, using it to embellish his sketchbooks or to create independent works for exhibition. Prendergast continued to find pleasure and artistic reward in the spontaneity and fluidity of the medium, which provided an antidote to his carefully planned and executed paintings in oil.   *CC*

1. For further discussion of the mural project, see Dennis A. Nawrocki, "Prendergast and Davies: Two Approaches to a Mural Project," *Bulletin of the Detroit Institute of Arts* 56, no. 4 (1978): 243–52.

2. *Gloucester Park* acquired its title in 1941 upon purchase by the Worcester Art Museum from William Macbeth, Inc. See the letter from Robert G. McIntyre to Benjamin H. Stone, July 1, 1941, Worcester Art Museum files. *Picnic* is at the Museum of Art, Carnegie Institute, Pittsburgh; and *Promenade* is at the Detroit Institute of Arts. The sketch for *Picnic* is in a private collection.

3. Gwendolyn Owens first observed this, in *Watercolors by Maurice Prendergast from New England Collections* (Williamstown, Mass.: Sterling and Francine Clark Art Institute, 1978).

Provenance
Charles Prendergast; Lizzie P. Bliss; (William Macbeth, Inc., New York); museum purchase, 1941

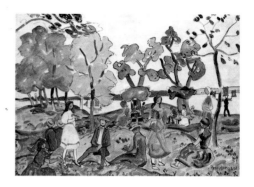

93a
Maurice Prendergast
Picnic, c. 1914–15
77 × 106½ in. (195.6 × 270.5 cm.)
Museum of Art, Carnegie Institute, Pittsburgh; Gift of the People of Pittsburgh in honor of the Sarah Scaife Gallery, through the Women's Committee of the Museum of Art

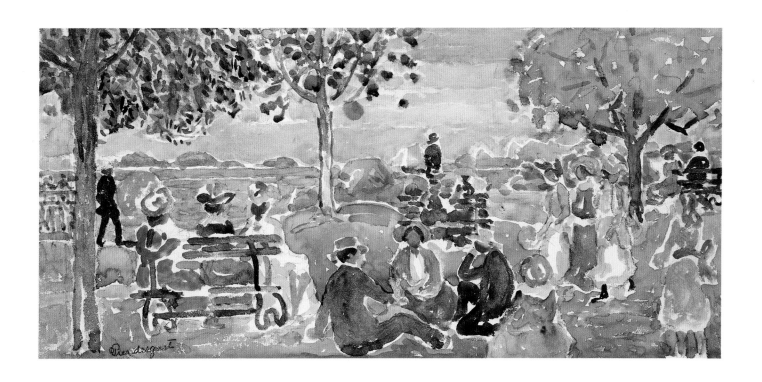

151

94
Childe Hassam (1859–1935)
Looking into Beryl Pool, 1912

Watercolor was a particularly important medium for Childe Hassam, one that he used regularly throughout his career. While working as an illustrator, he produced his first significant body of noncommercial work, a group of small, freely brushed watercolor sketches painted in 1882 in and around his native Dorchester, Massachusetts. In their literal depictions of nature, these youthful works emphasize the artist's naturalistic view of the world around him, an attitude that underlies much of his art. His first one-man exhibitions, held at the Boston art galleries of Williams and Everett in 1882 and 1884, were composed solely of watercolors, indicating his interest in the medium from the outset. Hassam was active in several watercolor clubs, most notably the American Water Color Society and the New York Water Color Club, of which he was a founding member and first president (1890–95). Similarly, he promoted watercolor as a legitimate medium for serious works of art, advising both museums and collectors to acquire watercolor paintings and drawings.[1]

Over the course of his long and extremely prolific career, watercolor seemed to suit Hassam's active, peripatetic moods by allowing him to capture nature spontaneously, in a rapid and direct fashion. Hassam sketched *Looking into Beryl Pool* in 1912 at the Isles of Shoals, a group of rocky islands off the Maine–New Hampshire coast. He first visited this vacation spot in the early 1880s, after meeting in Boston Mrs. Celia Thaxter, whose family owned the islands and made the main Appledore Island into a summer haven for many distinguished writers and artists.[2] Hassam maintained a studio on the Shoals and made regular visits there even after Mrs. Thaxter's death in 1894. He painted dozens of oils and watercolors of the rugged coastline and interior pools of the islands, as well as Mrs. Thaxter's vibrant flower gardens.[3] It was characteristic of him to paint a familiar subject over and over, each time depicting it in different weather or from a new vantage point.

This glimpse into a coastal pool nestled among the rugged granite rocks is a thoroughly Impressionist work—one of Hassam's many attempts to capture the fleeting effects of brilliant sunlight upon moving tidal waters. Although he painted similar scenes in oil, watercolor provided him with a more flexible medium. Certainly Hassam presented an accurate, though generalized, description of the terrain; yet his primary focus was on the abstract possibilities in the subject. Choosing a close-up vantage point, he cropped the scene and eliminated any view into the distance. As a result, the image appears flat and two-dimensional, factors that enhance its decorative quality. Quick, angular strokes indicate the faceted, almost architectural wall of rock that encloses the composition. Watery washes of oranges and gray-greens suggest the variegated texture of the granite, while in the foreground the reserve of white paper implies the blanching effects of intense sunlight. Similarly, the rich midnight blue of the deep waters cast in shadow contrasts with lively staccato notes of color on the rippling surface, which reflects the multicolored rocks above. Although not technically complex, this work is evidence of Hassam's mastery of the medium.

During the first two decades of this century Hassam often hung similar subjects as "sets" within a single exhibition. In November 1915 the Montross Gallery in New York mounted a show of more than one hundred pictures by Hassam, over half of which were watercolors. Twenty-one belonged to the Isles of Shoals group, including one watercolor entitled *Looking into Beryl;* although not conclusively documented, that work may well have been the watercolor now in the Worcester Art Museum.[4]

KMB

1. In a letter of October 2, 1912, to Mrs. Charlotte E. W. Buffington, a trustee and patron who gave four Hassams to the museum, the artist wrote: "I very much want [the museum] to have a set of drawings of mine someday. I think museums will do more of this in the future, having drawings in watercolor and pastel"; Worcester Art Museum files. Hassam also encouraged the Carnegie Institute to buy a group of his drawings and watercolors: see Gail Stavitsky, "Childe Hassam in the Collection of the Museum of Art, Carnegie Institute," *Carnegie Magazine* 6, no. 4 (July–August 1982): 27–39, and "Childe Hassam and the Carnegie Institute: A Correspondence," *Archives of American Art Journal* 22, no. 3 (1982): 2–7. He also advised private collectors to acquire drawings: see Hassam to Col. Charles E. S. Wood, October 21, 1919, C.E.S. Wood Papers, Huntington Library, San Marino, California.

2. For an excellent introduction to the cultural life of the Isles of Shoals during the late nineteenth century, see Susan Faxon, Alice Downey, and Peter Bermingham, *A Stern and Lovely Scene: A Visual History of the Isles of Shoals* (Durham, N.H.: University of New Hampshire Art Galleries, 1978).

3. Other related watercolors from 1912 include Worcester Art Museum's *Lyman's Pool* as well as *The Gorge, Appledore* (Brooklyn Museum), *Diamond Cove* (San Diego Museum of Art), and *The Dark Pool* (private collection, New York). The Worcester Art Museum also owns an oil painted at the Isles of Shoals, *Sylph's Rock, Appledore* (1907), which was a gift of Mrs. Buffington (see plate 19).

4. The museum's watercolor may have been no. 93 in the Montross Gallery's *Exhibition of Pictures by Childe Hassam*, New York, November 27–December 11, 1915.

Provenance
(Montross Gallery, New York); Mrs. Charlotte E. W. Buffington, Worcester, until 1935; bequest of Mrs. Charlotte E. W. Buffington, 1935

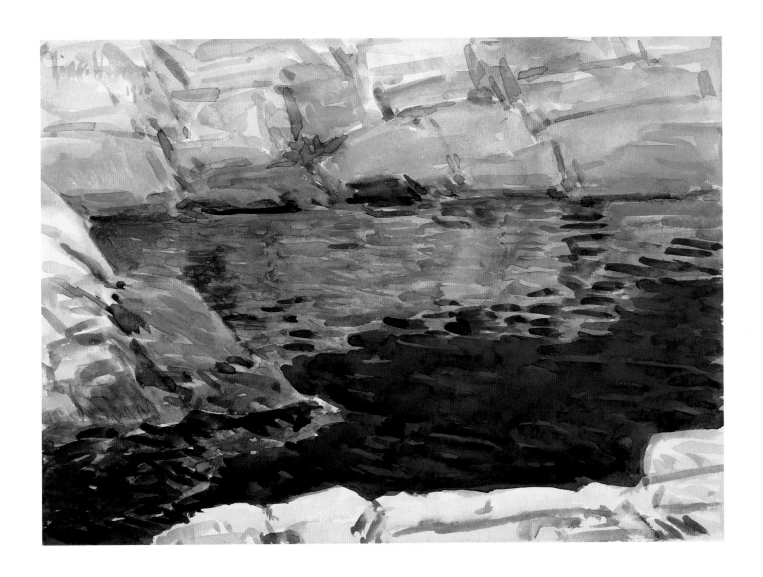

95

Childe Hassam (1859–1935)
Yonkers from the Palisades, **1916**

Painted in the autumn of 1916, *Yonkers from the Palisades* depicts a distant view of the New York town nestled on the eastern shore of the Hudson River. Hassam has captured this expansive scene from a high point on the New Jersey Palisades. His friendships with fellow artists Reynolds and Gifford Beal, whose family home was in Newburgh, New York, inspired a number of trips to this region in the 1910s. Hassam drew and painted numerous views of the historic villages and picturesque scenery along the Hudson between Manhattan and Newburgh, some fifty miles north. Eighteen of these works, composing the "Hudson River Set," were featured in the *Exhibition of Pictures by Childe Hassam* at the Montross Gallery in Manhattan in 1917.[1] Shortly after the close of the exhibition, a group of nine of these watercolors was sent on approval to the Worcester Art Museum; *Yonkers from the Palisades* was purchased from this group.

While Hassam's choice of subject matter was traditional, his treatment of it reveals an innovative vision and improvised technique. The artist blocked out the composition into a few broadly articulated areas: the foreground ledge and foliage; the broad expanse of the Hudson River; and the two horizontal bands of the far bank and sky. This division gives the design a striking decorative quality, which further accentuates the vibrant surface effects. This emphasis on the decorative elements of the work is in keeping with much of Hassam's production during the twentieth century, when he increasingly modified his Impressionist style to reflect an interest in vivid color, strong pattern, and, to a degree, flattened pictorial space, all presumably as a response to developments in modern art.

Close examination of *Yonkers from the Palisades* reveals graphite underdrawing used to denote both the placement of major elements and some details of the jagged ledge. Very subtle shading was applied in pink colored pencil on the face of the cliff, in the autumnal foliage above, and on the far riverbank, giving a purplish hue

where it mixes with the blue watercolor wash. Similar shading in yellow was applied to the reserved white paper in the cliff, enhancing the effects of brilliant sunlight. The shimmering expanse of the river was created by layering blue and yellow washes, which were then tamped with a fibrous material, probably a wad of cotton. With controlled dexterity, Hassam subtly animated the composition with tiny reserves of white paper that suggest houses and buildings in the distant village and a lone sailboat on the river.

Interestingly, at the same time he was executing *Yonkers from the Palisades,* Hassam was beginning to make prints. Some of his lithographs—especially those employing liquid tusche, painted directly on the stone with a brush, much as he applied wash to his watercolors—are among the most original American lithographs of the period, and their innovative character suggests a kinship with the artist's broadly painted watercolors of the mid-1910s. Even twenty years earlier Hassam had experimented in his watercolors, combining pencil, charcoal, pastel, gouache, and opaque chinese white to achieve special atmospheric effects in his urban nocturnes. The artist's creative integration of different media within his watercolors may, in part, have stemmed from his facility with so many of them. The complicated surface of this particular painting reveals Hassam to be an artist whose work, particularly in watercolor, was more inventive than is often realized.   *KMB*

1. The exhibition at Montross Gallery was held January 4–20, 1917. A smaller watercolor of 1916, *On the Palisades* (E. B. Crocker Gallery, Sacramento), is related to *Yonkers from the Palisades.*

Provenance
(Montross Gallery, New York, 1917); museum purchase, 1917

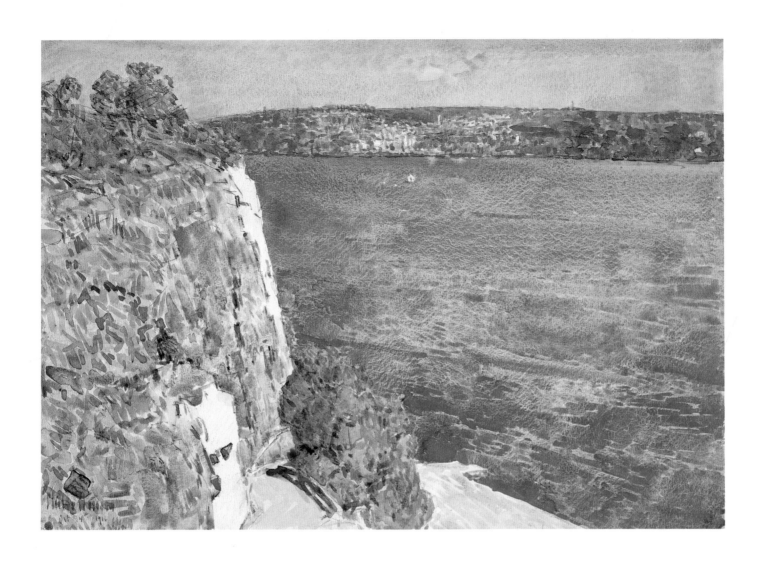

155

96

Frank W. Benson (1862–1951)
Eider Ducks in Winter, about 1913

Frank W. Benson was one of the most successful and prolific artists of his generation. Having studied at the School of the Museum of Fine Arts in Boston and the Académie Julian in Paris, by the early 1890s he was working in the Impressionist style and in 1897 became a founding member of the Impressionist group, Ten American Painters. By the early years of this century he was a leader in the Boston art world, locally important as a painting instructor at the School of the Museum of Fine Arts and nationally acclaimed for his bright, colorful portraits and figural pictures, which often featured his beautiful daughters at leisure. He was a lifelong outdoorsman, and his fishing and shooting experiences provided him with subjects for oil paintings, watercolors, etchings, and drypoints with increasing frequency in the 1910s and 1920s. At the height of his career, Benson's subjects ranged from the domestic world—interiors, still lifes, formal portraits—to wild-bird pictures and hunting scenes. His work appealed to a wide range of temperaments, and he attracted patrons of different financial circumstances by producing many prints and watercolors in addition to oils.

When the Worcester Art Museum acquired *Eider Ducks in Winter* in 1913, it made a timely and insightful purchase of a new work by a local master.[1] Benson was not yet widely acclaimed as a watercolorist and had exhibited very few works in this medium. Furthermore, his professional interest in sporting art was forming at this time; although his first etchings of birds date from 1912, none was exhibited until 1915.

Despite its monochrome palette, this watercolor exemplifies Benson's interest in the Impressionist style: the washes in the foreground have a painterly flourish, which enhances the sense of liveliness and spontaneity. There is none of the minute detail and frozen classical effect of the traditional naturalist watercolor associated with John James Audubon and his followers. However, Benson's ornithological expertise is evident in his drawing, and although the ducks are impressionistically rendered, they contain enough truthful observation and expressive gesture to please the most serious birder. *Eider Ducks in Winter* is a good example of the way Benson transformed his observations of nature to suit his own artistic purposes. Female eider ducks are mottled and barred in various browns; Benson confidently adapted their actual coloring to his black and white scheme so that even those farthest from the viewer are readily distinguishable.

It might be imagined that the restricted black and gray palette of *Eider Ducks in Winter* developed from the artist's growing interest in etching; in fact, the hallmarks of Benson's etchings—the boldly simple arrangements, the immediacy and sketchlike freedom of the drawing, the naturalistic accuracy of the movements—were all established in watercolors such as this one, and several of Benson's grisaille watercolors predate his printmaking period, which began in 1912.[2] Benson may have been inspired by Winslow Homer, whose hunting pictures offered a precedent for Benson's and who occasionally made grisaille watercolors. But the greatest inspiration for Benson's use of monochrome was more likely the ink paintings of Japan, particularly the eighteenth-century animal and bird pictures of the Edo period. Benson was surely aware of the outstanding examples in the William S. Bigelow Collection acquired by the Museum of Fine Arts, Boston, in 1911.

Several aspects of *Eider Ducks in Winter* recall Japanese art and enhance the abstract qualities of the design: the nervous calligraphic lines denoting ripples in the water; the decorative unity of the composition, with the birds grouped in a succession of receding diagonals; the choice of a vantage point with neither horizon nor foreground devices, which keeps the landscape setting minimal but no less evocative. The black pigment is used to great visual effect, sparingly at the top of the sheet but boldly at the bottom, where it dramatically articulates the forms and movements of the two central ducks. Benson's Impressionist style, his admiration for Japanese ink painting, and his love and knowledge of birds are all allied in this watercolor. The sources may seem disparate and eclectic, but they combine in a style that synthesizes the expressive, the decorative, and the naturalistic.   *TJF*

1. The Worcester Art Museum purchased at the same time a second watercolor by Benson, *Eider Ducks Flying.* See Adam E. M. Paff, *Etchings and Drypoints by Frank W. Benson* (Boston: Houghton Mifflin, 1917), p. x.

2. For example, the monochrome *Redhead Ducks,* bequeathed to the Museum of Fine Arts, Boston, in 1942 by Benson's friend and fellow sportsman Arthur Tracy Cabot, is signed and dated 1907.

Provenance
(Copley Gallery, Boston, 1913); museum purchase, 1913

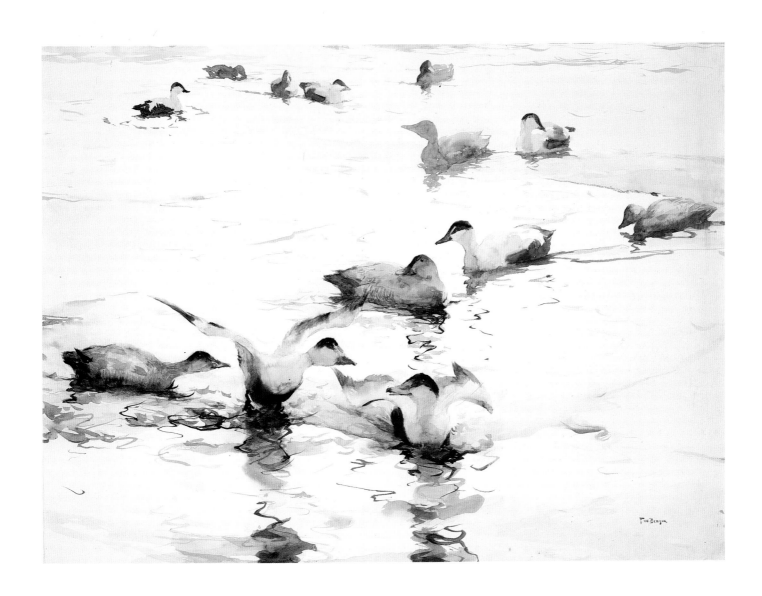

157

97A and 97B
Arthur B. Davies (1862–1928)
Castello, Edge of the Alps, about 1928
Italian Coast Port, about 1928

During the course of his long and successful career Arthur B. Davies espoused some of the most progressive tendencies in European and American art of the early twentieth century. Curiously, however, none of his extensive body of paintings, sculpture, prints, and decorative arts can be considered as the most innovative examples then being produced. In the 1910s Davies emerged from the Whistlerian tonalist tradition of the late nineteenth century to develop a unique decorative style that summoned a wide range of sources: the linear rhythms of Sandro Botticelli; the idyllic classicism of Pierre Puvis de Chavannes; the faceted surfaces of Cubism and Futurism; and a Romantic mysticism that aligned Davies with William Blake, Odilon Redon, Albert Pinkham Ryder, and Ralph Blakelock. Landscape was an integral part of Davies's art from the beginning of his career, both as a backdrop to his figural subjects and as an important element in establishing a mood. He worked in watercolor sporadically throughout his career, generally using it for landscapes.

From 1924 until his death four years later Davies spent about six months of every year in Europe. Working outdoors, he painted a large group of landscape watercolors in France, Spain, Italy, and northern Africa. These forthright watercolors represent a sharp break from the lyrical studio-composed work that he had produced in a variety of media throughout his career. His late watercolors were begun at the suggestion of his friend and patron Duncan Phillips, who reputedly urged him to eliminate the classical or Cubist-inspired figures that usually inhabited his landscapes.[1]

Castello, Edge of the Alps and *Italian Coast Port* were both executed on smooth-textured wove paper, probably sometime during the summer or early fall of 1928, just prior to Davies's death on October 28.

The principle features of the dramatic *Castello, Edge of the Alps* and the more tranquil *Italian Coast Port* were established with translucent washes: some of the washes were applied to paper wetted by previous washes and some were painted on dry paper. Small touches of pigment were then added to create highlights and define details, with pencil used to clarify the architectural details, as he did in the watercolors of this period. In *Italian Coast Port*, Davies covered the buff paper with a glowing salmon-colored wash. In *Castello, Edge of the Alps* he was apparently confident enough in his control over the design to leave large sections of the foreground unpainted.[2] Although the web of washes in the foreground conveys traditional illusionistic effects, it is laid down with a seeming casualness that underscores the painter-critic Bryson Burroughs's insight that Davies "trusted accidents and many a charming and capricious effect was due to them."[3]

In subject matter these works relate to several other views of Italy and Spain that were among the 118 of Davies's last watercolors exhibited by the artist's dealer, Frederick Newlin Price, in March and April 1929.[4] This show was widely praised, and elicited from critic Royal Cortissoz the following comparison with one of England's greatest masters: "One thinks again and again of Turner in this exhibition, of the genius which wrought out of the visible world a beauty allying it to a higher sphere. But where Turner worked so often in a high key, Davies is curiously restrained, dealing in tender blues and greys, in the delicate expression of fleeting effects."[5]

The absence of foreground details in both works suggests that Davies did not rely upon the conventions of the picturesque landscape, but was keenly aware of contemporary artistic currents. The distant mountain peak in *Italian Coast Port* seems reminiscent of Hokusai's many views of Mount Fuji, whereas *Castello, Edge of the Alps* calls to mind the majestic, colorful,

and economically rendered Alpine views by the Swiss painter Ferdinand Hodler, whose works Davies would have seen at the 1913 Armory Show. Davies appears to have sought effects that were primarily optical rather than cerebral—unlike Paul Cézanne, for example, or even John Marin, two artists whose watercolors reveal a concern for rigorous internal structure. Davies's interest in optical effects at the expense of structure in these late landscapes is comparable to his superficial adaptation of the formal complexities of Cubism in some of his figural paintings.

Recalling Davies, the critic and historian Sadakichi Hartmann wryly noted that the artist was known as "The Echo" because of his eclectic borrowing. Although the epithet seems justified, the watercolors that Davies created at the end of his career reveal a new freedom and originality that would probably have influenced his oil paintings had he lived longer. Unfortunately, these remarkable late watercolors have been overshadowed by Davies's earlier pictures and by the pivotal role he played in advancing the cause of modern art in America.   *PDS*

1. See Brooks Wright, *The Artist and the Unicorn: The Lives of Arthur B. Davies (1862–1928)* (Rockland, N.Y.: Historical Society of Rockland County, 1978), p. 92.

2. The formal characteristics of the museum's two watercolors are discussed by Ellen Berezin in "Arthur B. Davies: Artist and Connoisseur," *Worcester Art Museum Bulletin* 6 (November 1976): 16.

3. Bryson Burroughs, "Arthur B. Davies," *The Arts* 15 (February 1929): 86.

4. *Arthur B. Davies, Watercolors [and] Bronzes*, Ferargil Galleries, New York, March 25–April 8, 1929. The titles of the museum's two watercolors are not in the checklist that accompanied this show; the earliest record of these titles appears in a letter dated February 26, 1941, from William Macbeth to Charles H. Sawyer, in the curatorial files at the Worcester Art Museum.

5. Royal Cortissoz, "A Group of Water Colors and Bronzes," *New York Herald Tribune*, March 31, 1929, p. 10.

Provenance
Castello, Edge of the Alps and *Italian Coast Port*
Gift of Mrs. Cornelius N. Bliss, 1941

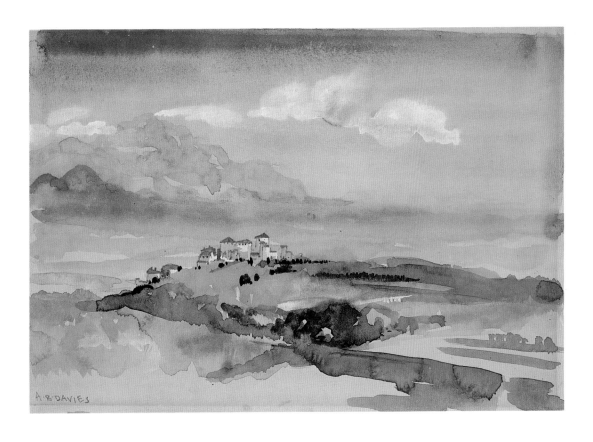

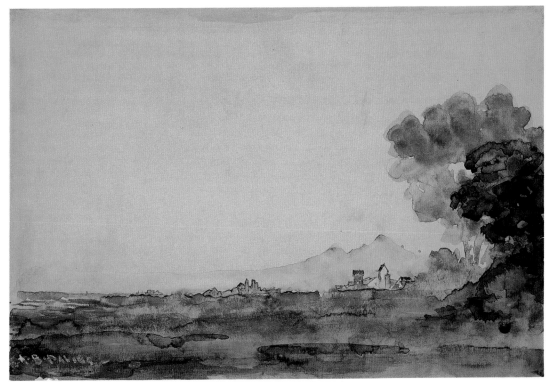

159

98
Lyonel Feininger (1871–1956)
The River, **1940**

Lyonel Feininger was one of the great marine painters of the twentieth century. In his many seascapes he harmoniously joined the stylistic innovations of modern art to traditional subject matter, creating a private, ideal world. For Feininger, the combination of shoreline, water, ships, and sky was especially resonant, and it recurs in multiple variations in his painted, drawn, and printed oeuvre. In the words of his biographer Hans Hess, "The place where land and sea meet, where two great forces face each other . . . held a strange fascination for Feininger. It was the end of one world and the beginning of another. It was neither quite here nor quite there."[1] The theme probably draws upon the artist's early childhood memories of boats on New York's Hudson and East rivers and of model ships on the pond in Central Park.[2]

These roots in a distant time and place help to account for the air of unreality that pervades this serene watercolor, as it does so much of Feininger's work. The location of the scene is left unidentified, and the vessels, while apparently belonging to a different century, evoke not so much real schooners, brigs, and cutters as the meticulously constructed models that the artist so passionately loved to build. The diluted Cubist style of *The River*—with its network of splintery pen lines, loosely interpenetrating angular planes, and quasigeometrical forms—is also of another time, since these elements were most prevalent in Feininger's work of the late 1920s and early 1930s. *The River* reflects nothing of its date of composition: the first year of total war unleashed on Europe by the Nazi tyranny, which three years earlier had forced the artist into impoverished exile in America at the height of his career in Germany. At a time when Feininger was adjusting to his new surroundings and just beginning to address recognizably modern American themes, he turned to a trusted subject. With restraint and order, he constructed a comfortable, familiar image, making it sufficiently artificial to create a sense of distance and insubstantiality.

This oscillation between the actual and the abstract was inherent in Feininger's working method. An obsessive draftsman, he made many thousands of sketches from nature, which he would then generalize into a final composition, translating the depicted scene into a more universal, timeless statement. He explored the traditional symbolic potential of ships and shores in his meditative, almost spiritual evocations of another world. While Feininger may not have shared the conscious symbolism of a Caspar David Friedrich, the German Romantic artist whose paintings were so charged with religious meaning, a nostalgic or utopian urge does clearly inform a work such as *The River*.[3]

In subject, color range, and technique, *The River* recalls another great nineteenth-century seascape painter, English artist J.M.W. Turner, whom Feininger much admired. Both masterfully used watercolor to render the effulgence of light and its atmospheric refractions, but Feininger exploited the medium less for naturalistic intensity than for its brilliant translucency. Fascinated by translucency in film as well, Feininger experimented with positive and negative photographic images, and in the last years of his life he painted his characteristic caricature figures on a series of slides—a peculiarly modern version of stained glass.[4] By using translucency to dissolve the solidity of objects, he could express the unity of all things that was so important in his introspective, idealist world. This may have prompted the artist to quote an old French tag on one of his watercolors: "La peinture à l'huile, c'est plus difficile; la peinture à l'eau, c'est peut-être plus beau."[5]   *PN*

1. Hans Hess, *Lyonel Feininger* (New York: Harry N. Abrams, 1961), p. 66.

2. See ibid., p. 3.

3. Feininger wrote to his wife: "How apt is the ocean, spread out in front of one with the immeasurably bright sky above, to conjure thoughts from one's hidden inner depths" (June 4, 1932, Lyonel Feininger Archive BR1963.70F, Busch-Reisinger Museum, Harvard University Art Museums).

4. These unpublished slides and several of the photographs are now in the collection of the Lyonel Feininger Archive, Busch-Reisinger Museum, Harvard University Art Museums.

5. Feininger, in Sara Campbell, ed., *The Blue Four: Galka Scheyer Collection* (Pasadena, Calif.: Norton Simon Museum of Art, 1976), p. 19. "Painting in oil is the most difficult; painting with watercolor is perhaps the most beautiful."

Provenance
(Buchholz Gallery, New York); museum purchase, 1942

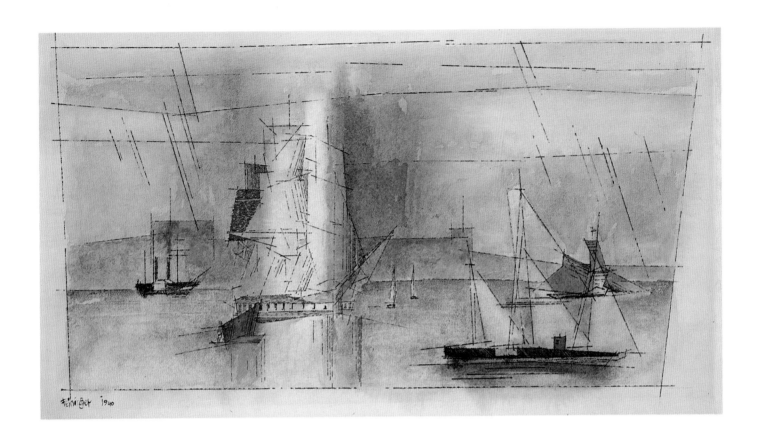

99

Walter Appleton Clark (1876–1906)
King He Is, of Thee Begot, Queen both Fair and Good!, 1899

Originally from Worcester, Walter Appleton Clark studied briefly at Worcester Polytechnic Institute before discovering that his talents were artistic rather than scientific. His desire to pursue art as a career took Clark to the Art Students League in New York City. He was only twenty-one years old when Robert Chapman, art editor for *Scribner's Magazine*, saw a few of his drawings at the League and asked to publish his work. By 1899 Clark was one of *Scribner's* leading illustrators.

The Christmas issue of *Scribner's* for 1899 contains some of Clark's finest work. He was teamed with poet Harrison S. Morris to illustrate Morris's poem ''The Three Kings,'' which ran six full pages and featured a double-page illustration, as well as a heading and a tailpiece.[1] For the double-page spread Clark drew *King He Is . . . ,* whose subject is the adoration of Mary by the three wise men and the shepherds. The separation between the two halves is the allowance for the magazine's gutter.

The extensive use of gouache in the illustration was unusual for Clark, who worked chiefly in wash and ink for black and white illustrations. Because of the high cost and the unpredictable quality of color reproductions, *Scribner's* limited its use of color to special illustrations. As an experienced illustrator, Clark was aware that bright colors in the original drawing often translated into muddy tones in the reproduction, and soft colors could be lost next to the heavy outlines of the key plate.

He carefully planned this drawing so that the color would work to best advantage. Addressing the limitations of the printing process as well as the difference a good printer could make, Clark made marginal notes to the printer: ''Keep all heavy outlines warm (red and yellow) underneath. Keep the whole thing *very dark* and rich with too little color rather than too much. Try most to keep the values and the drawing.''

The effect Clark desired was to contrast the shadowy, ponderous figures of the worshipers with the brightness of Mary, whose pious expression is highlighted by her halo. Never does the drawing give way to murkiness, thanks to Clark's attention to detail and to subtle color accents. The use of light and shade in setting a mood shows the influence of the artist Clark admired most, James McNeill Whistler. The silhouetting of the massive figures against a plain, shallow background was influenced by the famous French muralist Pierre Puvis de Chavannes. The strong contours of the figures, which are composed of broad, generalized forms with only minimal shading, underscore their supplicative gestures and attitude of adoration.

Clark's drawings are generally characterized by a meticulous accuracy. He was known to rummage through old shops, buying props and costumes, and to wander through the streets of New York, looking for the right face to sketch for a character in a story. Clark had both a sense of the decorative possibilities in his compositions and a firm command of draftsmanship. In an era when many young illustrators were imitating the saucy sweet faces of the ''Gibson Girls'' drawn by Charles Dana

Gibson, Clark chose to portray more profound subjects. After 1902 he no longer worked exclusively for *Scribner's* but also published drawings in both *Harper's* and *Collier's*; his name also appeared on the title pages of books by then-noted authors such as Richard Harding Davis, Margaret Deland, and Guy Wetmore Carryl. Unfortunately, Clark did not live long enough to enjoy his celebrity status. In 1906, after suffering from the flu, he was stricken with appendicitis. Weakened by the first illness, he did not survive surgery.[2]   *JLL*

1. The *Scribner's* files record Clark's payment as $160 for each drawing, plus $100 for the heading and $80 for the tailpiece—a total of $500. However, Scribner and Sons retained ownership of the original artwork. This policy changed in 1903, when the art dealer Frederick Keppel and Company offered Clark an exhibition. *Scribner's* returned this watercolor and several others to the artist for the purpose of exhibiting and selling them. This particular agreement was instrumental in changing the policies regarding ownership of originals both with *Scribner's* and with other leading publishers at the turn of the century. The illustration files of Charles Scribner and Sons are now part of the archives of the Brandywine River Museum in Chadds Ford, Pennsylvania.

2. His friend and fellow illustrator John Wolcott Adams helped Clark's wife settle the estate. The Worcester Art Museum purchased this drawing at that time.

Provenance
Charles Scribner and Sons, 1899–1903; Walter Appleton Clark, 1903–6; Mrs. Walter Appleton Clark, 1906–7; museum purchase, 1907

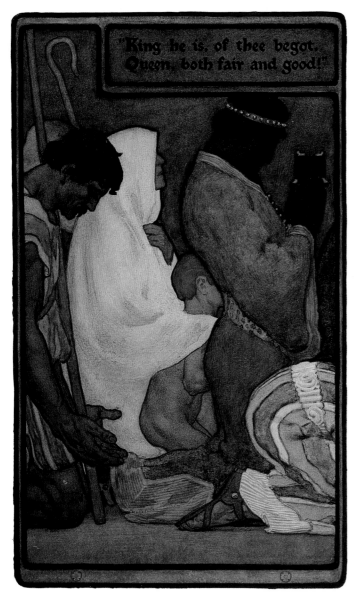

"King he is, of thee begot,
Queen, both fair and good!"

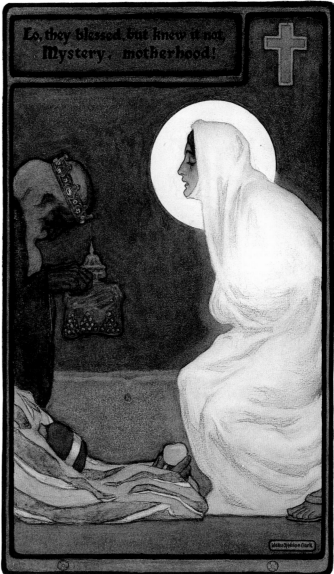

Lo, they blessed, but knew it not,
Mystery, motherhood!

163

100
Earl Horter (1881–1940)
Storage Tanks, **1931**

Earl Horter was an eclectic artist who experimented with the styles of numerous avant-garde European and American painters in the 1920s and 1930s.[1] His thorough knowledge of current artistic trends was acquired through his activities as a collector. Financial success working as a commercial illustrator and art director had enabled him to amass a fine collection of modern painting, including works by Henri Matisse, Pablo Picasso, Georges Braque, and Charles Sheeler, a fellow Philadelphian.

As early as the 1910s, while under the influence of Joseph Pennell, Horter had produced many etchings of New York City, including a series for the Consolidated Edison Company. These early architectural images were dark, romantic evocations of the mystery and power of the modern city, but by 1931 Horter's work revealed the influence of Sheeler's cool, rational appreciation of the pristine beauty of machines and buildings and his precise, hard-edged style. He and Sheeler were evidently friends at the time, perhaps drawn together by similar backgrounds and interests. Both had worked for the Philadelphia advertising firm of N. W. Ayer.[2] More important, each man had a fascination with architectural subjects.

The specific location of Horter's *Storage Tanks* is unknown, although the brick house at the lower left suggests that it may be near the port of Philadelphia.[3] Sheeler's photographs, drawings, and paintings of the Ford Motor Company plant at River Rouge, Michigan, may have also inspired Horter. This composition is much like that of Sheeler's 1931 drawing *Ballet Méchanique* (plate 100a), which was based on photographs of the Ford plant. Horter, like Sheeler, created abstract rhythms by cropping and isolating the central image in an almost photographic fashion, creating the impression that the viewer is in the midst of a vast industrial complex. In both works there is a visual tension between the delicate tracery of catwalks and ladders and the massive tanks and pipes, while the diagonal thrusts of each composition imbue the

architecture with a vital sense of energy and power.

Horter began his career as a printmaker and did not paint in watercolor or oil until the 1920s, when urged to do so by Arthur B. Carles, a fellow artist and close friend.[4] In painting *Storage Tanks*, Horter drew upon his background as a graphic artist and prepared an elaborate, precise pencil drawing. Where the washes of color are thin, much of this underdrawing is readily visible. Many long, straight pencil lines, like those defining the girders and braces around the four large tanks, suggest the artist's use of a ruler or drafting tools. Horter was a careful and deliberate worker, and a grid of lines extending beyond the visible portion of the image shows that he squared his composition before beginning to apply color.

In much the same way that Horter simplified the forms of his tanks and structures, so did he apply paint and color in a broad manner to suggest texture and light, especially the effects of brilliant sunlight on the hard surfaces of the tanks. He broadly brushed on washes to indicate smooth metallic surfaces. Moving from left to right, Horter applied the pigment more opaquely. Where the light gleams brightest, he let the paper—which has since yellowed slightly—show through. As the shadows darken, he built up the gray washes until they became quite thick and darker in value. Horter left certain passages unpainted—for example, where the girder bisects the middle gray tank—which suggests that he was grappling with the effect of light on the rounded tank. Although the work is signed, several other unpainted areas further the impression that Horter left the watercolor unfinished when similar problems appeared.

Storage Tanks may be incomplete, but it reveals the strong impact of Sheeler's architectonic vision. Like many other Americans in the 1930s, Horter saw the inherent abstract beauty of industrial subjects with a new appreciation because Sheeler's sanitized and intellectualized paintings stripped away the grime. For a

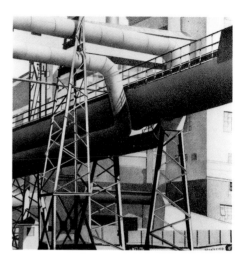

100a
Charles Sheeler (1883–1965)
Ballet Méchanique, 1931
Conte crayon
10¼ × 10 in. (26 × 25.4 cm.)
Memorial Art Gallery, University of Rochester;
Gift of Peter Iselin and his sister, Emilie I. Wiggin

brief time Horter seems to have shared Sheeler's idealizing approach to the modern scene. *WWS*

1. Little attention has been paid to the career of this inventive artist since his death in 1940. For the most authoritative, although brief, account, see Anne d'Harnoncourt, "Earl Horter," in *Philadelphia: Three Centuries of American Art* (Philadelphia: Philadelphia Museum of Art, 1976), p. 523.

2. Exact dates in the Horter chronology are difficult to ascertain. He seems to have worked for N. W. Ayer by the early 1920s, eventually becoming the art director, according to some accounts. Extensive use of photography eventually pushed illustrators like Horter out of advertising. It is unclear whether Horter and Sheeler were employed there at the same time.

3. According to David Shayt of the Smithsonian Institution's National Museum of American History, these structures are almost certainly silos used to store dry materials, most likely concrete or grain, and they could have been found in most American cities in the early twentieth century.

4. Carles was an especially close friend, whose name appears on a handwritten list of the pallbearers at Horter's funeral. That list, along with photographs of Carles, can be found in the Horter Papers in the library of the Philadelphia Museum of Art.

Provenance
Mrs. Earl Horter; David Medoff, c. 1940; gift of David and Selma Medoff, 1982

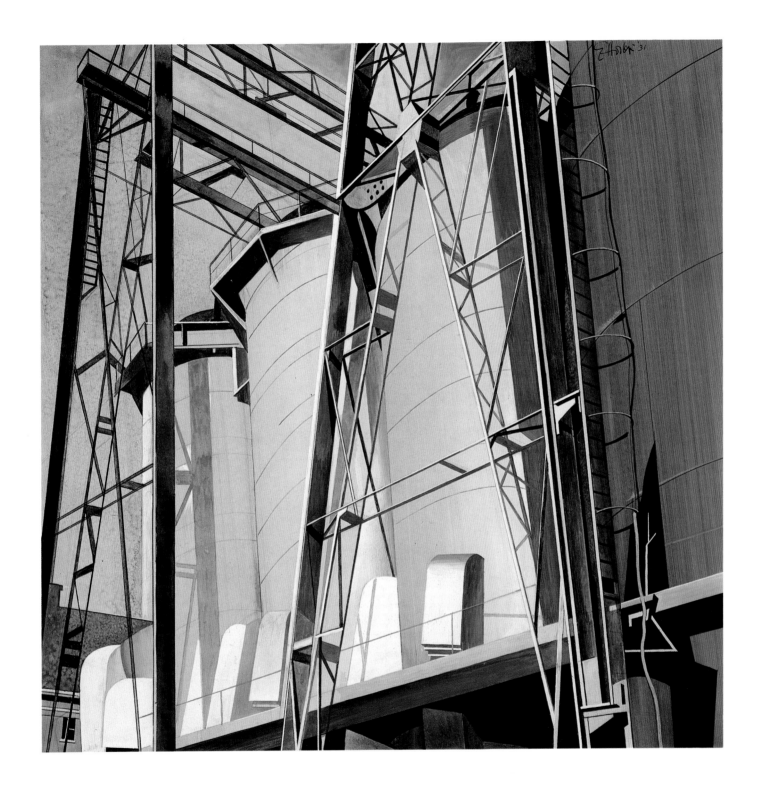

101
Rockwell Kent (1882–1971)
Cottage in a Landscape, probably 1926

Robust and opinionated, Rockwell Kent was not only a painter, printmaker, book designer, and illustrator but also an explorer, writer, sailor, and political activist. Influenced by the example of his teacher Robert Henri—for whom creativity and life were inextricably linked—Kent acknowledged that his own art, writing, and even socialist philosophy were shaped by an attraction to a vigorous lifestyle and the appeal of hard work. From the 1910s, when he worked on Monhegan Island off the Maine coast as a fisherman, well driller, and carpenter, Kent was drawn to distant, rugged places, where he seemed to thrive on the physical challenges of living close to the land, away from the comforts and pressures of urban society. His adventures in Alaska (1918–19), Tierra del Fuego (1922), and Greenland (1928, 1931, and 1934–35) were recounted in three popular books, and these trips provided inspiration for a large portion of his best-known paintings and prints.[1] Kent worked in watercolor throughout much of his career, but he seems to have used the medium more frequently for subjects from his trips to Greenland and Ireland.

Cottage in a Landscape was a product of one of Kent's less-documented trips, a five-month visit he made with his second wife, Frances, between late April and early October 1926 to the remote village of Glenlough in County Donegal on the isolated northwest coast of Ireland.[2] In June he wrote to his good friend Carl Zigrosser: "We're settled at last—in one of the most inaccessible spots in Ireland—ten miles over the boggy mountainside afoot, after twenty miles on increasingly bad road from the nearest railway. You'd love it, Carl, for

you'd not mind the difficulties of the journey for the grandeur of coastal scenery at last so near at hand. . . . It is so entirely, serenely, untamedly beautiful!"[3] There they converted an abandoned cottage, long used as a cow shed, into a modest dwelling and tiny studio. The Kents became warm friends with several farming families who lived in "white-walled, thatch-roofed houses on a little cove" overlooking the ocean, the same type of rustic, windowless structure depicted in this watercolor.[4]

Kent found Glenlough a sanctuary conducive to painting, and he produced a significant group of oils, watercolors, and drawings, many of which were seen in two successful exhibitions in New York the following spring at the Wildenstein and Weyhe galleries. *Cottage in a Landscape* is one of five watercolors of Irish subjects that the Worcester Art Museum purchased from E. Weyhe following the exhibition. Although Kent dated all five 1927, they were certainly inspired by, if not painted during, his months in Glenlough.[5]

This work reflects the formal ordering of Kent's distinctive landscape aesthetic, which emerged in his simplified Alaskan views and culminated in stark, monumental panoramas of Greenland. Drawn to the inherent geometry of Glenlough's primitive landscape, sculpted by fields and angular hills, Kent here conveyed his attraction to the austere terrain though generalized forms and masses, strong contrasts of light and shadow, and a striking, almost discordant, palette: orange and green fields and mountains boldly articulated by magenta shadows are silhouetted against a violet sky. The obvious omission of human activity and the bird's-eye vantage point from which we glance across the landscape into an infinite distance enhance the sense of isolation that appealed to the artist.

Kent constructed the composition from a faint graphite sketch. Working on moistened paper, he outlined the drawing in watercolor and filled in the contours with

washes of translucent color. His confident, straightforward technique suits the simple strength of his design. The result evokes both nature's stark quiescence and the romantic solitude of this faraway place. These qualities link Kent's work to the northern European Romantic landscape tradition, epitomized by the nineteenth-century German master Caspar David Friedrich, and to the winter Maine scenes that Winslow Homer painted in his final years.   *SES*

1. Kent documented his travels in *Wilderness: A Journal of Quiet Adventure in Alaska* (New York: G. P. Putnam's Sons, 1920); *Voyaging: Southward from the Strait of Magellan* (New York: G. P. Putnam's Sons, 1924); *N by E* (New York: Random House, 1930).

2. The Kents left for Ireland in late April, although their date of arrival is not clear. The Kent Papers in the Archives of American Art, Smithsonian Institution, Washington, D.C., and his correspondence in the Carl Zigrosser Papers, Van Pelt Library, University of Pennsylvania, were useful in documenting Kent's Irish trip.

3. Kent to Zigrosser, June 17, 1926, Carl Zigrosser Papers.

4. Kent's most in-depth description of his Irish trip appears in *It's Me O Lord: The Autobiography of Rockwell Kent* (New York: Dodd, Mead, 1955), pp. 415–22.

5. The exact dates for all five of Worcester's watercolors remain undetermined. Kent dated his oils precisely, often dating a painting a second time when he returned to it after some years. Many of his oils of Alaska and Greenland were painted after his trips from drawings he had made on location. It is not clear if Kent executed the Worcester watercolors in 1927, from drawings made the year before, or whether he misdated them about the time of the exhibition at E. Weyhe.

Provenance
The artist; (E. Weyhe, New York, 1927); museum purchase, 1927

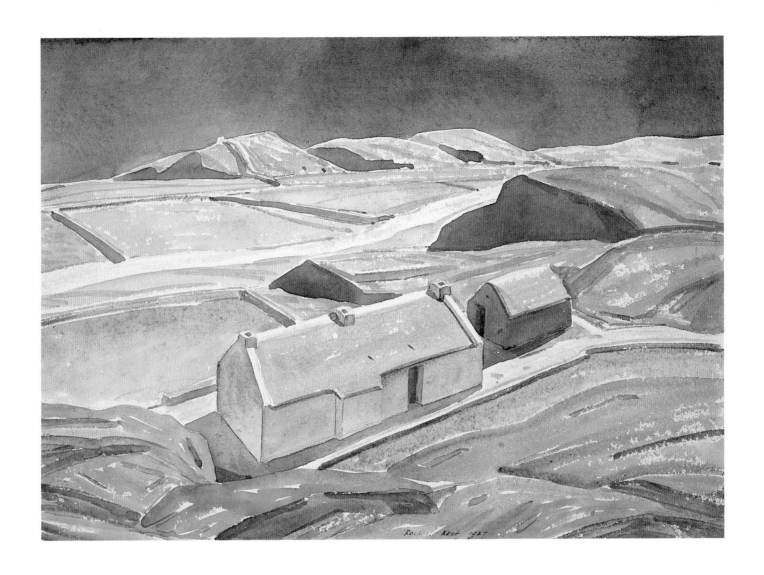

102
Rockwell Kent (1882–1971)
Woman Reaping, probably 1926

Whenever Kent made sojourns to faraway places, he became well acquainted with the local working people. In Ireland he and his wife, Frances, particularly enjoyed the company of Denis McGinley and Dan Ward and their families, with whom they drank homemade "poteen" and sang old Irish songs or danced to fiddle music.[1] Kent's visit to Ireland was extremely happy, and it was with mixed feelings that he left his Irish friends in early October 1926 to rejoin Frances, who had already returned to New York to find an apartment.

Woman Reaping depicts an activity the artist probably observed near the end of his stay in Glenlough: an Irish peasant woman—possibly Annie McGinley, who had posed for Kent in other pictures—reaping grain, her head covered with a kerchief in local fashion.[2] Although the pose of this faceless woman is decidedly contrived, it also expresses the strong physical appeal that common labor held for the artist. A farmer himself, Kent was "impressed by the strength and potential power of people who did work with their hands."[3] His empathy and respect for the working classes clearly reflected his socialist philosophy, which emerged more publicly in the years following his trip to Ireland.

Stylistically, the solitary and mysterious laborer in *Woman Reaping* relates to many of the monumental figural subjects that Kent executed in the 1920s and 1930s in wood engraving, a medium he took up in earnest following his Alaskan trip in 1918–19. The dramatic, gestural pose of the single figure set against a landscape, the strong linear design, and the emphasis on crisp contour all find parallels in Kent's engraved illustrations and separately published prints. These characteristics also recall the stylization of the Art Deco period. The repetition of curves and arcs throughout the watercolor—the blade of the sickle, the bow of the grain, the arch of the woman's back—and the distinct contrast of sunlight and shadow imply a sense of movement in an otherwise frozen composition. The harsh palette of intense orange-brown, yellow, and maroon enhances the feeling of exertion as the woman harvests the crop.

Worcester was the first museum to acquire a representative group of Kent's watercolors, according to Carl Zigrosser, director of Weyhe Gallery.[4] The artist's works in this medium still had not received much attention, despite their evocative strength. Museum director George W. Eggers, who acquired the watercolors, had planned an exhibition of Kent's work for the fall of 1927. However, Kent's outrage at the execution of Nicola Sacco and Bartolomeo Vanzetti in Massachusetts on August 23, 1927, led him to cancel the show. "I am compelled to take this action by my abhorrence of such murder," Kent explained, "and my conclusion that the citizens of the State must be held responsible for it."[5]
SES

1. See Rockwell Kent, *It's Me O Lord: The Autobiography of Rockwell Kent* (New York: Dodd, Mead, 1955), p. 420.

2. The date of this watercolor, like the other four in the museum's collection, is probably 1926.

3. Kent, in Merle Armitage, *Rockwell Kent* (New York: Alfred A. Knopf, 1932), p. 28.

4. Zigrosser to George W. Eggers, March 25, 1927, Worcester Art Museum Files.

5. Kent to Mrs. Walter H. Siple (curator of decorative arts), August 23, 1927, Worcester Art Museum files.

Provenance
The artist; (E. Weyhe, New York, 1927); museum purchase, 1927

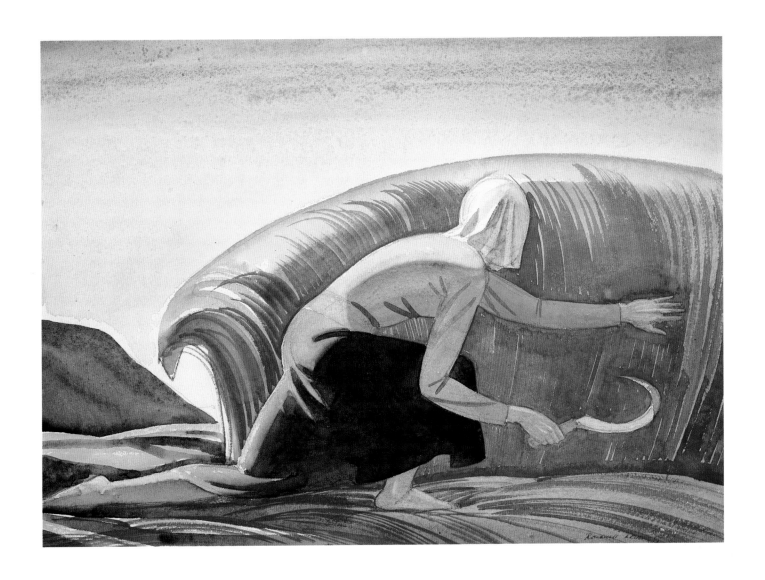

103
Edward Hopper (1882–1967)
Yawl Riding a Swell, 1935

Edward Hopper, one of America's leading twentieth-century realists, received his first recognition as a painter for his watercolors. While he continued to work sporadically in this medium until the end of his life, the main body of his work in it dates from the 1920s and 1930s. Hopper created watercolors as independent works of art, not as studies, and only in a few rare cases did he transform a watercolor composition into an oil painting.

Yawl Riding a Swell was painted on Cape Cod, where Hopper and his wife had summered since 1930. Nautical themes recur in the artist's oeuvre, from his boyhood sketches to his masterful *The Martha McKean of Wellfleet* (1944; Thyssen-Bornemisza Collection), his final canvas of a sailing subject. At that time Hopper was sixty-two and his wife, Jo, who feared the sea, was increasingly concerned about his sailing, even in someone else's boat, claiming "He's too good a man to lose that way."[1] This perhaps explains Hopper's abandonment of a theme that had interested him since his early days in Nyack, New York, a Hudson River town with a thriving shipyard that built racing yachts. As a child, Hopper had built his own boat and later considered a career as a naval architect.

Hopper always painted his watercolors on location, recording his subjects—architecture and landscape for the most part—as he observed them. He usually sketched the composition lightly in pencil and then painted over it in watercolor, improvising as he proceeded. His technique was simple and straightforward. For example, in *Yawl Riding a Swell* he reserved the white of the paper for the sails and wisps of clouds, rather than delineating them with an opaque application of chinese white. Similarly, he sought to convey form primarily through the drama of light, and most of his watercolors are, like this example, painted in sunlight; he had little interest in the rendering of textures. Neither was he naturally adept at depicting movement; rather, he was drawn to subjects where stillness predominated. When he did attempt to suggest motion, the result was often a sense of frozen action, and this crisp, brittle quality is readily apparent in *Yawl Riding a Swell,* in which the waves seem artificially calm and solid, only hinting at the rolling motion of the sea.

In his formative period of the 1910s, while under the influence of James McNeill Whistler, Hopper had briefly experimented with the limited, muted palette typical of tonalism. Here the entire composition is economically conveyed in azure contrasted against the white of the paper and accented by the yellow deck and black-green hull. The boldness and simplicity of the palette enhance the sculptural quality of both the yawl and the swelling sea.

Through his dealer, Frank Rehn, Hopper sent this newly completed watercolor to represent him in Worcester's second biennial exhibition, *American Painting of Today.*[2] The museum awarded Hopper a purchase prize for the watercolor—a bright note for the painter, who, struggling to earn his living in the midst of the Great Depression, was forced to live on his savings.   *GL*

1. Jo Hopper, quoted by the late John Clancy (Hopper's dealer at the Frank K. M. Rehn Gallery, New York), interview with the author, 1977.

2. The exhibition extended from November 2 to December 15, 1935.

Provenance
The artist; (Frank K. M. Rehn, New York, 1935); museum purchase, 1935

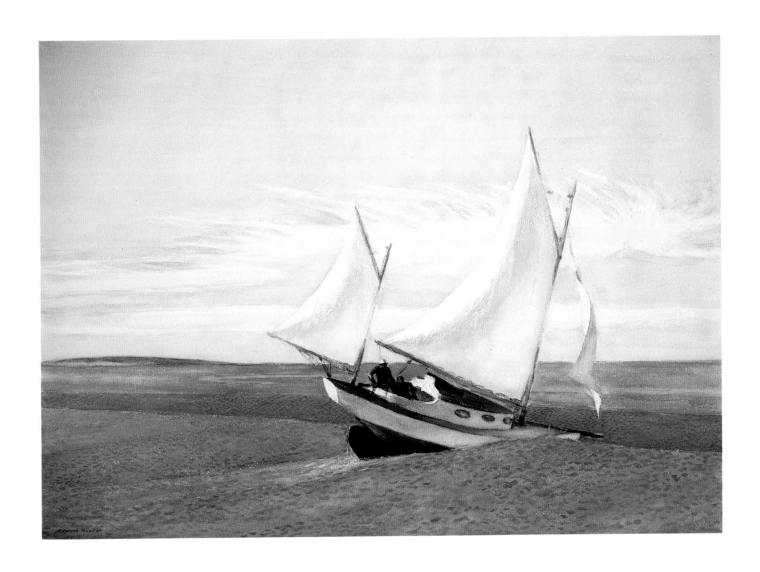

104
Edward Hopper (1882–1967)
Cobb House, **1942**

In September 1942, Hopper painted the back end of this weathered house, located not far from his own home in South Truro on Cape Cod. He had first painted the Cobb family home and farm buildings during his first summer on the Cape in 1930. In fact, before the Hoppers built their own home in 1934, they had rented a small cottage from Burly Cobb. Thus the family's home, farm, and surrounding land were especially familiar to the artist.

By 1942 Hopper had been painting on the Cape for thirteen consecutive summers. He had become bored with his immediate surroundings in isolated Truro, with its exotic Cape Cod beauty, and preferred to drive to such communities as Eastham, where he found the more traditional, small-town architecture more to his liking. He frequently painted subjects while sitting in his automobile. But the summer of 1942 brought a wartime rationing of tires, and Hopper could not afford to risk wearing out the only set that could transport him and his wife back to New York at the end of the season. Confined to subjects closer to home, he produced few watercolors at this time. Hopper's work in watercolor after the 1920s is generally larger in format, less spontaneous in execution, and painted on heavier paper, which allowed for more layers of transparent glazes, applied in a manner more like oil painting.

The simple composition of *Cobb House,* with its three distinctive horizontal registers—foreground grass, building and hillside, sky—is characteristic of Hopper. A devoted realist, he intended to record only his direct observations of nature, forgoing arbitrary departures from reality in either style or palette. From his wife's diary entries of September 5 and 7, 1942, we know that Hopper worked on this watercolor for several days.[1] He was eager to be out painting by four o'clock in the afternoon, presumably to catch just the right angle of the sun and the long shadows cast late in the day. The green kitchen door, all in shadow, the bleached-out shutters, and the worn gray shingles are evocative elements, so charac-teristic of Cape Cod houses. The soft tones of the house contrast with the blue sky marbled with white clouds and the rich green lawn partially darkened by shadow. The approach of autumn is evident in the foreground, where the timothy grass is already beginning to turn the golden brown that marks the end of the summer season on Cape Cod. Hopper particularly liked staying on after August, even until the end of October, when the tourists had left and tranquility returned.

Throughout his career, for both his oils and watercolors, Hopper was drawn to manmade rather than natural subjects. For his watercolors he also preferred architectural subjects to human figures, a preference that recalled the days when he had been forced to earn a living as a commercial illustrator. "I was always interested in architecture, but the editors wanted people waving their arms," he recalled.[2] "Maybe I am not very human. What I wanted to do was to paint sunlight on the side of a house."[3]

GL

1. Jo Hopper listed this watercolor as *Cobb House* in her record book of her husband's work.

2. Hopper, in Archer Winsten, "Wake of the News: Washington Square Boasts Strangers Worth Talking To," *New York Post,* November 26, 1935.

3. Hopper, in Lloyd Goodrich, *Edward Hopper* (New York: Harry N. Abrams, 1971), p. 31.

Provenance
(Frank K. M. Rehn Gallery, New York); gift of Stephen C. Clarke, 1943

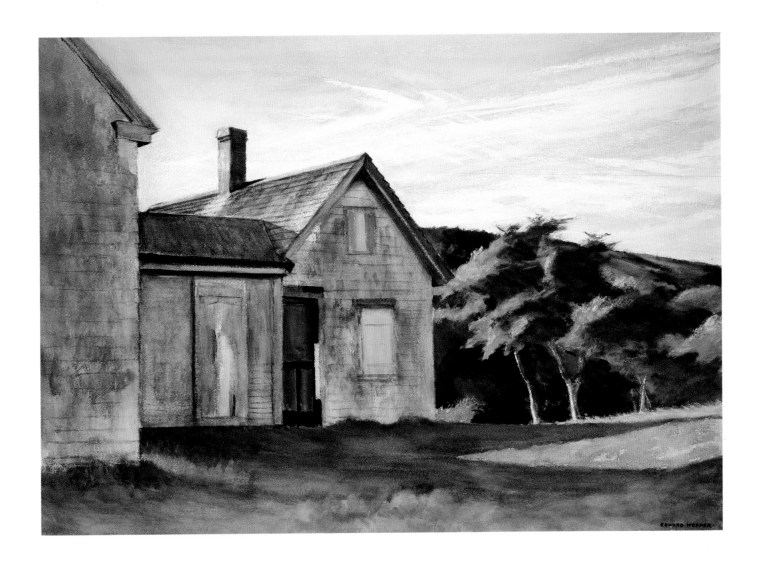

173

105
Charles Sheeler (1883-1965)
City Interior No. 2, 1935

Early in 1935 Charles Sheeler traveled to Detroit with his dealer, Edith Halpert, to see an exhibition of his paintings and works by Charles Burchfield at the Detroit Society of Arts and Crafts. It was his first visit to Michigan since 1928, when, on commission from Edsel Ford, he spent six weeks at River Rouge photographing the Ford Motor Company plant. The photographs were reproduced in various Ford publications and advertisements and, when exhibited as works of art, cemented Sheeler's reputation as one of the preeminent photographers in America. They also served as the basis for several drawings and oils that Sheeler produced over the next few years. Some of these were included in his first solo show at the Downtown Gallery in 1931, and they were so well received that Sheeler, up until then only moderately successful as a painter, was established as the premier artistic spokesman for the new industrial age.[1] Subsequently, however, he turned away from industrial imagery and concentrated instead on such domestic themes as rural interiors and Shaker buildings, subjects that celebrated the simplicity and clarity of indigenous American design.

Sheeler's 1935 visit to Detroit seems to have rekindled his interest in industrial subjects. On his return to his studio, he produced a group of modest-sized temperas that included this view of a blast furnace at the heart of the Ford plant. The following year he completed a large oil of the same subject: *City Interior* (plate 105a). While the tempera's composition forms the core of the larger work, it is so finished and satisfying a painting that it can in no way be considered merely a study.[2] Together the two paintings of the blast furnace constituted Sheeler's most complex and rigorous work to date.

City Interior No. 2 shows the west side of the blast furnace at River Rouge. At

the right of the composition is the cast house, where the by-product slag is separated from molten steel and channeled through a pipe, shown at center right, into waiting slag buggies. Another group of buggies is being taken away to the slag yard to be emptied. At left is the wall of the sintering (or heating) plant; overtop is the gas main for the blast furnace.[3]

This painting incorporates details recorded in several of the thirty-two photographs Sheeler submitted for the Ford commission.[4] He took many more photographs than the ones he presented to Ford, but those working shots, including any that might have captured the entire scene pictured in *City Interior No. 2,* do not survive. Ironically, the photographs Sheeler made of this area of the plant show no figures; he added the two tiny, faceless figures to the tempera to dramatize the overwhelming scale of the River Rouge complex.

City Interior No. 2 is exceptional in Sheeler's work of this period, in both complexity of design and bold penetration of space and in Sheeler's brilliant control over the medium. Here he used tempera as though it were oil, applying the pigment in thick strokes over his graphite underdrawing, creating an opaque, matte surface in which his brushwork is barely visible. Only occasionally did he thin down his color to produce a translucent passage, as in tiny sections of the sky at upper left; more frequently—as in the floor of the rail yard— he brushed one tone over another to produce a more lively texture. Certain edges were then reinforced by pencil to achieve crisp contours and, in the case of the rail tracks, to produce an effect both dramatic and witty: the metallic tone gives greater prominence to the metallic form and emphasizes the lines plunging into deep space.

Sheeler's technique, with its complex brushwork and intricately varied surface textures, demands intimate inspection; yet it is under just such inspection that the rational, legible aspect of the image disin-

tegrates and the picture becomes abstract— a flat, fascinating patterned surface of alternating darks and lights and rhythmically arrayed geometric shapes. At the same time, this modest-sized work contains a grand, dramatic view, which for all its realistic detail seems somehow artificial. The blast furnace had been in operation some ten years when Sheeler first visited it, yet in neither painted version is there the least sign of rust or decay, debris or disorder: it is "the industry of our dreams," in the words of a contemporary admirer.[5] Similarly, Sheeler's elegant palette is improbable for an industrial scene: pale blue, lavender, grayed blues and white, with the creamy color of the heavy watercolor paper playing an active role. Far more than in the larger *City Interior,* in this picture the tension between the hurtling deep space and the compelling abstract surface pattern, between the vividness of the scene and its unsettling artificiality, creates an image that is one of Sheeler's most dynamic.   *CT*

1. See Henry McBride, "Paintings by Charles Sheeler. Landscapes and Still Life That Are Unquestionably of the Machine Age," *New York Sun,* November 21, 1931.

2. Sheeler painted the present composition (which a former owner designated as "No. 2" to distinguish it from the larger work) in 1935, probably shortly after his return from Michigan.

3. See Mary Jane Jacob and Linda Downs, *The Rouge: The Image of Industry in the Art of Charles Sheeler and Diego Rivera* (Detroit: Detroit Institute of Arts, 1978), p. 40.

4. See especially *Row of Slag Buggies under the Blast Furnace* (1927; Ford Archives, Henry Ford Museum, Dearborn, Michigan).

5. Winslow Ames, "A Portrait of American Industry," *Worcester Art Museum Annual* 2 (1936–37): 97.

Provenance
Raphael Soyer, New York; (The New Gallery, New York); William H. Lane, Leominster, Mass., 1955; gift of William H. and Saundra B. Lane, 1977

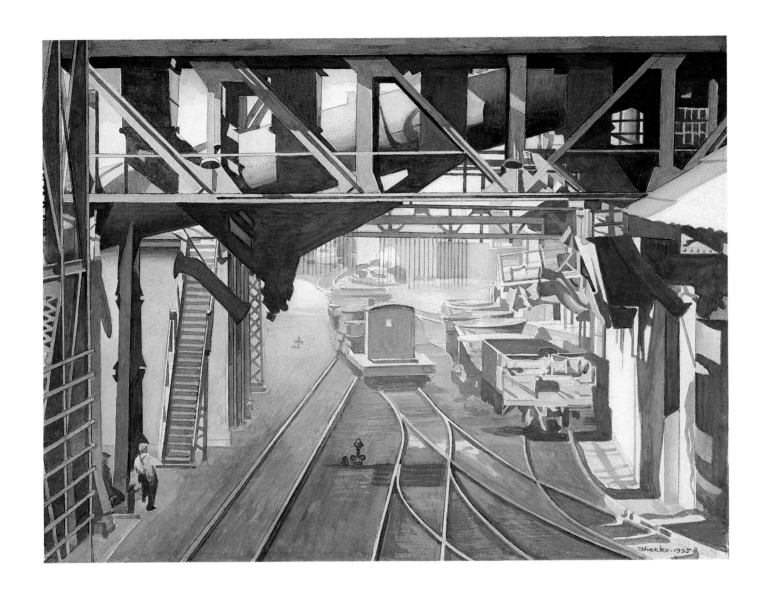

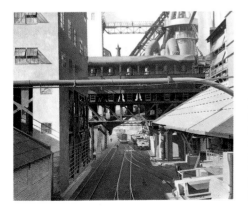

105a
Charles Sheeler
City Interior, 1936
Aqueous adhesive and oil on composition board
22⅛ × 26⅞ in. (56.2 × 68.4 cm.)
Worcester Art Museum; Bequest of Elizabeth M.
Sawyer in memory of Jonathan and Elizabeth
M. Sawyer

106
Mark Tobey (1890–1976)
The Cycle of the Prophet, 1945

The Cycle of the Prophet belongs to Mark Tobey's overtly religious work, most of which he executed during the 1940s. Less known than the artist's calligraphic abstractions of the 1950s and 1960s, these paintings clearly express the religious content that, in fact, underlies all the artist's work. Although he is celebrated mostly as a technical innovator—creator of "white writing" and the "all-over" painting style associated subsequently with Jackson Pollock—Tobey approached painting not as abstraction but as a vehicle for expressing a deeply felt and carefully pondered philosophy. He was born in Wisconsin to a family of devout Congregationalists and later converted to the Baha'i World Faith, to which he was introduced in New York in 1918. While Christianity was a source for Tobey's themes, Baha'i gave him a more complex framework for treating those themes. As Tobey wrote in a letter to a friend in 1963, "There is no official Baha'i art, as this is not a new religion, but religion renewed."[1] Thus the Bible is included among the Baha'i books of revelation as well as the Koran. The Bible was naturally one of the religious texts with which Tobey was most familiar, and most of his religious imagery is biblical.

Many of Tobey's religious paintings of the 1940s, including *The Cycle of the Prophet*, consist of a series of figural scenes suggesting a narrative. The composition is frequently divided into registers, as here, in which individual scenes are framed by an architectural setting, often an arch or window. In *The Cycle of the Prophet* smaller scenes are arranged around a central one, reflecting the Baha'i view that all the religions of the world are manifestations of one spirit and are all embraced by the Baha'i World Faith.[2]

The writings of Baha'u'llah, the founder of the Baha'i faith, include an entry on the "prophetic cycle," in which he affirms the manifestation of God in prophets of earlier times but states that "the Prophetic Cycle has verily ended. The eternal truth is now come."[3] Tobey's painting deals largely with the life of one of the cycle's "prophets," specifically Christ. Although some of the scenes in it remain obscure, others can be securely identified. In the lower right corner, just above Tobey's signature, is the Annunciation, with the angel Gabriel bowing to the Virgin, who is seated at the left under an arch, in keeping with medieval and Renaissance depictions of the scene. Between the two is a table or lectern with a dove hovering above. Directly over this scene, toward the upper right corner, is a kneeling figure, presumably the Virgin of the Nativity adoring the Christ child. To the immediate left is a chalice, below which may be a representation from the Old Testament of the sacrifice of Isaac, a prefiguration of the Crucifixion. To the far side of the enigmatic central group, two figures appear to represent the Entombment of Christ, one prone, the other leaning forward slightly, arms extended. Crowning the composition is a robed figure standing by a stool before a large painting or tablet. A torch illuminates the scene. The figure suggests Moses, but also, more fittingly, Baha'u'llah; it may also refer to the artist himself. For Tobey, all are revealers of the spirit.

Like Tobey's other Baha'i paintings of the mid-1940s, *The Cycle of the Prophet* looks as if it were rendered in chalk on stone.

Using gouache with a large amount of white in it, the artist created subtle tonality: beiges and grays predominate, but blue, green, and oxblood red also emerge. Some figures are merely suggested, like apparitions that have been conjured out of the past. *The Cycle of the Prophet* is thinly painted, so that the cardboard ground shows through, particularly in the more loosely worked upper portions. It is there that Tobey's calligraphic brush stroke is most evident; the loose gestural strokes have a rhythmic flow that unifies the elements of the composition. It was during the same period in which he produced this watercolor that Tobey became known in New York for the all-over linear style of his abstractions. *EER*

1. Tobey, quoting Shoghi Effendi, Guardian of the Baha'i Faith, in *Mark Tobey: Paintings from the Collection of Joyce and Arthur Dahl* (Palo Alto, Calif.: Stanford Art Gallery, Stanford University, 1967), p. 15.

2. The work was first exhibited as *The Cycle* at the Willard Gallery in 1947. The title was soon expanded to *The Cycle of the Prophet*, more clearly denoting its religious content as well as its Baha'i source.

3. *Baha'i World Faith: Selected Writings of Baha'u'llah and Abdu'l-Baha* (1956; Wilmette, Ill.: Baha'i Publishing Trust, 1971), p. 28.

Provenance
(Willard Gallery, New York, 1947); William H. Lane Foundation, 1955–76; gift of William H. and Sandra B. Lane, 1976

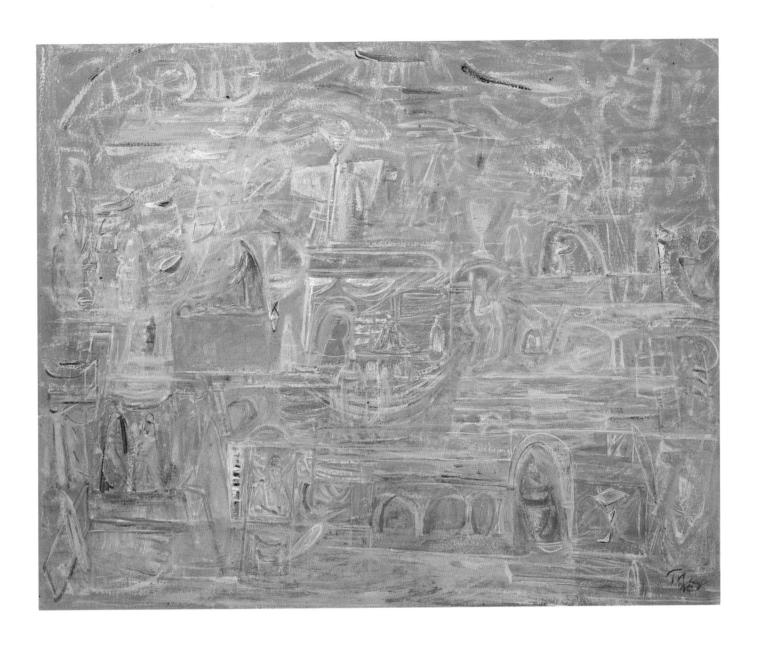

107
Charles Burchfield (1893–1967)
June Wind, 1937

Chiefly a self-taught artist, who worked almost exclusively in watercolor, Charles Burchfield was a solitary and visionary poet of nature. His intuitive understanding of the natural world, which developed during his adolescence, was shaped by such diverse influences as the great pantheists Ralph Waldo Emerson and Henry David Thoreau, the American naturalist John Burroughs, and Hindu and Buddhist philosophies in which natural phenomena are personified. Burchfield's response to nature was often mystical and always intensely personal. It was the small, commonplace creature—the dandelion, crow, songsparrow, or frog—that attracted him, rather than nature's grandiose or exotic aspects. His own letters and journals are replete with highly sensitive responses to his walks through woods or fields. Both his writings and pictures clearly reflect the essential role that nature played in sustaining him spiritually and artistically.

Burchfield's oeuvre falls into three distinct periods. His early mature watercolors from about 1915 to 1921 are small, decorative compositions, usually brightly colored and whimsical pictures of backyard gardens and neighboring fields near his home in Salem, Ohio. During the 1920s and 1930s, after he had moved to Buffalo, New York, his primary theme became the depressed villages, farms, and industries of New York, eastern Ohio, and Pennsylvania. His compositions became larger, his style more realistic, and his tone more sober. By 1943 nature resurfaced as his foremost

muse, and he produced vibrant, expressionist landscapes that recapture the fantasy of his early watercolors. These final watercolors remain among his best-known works.

June Wind dates from Burchfield's middle period, when he turned to nature for emotional respite from the gravity of manmade subjects. Painted not long after Burchfield had suffered a period of depression, during which he found it virtually impossible to paint, it depicts a sunlit field, probably outside Buffalo.[1]

The large scale of this composition, the simple solidity of its design, and the rich, if limited palette and straightforward style all recall the moody realism of Burchfield's concurrent architectural subjects. These elements also reflect his efforts to give his watercolors the legitimacy of oil paintings. The rich application of opaque pigments in *June Wind*—typical of his technique for much of the previous twenty years—suggests the consistency of oil rather than the translucency of an aqueous medium. In the colored bands of grass speckled with dandelions, the artist used a stiff-bristled brush to indicate the texture of individual blades. As in many of his landscapes from the 1930s, the sky is a palpable and evocative element: the billowing cumulus clouds against the bright blue sky provide an active, stylized backdrop for the swaying boughs of the slender trees. The repetitious rhythm of the arcs of these forms and the directional brushwork in the sky and grass convey the effects of the brisk summer breeze that was Burchfield's inspiration. The approach here is fairly conventional, with only slight reference to the strong patterns of his early work. Burchfield often attempted to pictorialize the sounds and sensations of nature. In his

later landscapes, in particular, he developed highly inventive notations to depict such nonvisual phenomena as the chirping of birds and locusts, the breath of the wind, or a clap of thunder.

In a letter of 1944 to his dealer Frank Rehn, Burchfield expressed concern over the turn toward a more objective realism that his work had taken:

> To me the 1920–1940 period (roughly speaking) has been a digression, a necessary one but not truly in the main stream that I feel I am destined to travel. . . . I was searching for an appreciation of form and solidity, and a painting quality the 1917 things lacked. Now it seems to me, I am in danger of painting too realistically, and must try to recapture the first imaginative and romantic outlook.[2]

Although romantic in its evocation of a windswept, sun-dappled day, *June Wind* reflects the culmination of Burchfield's more objective response to the landscape not long before he embarked on a highly personal and fanciful exploration of nature in his final years.   *SES*

1. This depression occurred in April and May 1937, and he felt a complete aversion to painting. He had first experienced such bouts in about 1930, and they continued throughout his career. See John I. H. Baur, *The Inlander: Life and Work of Charles Burchfield, 1893–1967* (East Brunswick, N.J.: Associated University Presses; London: Cornwall Books, 1982), p. 151.

2. Burchfield to Rehn, September 21, 1944, in Baur, *The Inlander*, p. 196.

Provenance
(Frank K. M. Rehn Gallery, New York, until c. 1944); Arthur Bradley Campbell; (Parke-Bernet Galleries, New York, Campbell Collection sale, October 27, 1954); gift from the Chapin and Mary Alexander Riley Collection, 1986

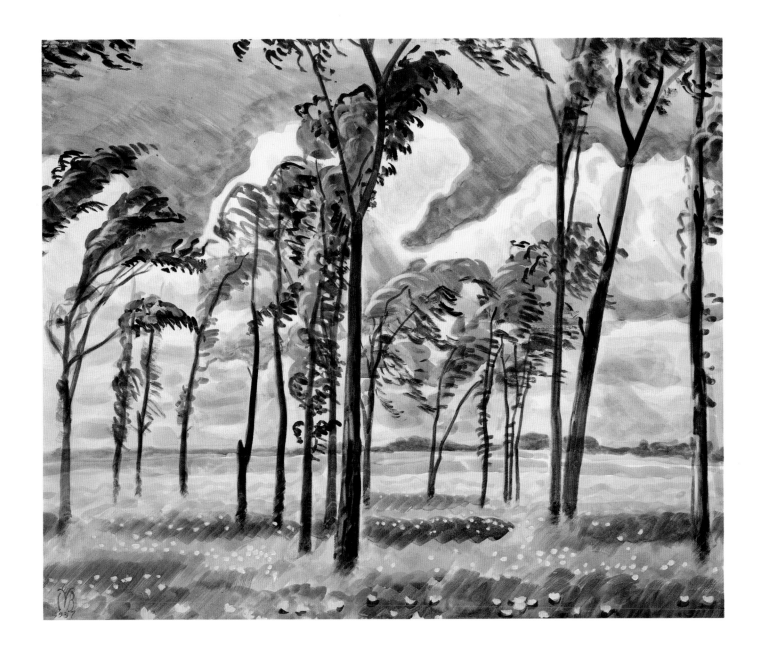

108
Reginald Marsh (1898–1954)
View of Manhattan, 1929

A painter, printmaker, and illustrator, Reginald Marsh is perhaps best remembered for his figural works that chronicle the crowded and often chaotic lives of New Yorkers, from the beaches of Coney Island to the movie houses and burlesque shows of Manhattan. He also depicted the physical presence of the city itself, its bridges, piers, and skyscrapers. His watercolor *View of Manhattan* offers a picturesque, panoramic vista of lower Manhattan seen behind the Manhattan Bridge, which crosses the East River to Brooklyn. Such dramatic skyline views had provided Marsh with subject matter since the early 1920s, and he continued to document the cityscape in both etchings and watercolors well into the 1940s. Painted on the threshold of the Great Depression, *View of Manhattan* depicts a city of progress, with unfinished construction visible on the horizon. The bridge separates the towering modern architecture from the low-lying tenements and warehouses, just as, in retrospect, the year 1929 separated prosperity from hardship.

Marsh worked in watercolor as well as in the related media of wash drawings and tempera throughout much of his career. His *View of Manhattan* is painted in a realistic manner, reminiscent of his work as an illustrator. His handling of the medium is at once confident and controlled. Pencil drawing is visible beneath the color. A hazy sky is evoked by a loose blue wash, but sunlight nonetheless breaks through, illuminating the skyscrapers, which are subtly rendered in shades of blue and gray with warm highlights. The foreground tenements and warehouses are painted in warmer earth tones, but they too are animated by the play of light and shadow. The dark band of the bridge dramatically separates these two zones.

Unlike Marsh's scenes of people at work or leisure, his objective views of the cityscape, such as this one, are not firmly rooted in the anecdotal tradition of so-called Ash Can School painters, such as Robert Henri and John Sloan, who depicted city life with documentary specificity. Rather, the distant vantage point from which Marsh captured the panorama of the skyline suggests his awareness of the modernist painters and photographers in the circle of the photographer Alfred Stieglitz.[1] For many of these artists, including John Marin, Georgia O'Keeffe, Charles Sheeler, and Stieglitz himself, the architecture of the cityscape, with its simple geometric forms, was an important theme at some point in their careers, as it was here for Marsh.

The spontaneity of *View of Manhattan* surely represents a direct observation, probably recorded on location. However, Marsh often produced his figural works in the studio, basing them on sketches or photographs he had made elsewhere. This scene of New York's skyline is more subtle than many of Marsh's figural compositions, yet it makes a definite statement about the evolution of the city at a pivotal moment.

GL

1. Marsh himself worked in the medium. His own photographs, almost exclusively of figural subjects, are in the documentary tradition of Walker Evans and Dorothea Lange.

Provenance
The artist, 1929–54; the artist's widow, Felicia Meyer Marsh, 1954–78; bequest from the Estate of Felicia Meyer Marsh, 1979

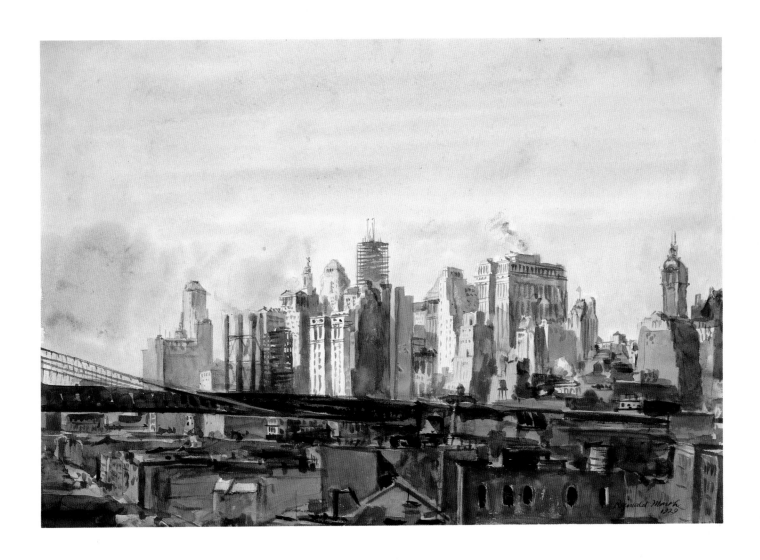

109A and 109B
Reginald Marsh (1898–1954)
Tessie's Bridal Shop, 1946

Possessing intense powers of observation, Marsh often included explicit social commentary and satire in his depictions of city life such as *Tessie's Bridal Shop*. He developed this composition on both sides of the sheet. The more finished image, which has touches of color, seems to have been worked up from the wash drawing on the verso.

In his city scenes Marsh frequently included a caption in the form of a newspaper or a sign, perhaps recalling his days as a newspaper and magazine illustrator.[1] Often he used these devices to focus on the irony of a situation, and in *Tessie's Bridal Shop* he comments on the frivolity of a shop for brides in the tumultuous period immediately after World War II by including the headline: "11 NAZI LEADERS HANG IN 15 DAYS." The story, which announces the verdict of the Allied trials at Nuremberg, is clearly legible only on the later version of this work: "3 Get Life/4 Jailed/5 Freed." In perfecting the clarity of the headline, which he adapted from the October 2, 1946, headline of the *New York Daily News*, Marsh evidently sought to convey the lingering effect of the war on the lives of so many.[2] The storefront evokes the image of war brides and postponed marriages. The sign in the window—"THIS IS OUR ONLY STORE. TESSIE'S BRIDAL SHOP"—adds to the reality of the scene and provides contrasting commentary to the headline in much the same way that the old man and teenage girl stand in contrast to one another.

In his choice of the mannequin image in the second version of this subject, Marsh seems to have been influenced by the art of the many European Surrealists living in exile in New York during the war years. He depicts one of the mannequins, garbed in a bridal gown and veil, as virtually coming alive as she turns toward the newspaper; her countenance suggests that she is actually reading it through the window, like a passenger on a bus stealing a glance at a neighbor's paper. The Surrealists had frequently included mannequins in their work, often in bizarre or unexpected situations.[3] In rendering the mannequins so much more lifelike in the second version, Marsh endowed the composition with an uncanny atmosphere in which an inanimate object suddenly comes alive. Even subtle details added in the later image help to fill out the narrative: the man's lit cigarette, casually hanging from his lips, seems about to drop ash on his paper, suggesting the smoldering aftermath of the war's immense destruction.

Similarly, the transformation of the female figure at the left changes the tone of the scene. In the first version, the sophisticated, well-coiffured woman wearing high-heeled shoes and a chic suit seems oblivious to the newspaper headline or the shop window as she briskly walks by. In the later composition, Marsh transformed her into a teenage girl, wearing flat sandals, a short skirt, and dark sunglasses. She pauses just after she has passed the shop sign and turns her head slightly toward the viewer, in contrast to the unresponsive profile of her counterpart in the earlier sketch. Perhaps Marsh meant the teenager to seem more aware of both the gravity of the newspaper headline and the sharply contrasting romance and festivity promised by the shop window; she appears almost contemplative. Her thoughts might be those of relief, for the end of the war, the return of the young men who had fought in it, and the promise of a future for her, including marriage. Marsh contrasted the bleak past represented by the stooped old man with the hope of the future in a postwar society alluded to by the voluptuous girl. Similarly, the girl and the old man are emblematic of the different messages conveyed by the shop sign and the headline. Marsh's social commentary and historical awareness are among his most powerful and fascinating aspects.   *GL*

1. Marsh worked as a staff artist for the *New York Daily News* from 1921 to 1925 and for such magazines as the *New Yorker* and *Vanity Fair*.

2. The actual *Daily News* headline for October 2, 1946, reads: "Goering and 10 Hang in 15 Days. 3 Get Life, 4 Jailed, 3 Freed." I wish to thank Susan Strickler for providing this information.

3. For examples of the Surrealists' use of mannequins, see the work of André Masson, Salvador Dali, and Hans Bellmer.

Provenance
The artist, 1946–54; the artist's widow, Felicia Meyer Marsh, 1954–78; bequest from the Estate of Felicia Meyer Marsh, 1979

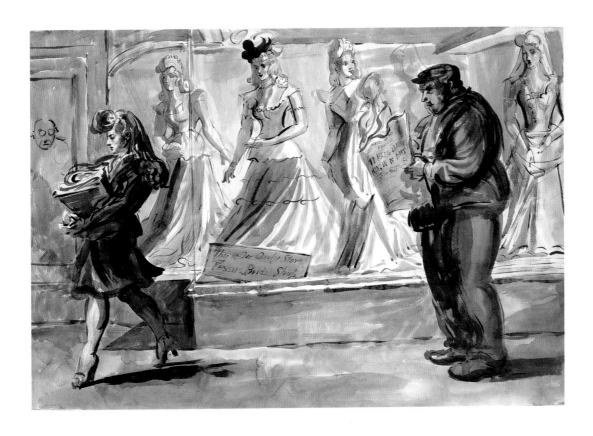

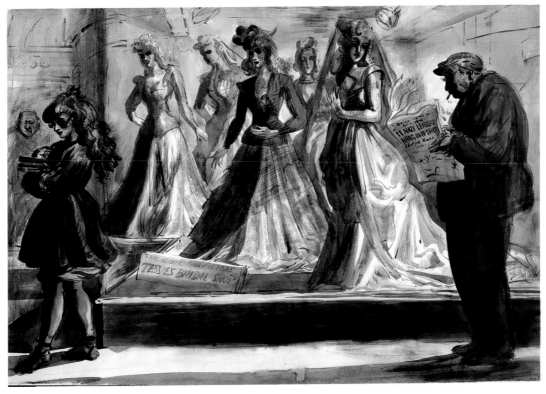

110
Morris Graves (b. 1910)
Ibis Feeding on Its Own Breast, 1947

Morris Graves's work gained wide public attention during World War II, when some thirty of his paintings were presented in the Museum of Modern Art's exhibition *Americans 1942: 18 Artists from 9 States*.[1] Impressed with Graves's ability to create inventive and emotional works that integrate elements of Asian and European art, Duncan Phillips described the artist as "an original genius" whose images represented a "poignant commentary on the crucial period through which we are passing."[2]

Born on a remote homestead in Fox Valley, Oregon, and raised in Seattle, Graves suffered from frail health and often was forced to remain at home for extended lengths of time. During these periods of convalescence he frequently accompanied a neighborhood gardener and became intimately acquainted with the birds and flowers that would later become his personal symbols. His interest in art expressed itself early, and he was respected by his high school peers for his talent as an illustrator.

Graves made two important trips to the Orient, in 1928 and 1930, as a common seaman aboard a commercial steamer. His experience of the East had a profound effect on him. As a young artist in his mid-twenties he began to adopt the religious orientation of Eastern aesthetics, which emphasized the growth of spiritual awareness and benign cooperation with nature. He also became exposed to the avant-garde modernism of Europe through reproductions in popular magazines. In his early work of the mid-1930s we see Christian themes reflective of his family upbringing gradually merging with influences from European Surrealism and Asian art; by the late 1930s Graves had developed an original visual vocabulary of provocative wild-life symbols, painted on densely soaked pages in earthen-hued watercolor. The religious ardor that may be felt in the best of his work proceeds from Graves's attempt to awaken the viewer to the transcendental consciousness that underscores his personal aesthetics. Indeed, he has described many of his paintings as virtual tracings of images that have appeared to him in meditation on "the screen of inner vision."[3]

The dying or wounded bird appeared in Graves's work as early as 1937, with the distinctive Dying Pigeon series of life studies he made during a six-month visit to Father Divine's mission in New York City. In 1943, shortly after a painful period of six months' imprisonment for his conscientious objection to military service, Graves painted a series of perishing wounded gulls that reflects his ordeal.[4]

Ibis Feeding on Its Own Breast was completed following the atomic blasts in Hiroshima and Nagasaki. Appalled by the events, Graves tried to travel to Japan in order to assist in restoring the Japanese culture that he believed had so much to contribute to the Western world. In Honolulu, the U.S. State Department refused to issue him an entry visa to Japan. However, he was able to view the significant collection of ancient Chinese bronzes at the Honolulu Academy of Art. These Shang and Chou period bronzes, which often employ animal and birdlike features in both their form and rich surface decoration, inspired Graves to paint a series of watercolors in which he transformed these vessels into personal symbols of self-contemplation. In these watercolors his birds become humanity confronting the chaos and disintegration it has brought upon itself in the modern world.

The characteristic blending of allegory and elusive naturalism apparent in Grave's work at this time was derived neither from Surrealist sources nor from examples of European or Asian religious painting. Rather, his images communicate in an uncanny way with an emotional consciousness more supernatural than surreal. Furthermore, by the 1940s Graves fundamentally adhered to the Eastern belief that a picture's worth is partly dependent on the observer's ability to see into it and realize its deeper meaning. As Graves noted, "I paint to evolve a changing language of symbols, a language with which to remark upon the qualities of our mysterious capacities which direct us toward ultimate reality. I paint to rest from the phenomenon of the external world—to pronounce it—and to make notations of its essences with which to verify the inner eye."[5] The role of the audience in completing the communicative act of art became part of the meditative procedure in Graves's painting.

In the same way Graves appropriated the forms of Chinese bronzes, he adapted the image of the ibis, which we may also associate with ancient Egyptian art, to convey his message. Graves's depiction of this graceful bird feeding upon its own breast is a powerful, ritualistic image of pain and alienation as well as transcendence; perhaps it may be best understood as a poignant self-portrait of Graves himself.   *RK*

1. See Dorothy C. Miller, *Americans 1942: 18 Artists from 9 States* (New York: Museum of Modern Art, 1942), p. 51; and Raymond Kass, *Morris Graves: Vision of the Inner Eye* (Washington, D.C.: Phillips Collection; New York: George Braziller, 1983), p. 32.

2. Duncan Phillips, "Morris Graves," *Magazine of Art* 40 (December 1947): 306, in Kass, *Graves*, p. 32. Phillips, founder of the Phillips Collection in Washington, D.C., was one of Graves's important patrons.

3. Graves, conversation with Kass, August 1980. For a detailed description of Graves's concepts pertaining to "space," see Nancy Wilson Ross, et al., *Morris Graves: A Retrospective* (Eugene, Ore.: University of Oregon Museum of Art, 1966), p. 41.

4. See Kass, *Graves*, p. 38.

5. Graves, in Miller, *Americans 1942*, p. 51.

Provenance
(Willard Gallery, New York); museum purchase, 1948

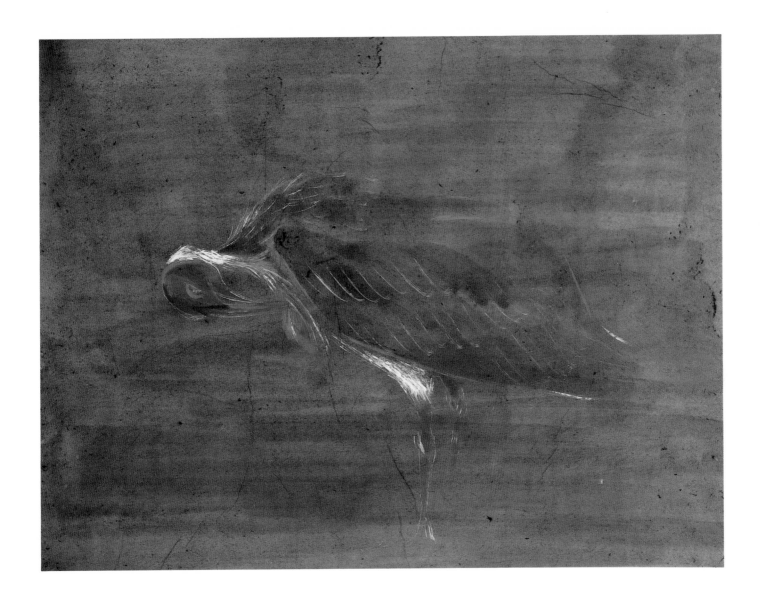

111
Andrew Wyeth (b. 1917)
The Rope, 1957

Andrew Wyeth is probably America's most famous and popular artist. He is also among the most influential realists, having inspired a generation of younger painters who have chosen watercolor as their primary medium to depict rural, indigenous subjects. Wyeth received his first public acclaim in 1937 for his bold watercolors of Maine subjects, which recalled the mature style of Winslow Homer.[1] Since then, watercolor has remained an important medium for Wyeth, one he uses not only for sketches leading up to final compositions in tempera but also for finished works, often rendered in dry-brush technique.

Wyeth has frequently been categorized as a regionalist because much of his painting has focused on two circumscribed environments: the farm of the Kuerner family, who were Wyeth's neighbors in his native Chadds Ford, Pennsylvania, and the farm belonging to Christina Olson and her brother Alvaro, who lived just a few miles from the artist's summer home in Cushing, Maine.[2] Although his paintings are most often praised for their striking realism, his vision includes a symbolic content—both private and universal—that transcends mere literal transcription of the seemingly picturesque lives of these withdrawn, self-sufficient individuals.[3] This dramatic element, which the artist never fully unveils for the viewer, derives from a strong sense of connection with his subjects.

The Rope belongs to a group of drawings and watercolor studies that culminated in the tempera painting *Hay Ledge* (1957; Arthur and Holly Magill Foundation), depicting the interior of Alvaro Olson's barn.[4] The artist first met the Olsons in 1939 through their neighbor Betsy James, whom Wyeth later married. For the next thirty years he spent most of his summers painting the Olsons and their farm. He remarked, "Through the Olsons I really began to see New England as it really was. . . . I stayed right within that environment. It was everything. The world of New England was in that house overlooking the mouth of the Georges River."[5]

Wyeth painted Christina numerous times; the most famous depiction is also his best-known work, *Christina's World* (1948; Museum of Modern Art, New York). But he only once painted her brother Alvaro (*Oil Lamp*, 1945; Museum of Fine Arts, Houston), who had given up his life as a fisherman to care first for his arthritic father and then for his crippled sister. To earn a living Alvaro turned to farming, which he disliked as much as he had loved fishing. Wyeth found the lives of Christina and Alvaro reflected in the objects around them, and his paintings of their implements and of the house and outbuildings became, in essence, metaphorical portraits of the Olsons.

The Rope presents a glimpse of the haymow where Alvaro stored the dory he no longer used. On the stern rests a chicken crate, easily mistaken for one of Alvaro's lobster traps.[6] A scythe is tossed on top of an old clamming hod. Hanging from a rafter is a frayed rope, possibly used to raise the hay into the loft, highlighted by the sun against the dim recess of the barn. The focal point of the composition, the rope casts an enigmatic presence. Its form conjures up many images: a noose, the pulley lines of a lobster boat, even a human figure. Although the composition clearly relates to Alvaro's transition from fisherman to farmer, the ambiguity of the imagery lends a contemplative note to the work. Perhaps its ultimate message is more universal than just the predicament of one man and refers to the changes that all men face during their lives.

The immediacy of this composition is conveyed, in part, by the artist's varied manipulation of the medium. The roughness of the barn wall is suggested through gestural strokes worked with a stiff-bristled brush in a relatively rich application of the pigments. Sgraffito, or scratching of the paint surface with a pointed implement, was used to define the dory's green gunwale. Painting with his finger, the artist articulated a post visible above the chicken crate at the far right. Wyeth applied pale washes over the cream paper to create shadows on the dory's hull, and with graphite he delineated its lapstrake siding. A few drips or splatters of paint suggest bits of hay on the foreground rafter. The active use of the medium underscores the textural "rawness" implicit in this rural subject and also enhances the sense of abandonment created by the discarded objects.

Wyeth continued to paint the Olsons through the summer of 1967. That winter, both Alvaro and Christina died. The following year he made sketches for his final painting of the deserted property, a tempera called *End of the Olsons* (1969; Arthur and Holly Magill Foundation). But his feeling for the farm had changed with the loss of his friends. In an interview he said, "Without Alvaro and Christina, it's just an object, nothing more—interesting perhaps, but not emotionally interesting."[7]   SES

1. These were shown in the *First Exhibition of Water Colors by Andrew Wyeth*, at the Macbeth Gallery, New York, October 19–November 1, 1937.

2. See Betsy Wyeth, *Wyeth at Kuerners* (Boston: Houghton Mifflin, 1976) and *Christina's World* (Boston: Houghton Mifflin, 1982).

3. See Wanda Corn's sensitive discussion in *The Art of Andrew Wyeth* (Greenwich, Conn.: New York Graphic Society, 1973), pp. 97ff. and 150ff.

4. For illustrations of some related works, see Betsy Wyeth, *Christina's World*, pp. 66–68, 70. Andrew Wyeth has stated that he was attracted to this subject by the way the sunlight shone through the rafters against the white dory, an effect captured in the *Hay Ledge*.

5. Wyeth, interview with Thomas Hoving, *Two Worlds of Andrew Wyeth: Kuerners and Olsons* (New York: Metropolitan Museum of Art, 1976), p. 42.

6. Betsy Wyeth identified this object as a chicken crate in *Christina's World*, p. 70.

7. Wyeth, in Hoving, *Two Worlds of Andrew Wyeth*, p. 171.

Provenance
(Weintraub Gallery, New York); private collection; anonymous promised gift

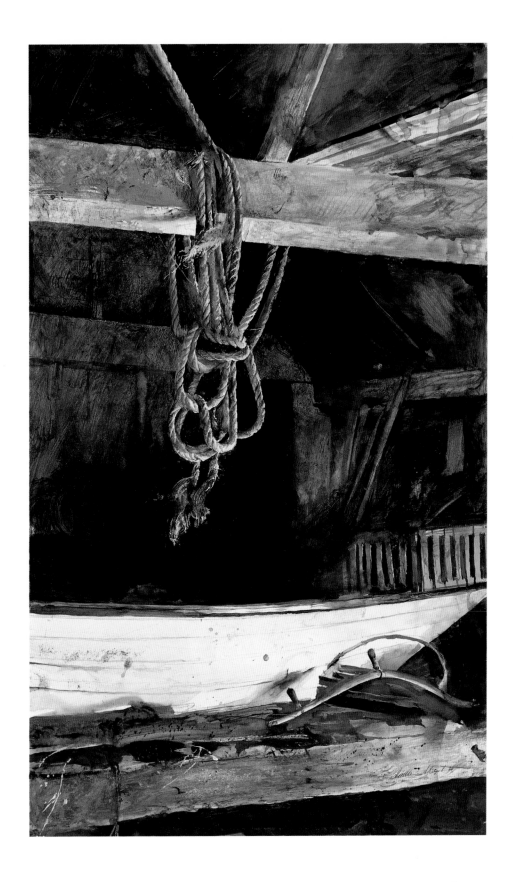

112
William T. Wiley (b. 1937)
Construct a Vista, 1981

William T. Wiley developed a distinctive approach to art in California during the late 1960s and 1970s. Like his contemporaries Robert Rauschenberg and Jasper Johns in the East, Wiley draws upon everyday life in his art, but his explorations are more intuitive and autobiographical, idiosyncratically combining his interests in Dada, Surrealism, and Zen Buddhism with a predilection for magic, metaphor and myth, puns and low-key humor.[1]

While Wiley is also a painter, printmaker, and sculptor, watercolors have been an important part of his oeuvre since he first picked up a portable set of watercolors in 1967. The style and technique he developed then is evident in *Construct a Vista*. First, he outlines the images with a felt-tip pen and then fills in the network of black lines with watercolor, blotting the clear, delicate colors with a paper towel to maintain an even texture as he moves from one area to the next. One of the most virtuoso and exciting draftsmen of his generation, Wiley creates a jewellike jigsaw puzzle out of his nervous, broken lines and tinted watercolor washes, which rely as much on Leonardo's sketchbook scribbles as on Wiley's childhood love for picture books.

The objects in *Construct a Vista* appear in various guises and combinations elsewhere in Wiley's work in all media. Some are taken from his immediate surroundings; others are part of a repertoire of abstract forms with personal and metaphorical associations. In *Construct a Vista* these objects, signs, and symbols are accompanied by an equally enigmatic text, a device Wiley uses here and elsewhere to express thoughts he cannot present visually but that reinforce understanding of his imagery.

The title of the watercolor may offer clues to meaning. The exhortation to "Construct a Vista" suggests a challenge both to the artist and to everyman: the artist must somehow schematically represent vast spaces, just as each of us must chart our own life's course. Prominent in the watercolor are references to the artist's world. The scene depicts his studio, complete with wood-burning stove and tools of the trade: easel, brushes stored in an empty can, a pencil tossed on the floor, and an acetylene torch next to one of Wiley's sculptures, a mysterious construction with an arrow.[2]

More enigmatic images emerge upon closer inspection. A shadowy palette with brushes materializes out of the floor patterns, which also yield the ghostly shape of a world map. Having grown up in various states from Texas to Washington, Wiley is fascinated with metaphors for travel, which symbolize for him the process of artistic creation, the journey of the mind, and the passage of life. Maps appear in the arrow sculpture and tacked to the furniture on the right; even the edges of the image are tattered like a well-used map. Ships and navigation are suggested by the boatlike shape in the center of the floor and the sailboat beneath the arrow.

Among other surreal patterns on the floor is a silhouetted figure who appears to be "walking the line." This traveler, probably a variation of a favorite Wiley persona, Nomad, may refer to the Zen concept of No-Mind, a state of complete self-understanding and enlightenment, which is the ultimate goal of life's journey. The only other figural reference is less enigmatic. In two silhouette profiles (one with its tongue rudely stuck out) flanking the arrow sculpture, Wiley acknowledges his debt to Marcel Duchamp, who inspired his delight in ordinary objects, word plays, and nonart materials—and his irreverence.

Scattered around the artist's studio are many of Wiley's favorite abstract symbols. The infinity sign is visible, almost completely disguised as the creases in the blue pillow on the chair at left. Wiley recalls that the triangle, which appears repeatedly in *Construct a Vista*, was suggested by a sign he saw as a child in a chiropractor's office, inscribed, "God, Patient, Chiropractor"; it is also a universal religious symbol.[3] The striped rod at bottom left is an important image to Wiley. As a child he had been intrigued by his father's surveyor's rod. Here he heightened the mystical properties he has attached to this tool by associating it with the staff carried by Zen Buddhists: according to Zen philosophy, when the meaning of this staff is understood, enlightenment is reached. Even the partially filled bucket may allude to enlightenment, which is described as "the bottom of a pail broken through."[4]

These multiple meanings, an important part of Wiley's art and his view of the world, are apparent in the pun-filled writings that complement his images. In *Construct a Vista*, as in his other works, Wiley draws on the tradition of the Koan, a Zen form of instruction. In this intentionally irrational and inexplicable dialogue between Bore us (Boris) and Elict sigh (Alexis) Wiley seems to discuss the nature and style of art (including Russian Constructivism). Like his protagonists, Wiley does not come up with any answers but accepts art, life's variety, and the universality of man with humor and gentleness. For him, the path to understanding is realized not through logic but through the exploration and celebration of the mystery of the mundane.   *RW*

1. For an informative discussion of Wiley's work, see Graham Beal and John Perreault, *Wiley Territory* (Minneapolis: Walker Art Center, 1979) and Brenda Richardson, *William T. Wiley* (Berkeley: University Art Museum, 1971).

2. This sculpture, also entitled *Construct a Vista* (mixed media, 1981), is reproduced in Ted Lindberg, *William T. Wiley* (Vancouver, B.C.: Emily Carr College of Art; New York: Allan Frumkin Gallery, 1982).

3. Wiley, in Emily Wasserman, "William T. Wiley and William Allan: Meditating at Ford Prank," *Artforum* 60, no. 4 (December 1970): 63.

4. The Zen teaching popular in San Francisco in the 1960s and 1970s was essentially that of D. T. Suzuki, author of the *Zen Mind, Beginner's Mind*. This quotation is from *Zen Buddhism, Selected Writings of D. T. Suzuki*, ed. William Bennett (New York: Doubleday, 1956), p. 85.

Provenance
(Allan Frumkin Gallery, New York); museum purchase through the National Endowment for the Arts Museum Purchase Plan, 1984

CHOOSING NOT TO TELL — THE FIR STORY — ELECT SIGH..
IS ... SPEAKING TO BORE US..
RUSHIN TO CONSTRUCT A VISTA — THESE WORDS HE
MURDERED TO IS ELF —
REVOLUTION .. SCHMEVELUTION (E.N.W.80) NOTHING
IS INVENTED .. OF COURSE .. WRONG — SCHMONG
WHO'S AFRAID? OF FODDER LAND — MUDDER LAND?
I DO AS VISH .. PAINT AS X PLEASE .. DESE
VISENHEIMERS DARE JUST JUNG UPSTARTS
HLIKE A BAD REAM .. CUSHION CULTURE .. PUNK
SCHMONK ..   THE L FANGERS
NO BUT ELECT SIGH .. WHEE ARE A'IN TAUS
AIM — NOT AS CULT SURE MAYBE ?! BUT AS
HUE MAN BEINGS .. IS TROUE NO .. ALL HUMAN
NEEDS AIM .. ? EA!!?
BORE US ARE HUE NUTS OR SOMETHIN?
MAYBE — I DON'T KNOW WHY?
AHH BORE US IF YOU MUST TO ASK .. THEN
WHAT CAN I SAY ..
WELL ONE NOTE OR COVE DON'T ITS ALL
THE SAME TO ME .. THUS AIM THUSAIM
SO SO SO ALL A LOT OF WHIRD GAMES ..
YOU REVEAL .. NOTHING.
AHH BUT ELECT SIGH .. THATS A LOT ..
DATS A LOT ALL RIGHT .. A LOT A P—
HODEL!
NO NOTHING!
OH YEAH — YOU CAN'T EVEN CONCIEVE OF
THIS NOTHING ..
THE L FALL SILENT.
NOTHING IS MUTE.
YAS YAS .. OR QUITE THAT SERIOUS ..
SURE ELECTS EYE — YOU AND YOUR SO CALLED
OBJECTIVE .. DE-TATCHED .. DISSA DENT SCHMISSADENT..
VIEW..
SO ARE YOU FINISHED — YES FINISHED!
WHY DON'T YOU SAY SO .. O.K. I'M
FINISHED! WHAT DO YOU MEAN?
I'VE HAD ENOUGH .. WHAT DO YOU MEAN
BY THAT.?? I DON'T KNOW, CAUSE IT
ISN'T TRUE ..
          VAN.TUYL
          1981 ©

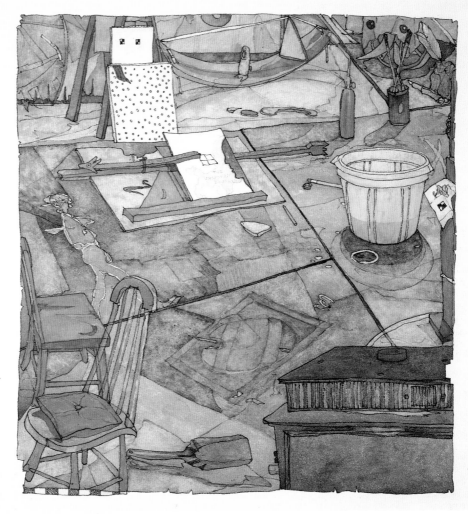

113
Carolyn Brady (b. 1937)
Last Red Tulips (Baltimore Spring 1984), 1984

Through the sheer size and power of her work, Carolyn Brady has been particularly instrumental in reestablishing watercolor as a major means of expression, following its decline in popularity with the advent of Abstract Expressionism after World War II. After several years as a commercial textile designer in New York, Brady moved to the Midwest in 1967 to concentrate on her own work, chiefly large images appliquéd on brightly colored pieces of cloth. She first used watercolor in preparatory sketches and then in the early 1970s as a source of increasingly realistic images for the sewn works. By mid-decade she considered her watercolors her most "potent" work and was spending most of her time exploring this medium.

Brady is usually linked with Photo-Realism, a style that draws upon Pop Art and its sources in commercial art and photography and upon the compositional concepts of Abstract Expressionism. She paints subjects from everyday life: still lifes, interiors, and gardens, often dominated by flowers. Like the Photo-Realists, she works from photographs rather than directly from life: she takes numerous 3-by-5-inch color snapshots and from these selects a promising few, which are enlarged to 11-by-14-inch prints. She then chooses one as the subject of her watercolor, mounts the color negative as a slide, projects it onto her watercolor paper, and makes a free-line drawing, defining the composition, sometimes correcting the camera distortion, other times preferring the interesting effects that result.[1]

Brady based Last Red Tulips (Baltimore Spring 1984) on a color photograph of her garden. Using delicate pencil notations, she quite closely followed the outlines of the projected color negative. The photograph continued to serve as an artist's sketch during the working process. The dramatic scale and strong design, conceived edge to edge, is related to the work of the Photo-Realists and their Pop Art predecessors: in Last Red Tulips, the huge, fiery petals threaten to penetrate into the viewer's space.

Brady structured this dramatic composition carefully, consulting or disregarding the color photograph as it served her artistic needs. She had conceived in the camera the lyrical, dynamic composition of the tulips, framed by the S-curve of daffodils on the left and the radiating patterns of leaves on the right. Echoing the camera's vision, which sharply focuses on only a single point, she emphasized the tulips' central position by rendering them sharp edged and clear, while the daffodils, earth, and leaves are more abstractly painted as they recede into the background. She altered the light and space to enhance this arrangement and added glowing highlights on the tulip petals and subtle color variations in the broad leaves to bring the central cluster even closer to the viewer. Her painting method reinforced the primacy of the tulips: she painted from background to foreground so that the final overlapping edge of watercolor was reserved for the tulips.

Although Brady shares with the Photo-Realists and the Pop Artists an interest in common subjects conceived and composed in an all-over design, she does not adopt their cool, objective attitude. Like much of the work of her contemporaries the New Imagists and Neo-Expressionists, Brady's watercolors are personal and autobiographical. Last Red Tulips (Baltimore Spring 1984) resonates with the artist's response to a fragment of nature in a moment of time. Through every artistic device at her disposal—composition, scale, color, light, and the freshness of the medium—Brady vividly communicates her sensual and intellectual pleasure in the beauty and drama present in a small patch of earth, a deeply felt part of her personal world. She rejects the airbrush often used by Photo-Realists; her handling of the watercolor medium is also autographic and personal. As she says, "My paintings are more of a diary for me. . . . I think that people sense that there are more memories attached to the objects I choose."[2]

Brady's gesture has grown in breadth, freedom, and power as the scale of her work has expanded, but it has remained at once loose and controlled. She does not work over an area, but allows the white of the paper to give light and life to the medium. This spontaneity makes it possible to "see the thought of the artist" as well as the artist's personal touch.[3]   RW

1. Brady, interview with the author, November 28, 1984.

2. Brady, in Alan D. Singer, "Carolyn Brady," American Artist 49 (May 1985): 95.

3. Janice C. Oresman, Twentieth Century American Watercolor (Hamilton, N.Y.: Gallery Association of New York State, 1983), p. 43.

Provenance
Collection of the artist; (Nancy Hoffman Gallery, New York); Museum purchase through the National Endowment for the Arts Purchase Plan, 1984

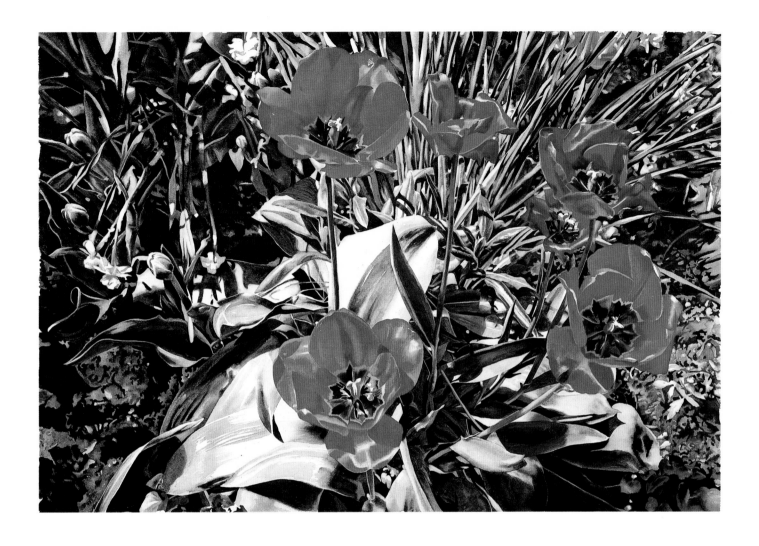

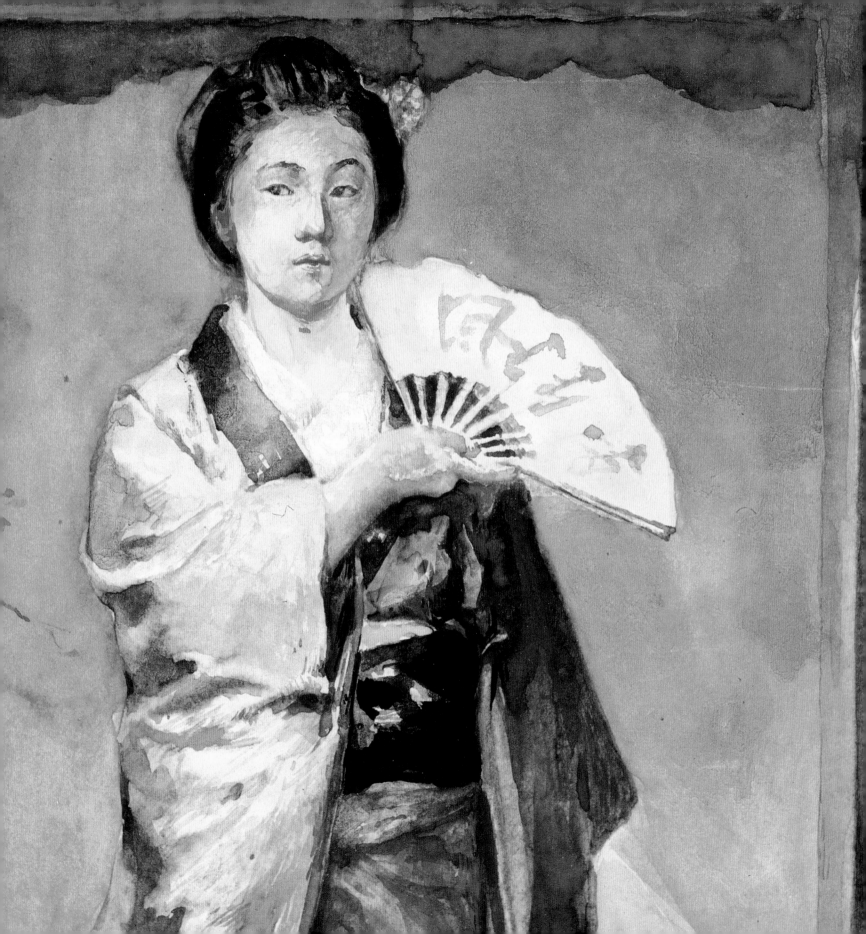

Compiled by
Norma Steinberg

Illustrated Checklist of the Collection

Explanation of the Checklist

General arrangement

Works are arranged alphabetically according to the artist's surname, with the anonymous works listed first. Where there are two or more works by a single artist, they are listed chronologically. Only images on the fronts of sheets are illustrated, although verso images are noted in the entry. Plate numbers are noted in the checklist for those works illustrated in color or black and white in the preceding essays.

Title and date

The artist's original title or a previously published or historically relevant one is given if known; otherwise, a descriptive title has been used. In the few cases where a date cannot be determined from inscriptions, documentation, or style, no date has been indicated.

Medium and support

A liberal interpretation of the watercolor medium has been used for the purposes of inclusion. Works that incorporate transparent watercolor, gouache (opaque watercolor), and, in one case, tempera, are included. All other media in each work are described as accurately as possible. The general character of the paper, watermarks, and blind stamps is noted.

Dimensions

Image size is given in both inches and centimeters, with height preceding width.

Inscriptions

All inscriptions on the front and important inscriptions on the back are included. Slashes are used to indicate lineation.

Accession number

The manner of acquisition (gift or purchase) is noted, followed by the museum's accession number, which designates the year the work was accessioned and the serial number within that year (e.g., 1985.1 indicates the first work to be accessioned in 1985).

114
John La Farge
Musicians in Ceremonial Costume, 1887
(detail of plate 56)

Anonymous (19th century)

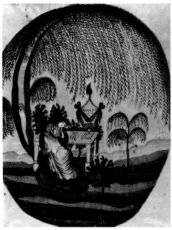

Mourning Piece
Watercolor, graphite, ink on off-white silk
12⅛ × 9¼ in. (30.8 × 23.4 cm.)
Inscribed on tablet: to the/memory/of Mrs./
Mary Grovsn/or
Bequest of Stephen Salisbury III   1907.17

Anonymous (19th century)

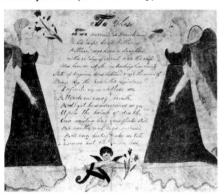

Birth Certificate of Mary Warner, 1824
Watercolor, ink over graphite on buff wove
paper
7⅞ × 10 in. (20 × 25 cm.)
Gift of Nicholas Joost   1966.66

Anonymous (19th century)

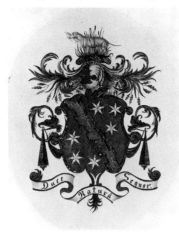

Coat of Arms of Paine Family
Watercolor, metallic paint over graphite on
ocher wove paper
9⅛ × 7¾ in. (23.3 × 19.8 cm.)
Lettered in riband: Duce Natura Segnor
Bequest of Eliza Sturgis Paine   1945.89

Anonymous (19th century)

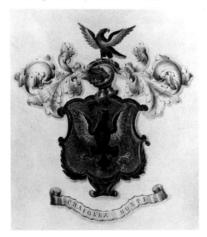

Coat of Arms of Weston Family
Watercolor, gold leaf, shell gold over graphite
on beige wove paper
12¾ × 9¾ in. (32.6 × 24.8 cm.)
Lettered in riband: CRAIGNEZ HONTE
Bequest of Eliza Sturgis Paine   1945.88

Anonymous (19th century)

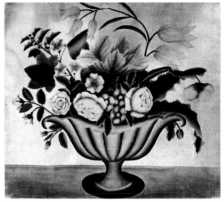

Bowl of Flowers
Watercolor on cream-colored velvet
16⅛ × 18½ in. (41 × 47 cm.)
Gift of Admiral and Mrs. Ralph
Earle, Jr.   1962.14

Lewin Alcopley (b. 1910)
Born Germany. Studied in Dresden. 1935–
37, lived in Switzerland. 1937, became
U.S. citizen. Member of American Abstract
Artists. 1945–47, worked in Stanley Hayter's Atelier 17 in New York. 1949, founding
member of The Club, New York. 1952–59,
lived in Paris and London. 1960, settled
in New York. Painter and graphic artist.

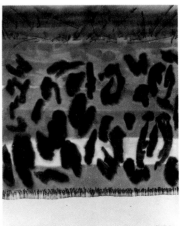

Untitled, 1957
Watercolor on off-white laid paper
20½ × 16½ in. (52.1 × 42 cm.)
Signed and dated lower right: alcopley
1957
Gift of Betty Parsons Foundation   1985.267

Manuel Ayaso (b. 1934)

Born La Coruña, Spain. 1947, immigrated to U.S. 1955, became U.S. citizen. 1953–56, studied at Newark (N.J.) School of Fine and Applied Arts. 1956–58, served in U.S. Army as illustrator. 1959, in Madrid. 1963, on Tiffany Foundation scholarship, painted in Spain for eighteen months. Works chiefly in goldpoint with watercolor washes.

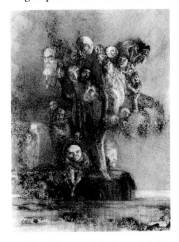

Judios, Moros y Cristianos, 1968
Goldpoint, watercolor on white wove paper (prepared for metalpoint)
10⅜ × 7¾ in. (26.3 × 19.7 cm.)
Signed lower left: Ayaso
Director's Discretionary Fund   1969.2

Alice Baber (1928–1982)

Born Charleston, Ill.; died New York. 1951, B.A. Indiana University. 1951–58, in New York. 1959–68, studios in Paris and New York. 1968, settled in New York when marriage to painter Paul Jenkins ended. 1971–78, traveled and exhibited in Asia, Russia, Europe, and Latin America. 1977–81, taught and lectured widely on painting, design, and color lithography. Her abstract serial paintings reflect her interest in the psychology of color.

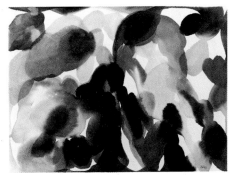

Green Dervish Turns to Blue, 1973
Watercolor over graphite on white wove paper
Watermark: ARCHES FRANCE
29⅝ × 41½ in. (75.2 × 105.2 cm.)
Signed lower right: Baber/73
Inscribed verso: Alice Baber/New York/1973/Green Dervish Turns to Blue
Gift of Mr. Adin Baber   1974.269

Henry Bacon (1839–1912)

Born in Haverhill, Mass.; died Cairo, Egypt. Worked as field artist for *Leslie's Weekly* during Civil War. 1864, studied in Paris with Jean-Léon Gérôme and Alexandre Cabanel; 1866–67, at Ecouen, France, with Edouard Frère. 1868–96, in Paris. From 1897, traveled extensively in Egypt, Greece, Sicily, Ceylon, and Italy. About 1900, settled in London; wintered in Egypt. Last fifteen years spent painting watercolors of Egypt and Greece. Note: Titles for the Bacon watercolors are derived from those published in *Catalogue of a Memorial Exhibition of Water Colors of Egypt, Greece, France, Italy and England by Henry Bacon* (Washington, D.C.: National Gallery of Art, 1931).

Plate 77

Queen Arsinoë in the Form of Isis Presenting the Wand of Everlasting Life to Ptolemy, c. 1900
Watercolor over graphite on cream wove paper
19⅝ × 13¼ in. (49.7 × 33.6 cm.)
Signed lower right: Henry Bacon
Inscribed lower left: Arsinoë/Wife of Philopater I BC 805
Inscribed verso: Queen Arsinoë under the form of/the Goddess of Isis/From the Temple of Isis—Island of Philae-Egypt.
Gift of Mrs. Frederick L. Eldridge in memory of Henry Bacon   1943.26

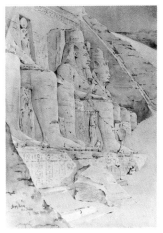

''Where Afric's Sunny Fountains Roll Down Their Golden Sand,'' 1902
Watercolor over graphite on cream wove paper
22¼ × 15¼ in. (56.3 × 38.8 cm.)
Signed and dated lower left: Henry Bacon/Abu Simbel/1902
Inscribed lower right: ''afric's sunny fountains/roll down their golden sand''
Inscribed verso: Temple at Abou Simbel/''Where Afric's Sunny Fountains/roll down their golden sand''/Memorial exhibition/No. 65
Gift of Mrs. Frederick L. Eldridge in memory of Henry Bacon   1943.21

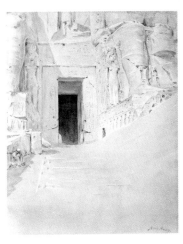

Rock Temple of Abou Simbel, Nubia, 1902

Bacon (continued)
Watercolor over graphite on cream wove paper
23¾ × 18⅞ in. (60.3 × 47.8 cm.)
Signed lower right: Henry Bacon
Inscribed lower right: Queen Nefert—Ard BC 1400
Gift of Mrs. Frederick L. Eldridge in memory of Henry Bacon   1943.22

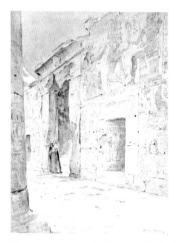

The Forecourt of the Temple of Abydos, **1902**
Watercolor over graphite on cream wove paper
Watermark: J WHATMAN [partial]
21½ × 15½ in. (54.5 × 39.2 cm.)
Inscribed lower right: Abydos Dec. 1902
Inscribed verso: Forecourt Temple of Abydos/Memorial Exhibition/No. 68
Gift of Mrs. Frederick L. Eldridge in memory of Henry Bacon   1943.36.4

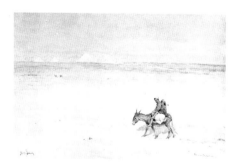

Provisions for My Camp at Sakkarah, **1903**
Watercolor over graphite on cream wove paper
Watermark: J WHATMAN [partial]
13⅞ × 20⅞ in. (35.2 × 53.1 cm.)
Signed lower left: Henry Bacon
Inscribed lower right: Provisions for Sakkarah/Dec. 1903
Gift of Mrs. Frederick L. Eldridge in memory of Henry Bacon   1943.27

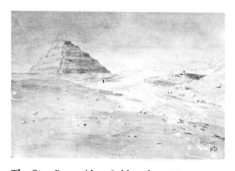

The Step Pyramid at Sakkarah at Noon, c. 1903
Watercolor over graphite on cream wove paper mounted on board
14 × 21 in. (35.5 × 53.4 cm.)
Signed lower right: HB
Gift of Mrs. Frederick L. Eldridge in memory of Henry Bacon   1943.29

Plate 78
The Colossi of Thebes, **1904**
Watercolor over graphite on cream wove paper
15⅜ × 21½ in. (38.8 × 54.3 cm.)
Signed lower left: Henry Bacon 1904
Inscribed verso: Memorial Exhibition/No. 62/The Colossi of/Thebes
Gift of Mrs. Frederick L. Eldridge in memory of Henry Bacon   1943.36.3

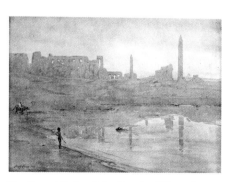

The Sacred Lake of the Temple of Karnak (evening), **1905**

Watercolor over graphite on cream wove paper mounted on board
15⅞ × 22⅞ in. (40.4 × 58.2 cm.)
Signed lower left: Henry Bacon 1905/Sacred Lake Karnach
Gift of Mrs. Frederick L. Eldridge in memory of Henry Bacon   1943.28

Plate 79
Street in Cairo, **1905**
Watercolor over graphite on cream wove paper
Watermark: J WHATMAN [partial]
13½ × 19⅞ in. (34 × 50.6 cm.)
Signed and dated lower left: Henry Bacon Cairo 1905
Gift of Mrs. Frederick L. Eldridge in memory of Henry Bacon   1943.31

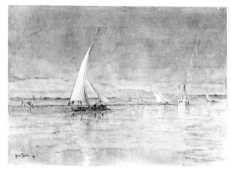

The Nile (near Luxor, Pink Hills of Thebes in the Distance, Very Early Morning), **1905**
Watercolor over graphite on cream wove paper
16 × 22¹³/₁₆ in. (40.5 × 57.9 cm.)
Signed and dated lower left: Henry Bacon 1905
Inscribed verso: An Egyptian Shissah (freight boat)/and hills opposite Luxor
Gift of Mrs. Frederick L. Eldridge in memory of Henry Bacon   1943.36.7

Bacon (continued)

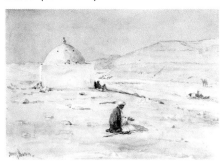

The Sheik's Tomb in the Desert (Abou Shreer, Midday), c. 1905
Watercolor over graphite on cream wove paper
13⅜ × 20 in. (34 × 50.8 cm.)
Signed lower left: Henry Bacon
Inscribed verso: The Sheik's Tomb in the Desert
Gift of Mrs. Frederick L. Eldridge in memory of Henry Bacon   1943.36.5

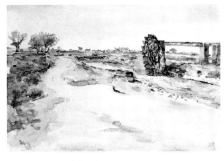

Along a Canal in the Fayoum, c. 1905
Watercolor over graphite on cream wove paper
13½ × 20 in. (34.2 × 50.8 cm.)
Signed lower right: HB
Inscribed lower left: Feb 19
Inscribed verso: Along a Canal in the/ Fayoum Memorial/Exhibition, no. 14
Verso: graphite sketch of similar subject
Gift of Mrs. Frederick L. Eldridge in memory of Henry Bacon   1943.36.6

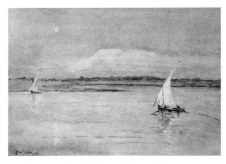

Sunrise on the Theban Hills, 1907
Watercolor over graphite on cream wove paper
13¼ × 20⅛ in. (33.6 × 51.1 cm.)
Signed and dated lower left: Henry Bacon 1907
Inscribed lower right: [illegible] Luxor Dawn
Gift of Mrs. Frederick L. Eldridge in memory of Henry Bacon   1943.25

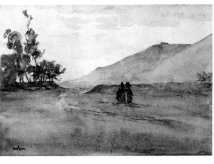

Women Fetching Water at Dawn in the Plain of Thebes, c. 1907
Watercolor over graphite on cream wove paper
13½ × 20 in. (34.2 × 51.8 cm.)
Signed lower left: Henry Bacon
Gift of Mrs. Frederick L. Eldridge in memory of Henry Bacon   1943.30

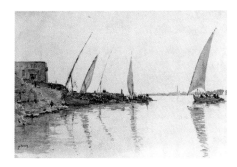

The Pharaoh's Boat Landing-place (near Luxor), c. 1907
Watercolor over graphite on cream wove paper
13⅛ × 19⅞ in. (38.3 × 50.6 cm.)
Signed lower right: H Bacon
Inscribed verso: The Pharaoh's Landing Pier/Luxor/Memorial Exhibition/No. 58/The Pharaoh's boat landing near Luxor
Gift of Mrs. Frederick L. Eldridge in memory of Henry Bacon   1943.36.2

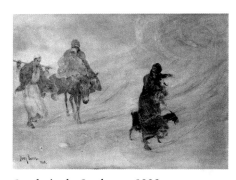

Caught in the Sandstorm, 1908
Watercolor over graphite on ocher (discolored) wove paper
14 × 20½ in. (35.5 × 52 cm.)
Signed and dated lower left: Henry Bacon 1908
Gift of Mrs. Frederick L. Eldridge in memory of Henry Bacon   1943.32

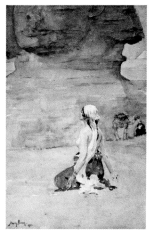

An Appeal to the Great Abel Hone, 1910

Bacon (continued)
Watercolor over graphite on cream wove paper
20⅜ × 13½ in. (51.7 × 34.4 cm.)
Signed and dated lower left: Henry Bacon 1910
Gift of Mrs. Frederick L. Eldridge in memory of Henry Bacon   1943.20

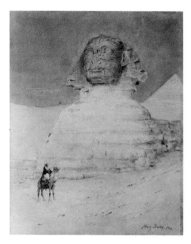

The Great Sphinx (Sunrise), 1910
Watercolor over graphite on cream wove paper
23⅞ × 18¾ in. (60.5 × 47.8 cm.)
Signed lower right: Henry Bacon 1910
Gift of Mrs. Frederick L. Eldridge in memory of Henry Bacon   1943.23

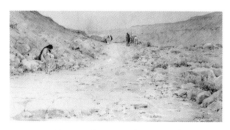

An Egyptian Mother (Road near Cairo, Evening), 1911
Watercolor over graphite on cream wove paper
18⅝ × 36½ in. (47.3 × 92.5 cm.)
Signed and dated lower right: Henry Bacon/1911
Gift of Mrs. Frederick L. Eldridge in memory of Henry Bacon   1943.16

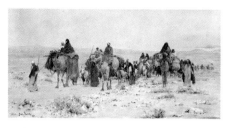

Bedouins on Annual Pilgrimage to the Desert Shrine of ''Abou Shreer,'' in the Hill Country near the Red Sea, 1911
Watercolor over graphite on buff wove paper
18⅝ × 36⅜ in. (47.2 × 92.2 cm.)
Signed and dated lower left: Henry Bacon/1911
Gift of Mrs. Frederick L. Eldridge in memory of Henry Bacon   1943.17

Plate 80
Bedouin Camp Fires, c. 1911
Watercolor over graphite on cream wove paper
16⅝ × 25½ in. (42.2 × 64.7 cm.)
Signed lower left: Henry Bacon
Inscribed lower right: Halt in the valley of [illegible]
Gift of Mrs. Frederick L. Eldridge in memory of Henry Bacon   1943.18

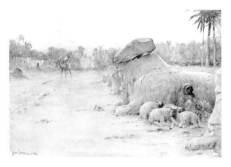

The Last of Krio Sphinxes between Karnak and Luxor, 1911
Watercolor over graphite on cream wove paper
16½ × 25⅝ in. (42 × 65 cm.)
Signed and dated lower left: Henry Bacon Luxor 1911
Gift of Mrs. Frederick L. Eldridge in memory of Henry Bacon   1943.19

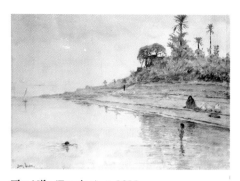

The Nile (Evening), c. 1911
Watercolor over graphite on cream wove paper
15⅞ × 22⅞ in. (40.3 × 58.1 cm.)
Signed lower left: Henry Bacon
Gift of Mrs. Frederick L. Eldridge in memory of Henry Bacon   1943.24

Frank W. Benson (1862–1951)
Born and died Salem, Mass. 1880–83, studied at School of the Museum of Fine Arts, Boston; 1883–85, in Paris at Académie Julian. 1885–87, taught at the Portland (Me.) Society of Art; 1889–1917, at School of the Museum of Fine Arts, Boston. Benson, with friends Joseph De Camp and Edmund C. Tarbell, were the ''Boston Men'' of The Ten, a group of American Impressionists who exhibited together for two decades beginning in 1897. A leading figure in Boston's art world, Benson was a successful portraitist, watercolorist, and printmaker and an influential teacher.

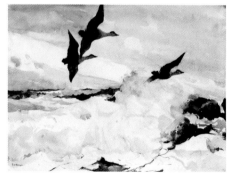

Eider Ducks Flying, c. 1913
Watercolor over graphite on off-white wove paper
Watermark: J WHATMAN 1911/ENGLAND
20 × 27 in. (50.6 × 68.5 cm.)
Signed lower right: F. W. Benson
Museum purchase   1913.60

Benson (continued)
Plate 96
Eider Ducks in Winter, c. 1913
Watercolor, gouache over graphite on off-white wove paper
19¾ × 26⅞ in. (50.1 × 68.1 cm.)
Signed lower right: F. W. Benson
Museum purchase   1913.61

Robert Birmelin (b. 1933)
Born Newark, N.J. Studied at Cooper Union, New York; 1951–54, at the Skowhegan School of Painting and Sculpture, Me. 1956, B.F.A. and 1960, M.F.A. Yale. 1961–64, in Rome on a Prix de Rome. Since 1964, professor at Queens College, N.Y. Summers of 1965 and 1966 taught at Columbia University; 1967, at Skowhegan. A painter, etcher, and draftsman, Birmelin has focused on the crowded streets of Manhattan as his subject since the 1970s.

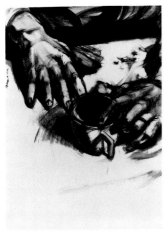

Two Hands with a Cup, 1962
Watercolor on cream wove paper
39 × 27½ in. (99 × 69.9 cm.)
Signed and dated left margin: Birmelin 12–62
Inscribed verso: Robt. Birmelin Rome/Dec/1962/Two hands with a cup
Director's Discretionary Fund   1964.10

Carolyn Brady (b. 1937)
Born Chickasha, Okla. 1959, B.F.A. and 1961, M.F.A. University of Oklahoma, Norman. 1961–67, worked in New York as a textile designer and met fellow realists Joseph Raffael and Audrey Flack. About

1967–71, made brightly colored appliqué "cloth" paintings. 1971, focused on watercolor. 1974, taught at University of Missouri. Associated with Photo-Realism, Brady paints still-life subjects primarily in watercolor.

Plate 113
Last Red Tulips (Baltimore Spring 1984), 1984
Watercolor over graphite on white wove paper
38 × 55½ in. (96.4 × 140.8 cm.)
Signed lower right: Carolyn Brady 1984 ©
Inscribed verso: Carolyn Brady 1984 copyright/*Last Red Tulips (Baltimore Spring 1984)*
Acquired through the National Endowment for the Arts Museum Purchase Plan 1984.132

Charles Burchfield (1893–1967)
Born Ashtabula, Ohio; died Buffalo, N.Y. 1912–16, studied at Cleveland Institute of Art. Supported himself with clerical jobs; painted scenes of countryside in spare time. 1921, to Buffalo. 1921–29, worked as wallpaper designer. For next twenty years, painted depressed villages near Buffalo, in eastern Ohio and Pennsylvania. About 1940, turned again to landscape. One of the major watercolorists of this century, Burchfield imbued depictions of rural surroundings with his own sense of fantasy.

Plate 107
June Wind, 1937
Watercolor on buff wove paper mounted on chipboard
23 × 27⅞ in. (58.4 × 70.8 cm.)
Signed in monogram and dated lower left: CEB/1937
Gift from the Chapin and Mary Alexander Riley Collection   1986.45

Alexander Calder (1898–1976)
Born Philadelphia; died New York. Son and grandson of sculptors. 1919, graduated from Stevens Institute of Technology, Hoboken, N.J. 1923–25, studied at Art Students League, New York. 1926, made first

wooden sculptures. 1926–33, in Paris; made first wire sculptures, first nonobjective constructions and mobiles. 1933, settled at Roxbury, Conn. In 1940s, sculptures grew more monumental in scale. 1953, established a second residence near Tours, France. A versatile sculptor, designer, painter, and printmaker, Calder worked in watercolor and gouache most actively during the last thirty years of his life.

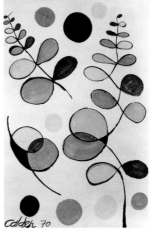

Untitled, 1970
Watercolor on white wove paper
Blind stamp: ANCᴺᴱ MANUFRE CANSON & MONTGOLFIER. VIDALON-LES-ANNONAY
43⅛ × 29³/₁₆ in. (109.5 × 74.2 cm.)
Signed and dated lower left: *Calder 70*
Anonymous promised gift

Walter Appleton Clark (1876–1906)
Born Worcester; died New York. 1891, studied with Worcester artist Anna C. Freeland; 1892–94, at Worcester Polytechnic Institute. Studied at Art Students League, New York, with H. Siddons Mowbray and William Merritt Chase. Taught at Art Students League; Cooper Union, New York; Pennsylvania Academy of the Fine Arts, Philadelphia. Employed from 1897 by *Scribner's Magazine* as an illustrator. 1900, to Paris; 1903–5, at Giverny and Paris. Clark continued to provide illustrations for several American magazines and to design books and murals for the remainder of his short career.

Clark (continued)
Plate 99
King He Is, of Thee Begot, Queen both Fair and Good!, 1899
Gouache, ink, collage, graphite on off-white wove paper
Each panel: 12 × 7¼ in. (30.6 × 18.3 cm.)
Signed lower right of right panel: Walter Appleton Clark
Lettered at upper left: King he is, of thee begot/Queen both fair and good!
Lettered at right: Lo, they blessed, but know it not,/mystery, motherhood!
Inscribed around margins with instructions to printer
Museum purchase   1907.85

Jasper F. Cropsey (1823–1900)
Born Staten Island, N.Y.; died Hastings-on-Hudson, N.Y. 1837–42, worked as architect's apprentice; studied watercolor. 1847–49 and 1856–63, in England and Europe. Made regular sketching trips to New England, New York, Pennsylvania. 1867, elected member of American Society of Painters in Water Colors. 1885, settled at Hastings-on-Hudson as patronage declined. Worked increasingly in watercolor during last 15 years. A second-generation Hudson River School painter, Cropsey is noted for a brilliant autumnal palette.

Plate 54
On the Susquehanna River, 1889
Watercolor, gouache over graphite on cream wove paper
Watermark: 1886 B
10 × 17¹/₁₆ in. (25.4 × 43.8 cm.)
Signed and dated lower left: J. F. Cropsey 1889
Inscribed lower right: On the Susquehanna River
Gift of Mrs. John C. Newington   1985.304

Charles Culver (1908–1967)
Born Chicago; died Huntington Woods, Mich. 1926–30, studied at Wicker School of Fine Arts, Detroit; 1932, at Cranbrook Academy of Art, Bloomfield Hills, Mich.

1946–58, painted wildlife subjects near his home in Bellaire, Mich., and worked as a commercial artist in Detroit. 1960–67, head of department of watercolor and editor for the Society of Arts and Crafts. 1966–67, art critic for the *Detroit Free Press.*

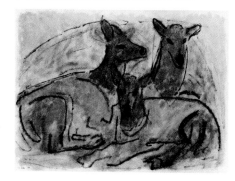

Three Deer Resting, 1948
Watercolor over graphite on off-white wove paper
Watermark: HAND MD LINEN
Blind stamp: ALL PURE LINEN, GRUMBACHER
21 × 29½ in. (53 × 74.5 cm.)
Signed and dated lower left: Three deer resting/C. Culver 1948
Verso: canceled watercolor image
Museum purchase   1948.32

Arthur B. Davies (1862-1928)
Born Utica, N.Y.; died Florence, Italy. 1878, studied at Chicago Academy of Design; c. 1883, at Art Institute of Chicago; 1886–88, at Art Students League and Gotham Art School in New York. 1887, worked as illustrator. Traveled extensively in U.S. and Europe throughout his life. 1908, exhibited with The Eight. 1911, became president of the Association of American Painters and Sculptors, which organized the 1913 Armory Show. An adviser to leading collectors of modern art, Davies was a sculptor, designer, printmaker, and painter.

Plate 97A
Castello, Edge of the Alps, c. 1928
Watercolor over graphite on buff wove paper
7½ × 11 in. (19 × 27.9 cm.)
Signed lower left: A.B. DAVIES
Gift of Mrs. Cornelius N. Bliss   1941.3

Plate 97B
Italian Coast Port, c. 1928
Watercolor over graphite on buff (prepared to coral) wove paper
7½ × 11 in. (19 × 27.9 cm.)
Signed lower left: A.B. DAVIES
Gift of Mrs. Cornelius N. Bliss   1941.4

Alice Preble Tucker de Haas (?–1920)
Born Boston; died New York. Studied at Cooper Union, New York; privately with R. Swain Gifford, William Merritt Chase, Rhoda Holmes Nicholls, and her own husband, Mauritz Frederick de Haas, a Dutch marine painter. Equally well known in her day for watercolors of landscapes and seascapes and for portrait miniatures.

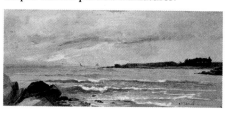

York Bay, Maine
Watercolor over graphite on paper-faced board
9 × 20⅞ in. (22.8 × 53.3 cm.)
Signed lower right: A.P.T. de Haas
Bequest of Stephen Salisbury III   1916.62

Khoren Der Harootian (b. 1909)
Born Ashodavan, Armenia. 1921, immigrated to U.S. 1925-29, studied at School of the Worcester Art Museum with O. Victor Humann. 1931–38, in West Indies; 1938–39, in London. After returning to Jamaica, produced first sculptures in indigenous woods. Present studio near New York. Occasionally visited Italy to work in bronze. Der Harootian's early work focuses on the life of Jamaicans, but his recent expressionist work records Greek mythology and Armenian legends in watercolor and sculpture.

Der Harootian (continued)

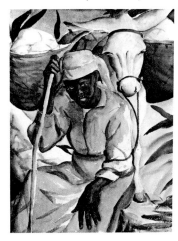

Patience, 1931
Watercolor over graphite on white wove paper
22¹⁄₁₆ × 16⅛ in. (56 × 41.2 cm.)
Signed and dated lower right: Koren Der Harootian/1931
Museum purchase   1932.16

Toni Dove (b. 1946)
Born Flushing, N.Y. 1968, B.F.A. Rhode Island School of Design. 1974–79, taught at Brown University and Pine Manor College; 1979–81, at Boston College. Lives and works as a graphic artist and illustrator in Cambridge, Mass.

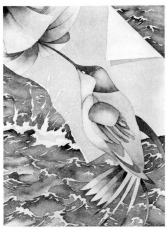

Land Bird, 1974
Watercolor over graphite on cream wove paper
Watermark: ARCHES, FRANCE

30⅞ × 22⅞ in. (78.6 × 58 cm.)
Signed and dated lower right: © Toni Dove '74
Alexander and Caroline M. DeWitt Fund 1974.117

Louis Michel Eilshemius (1864–1941)
Born Arlington, N.J.; died New York. Spent childhood years in Europe. 1884–86, studied at Art Students League, New York; 1886, at Académie Julian, Paris, and that summer in Antwerp. 1888, returned to New York. Traveled widely to Europe, North Africa, Hawaii, and South Pacific. Discovered by Marcel Duchamp at the 1917 Society for Independent Artists exhibition. About 1920, ceased painting to devote energies to musical composition, inventions, and writing.

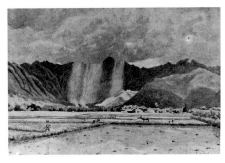

Rice Paddy, c. 1908
Watercolor over graphite on off-white laid paper.
12 × 18 in. (30.5 × 45.7 cm.)
Signed lower right: Elshemus
Gift from the Estate of Dorothy K. Hartwell   1978.53

Dean Fausett (b. 1913)
Born Price, Utah. Studied at Brigham Young University; 1931–36, at Art Students League and National Institute for Architectural Education, New York; 1936, at Colorado Springs Fine Arts Center with muralist Boardman Robinson. 1936–39, taught at Henry Street Settlement House Arts and Crafts School, New York. 1938–44, received several U.S. government commissions for murals. Founder of the Southern Vermont Art Association. Also an etcher and sculptor.

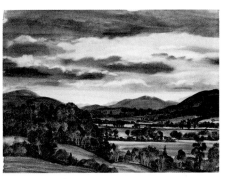

Vermont Landscape, 1940
Watercolor on off-white wove paper
21⅞ × 29⅞ in. (55.4 × 76 cm.)
Signed and dated lower left: Dean Fausett/ 1940
Gift of Friends of Southern Vermont Artists   1940.25

Paul Feeley (1913–1966)
Born Des Moines, Iowa; died New York. 1922–31, lived in California. About 1931, moved to New York. Studied with Cecilia Beaux; with Thomas Hart Benton at Art Students League and Beaux-Arts Institute of Design, New York. 1932–37, taught at Cooper Union, New York. 1946–66, taught painting at Bennington College, Vt., where he mounted early exhibitions of work by Jackson Pollock, David Smith, Hans Hofmann. First worked in Abstract Expressionist manner; c. 1954, turned to more objective, classical style. 1965, began working in sculpture.

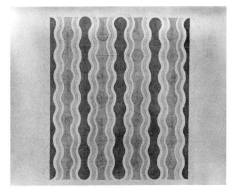

Venice, 1966
Watercolor over graphite on cream wove paper
14⅞ × 19⅝ in. (37.8 × 49.8 cm.)

Feeley (continued)

Inscribed and dated lower right: Venice 29 Jan 66
Gift of Betty Parsons Foundation 1985.279

Lyonel Feininger (1871–1956)

Born and died New York. 1880–87, studied violin. 1887–93, studied art in Hamburg, Berlin, Liège, and Paris. 1893–1906, worked in Berlin as cartoonist and illustrator. 1906, moved to Paris; associated with Jules Pascin and Robert Delaunay. Exhibited in 1911 Salon des Artistes Indépendents and in 1913 with The Blue Rider group in Berlin. 1924, founding member of The Blue Four with Kandinsky, Klee, and Jawlensky. 1919–33, taught at Bauhaus in Weimar and Dessau. 1937, settled in New York. Feininger's paintings and graphics reflect the influences of European modernism, especially Cubism, Futurism, and Expressionism.

Plate 98

The River, 1940
Watercolor over graphite with ink on buff laid paper
9⅝ × 17 in. (24.2 × 43 cm.)
Signed and dated lower left: Feininger 1940
Inscribed verso: The River
Museum purchase   1942.48

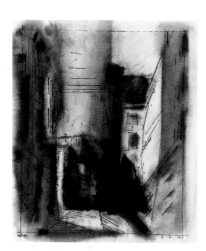

Dead End, 1942

Watercolor, India ink over charcoal on off-white laid paper
Watermark: FABRIANO (Italy)
18¼ × 15¼ in. (46.5 × 38.7 cm.)
Signed lower left: Feininger
Dated lower right: 3. ix. 42
Inscribed lower center: DEAD END
Museum purchase   1943.15

Mary Frank (b. 1933)

Born London. 1950, studied in New York with Max Beckmann; 1951, with Hans Hofmann. Traveled in Spain, France, and England. 1965–70, taught at New School for Social Research, New York; 1970–75, Queens College; 1976, Skowhegan School of Painting and Sculpture, Me. An illustrator and printmaker, Frank is best known for her expressionist terra-cotta sculpture.

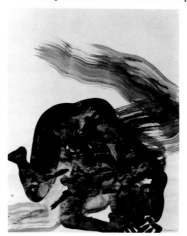

Nude, 1975
Watercolor, ink on ocher laid paper
25⅞ × 19⅞ in. (65.5 × 50.5 cm.)
Signed and dated lower right: Mary Frank 75
Charlotte E. W. Buffington Fund   1976.123

David Fredenthal (1914–1958)

Born Detroit; died Rome. 1934, scholarship from Museum of Modern Art to travel in Europe; 1935–37, scholarship from Cranbrook Academy of Art, Bloomfield Hills, Mich. An early meeting with Diego Rivera influenced him to work in murals. 1937, assistant on Boardman Robinson's murals at Colorado Springs Art Center. 1937–39,

WPA muralist. Worked as an artist-correspondent during World War II on both European and Asian fronts.

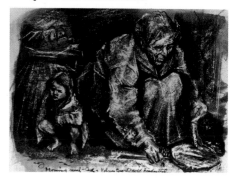

Morning Meal—Cave—Volmen Cove, c. 1947–48
Watercolor, colored ink washes, pen on buff wove paper
8⅜ × 12¼ in. (21.3 × 28.7 cm.)
Signed and inscribed lower margin: Morning Meal—Cave—Volmen Cove—David Fredenthal
Museum purchase   1948.30

Madeleine Gekiere (b. 1919)

Born Zurich. Studied at Slade School, London; at Stanley Hayter's Atelier 17, Paris; with Morris Kantor at Art Students League, New York; with Rufino Tamayo at the Brooklyn Museum School; with Sam Adler at New York University. 1958–67, taught at New York University; since 1967, at City College, New York. Also an active author and illustrator of children's books.

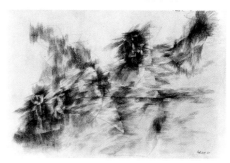

Space Ride, 1960
Graphite, watercolor on off-white laid paper
Watermark: CICONA surmounted by crane
12½ × 18⅞ in. (31.8 × 48 cm.)
Signed and dated lower right: Gekiere 60
Verso: canceled graphite drawing
Director's Discretionary Fund   1961.15

Lev Vladimir Goriansky (1897–1967)

Born near Kharkov, Russia; died Andover, Mass. Served in Russian Imperial Navy during World War I. Immigrated to U.S. 1923, B.S. Architecture and 1925, M.S. at M.I.T. 1933, M.A. Harvard University. 1925-27, practiced architecture with Ralph Adams Cram in Boston; c. 1927–31, with Cross and Cross in New York. About 1942–60, worked as a commercial artist, living in Andover and summering in Northeast Harbor, Me.

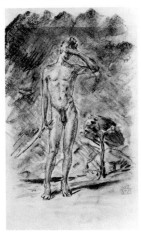

Figure
Watercolor, graphite, black and red chalk on ivory wove paper
14 × 8½ in. (35.5 × 21.5 cm.)
Signed lower right in rectangle: LVG/BTS
Signed upper left margin: Lev Vladimir Goriansky
Gift of Buchanan Charles   1953.58

Morris Graves (b. 1910)

Born Fox Valley, Oreg. Chiefly self-taught, studied briefly in 1937 with Mark Tobey. 1928–30, worked as a seaman sailing to Far East. 1933, work discovered by Seattle Art Museum. 1934–57, lived in Seattle. 1936–39, worked for WPA Federal Art Project. 1943, imprisoned as conscientious objector. 1957–63, resided near Dublin. 1964, settled in Loleta, Calif., where he lives today. Watercolor, gouache, and tempera have been his preferred media.

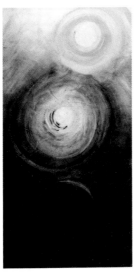

Moon Rising, 1944
Watercolor, gouache on ocher Japanese paper
27¼ × 13⅞ in. (69.2 × 35.2 cm.)
Signed lower right: M Graves
Inscribed lower left: Moon Rising
Gift of William H. and Saundra B. Lane
1976.179

Plate 110

Ibis Feeding on Its Own Breast, 1947
Gouache over ink (?) wash on ocher Japanese paper
23⅛ × 30⅛ in. (58.7 × 76.4 cm.)
Signed lower right: M Graves
Inscribed lower left: Ibis
Museum purchase   1948.31

Chaim Gross (b. 1904)

Born Kolomea, Austria. 1921, immigrated to U.S. 1919, studied briefly in Budapest; 1921, at Educational Alliance Art School, New York; 1922–26, at National Institute for Architectural Education, New York, with sculptor Robert Laurent. An active teacher of sculpture, Gross was a strong advocate of direct carving. In late 1950s began to cast work in bronze from plaster models.

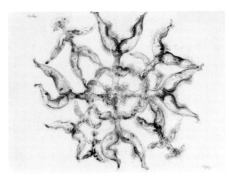

Untitled (sketch for sculpture), 1967
Watercolor over graphite on off-white wove paper
Watermark: [illegible]
22 × 30½ in. (55.8 × 77.5 cm.)
Signed and dated upper and lower right: Chaim Gross/'67
Gift of the artist in honor of Frances and Jacob Hiatt   1974.334

George C. Halcott (?–1930)

Born Albany; died Worcester. Studied architecture with Fuller and Whaler in Albany. 1896, moved to Worcester. Worked with architects Stephen Earle and Clelland W. Fisher. 1904–25, active as architect and served as superintendent of public buildings for the City of Worcester. Although no documentation exists, presumably he signed this rendering of the original Worcester Art Museum building designed by Earle.

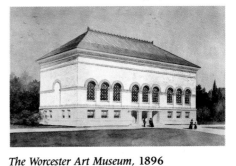

The Worcester Art Museum, 1896
Watercolor over graphite on discolored wove paper
15¾ × 24⅛ in. (40 × 61.2 cm.)
Signed and dated lower right: G. C. Halcott . . . 96
Inscribed lower margin (partially trimmed): Worcester Art Museum, Earle & Asher Architects
Bequest of Stephen Salisbury III   1907.86

203

Lee Hall (b. 1934)
Born Lexington, N.C. B.F.A. University of
North Carolina, Greensboro; M.A. and
Ph.D. New York University. 1965–74,
chairman of art department, Drew University, Madison, N.J. 1974–75, dean of visual
arts, State University of New York, Purchase. 1975–83, president, Rhode Island
School of Design. Hall works in tempera,
acrylic, and watercolor.

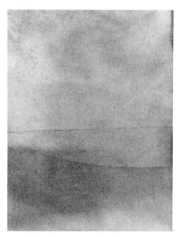

Betty's View/Connecticut Horizon, 1981
Watercolor on Japanese paper mounted on
paper
7⁵⁄₁₆ × 5⁵⁄₈ in. (18.6 × 14.2 cm.)
Signed and dated on mount: Lee Hall '81
Inscribed on mount: Betty's View/Con-
necticut Horizon
Gift of the Betty Parsons Foundation
1985.268

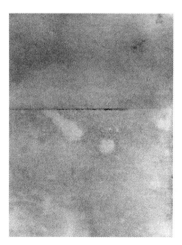

204   *Shore Distance/Betty's Ledge,* 1981

Watercolor on Japanese paper mounted on
paper
7⁵⁄₁₆ × 5⁵⁄₈ in. (18.6 × 14.2 cm.)
Signed and dated on mount: Lee Hall '81
Inscribed on mount: Shore Distance/Betty's
Ledge
Gift of the Betty Parsons Foundation
1985.269

Robert Hallowell (1886–1939)
Born Denver; died New York. 1910, B.A.
Harvard. 1914–25, founder and executive
of the *New Republic.* Studied with illustrator
Howard Pyle; established reputation as
portraitist and illustrator as well as editor
and writer. Traveled to France, Spain, Morocco, and Cuba. 1935–36, assistant director, WPA Federal Arts Project, Washington,
D.C.

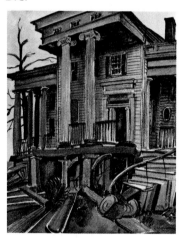

Gloire Passée, 1931
Watercolor over graphite on buff wove paper
23⁷⁄₈ × 19 in. (60.6 × 48.2 cm.)
Signed and dated lower right: R. Hallowell/
'31
Gift of Lee Simonson   1942.46

DeWitt Hardy (b. 1940)
Born St. Louis. 1962, B.A. Syracuse University. Settled in Maine shortly after grad-
uation. About this time turned from
Abstract Expressionism to realism. 1964–
77, curator and associate director of the
Museum of Art, Ogunquit, Me. 1978–81,
scenic designer for Hackmatack Theater,
Berwick, Me. A printmaker and watercolorist, Hardy depicts subjects from his imme-

diate surroundings—town and landscapes
and portraits of family and friends.

Plate 27
View of Dover, New Hampshire, 1976
Watercolor over graphite on white wove
paper
21⁵⁄₈ × 24⁷⁄₈ in. (55 × 62.9 cm.)
Signed lower right: D. Hardy
Gift of Dr. and Mrs. Robert A. Johnson
1985.4

William Stanley Haseltine (1835–1900)
Born Philadelphia; died Rome. 1854, studied with German landscape painter Paul
Weber in Philadelphia. 1855–56, studied
in Düsseldorf with Andreas Achenbach.
1856, visited Switzerland and Italy with
Albert Bierstadt, Emanuel Leutze, and
Worthington Whittredge; lived in Rome
until 1858. 1858–66, in New York. 1866,
in Paris, where he associated with Barbizon
School landscape painters. 1867, settled in
Rome. A leader of the American expatriate
art community in Rome, Haseltine was a
founder of the American Academy there in
the 1890s. He was also a popular painter
of coastal scenes.

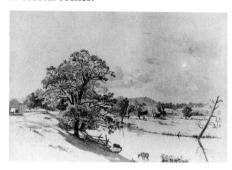

Delaware River, c. 1860
Black wash, pen over graphite on off-white
wove paper
14³⁄₄ × 22 in. (37.6 × 55.8 cm.)
Inscribed lower left: 170
Gift of Helen Haseltine Plowden   1952.20

Childe Hassam (1859–1935)

Born Dorchester, Mass.; died East Hampton, N.Y. 1877–83, active as illustrator in Boston. 1883, first trip to Europe. 1886–89, studied at Académie Julian, Paris; influenced by French Impressionists. 1890, settled in New York and began to summer at various spots along the New England coast; a founder and first president of the New York Water Color Club. 1897, a founder of American Impressionist group, The Ten. 1913, exhibited in Armory Show. 1915, began to work in etching and lithography. Worked extensively in pastel, watercolor, and oil throughout his career.

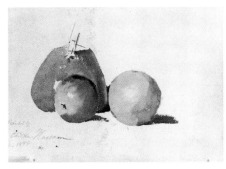

Still Life, 1886
Watercolor over graphite on off-white wove paper
9¾ × 14 in. (24.8 × 35.5 cm.)
Inscribed lower left: Painted by/Childe Hassam/in 1886
Anonymous gift   1941.41

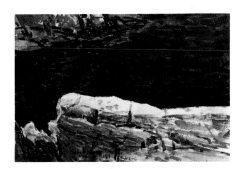

Lyman's Pool, 1912
Watercolor on off-white wove paper
12 × 18 in. (30.3 × 45.8 cm.)
Signed and dated lower center: Childe Hassam/1912
Bequest of Charlotte E. W. Buffington
1935.52

Plate 94

Looking into Beryl Pool, 1912
Watercolor on off-white wove paper
Watermark: J. WHATMAN
10⅞ × 15⅛ in. (27.6 × 38.6 cm.)
Signed and dated upper left: Childe Hassam/1912
Bequest of Charlotte E. W. Buffington
1935.53

Plate 95

Yonkers from the Palisades, 1916
Watercolor over colored pencil and graphite on off-white wove paper
13⅞ × 19⅞ in. (35.2 × 50.5 cm.)
Signed and dated lower left: Childe Hassam/Oct 14th 1916
Museum purchase   1917.40

John William Hill (1812–1879)

Born London; died West Nyack, N.Y. 1823–30, apprenticed to his father, the aquatinter John Hill, who engraved plates for William G. Wall's *Hudson River Portfolio*. 1850, a founding member of New York Water Color Society. About 1855, read Ruskin's *Modern Painters*, which profoundly influenced his style. 1863, president of Association for the Advancement of Truth in Art. A major figure among the American Pre-Raphaelites, Hill worked chiefly in watercolor.

Plate 53

Mountain River, 1868
Watercolor, gouache over graphite on off-white wove paper
Watermark: J WHATMAN 1860
15⅞ × 13¾ in. (40.3 × 35 cm.)
Signed and dated lower left: J. W. Hill/1868
Loring Holmes Dodd Fund   1985.303

Winslow Homer (1836–1910)

Born Boston; died Prout's Neck, Me. About 1854, lithographer's apprentice. 1857, began career as illustrator; artist-reporter for *Harper's* during Civil War. 1862, began to paint regularly. 1866–67, trip to France. 1872, moved to New York. 1873, produced first serious watercolors at Gloucester, Mass.

1881–82, in England. 1883, settled in Prout's Neck, where he first painted seascapes and developed theme of man's relationship to nature. 1884, began winter trips south to Caribbean, Florida, and Bermuda. 1890s, visited Adirondacks and Quebec frequently. 1905, painted last watercolor. 1906, health declined. 1909, completed last major oil.

Plate 59

Boys and Kitten, 1873
Watercolor, gouache over graphite on cream wove paper
9⅝ × 13⅝ in. (24.4 × 34.6 cm.)
Signed lower right below a partial signature: Homer
Sustaining Membership Fund   1911.1

Plate 60

The Swing, probably 1879
Watercolor, pen, graphite on off-white wove paper
7³⁄₁₆ × 9⅝ in. (18.2 × 24.4 cm.)
Signed lower right: Homer
Gift of Mrs. Howard W. Preston in memory of Dr. and Mrs. Loring Holmes Dodd
1969.128

Plate 61

Girl with Shell at Ear, 1880
Gouache, charcoal over graphite on gray (discolored to brown) paper
11⅞ × 11¹³⁄₁₆ in. (30.2 × 30 cm.)
Signed and dated lower right: Homer/1880
Bequest of Grenville H. Norcross   1937.14

Plate 62

Crab Fishing, 1883
Watercolor over graphite on off-white wove paper
Watermark: J WHATMAN
14⁹⁄₁₆ × 21¾ in. (37 × 55.2 cm.)
Signed and dated lower right: Winslow Homer '83
Bequest of Grenville H. Norcross   1937.13

Homer (continued)

Plate 63
Prout's Neck, Rocky Shore, 1883
Watercolor over graphite on off-white wove paper
11½ × 19¾ in. (29.2 × 50 cm.)
Signed and dated lower right: Winslow Homer/1883
Signed lower left: Winslow Homer
Inscribed verso: Prout's Neck Rocky Shore
Museum purchase   1911.16

Plate 64
The Garden Gate, Bahamas, 1885
Watercolor over graphite on off-white wove paper
18½ × 14½ in. (47 × 36.6 cm.)
Signed and dated lower left: Winslow Homer 1885
Bequest of Miss Miriam Shaw   1983.26

Plate 65
In a Florida Jungle, probably 1885–86
Watercolor over graphite on off-white wove paper
14 × 20 in. (35.4 × 50.8 cm.)
Signed lower right: Homer
Inscribed verso: In a Florida Jungle
Museum purchase   1911.19

Plate 66
Old Friends, 1894
Watercolor over graphite on off-white wove paper
21⅜ × 15⅛ in. (54.3 × 38.3 cm.)
Signed and dated lower left: Winslow Homer 1894
Inscribed verso: no. 6 An old Settler/Old Friends
Museum purchase   1908.3

Plate 67
Sunset, Prout's Neck, 1895
Watercolor over graphite on off-white wove paper
13¾ × 19½ in. (34.5 × 49.5 cm.)
Signed and dated lower left: HOMER/1895
Inscribed verso (not by artist): Sunset Gloucester Mass.
Museum purchase   1911.13

Plate 68
Prout's Neck, Surf on Rocks, 1895
Watercolor over graphite on off-white wove paper
15⅛ × 21½ in. (38.4 × 54.5 cm.)
Signed and dated lower right: Winslow Homer/1895
Inscribed verso: Prout's Neck, Surf on Rocks
Museum purchase   1911.20

Plate 69
Grand Discharge, Lake St. John, probably 1897
Watercolor over graphite on off-white wove paper
13⅞ × 21¾ in. (35.3 × 55.3 cm.)
Inscribed lower right: Winslow Homer/by C.S. Homer executor
Inscribed verso: Gr. Discharge, Lake St. John
Museum purchase   1911.18

Plate 70
Saguenay River, Lower Rapids, 1897
Watercolor over graphite on off-white wove paper
14 × 20¹⁵⁄₁₆ in. (35.3 × 53.1 cm.)
Signed and dated lower left: Homer '97
Inscribed verso: Saguenay River Lower Rapids
Museum purchase   1911.21

Plate 71
Rum Cay, 1898–99
Watercolor over graphite on off-white wove paper
14⅞ × 21⅜ in. (37.7 × 54.2 cm.)
Signed lower right: Homer
Inscribed verso: Rum Cay/Bermuda/Winslow Homer/about to turn turtle
Museum purchase   1911.17

Plate 72
The Light House, Nassau, 1899
Watercolor over graphite on cream wove paper
Watermark: J WHATMAN
14½ × 21 in. (36.5 × 53.4 cm.)

Inscribed lower right: Winslow Homer/by C.S. Homer executor
Inscribed lower left: Nassau—99
Inscribed verso: Light House/Nassau
Museum purchase   1911.14

Plate 73
Bermuda Settlers, 1901
Watercolor over graphite on cream wove paper
14 × 21 in. (35.2 × 53.2 cm.)
Signed and dated lower right: Homer/1901
Inscribed verso: Bermuda (The Settlers)
Museum purchase   1911.12

Plate 74
Coral Formation, 1901
Watercolor over graphite on off-white wove paper
14 × 21 in. (35.5 × 53.4 cm.)
Signed and dated lower right: Winslow Homer 1901
Museum purchase   1911.15

Plate 75
Fishing Boats, Key West, 1904
Watercolor over graphite on off-white wove paper
Watermark: J WHATMAN
13⅞ × 21¾ in. (35.3 × 55.2 cm.)
Signed on hull of boat: Homer
Inscribed lower left: Key West 1904
Inscribed verso: Key West/a Norther/Fishing Boats/Key West
Museum purchase   1911.22

Plate 76
The Turkey Buzzard, 1904
Watercolor over graphite on cream wove paper
13⅞ × 19⅝ in. (35 × 49.8 cm.)
Signed and dated lower left: Homer 1904
Museum purchase   1917.6

Charles Sydney Hopkinson (1869–1962)

Born Cambridge, Mass.; died Manchester, Mass. 1891, B.A. Harvard. 1893–95, studied at Art Students League, New York, with H. Siddons Mowbray and John Twachtman; 1896–98, in Paris at Académie Julian with Adolphe William Bouguereau. Returned to Cambridge. Founding member of the Boston Five, a group of watercolorists who exhibited together in New York and Boston, c. 1925–35. Best known as a formal portrait painter.

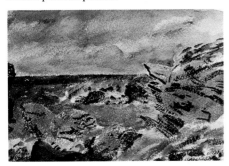

Wind in Bermuda, 1940
Watercolor over graphite on off-white wove paper
14⅞ × 21⅞ in. (37.8 × 55.6 cm.)
Signed lower left: Hopkinson/Bermuda
Museum purchase   1942.49

Edward Hopper (1882–1967)

Born Nyack, N.Y.; died New York. 1900–1905, studied at New York School of Art with Robert Henri, William Merritt Chase, and Kenneth Hayes Miller. 1906–10, three trips to Europe, chiefly Paris. 1908, settled in New York; worked as a commercial artist and illustrator until 1924. 1913, exhibited in Armory Show. 1915–23, worked in etching. 1924, show of watercolors at Frank Rehn Gallery in New York completely sold out, establishing Hopper's reputation. 1934, built summer studio at South Truro on Cape Cod, where he summered throughout his life. 1940s and 1950s, traveled extensively in U.S. and Canada. 1965, stopped painting.

Plate 103
Yawl Riding a Swell, 1935
Watercolor over graphite on off-white wove paper
19⅞ × 27¾ in. (50.5 × 70.4 cm.)
Signed lower left: Edward Hopper
Museum purchase   1935.145

Plate 104
Cobb House, 1942
Watercolor over graphite on off-white wove paper
Watermark: J WHATMAN 1938 ENGLAND
19⅞ × 27¾ in. (50.5 × 70.4 cm.)
Signed lower right: Edward Hopper
Gift of Stephen C. Clarke   1943.9

Earl Horter (1881–1940)

Born and died Philadelphia. Early etchings reflect influences of Whistler and Pennell. 1917–23, worked as commercial artist in Philadelphia. Mid-1920s, lived in Paris, where he met the French modernists and began to collect their work. Also collected work by his Philadelphia friends Charles Sheeler and Arthur B. Carles. 1915–40, exhibited frequently at Pennsylvania Academy of the Fine Arts, Philadelphia. 1933–39, taught at Graphic Sketch Club; Philadelphia Museum School of Art; Tyler School of Art, Philadelphia. Horter was influential in introducing modern art to the Philadelphia public.

Plate 100
Storage Tanks, 1931
Gouache, ink over graphite on off-white wove paper
15¾ × 15¾ in. (40 × 40 cm.)
Signed and dated upper right: E. Horter '31
Gift of David and Selma Medoff   1982.86

Leon Hovsepian (b. 1915)

Born Bloomsburg, Penn. Studied at School of the Worcester Art Museum and at Fogg Art Museum, Cambridge, Mass. 1940, B.F.A. Yale. 1940–81, taught at Worcester Art Museum School; since 1981 at Clark University, Worcester. Awarded numerous public mural commissions in Worcester and New England. 1979, Ford Foundation Fellowship to exhibit in Armenia. Works in stained glass, mosaic, fresco, and bronze as well as oil and watercolor.

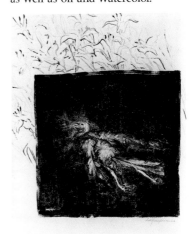

The Flight of a Song, c. 1968
Watercolor, ink over graphite on off-white wove paper mounted on board
27½ × 21⅝ in. (69.8 × 55.1 cm.)
Signed lower right: Leon Hovsepian
Museum purchase   1968.40

O. Victor Humann (1874–1951)

Born Chicago; died Worcester. 1898, graduated from Art Institute of Chicago. 1904–5, studied at Art Students League, Chicago; 1905–7, at Columbia University Teacher's College, New York; 1906, with Arthur W. Dow. 1901–10, taught at Columbia; 1910–38, at School of the Worcester Art Museum. Summered at Monhegan, Me., and Ipswich, Mass.

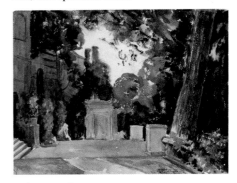

Vatican Gardens

Humann (continued)
Watercolor over graphite on white wove
paper mounted on chipboard
11 × 15⅛ in. (27.8 × 38.5 cm.)
Signed lower right: O. V. Humann
Gift of Mr. and Mrs. O. Victor Humann in
memory of Francis Henry Taylor   1959.75

Joel Janowitz (b. 1945)
Born Newark, N.J. 1967, B.A. Brandeis
University; 1969, M.F.A. University of California, Santa Barbara. Honors include fel-
lowships from National Endowment for the
Arts in 1976 and 1982. Has taught and
exhibited widely, chiefly in New England.

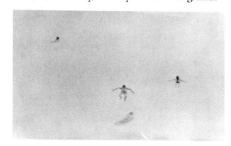

Quiet Water, 1975
Watercolor on white wove paper
Blind stamp: J GREEN
16⅜ × 27¾ in. (41.7 × 70.4 cm.)
Signed and dated lower left: © Janowitz
1975
Inscribed verso: Quiet Water
Gift of Ralph Rose in memory of his mother,
Mary D. Rose   1983.73

Rockwell Kent (1882–1971)
Born Tarrytown, N.Y.; died Plattsburg, N.Y.
1900, studied with William Merritt Chase;
1904, with Robert Henri, Kenneth Hayes
Miller, and Abbott Thayer. An organizer of
1910 Exhibition of Independent Artists;
subsequently involved in such politically
active organizations as the American Artists' Congress. Beginning in 1918, traveled
widely to Alaska, Europe, Latin America,
and Greenland. 1967, awarded Lenin Peace
Prize in Moscow. A versatile artist, Kent
worked in wood engraving, lithography,
textiles, oil, and watercolor.

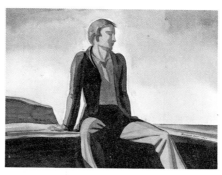

Man Seated, probably 1926
Watercolor over graphite on off-white wove
paper
9¾ × 13¾ in. (24.7 × 34.8 cm.)
Signed and dated lower right: Rockwell
Kent 1927
Museum purchase   1927.12

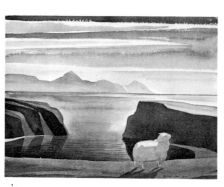

Landscape with Sheep, probably 1926
Watercolor over graphite on off-white wove
paper
9¾ × 13¾ in. (24.7 × 34.8 cm.)
Signed and dated lower right: Rockwell
Kent 1927
Museum purchase   1927.13

Plate 101
Cottage in a Landscape, probably 1926
Watercolor over graphite on off-white wove
paper
9¾ × 13¾ in. (24.7 × 34.8 cm.)
Signed and dated center lower margin:
Rockwell Kent 1927
Museum purchase   1927.15

Plate 102
Woman Reaping, probably 1926
Watercolor over graphite on off-white wove
paper
9¾ × 13¾ in. (24.7 × 34.8 cm.)
Signed and dated lower right: Rockwell
Kent 1927
Museum purchase   1927.16

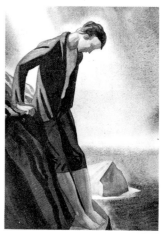

Boy on a Cliff, probably 1926
Watercolor over graphite on off-white wove
paper
13¾ × 9¾ in. (34.8 × 24.7 cm.)
Signed and dated lower left: Rockwell Kent
1927
Museum purchase   1927.14

Franz Kline (1910–1962)
Born Wilkes-Barre, Penn.; died New York.
1919–25, attended Girard College, Philadelphia; 1931–32, Boston University;
1936–38, Heatherley's School of Fine Art,
London. 1938, settled in New York. During
1940s painted portraits, figures, and street
scenes in a variety of styles. 1952, taught
at Black Mountain College, Asheville, N.C.;
1953–54, at Pratt Institute, New York. A
member of the New York School of Abstract
Expressionism.

Kline (continued)
Plate 24
Untitled, c. 1952
Watercolor, oil wash on white typing paper
10⅞ × 8½ in. (27.7 × 21.6 cm.)
Signed lower right of support: Kline
Gift of Mrs. Helen Sagoff Slosberg   1980.3

Lois Jean Knobler (b. 1929)
Born New York. 1950, B.F.A. Syracuse
University; 1951, M.F.A. Florida State University. Has exhibited widely in New England. Knobler works in acrylic, tempera,
watercolor, and, more recently, in multimedia sculpture.

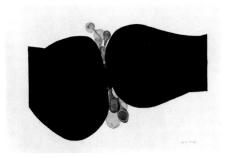

Drawing 2, 1962
Gouache on white wove paper mounted on
chipboard
10 × 15 in. (25.4 × 38 cm.)
Signed lower right: Lois Jean Knobler
Director's Discretionary Fund   1963.97

Florence Koehler (1861–1944)
Born in western U.S.; died in Rome. Lived
in Europe, chiefly London, Paris, and Rome.
Active as a potter, interior and jewelry
designer. Exhibited in 1893 Columbian
Exposition. Traveled widely in Europe and
Far East. About 1912–13, turned to painting. Acquaintances included Roger Fry,
Henry James, and Isabella Stewart Gardner.
An artist of eclectic tastes, Koehler drew
on diverse influences from Coptic and
Byzantine art to the modernism of Matisse.

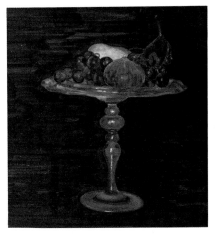

Fruit, No. 2
Gouache on paper mounted on chipboard
16⅝ × 15¼ in. (42.3 × 38.6 cm.)
Gift of Mrs. Henry D. Sharpe   1951.36

Yayoi Kusama (b. 1929)
Born Matsumoto, Japan. 1949, graduated
from Kyoto Arts and Crafts School. 1957,
settled in New York. 1966, became U.S.
citizen. Presently lives in Tokyo. Has exhibited widely in Europe and America.
About 1960, began to achieve recognition
for aggressive, highly personal work, which
relates to performance art, environments,
and ''happenings.''

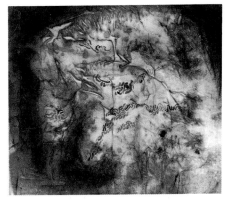

Pacific Ocean (No. 1), 1959
Watercolor, charcoal, pastel on laid Oriental
paper mounted on board
23¾ × 28¼ in. (60.3 × 71.4 cm.)
Signed and dated lower left: 1959/Yayoi
Kusama

Inscribed verso: Pacific Ocean/Yayoi Kusama/No. 1 1959
Gift of Mrs. Helen Sagoff Slosberg   1973.1

John La Farge (1835–1910)
Born New York; died Providence, R.I. Instructed in art by his grandfather. 1856–
57, briefly studied painting with Thomas
Couture in Paris; 1859, with William Morris Hunt in Newport, R.I. 1860s, painted
landscapes and still lifes and did illustrations. 1876, executed his first large-scale
mural at Trinity Church, Boston. Late
1870s, established a workshop to fulfill
large-scale decorative commissions. Traveled to Europe in 1873; with writer Henry
Adams to Japan in 1886 and to South
Pacific in 1890–91. A versatile artist who
worked in several media, La Farge collaborated with some of the foremost architects
and artists of his time.

Plate 55
Sacred Font, Iyémitsu Temple, Nikko, 1886
Watercolor over graphite on off-white wove
paper
8¾ × 11⅛ in. (22.1 × 28.3 cm.)
Signed and dated lower left: Nikko 1886.
LF
Inscribed upper left: Sacred font Iyémetsu
Temple/from platform of 2nd Gate
Gift of Dr. Samuel B. Woodward   1939.48

Plate 56
Musicians in Ceremonial Costume, 1887
Watercolor, gouache, gum glaze over
graphite on buff Japanese paper
10 × 9 in. (25.6 × 22.9 cm.)
Signed and dated lower right: JLF 1887
Gift of Dr. Samuel B. Woodward   1939.49

Plate 57
*The Three Marys: Study for the Southworth
Window, Church of the Ascension, New York*,
1889
Watercolor, gouache over graphite on buff
architect's tracing paper
15⅛ × 7¼ in. (38.4 × 18.5 cm.)
Signed and dated lower left: La Farge 1889
Gift of Felix A. Gendrot   1935.113

La Farge (continued)
Plate 58
The Last Sight of Tahiti: Trade Winds, 1891
Watercolor, gouache over graphite on buff
wove paper
8¾ × 16⅝ in. (22.2 × 42.2 cm.)
Dated lower right: June 7, 91
Inscribed verso: No. 21/The Last Sight of
Tahiti. Trade Winds
Gift of Dr. Samuel B. Woodward   1939.52

Jacob Lawrence (b. 1917)
Born Atlantic City, N.J. 1920, settled in
Harlem, N.Y. 1934–38, studied with
Charles Alston at Harlem Workshop; 1934–
37, with Henry Bannarn at College Art
Association, New York; 1937–39, with
Anton Refrigier at American Artists School.
1939–40, worked at WPA Federal Art Project. 1946, taught at Black Mountain College, Asheville, N.C., and then elsewhere.
Since 1971, at University of Washington,
Seattle. Lawrence paints serial narratives of
historical or contemporary black experience in America, chiefly in tempera or
gouache.

Plate 26
They Live in Fire Traps, 1943
Gouache on off-white wove paper
21½ × 14⅜ in. (54.7 × 36.6 cm.)
Signed and dated lower right: J. Lawrence
43
Museum purchase   1943.14

Elizabeth Lee (b. 1906)
Born Boston. Studied with Charles W.
Hawthorne. Member of Provincetown Art
Association. Married Allan McKissock.
Exhibited at the Grace Horne Galleries,
Boston. Little else known about her career.

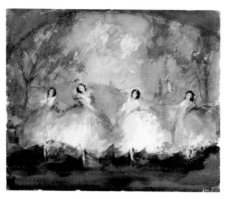

Russian Ballet Dancers
Watercolor on off-white wove paper
15⅛ × 18¾ in. (38.3 × 47.5 cm.)
Signed lower right: Lee
Museum purchase   1934.91

Mong Q. Lee (1923–1960)
Born Canton, China; died Boston. Began
to exhibit in U.S. in mid-1950s after studying in New England schools. Lived in
Lynn, Mass., and Rockport, Me. Worked
only in watercolor.

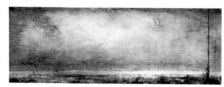

Waiting, 1956
Watercolor over ink on Oriental laid paper
13¾ × 40⅛ in. (34.9 × 101.7 cm.)
Signed lower left: Mong Q. Lee
Signed and dated at right margin in
Chinese characters above artist's seal: Mong
Q. Lee 1956
Director's Discretionary Fund   1956.81

Edmund Darch Lewis (1835–1910)
Born and died Philadelphia. About 1850–
55, probably studied with Paul Weber, a
German-born landscape painter in Philadelphia. 1854, first exhibited at Pennsylvania Academy of the Fine Arts, Philadelphia;
1862, elected Academician. In 1860s and
1870s, painted landscapes chiefly in mid-
Atlantic states, and New England. By 1880s,
he amassed a fortune from artistic success
and focused on collecting European fine

and decorative arts. Reputation as painter
declined, and he turned to watercolor as
primary medium.

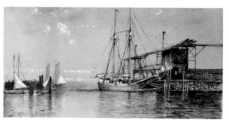

Harbor Scene, 1881
Watercolor over graphite on pale green
(discolored to ocher) wove paper
9⅞ × 20 in. (24.9 × 50.7 cm.)
Signed and dated lower right: Edmund D.
Lewis 1881
Gift of Mr. and Mrs. Hall James
Peterson   1982.106

Sol LeWitt (b. 1928)
Born Hartford, Conn. 1949, B.F.A. Syracuse
University. 1954–60, graphic designer.
1964–71, taught in New York at Museum
of Modern Art School, Cooper Union, the
School of Visual Arts, and New York University. 1976, founded *Printed Matter*, a
publisher and distributor of artists' books.
Associated with Minimalism and concep-
tual art, LeWitt has focused on the grid
and cube as the primary elements for his
serial paintings, sculptures, and prints.

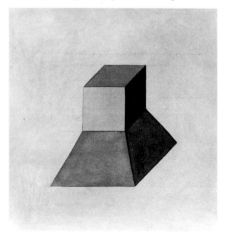

Form Derived from a Cube, 1982
Watercolor over graphite on off-white wove
paper

LeWitt (continued)

20⅜ × 20⅜ in. (51.7 × 51.7 cm.)
Signed and dated lower right: S. LeWitt
1982
Acquired through the National Endowment
for the Arts Museum Purchase Plan
1984.134

Charles H. Lincoln (1861–1943)

Born Petersham, Mass.; died Worcester.
1891–1920, practicing architect; 1891–94,
in partnership with J. W. Patston. Winner
of 1899 competition for the design of the
Worcester Art Museum's seal.

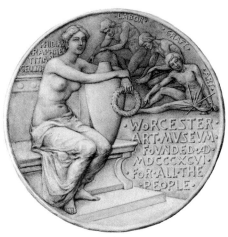

Design for Worcester Art Museum Seal, 1899
Watercolor, ink over printed tone on buff
wove paper
Image: 4¼ in. (10.6 cm.) diameter
Plate size: 9⅞ × 7⅞ in. (25.2 × 20 cm.)
Signed and dated lower right: Charles H.
Lincoln/Des et del–1899
Gift of the artist   1899.27

Jacques Lipchitz (1891–1973)

Born in Druskieniki, Lithuania; died Capri.
1901–10, studied sculpture at Académie
Julian, Paris; at École des Beaux-Arts and
Académie Colarossi, Paris. 1912–16, met
many important avant-garde artists, including Modigliani, Picasso, and Gris. By
1920s, established an international reputation as Cubist sculptor. 1941, immigrated
to New York. 1946, established a studio at
Hastings-on-Hudson, N.Y. 1958, became
U.S. citizen. Received many commissions
for monumental sculptures and exhibited

internationally. Chiefly a sculptor, Lipchitz
drew on biblical and classical myths for
his themes.

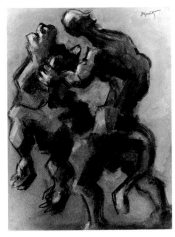

Study for Theseus and the Minotaur, 1942
Gouache, conté, wash, charcoal, over
graphite on gray laid paper
25½ × 19¼ in. (64.8 × 49 cm.)
Signed upper right: J. Lipchitz
Director's Discretionary Fund   1943.10

Dodge Macknight (1860–1950)

Born Providence, R.I.; died East Sandwich,
Mass. 1883, studied at Atelier Cormon,
Paris. 1886, traveled to Algeria, England,
and Spain. 1900, settled on Cape Cod. Remained chiefly in New England, making
brief visits to Mexico, Utah, and the Mediterranean. The patronage of Isabella
Stewart Gardner greatly enhanced his reputation. 1929, ceased painting. Acclaimed
in the 1920s as a great American watercolorist, Macknight was one of the first in
a long line of artists who emulated the
style of John Singer Sargent.

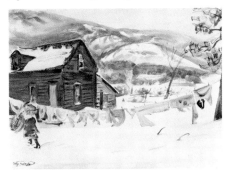

French Canadian Wash, c. 1918

Watercolor on white wove paper
Watermark: O.W.P. & A.O.W.
15¼ × 21⅝ in. (38.2 × 54.8 cm.)
Signed lower left: Dodge Macknight
Museum purchase   1918.16

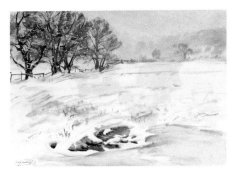

Meadow in Snow, c. 1918
Watercolor over graphite on off-white wove
paper
15⅜ × 22 in. (38.3 × 56 cm.)
Signed lower left: Dodge Macknight
Museum purchase   1918.186

Plate 20

*Grand Canyon of the Colorado (Looking West
Toward Havasupai Point)*, c. 1915
Watercolor over graphite on off-white wove
paper
Watermark: MADE IN ENGLAND [illegi-
ble] 19–
17¾ × 22¼ in. (45 × 56.6 cm.)
Signed lower right: Dodge Macknight
Gift of Henry H. and Zoe Oliver Sherman
1922.199

Reginald Marsh (1898–1954)

Born in Paris; died Dorset, Vt. Raised in
Nutley, N.J. 1920, B.A. Yale University.
1920–30, worked chiefly as an illustrator
in New York. 1919–24, studied at Art Students League, New York, with John Sloan,
Kenneth Hayes Miller, Boardman Robinson, and George Luks, all of whom influenced him. 1925–26, trip to Europe led to
increasing study of old masters. 1936–54,
taught at Art Students League. 1945, published *Anatomy for Artists*. Associated with
the Fourteenth Street School, which de-

Marsh (continued)

picted New York city life, Marsh was a muralist, painter, and printmaker.

Plate 108
View of Manhattan, 1929
Watercolor over graphite on off-white wove paper
13⅞ × 20 in. (35.3 × 50.6 cm.)
Signed and dated lower right: Reginald Marsh 1929
Stamped lower right: F. Marsh Collection/ WC29
Inscribed lower right: WC 29-39
Stamped verso: F. Marsh Collection/Cat #WC29-39
Bequest of Felicia Meyer Marsh   1979.25

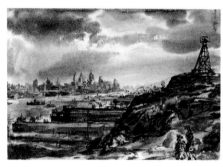

New York, from the Palisades, Weehawken, 1940
Watercolor over graphite on white wove paper
Watermark: J WHATMAN
15⅛ × 22½ in. (38.3 × 57.1 cm.)
Signed and dated lower right: Reginald Marsh 1940
Inscribed verso: New York from the Palisades $150
Gift of Friends of Southern Vermont Artists   1940.24

Plate 25
Street Scene, 1944
Watercolor on cream wove paper
13⅞ × 19⅞ in. (35.2 × 50.5 cm.)
Signed and dated lower right: Reginald Marsh 1944
Gift of Mr. and Mrs. Robert Warner 1984.56

Plates 109A and 109B
Tessie's Bridal Shop, 1946
Ink wash, watercolor over graphite on white wove paper
Watermark: J WHATMAN 1936 HAND-MADE ENGLAND
27⅜ × 40½ in. (69 × 102.8 cm.)
Stamped lower right: F. Marsh Collection Cat/#207
Verso: similar subject without watercolor
Bequest of Felicia Meyer Marsh   1979.24

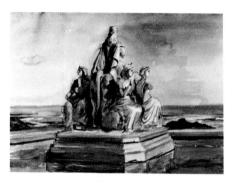

Monument on the Shore
Watercolor over graphite on white wove paper
13⅞ × 19⅞ in. (35.3 × 50.5 cm.)
Stamped lower right: F. Marsh Collection/ Cat #WC161
Inscribed verso: WC No-161
Bequest of Felicia Meyer Marsh   1979.26

Todd McKie (b. 1944)
Born Boston. 1966, B.F.A. Rhode Island School of Design. Since the mid-1970s, has exhibited widely in New England and New York. Chiefly a watercolorist, McKie also works in oil and makes silkscreen prints; his subjects poke fun at the formal heritage of modern art, especially Surrealism and Cubism.

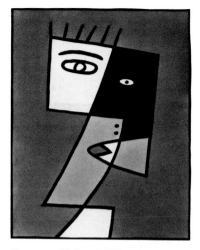

European Visitor, 1977
Watercolor on white wove paper
Watermark: ARCHES 14
26⅝ × 20¾ in. (67.5 × 52.7 cm.)
Signed and dated lower right: McKie 1977
Gift of Mr. and Mrs. B. A. King in honor of Richard Stuart Teitz   1981.346

Plate 7
Slide Show, 1978
Watercolor on off-white wove paper
Watermark: ARCHES FRANCE 12
24⅞ × 21⅛ in. (62.2 × 53.6 cm.)
Signed and dated lower right: McKie 1978
Gift of Sidney Rose in memory of his mother, Mary D. Rose   1983.64

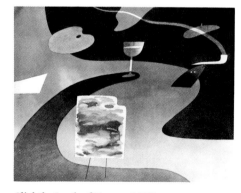

Slightly South of France, 1979
Watercolor on off-white wove paper
24⅝ × 32⅛ in. (62.3 × 81.6 cm.)
Signed and dated lower right: McKie 1979
Gift of Sidney Rose in memory of his mother, Mary D. Rose   1983.65

McKie (continued)

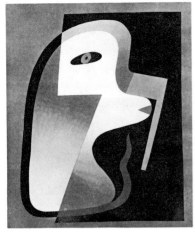

Woman with a Pipe, **1980**
Watercolor on off-white wove paper
49⅞ × 42⅛ in. (126.6 × 107.2 cm.)
Signed and dated lower right: McKie 1980
Inscribed verso: Woman with Pipe 1980
Gift of Sidney Rose in memory of his
mother, Mary D. Rose   1983.66

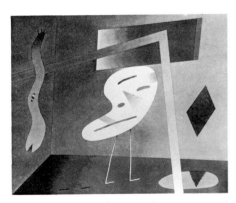

Simplicity Rears Its Ugly Head, **1981**
Watercolor on off-white wove paper
42⅛ × 53 in. (107.2 × 134.5 cm.)
Signed and dated lower right: McKie 1981
Inscribed verso: Simplicity Rears Its Ugly
Head 1981
Gift of Sidney Rose in memory of his
mother, Mary D. Rose   1983.67

Mary Melikian (b. 1927)

Born Worcester. 1955, B.F.A. Rhode Island
School of Design. 1957–59, studied at
Teachers College, Columbia University. First
specialized in textile design. 1961–67, on
staff of Grand Central Art Galleries, New
York. 1967, began to paint full-time. Melikian paints still life and landscape subjects,
chiefly in pastel and watercolor.

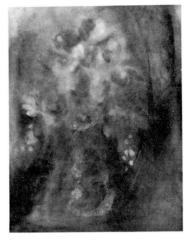

Roses, **1968**
Watercolor on white Japanese paper
11 × 8⅜ in. (27.9 × 21.2 cm.)
Signed lower right: Melikian
Gift of the artist   1969.41

Ludwig Mestler (1891–1959)

Born Vienna; died Cambridge, Mass. Studied architecture in Vienna. 1923, came to
U.S. Worked as architect in New York.
1929, turned to painting. 1931–38, traveled
in Austria, Germany, and Italy. 1938, settled in Cambridge, Mass. 1939, first one-
man show held at Worcester Art Museum.
Chiefly a graphic artist, Mestler specialized
in architectural and landscape subjects.

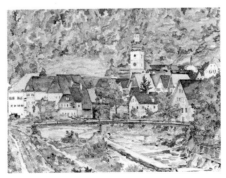

*Village of Lauffen on the Traun, Upper Aus-
tria*, **1932**
Watercolor over graphite on ivory wove
paper
9¾ × 13¼ in. (24.7 × 33.6 cm.)
Signed and dated lower right: Ludwig
Mestler/32
Museum purchase   1939.44

Barry Moser (b. 1940)

Born Chattanooga, Tenn. Studied at Au-
burn University, Montgomery, Ala.; University of Chattanooga; University of
Massachusetts; also with Leonard Baskin
and Jack Coughlin. Since 1967, he has
taught at high school and college levels.
Active as a book illustrator, Moser has
exhibited widely in New England since the
late 1960s.

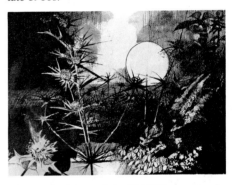

Landscape of Eternal Youth, **1976**
Ink, chalk, gouache on blue-gray laid paper
Watermark: G Wilmot 1914
Image: 5 1/16 × 7⅛ in. (12.9 × 18 cm.)
Signed lower right: B. Moser
Inscribed lower left: Study for Landscape of
Eternal Youth
Gift of the artist   1977.19

Robert Motherwell (b. 1915)

Born Aberdeen, Wash. Raised on West
Coast. 1936, B.A. Stanford University.
1937–38, studied philosophy at Harvard
University; 1940–41, art history at Columbia University with Meyer Schapiro, who
introduced him to leading European expatriate artists in New York. 1942, began
experimenting with Surrealist automatism.
By early 1940s, associated with young
Abstract Expressionists. 1945 and 1951,
taught at Black Mountain College, Asheville, N.C. A prolific painter, collage maker,
muralist, printmaker, teacher, and author,
Motherwell is a prominent figure among
the Abstract Expressionists.

213

Motherwell (continued)

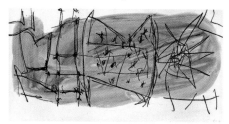

Cartoon for a Mural, 1951
Graphite over watercolor on white wove
paper laminate
14⅜ × 29 in. (36.5 × 73.5 cm.)
Sarah C. Garver Fund   1973.94

Antonia Munroe (b. 1952)
Born New York. 1969–72, studied at Simon's Rock Early College, Great Barring-
ton, Mass.; 1973, at San Francisco Art
Institute. 1975, textile designer in New York
for Fieldcrest Mills. Since the late 1970s,
she has exhibited widely in New England.
Currently living in Vermont, Munroe paints
chiefly still lifes and landscapes in gouache.

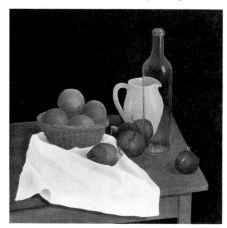

Still Life with Pink Onion and Blue Bottle
Gouache on white wove paper
19½ × 19⅛ in. (49.5 × 48.6 cm.)
Signed lower right: Antonia Munroe
Gift of Sidney Rose in memory of his
mother, Mary D. Rose   1984.156

Carl Gustaf Nelson (b. 1898)
Born Horby, Sweden. 1903, immigrated to
U.S. 1919, became U.S. citizen. 1920–21,
studied at Chicago Academy of Fine Arts;
1923–27, at Art Students League, New

York. 1934, worked in WPA Federal Arts
Project. 1934–42, taught at American People's School, New York. 1945, moved to
Boston, where he taught at a variety of
schools in the 1940s and 1950s. A painter
of landscape and still life subjects, Nelson
was influenced by Cubism.

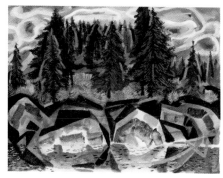

Maine Shore, 1946
Gouache, ink over graphite on off-white
wove paper
18¾ × 25⅞ in. (47.6 × 65.6 cm.)
Signed and dated lower right: C G Nelson/46
Inscribed verso: Maine Shore
Museum purchase   1947.15

Charles Hovey Pepper (1864–1950)
Born Waterville, Me.; died Brookline, Mass.
1889, B.A. and 1891, M.A. Colby College,
Waterville. Mid-1890s, studied at Art Students League, New York, and at Académie
Julian, Paris. Visited Europe and later Japan. About 1900, settled in the Boston
area. From 1912 often summered at Attean
Lake, Me. Pepper painted portraits and
landscapes in oil and watercolor.

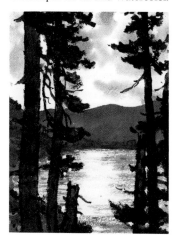

Attean Lake, c. 1939
Watercolor, gouache on ivory wove paper
15¼ × 11¼ in. (38.5 × 28.6 cm.)
Museum purchase   1939.40

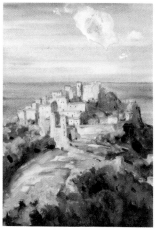

Eze, in Southern France, c. 1939
Watercolor, gouache on off-white wove
paper
21½ × 14¾ in. (54.5 × 37.6 cm.)
Inscribed verso: Stephen C. Pepper/Eze
France
Museum purchase   1939.41

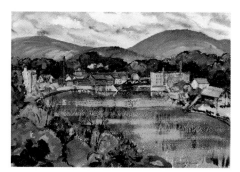

Skowhegan, Maine, c. 1941
Watercolor, gouache on white wove paper
15 × 22⅛ in. (38 × 56.2 cm.)
Signed lower right: Charles H. Pepper
Gift of the artist   1941.52

Gabor Peterdi (b. 1915)

Born near Budapest. 1929, studied at Academy of Fine Arts, Budapest. 1931, won Prix de Rome. 1932–34, studied at Académie Julian, Paris; with Stanley Hayter at Atelier 17. 1939, immigrated to U.S. 1942, settled in New York. 1947, worked again with Hayter. Traveled widely in Europe, Hawaii, and Alaska. 1949–53, taught printmaking at Brooklyn Museum School; 1951–60, at Hunter College; since 1960, at Yale. A prolific and influential printmaker and teacher.

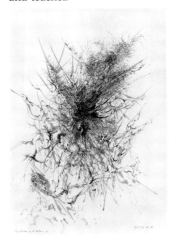

Temptation of St. Anthony, 1963
Wash, gouache on off-white wove paper
42 × 29¾ in. (106.6 × 75.7 cm.)
Signed and dated lower right: Peterdi 63 III
Director's Discretionary Fund   1963.100

Ogden M. Pleissner (1905–1983)

Born Brooklyn, N.Y.; died London. Studied at Art Students League, New York, with Frank Bridgman and Frank DuMond. 1930s, began painting in watercolor. 1942–43, served in U.S. Army Air Force. 1944, war artist-correspondent for *Life*. Traveled extensively in Europe and the American West, especially Wyoming. Lived in New York, summering in Vermont. Primarily a landscape painter, Pleissner is best known for precisely rendered architectural scenes of European cities and sporting subjects.

Plate 22

The Ramparts, St. Malo, 1950
Watercolor over graphite on off-white wove paper
19 × 27 in. (48.2 × 65.5 cm.)
Signed lower right: Pleissner
Museum purchase   1951.4

Maurice B. Prendergast (1858–1924)

Born St. John's, Newfoundland; died New York. Raised in Boston. Late 1870s, began to work as a commercial artist. 1886, traveled to England, the first of several trips abroad. 1891–94, studied in Paris at Atelier Colarossi and Académie Julian; saw work by James McNeill Whistler, Edouard Manet, Aubrey Beardsley. 1895–1914, chiefly in Boston. 1908, exhibited with The Eight; 1913, in Armory Show. 1914, moved to New York and began to summer on New England coast. Prendergast was among the first Americans to be consistently influenced by the Post-Impressionists and Nabis.

Plate 89

Low Tide, Beachmont, probably 1902–4
Watercolor over graphite, charcoal on off-white wove paper
19¼ × 22⅛ in. (48.8 × 56.2 cm.)
Signed and dated in different hands lower right: Prendergast 1897/1897
Museum purchase   1941.34

Plate 90

Across the Harbor, Salem, c. 1905–7
Watercolor, gouache over graphite on off-white wove paper
10¼ × 14¼ in. (26.3 × 36 cm.)
Signed lower left: Prendergast
Verso: graphite sketch of figures at the shore
Museum purchase   1941.35

Plate 91

Notre Dame, Paris, 1907
Watercolor over graphite on off-white wove paper
13¾ × 19⅞ in. (34.8 × 50.5 cm.)

Signed lower right: Maurice Prendergast
Inscribed verso: Prendergast/Paris 1907
Museum purchase   1941.36

Plate 92

Venice, probably 1911
Watercolor over graphite on buff wove paper
15 × 22 in. (38.2 × 55.9 cm.)
Signed lower right: Maurice B. Prendergast
Inscribed verso: Venice/1909 Bliss #1
Verso: graphite sketch of Venice
Museum purchase   1941.37

Plate 93

Gloucester Park, c. 1916
Watercolor over charcoal, graphite on off-white wove paper
Watermark: 1916 UNBLEACHED ARNOLD
10⅞ × 22½ in. (27.7 × 57.1 cm.)
Signed lower left: Prendergast
Inscribed lower right: Bliss #4
Museum purchase   1941.38

George Ratkai (b. 1907)

Born Budapest. 1929, became U.S. citizen. Lives in New York with a studio on Long Island. An artist and illustrator, Ratkai has also executed large sculptures in concrete and stainless steel.

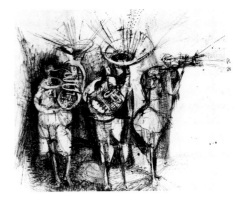

Men of Brass, 1960
Gouache, ink, watercolor on off-white wove paper
27⅛ × 33⅝ in. (68.8 × 85.2 cm.)
Signed lower right: G. Ratkai
Director's Discretionary Fund   1961.13

William Trost Richards (1833–1905)

Born Philadelphia; died Newport, R.I. 1848, studied in Philadelphia with German painter Paul Weber. 1850–55, worked as a designer of ornamental ironwork. 1855, traveled to Paris, Florence, and Düsseldorf; visited Europe frequently thereafter. 1863, member of Association for the Advancement of Truth in Art. 1874, established a studio at Newport. A landscape and marine specialist, Richards worked increasingly in watercolor after c. 1870.

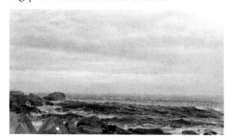

Sea and Rocks, c. 1875–80
Watercolor over graphite on gray wove paper
7¾ × 13¾ in. (19.7 × 35 cm.)
Gift of National Academy of Design from the Bequest of Mrs. William T. Brewster
1954.17

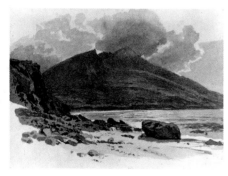

Slievemore, Achill Island, Ireland, 1893
Watercolor over graphite on buff wove paper
5⅛ × 7⅜ in. (13.1 × 18.7 cm.)
Inscribed verso: Slieve-More-Achill Island/Ireland
Gift of National Academy of Design from the Bequest of Mrs. William T. Brewster
1954.18

Chris Ritter (1906–1976)

Born Iola, Kans.; died Ogunquit, Me. B.A. University of Kansas; graduate study at Columbia University. Studied at Art Students League, New York, with Richard Lahey, George Grosz, and Morris Kantor. 1939–41, taught at Hunter College; 1947, at Cornell University; 1947–53, at Ballard School, New York; 1954, at Midland (Texas) Art Center. 1956, moved to Ogunquit. 1958–61, president of the Ogunquit Art Association. Ritter worked in oil, watercolor, and etching.

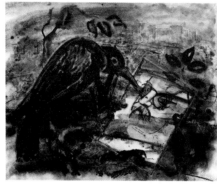

Crow and Self-Portrait of Matisse, 1942
Watercolor, collage, charcoal, ink, monoprint on off-white wove paper
Watermark: LAVIS J PERRIGOT ARCHES SPECIAL MBM (FRANCE) TRAIT
19¾ × 24¾ in. (50 × 63 cm.)
Signed and dated lower right: Chris Ritter '42
Museum purchase   1947.14

Ellen Robbins (1828–1905)

Born Watertown, Mass.; died Boston. Studied at New England School of Design in Boston with painter and author Stephen Tuckerman. Traveled widely in Europe and U.S. Lived in Boston and taught painting in her studio. Neoclassical sculptor Harriet Hosmer was a childhood friend and patron. Although few details of her life are known, her watercolors of wild flowers and autumn leaves were enormously popular during her lifetime; several were reproduced as chromolithographs by Louis Prang and Company.

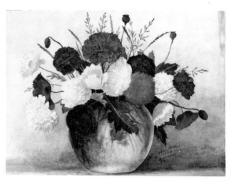

Carnations and Poppies, 1888
Watercolor, gouache over graphite on off-white wove paper
19 × 26 in. (48.2 × 66 cm.)
Signed and dated lower right: Ellen Robbins/1888/Appledore
Gift of Mrs. Gertrude Thaxter   1911.23

Olive Rush (1873–1966)

Born near Fairmount, Ind.; died Sante Fe, N.M. About 1890, studied at Corcoran School of Art, Washington, D.C.; 1900–1904, at Art Students League, New York, with John Twachtman and H. Siddons Mowbray; c. 1904, in Wilmington, Del., with illustrator Howard Pyle. Illustrations appeared in *St. Nicholas*, *Scribner's*, *Colliers*, and other magazines. By 1921, settled in New Mexico. Worked for U.S. Department of the Interior, becoming director of art at the Indian School of Santa Fe. Influenced by Oriental brushwork and by American Indian motifs, Rush is best known for watercolors of animals.

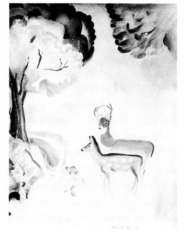

Edge of the Forest, c. 1928

Rush (continued)
Watercolor on off-white wove paper
Watermark: WHATMAN
9⅝ × 7¼ in. (24 × 18.5 cm.)
Signed lower right: Olive Rush
Museum purchase   1928.28

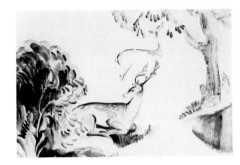

Fallow Deer, c. 1928
Watercolor over graphite on cream wove paper
Watermark: J WHATMAN
11¼ × 17¼ in. (28.5 × 43.8 cm.)
Signed lower right: Olive Rush
Museum purchase   1928.29

John Singer Sargent (1856–1925)
Born in Florence; died London. 1870, attended Academy in Florence. 1874, studied with Emile-Auguste Carolus-Duran in Paris, where he settled. 1879–80, studied old masters Diego Velázquez and Frans Hals, whose painterly styles greatly influenced his own. 1886, moved his studio from Paris to London. Soon became most sought-after painter of fashionable Anglo-American society. 1887, first working visit to U.S. Last twenty-five years were devoted to mural commissions in Boston, his American headquarters. Worked increasingly in watercolor, especially after 1900.

Plate 81
Venice, c. 1902
Watercolor over graphite on off-white wove paper
10 × 14 in. (25.2 × 35.4 cm.)
Signed and dated lower right: to my friend Rolshoven/John S. Sargent
Gift of Mr. and Mrs. Stuart Riley, Jr.
1974.332

Plate 82
Muddy Alligators, 1917
Watercolor over graphite on off-white wove paper
Watermark: WHATMAN
13⁹⁄₁₆ × 20⅞ in. (35.5 × 53 cm.)
Signed and dated lower left: John S. Sargent 1917
Sustaining Membership Fund   1917.86

Plate 83
The Pool, 1917
Watercolor over graphite on off-white wove paper
13⅝ × 20¹⁵⁄₁₆ in. (34.5 × 53.2 cm.)
Signed and dated lower left: John S. Sargent 1917
Sustaining Membership Fund   1917.93

Plate 84
Shady Paths, Vizcaya, 1917
Watercolor over graphite on cream wove paper
15⅝ × 21 in. (39.5 × 53.3 cm.)
Signed and dated lower right: John S. Sargent 1917
Sustaining Membership Fund   1917.88

Plate 85
The Bathers, 1917
Watercolor, gouache over graphite on off-white wove paper
15¾ × 20¾ in. (39.8 × 52.7 cm.)
Signed and dated lower left: John S. Sargent 1917
Sustaining Membership Fund   1917.91

Plate 86
Derelicts, 1917
Watercolor over graphite on off-white wove paper
Watermark: J WHATMAN (partial)
13½ × 21 in. (34.5 × 53.2 cm.)
Signed and dated lower right: John S. Sargent 1917
Sustaining Membership Fund   1917.87

Plate 87
Palms, 1917
Watercolor over graphite on off-white wove paper
15¾ × 21⅞ in. (40 × 55.6 cm.)
Signed and dated lower left: John S. Sargent 1917
Sustaining Membership Fund   1917.89

Plate 88
Boats at Anchor, 1917
Watercolor over graphite on off-white wove paper
15¾ × 20⅞ in. (40.1 × 52.9 cm.)
Signed and dated lower right: John S. Sargent 1917
Sustaining Membership Fund   1917.90

Plate 43
Fish Weirs, 1922
Watercolor over graphite on off-white wove paper
13½ × 21 in. (34.3 × 53.3 cm.)
Signed and dated lower left: John S. Sargent 1922
Gift of Mr. and Mrs. Richard C. Storey in memory of Richard C. Storey, Jr.   1975.674

Edward Savage (1761–1817)
Born and died Princeton, Mass. Originally a goldsmith, became an engraver and painter. Well known as portraitist during the 1780s. 1791–94, studied in London. 1796, established the Columbian Gallery in Philadelphia, moving it to New York in 1802 and to Boston in 1812. Savage painted miniature and life-size portraits, many of which, especially those of George Washington, were engraved and sold widely.

Plate 52A
Falls of the Passaic at Patterson, 1806
Gray wash over charcoal on pale ivory wove paper
Watermark: WD [in script]
9⅞ × 16⅛ in. (24.9 × 41.1 cm.)
Inscribed lower left: falls of Passaic at Patterson July 29, 1806
Museum purchase   1943.42

Savage (continued)

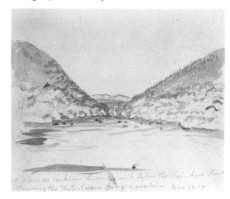

A View on Jackson River, Virginia, 1807
Gray wash over graphite on pale green
wove paper
Watermark: WD [in script]
8⅛ × 9¾ in. (20.7 × 24.8 cm.)
Inscribed across lower edge: a view on
Jacksons River ½ a mile below the Rainbow
Rocks/Shewing the Distent warm Springs
mountains June 1807
Anonymous Fund   1986.9

Plate 52B
Jefferson's Rock, probably 1807
Gray wash over charcoal on ivory wove
paper
Watermark: WD [in script]
8⅛ × 9¾ in. (20.7 × 24.8 cm.)
Inscribed lower left: Jefferson Rock
Museum purchase   1943.43

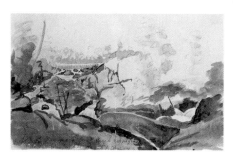

Falls of the Principio Creek, Chesapeake Bay,
1807
Gray wash over graphite on pale green
wove paper
Watermark: WD [in script]
9¾ × 16¼ in. (24.8 × 41.1 cm.)

Inscribed lower left: Falls of Principio a
Small Creek emptying/into the Chesapeake
Bay 9 July 1807
Anonymous Fund   1986.10

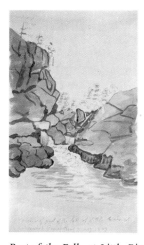

*Part of the Falls at Little River, Norwich,
Connecticut*, 1807
Gray wash, graphite on pale green wove
paper
Watermark: WD [in script]
16¼ × 9¾ in. (41.1 × 24.8 cm.)
Inscribed across lower edge: a view of part
of the falls of Little River at/Norwich, Con-
necticut 8 Aug 1807
Anonymous Fund   1986.11

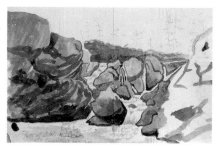

Little River Falls, Norwich, Connecticut,
1807
Gray wash, graphite on pale green wove
paper
Watermark: WD [in script]
9¾ × 16¼ in. (24.8 × 41.1 cm.)
Inscribed lower left: falls of Little River at/
Norwich, Connecticut Aug 1807
Anonymous Fund   1986.12

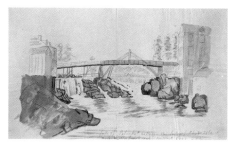

Pawtucket Falls, 1807
Gray wash, graphite on pale green wove
paper
Watermark: WD [in script]
9¾ × 16¼ in. (24.8 × 41.1 cm.)
Inscribed across lower edge: falls of Paw-
tucket between the S[t]ates of Rhode Is-
land/and Massachusetts August 1807 by E.
Savage
Anonymous Fund   1986.13

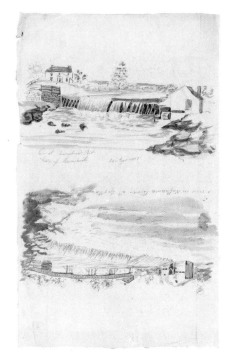

Nashua River, Groton, Massachusetts, 1807
and *Townsend Port, Massachusetts*, 1807
Gray wash, graphite on tan wove paper
Watermark: J LARKING/1806
16½ × 11 in. (41.9 × 27.9 cm.), both
images on one sheet

Savage (continued)
Inscribed across lower edge of each image:
a view on Nashawa River at Grotton Mas-
sachusetts 18 Aug 1807 [and] View at
Townshend Port/State of Massachusetts 18
August 1807
Anonymous Fund   1986.14

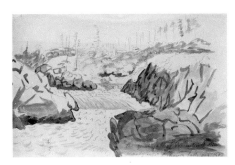

Bellows Falls, **1807**
Gray wash, graphite on tan wove paper
Watermark: J LARKING/1806
10⅜ × 16⅜ in. (26.4 × 41.7 cm.)
Inscribed lower right: the great falls of
Connecticut River/usually called Bellow's
falls Aug 1807
Anonymous Fund   1986.15

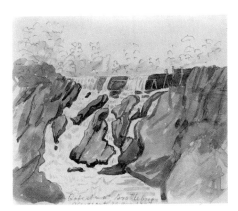

Cascade at Brattleboro, Vermont, **1807**
Gray wash, graphite on pale green wove
paper
Watermark: WD [in script]
8⅛ × 9¾ in. (20.7 × 24.8 cm.)
Inscribed lower edge: Cascade at Brattle-
boro/Vermont 24 Aug 1807
Anonymous Fund   1986.16

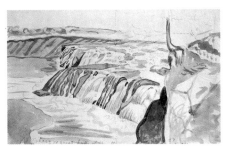

Cohoes Falls, Mohawk River, **1807**
Gray wash, graphite on pale green wove
paper
Watermark: WD [in script]
9¾ × 16⅛ in. (24.8 × 41 cm.)
Inscribed lower edge: The Cohoes or great
falls of the River Mowhawk Aug 27, 1807
Anonymous Fund   1986.17

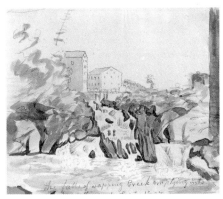

Falls of Wapping Creek, **1807**
Gray wash, graphite on pale green wove
paper
Watermark: WD [in script; partial]
8⅛ × 9¾ in. (20.7 × 24.8 cm.)
Inscribed lower right: the falls of Wapping
Creek emptying into/Hudson River, Sept
1807
Anonymous Fund   1986.18

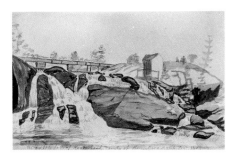

Middle Falls of Kenderhook, **1807**
Gray wash, graphite on tan wove paper
Watermark: J LARKING/1806
10⅜ × 16½ in. (25.3 × 41.9 cm.)
Inscribed lower edge: The middle falls of
Kenderhook county of Rensellaer, N. York
Sept 1807
Anonymous Fund   1986.19

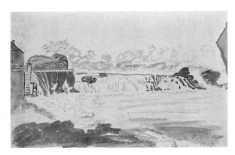

The Upper Falls of Kenderhook, **1807**
Gray wash, graphite on tan wove paper
Watermark: J LARKING/1806
10 × 16⅜ in. (25.2 × 41.7 cm.), with torn
edge
Inscribed lower edge: The upper falls of
Kenderhook a Creek emptying into Hudson
River/by E. Savage 1807
Anonymous Fund   1986.20

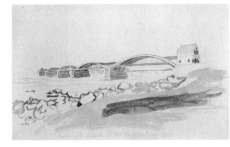

Bridge on the Delaware, **1807**
Gray wash, graphite on tan wove paper
Watermark: J LARKING/1806
10⅛ × 16½ in. (25.6 × 41.9 cm.)
Inscribed lower edge: Bridge on the Dela-
ware at Trenton, New Jersey Sept 1807
Anonymous Fund   1986.21

Savage (continued)

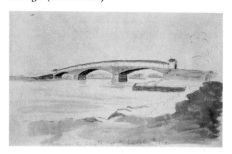

Bridge over the Schuylkill at Philadelphia,
1807
Gray wash, graphite on tan wove paper
Watermark: J LARKING/1806
10⅜ × 16½ in. (26.2 × 41.9 cm.)
Inscribed lower edge: Bridge over the
Schuylkill at Philadelphia Sep 1807
Anonymous Fund   1986.22

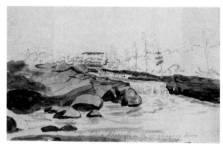

The Falls of the Ohiopyle on the Youghiogheny
River, **1807**
Gray wash, graphite on tan wove paper
Watermark: J LARKING/1806
10 × 16½ in. (25.4 × 41.9 cm.)
Inscribed lower edge: the falls of Ohiopyle
on the Youghiogany River/County of Fay-
ette, Pennsylvania Oct 1807 by E. Savage
Anonymous Fund   1986.23

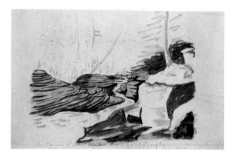

The Narrows of Great Meadow Run, **1807**

Gray wash, graphite on tan wove paper
Watermark: J LARKING/1806
10⅜ × 16½ in. (26.4 × 41.9 cm.)
Inscribed lower edge: the Narrows of great
Meadow Run a branch of Youghiogany
River emptying [illegible] below Ohiopyle
falls Pennsylvania Nov 1807
Anonymous Fund   1986.24

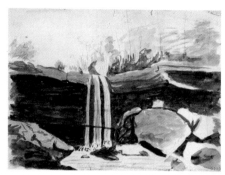

Cucumber Falls, **1807**
Gray wash, graphite on tan wove paper
Watermark: J LARKING/1806
12⅛ × 16½ in. (30.8 × 41.9 cm.)
Inscribed lower edge: the falls of Cucumber
River 100 yards above entrance into the
Youghiogany, Pennsylvania, 1807
Anonymous Fund   1986.25

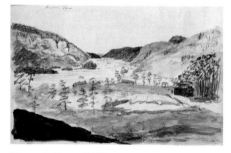

Harper's Ferry, **1807**
Gray wash, graphite on tan wove paper
Watermark: J LARKING/1806
10 × 16⅜ in. (25.3 × 41.8 cm.)
Inscribed in ink upper left: Harper's Ferry
Anonymous Fund   1986.26

George Schreiber (1904–1977)
Born Brussels; died New York. 1920–22,
studied at Arts and Crafts School in Elber-
feld, Germany; at Academy of Fine Arts
in Berlin; 1922, in Düsseldorf; 1923–28,
in London, Florence, Rome, and Paris.
1928, immigrated to New York. 1938, became U.S. citizen. War correspondent during World War II. From 1959, taught at
New School for Social Research, New York.
An author and illustrator of children's
books, poster designer, painter, and
lithographer.

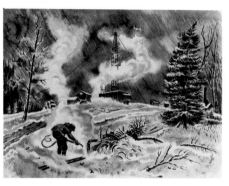

Seepage Lake, **1944**
Watercolor over graphite on off-white wove
paper
20⅝ × 27⅝ in. (52.3 × 70.1 cm.)
Signed and dated lower right: Schreiber/44
Verso: incomplete watercolor
Gift of Esso Standard Oil Company of New
Jersey   1951.100

Truman Seymour (1824–1891)
Born Burlington, Vt.; died Florence. 1842–
46, cadet at U.S. Military Academy at
West Point, where he studied drawing with
Robert W. Weir. 1850–53, became assistant
professor of drawing at West Point. 1852,
married Weir's eldest daughter, Louisa;
became brother-in-law of painters J. Alden
Weir and John F. Weir. 1859, first tour of
Europe. Sketched landscapes, fortifications,
camp scenes throughout his thirty-year
military career. 1877, retired from military
service in Europe. 1880s, worked extensively in watercolor, focusing on street
scenes and architectural views in Seville,
Cordova, Granada, and Florence and on
scenery in the lake region in northern Italy
and Switzerland.

Seymour (continued)

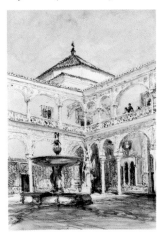

A Courtyard of the Casa de Pilatos, Seville, probably 1884
Watercolor over graphite on cream wove paper
10¹⁵⁄₁₆ × 7⁵⁄₁₆ in. (27.8 × 18.6 cm.)
Gift of the Reverend and Mrs. DeWolf Perry   1986.41

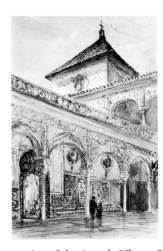

A View of the Casa de Pilatos, Seville, probably 1884
Watercolor over graphite on cream wove paper
11 × 7⅜ in. (27.9 × 18.7 cm.)
Gift of the Reverend and Mrs. DeWolf Perry   1986.42

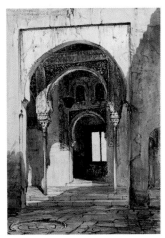

Patio de La Mezquita, 1884
Watercolor over graphite on cream wove paper
13⅛ × 6 in. (33.3 × 15.2 cm.)
Inscribed upper left and verso: Patio de la Mezquita/originally ''del Mexuar'' or of the Council/Oct 2ᵈ 84
Gift of the Reverend and Mrs. DeWolf Perry   1986.43

Charles Sheeler (1883–1965)

Born Philadelphia; died Dobbs Ferry, N.Y. 1900–1903, studied at School of Industrial Art, Philadelphia; 1903–6, at Pennsylvania Academy of the Fine Arts, Philadelphia, and in Europe with William Merritt Chase. 1908–9, visited Italy and Paris. 1912–c. 1932, worked as commercial photographer, specializing in architectural subjects. 1913, exhibited in Armory Show. By 1917, visited the New York salons hosted by Walter Arensberg, where he met European avant-garde artists. 1919, settled in New York. Mid-1930s, turned increasingly from rural and early American to urban, industrial subjects. 1959, a stroke forced him to cease painting.

Plate 105

City Interior No. 2, 1935
Tempera over graphite on off-white wove paper
7⅛ × 9¾ in. (18.2 × 24.7 cm.)
Signed and dated lower right: Sheeler–1935
Gift of William H. and Saundra B. Lane 1977.143

Roswell Morse Shurtleff (1838–1915)

Born Rindge, N.H.; died New York. 1857, B.A. Dartmouth College. 1857, worked in an architect's office in Manchester, N.H.; 1858, as a lithographer in Buffalo, N.Y.; 1859, as a wood engraver's draftsman in Boston. Studied art at Lowell (Mass.) Institute; 1860–61, at National Academy of Design. Maintained a studio in New York, spending summers in the Adirondacks. First worked as illustrator. 1870, began to paint in oils. Shurtleff's early paintings were animal studies; later he focused on landscapes.

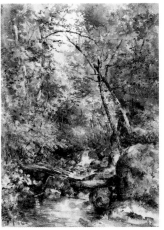

Chapel Brook
Watercolor over graphite on off-white wove paper mounted on chipboard
14 × 10 in. (35.4 × 25.5 cm.)
Signed lower right: R. M. Shurtleff
Gift of Jeanie Lea Southwick   1922.136

Ary Stillman (1891–1967)

Born near Minsk, Russia; died Houston. 1906, studied at Imperial Art School, Vilna. 1907, family immigrated to U.S. 1912, studied painting at Art Institute of Chicago; 1919–21, in New York at National Academy of Design, Art Students League, and Jewish Educational Alliance. 1921–33, studied and traveled in France, North Africa, and Near East. 1933, settled in New York. 1962, moved to Houston. Although his early work was figurative, Stillman turned to abstraction after World War II.

Stillman (continued)

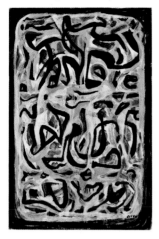

Enchantment, 1962
Gouache on off-white wove paper
20 × 13 in. (50.8 × 32.9 cm.)
Signed lower right: ary
Inscribed verso: 132 . . . Stillman/
Enchantment
Gift of the Stillman-Lack Foundation
1984.37

Dorothy Maria Thurn (b. 1907)
Born Providence, R.I. 1926, studied painting at Rhode Island School of Design with John Goss. 1930–34, member of Rockport Art Association and Providence Watercolor Society. Little else is known about her career.

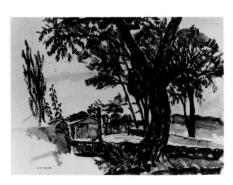

A Tree, c. 1931
Watercolor on off-white wove paper
15¼ × 22¼ in. (38.7 × 56.5 cm.)
Signed lower left: D. M. Thurn
Museum purchase   1932.17

222

Mark Tobey (1890–1976)
Born Centerville, Wis.; died Basel. 1907, studied at Art Institute of Chicago. 1909–17, worked as fashion illustrator in New York, where he studied briefly with Kenneth Hayes Miller. 1918, introduced to Baha'i World Faith. 1922–25, taught at Cornish School, Seattle. 1925–27, traveled in France, Spain, Greece, Turkey, and Near East. 1931–38, resident artist at Dartington Hall, Devonshire, England. 1934, traveled to Far East. 1940s, developed "white writing," a calligraphic style that pervaded his work. 1960, settled in Basel.

Plate 106
The Cycle of the Prophet, 1945
Gouache on off-white paper mounted on composition board
15⅞ × 19¾ in. (40.2 × 50.3 cm.)
Signed and dated lower right: Tobey/45
Inscribed verso: The Cycle
Gift of William H. and Saundra B. Lane
1976.180

Ross Sterling Turner (1847–1915)
Born Westport, N.Y.; died Nassau, Bahamas. Worked as draftsman. Turned to painting. 1876–82, studied in Munich with Frank Currier; 1882–83 in Italy. 1884, settled in Salem, Mass. 1885, opened a studio in Boston, where he taught painting. Frequently traveled to Europe, Mexico, and Bermuda. Wrote several books on watercolor technique.

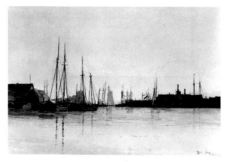

East Gloucester, 1884
Watercolor over graphite on buff wove paper
15⅛ × 23¼ in. (38.3 × 59.1 cm.)
Signed and dated lower right: Ross Turner/
E. Gloucester 84
Gift of Mrs. Kingsmill Marrs   1925.476

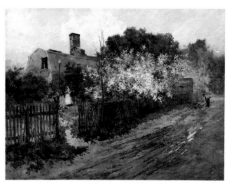

Village Street in Spring, 1893
Watercolor, gouache over graphite on off-white wove paper mounted on cardboard
22 × 28⅛ in. (55.7 × 71.5 cm.)
Signed and dated lower right: Ross Turner
May XCIII
Bequest of Charlotte E. W. Buffington
1935.51

David von Schlegell (b. 1920)
Born St. Louis. 1940–42, studied engineering at University of Michigan. 1946–48, studied painting at Art Students League, New York; 1945–50, with his father William von Schlegell. 1942–43, worked as an aircraft engineer; 1944–45, in an architect's office. 1960, visiting sculptor at University of California, Santa Barbara; 1969–70, at Cornell University. Since 1970, director of sculpture studies at Yale University.

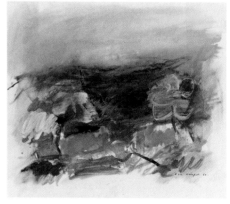

Untitled (landscape), 1964
Watercolor on buff wove paper
17¾ × 22⅜ in. (45 × 56.8 cm.)
Signed and dated lower right: D. von
Schlegell 64

von Schlegell (continued)
Gift of Robert Flynn Johnson in honor of his parents, Dr. and Mrs. Robert A. Johnson   1982.94

Herman Armour Webster (1878–1970)
Born New York; died France. 1900, B.A. Yale University. Studied in Paris with Alphonse Mucha. Reporter for his father's newspaper, *Chicago Record-Herald*. By 1904 resumed art studies in Paris at Académie Julian; left to study etchings of Charles Meryon. Studied etching with Canadian Donald Shaw MacLaughlin. 1908, elected associate of Royal Society of Painter-Etchers. Served with Allied forces during World War I; eyesight severely affected by mustard gas. 1920s, Webster worked chiefly in drawings and watercolors; later he returned to etching and drypoint.

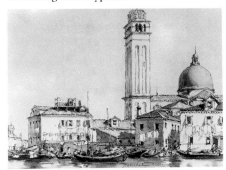

San Pietro di Castello, Venice
Watercolor over brown ink on cream laid paper
6¾ × 9¾ in. (17 × 24.8 cm.)
Signed bottom center: H A Webster
Inscribed on mount: S. Pietro di Castello, Venice
Thomas Hovey Gage Fund   1984.129

John Ferguson Weir (1841–1926)
Born West Point, N.Y.; died Providence, R.I. Son of the painter Robert W. Weir, who taught art at the U.S. Military Academy at West Point; half-brother of Impressionist Julian Alden Weir. 1861, moved to New York and studied at National Academy of Design. 1860s, established reputation with paintings of American industrial scenes. 1868–69, traveled to Europe. 1869–1913, first dean of Yale School of Fine Arts; re-

sponsible for developing art department and art collections. A painter, sculptor, writer, and teacher, Weir painted chiefly portraits and Impressionist landscapes during his later years.

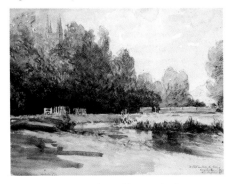

The Itchen, near the College, Winchester, England, 1913
Watercolor, gouache over charcoal on illustration board
10½ × 14½ in. (26.7 × 36.8 cm.)
Inscribed lower left: Winchester College
Inscribed lower right: The Itchen, near the College/Winchester, Engl./Itchen River Sept. 9th '13
Gift of the Reverend and Mrs. DeWolf Perry   1986.44

Cady Wells (1904–1954)
Born Southbridge, Mass.; died Sante Fe, N.M. First trained to be concert pianist. 1925, studied at Harvard University; 1933, at Fogg Art Museum, Cambridge, Mass. 1929–30, worked in stage design with Joseph Urban and Norman Bel Geddes. 1932, studied with Andrew Dasburg in New Mexico; settled in Sante Fe. 1952, traveled to France.

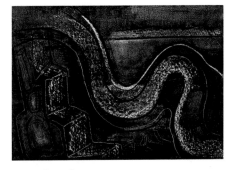

Ground Swell, 1950
Watercolor, ink on white wove paper

10⅝ × 15⅜ in. (27 × 39 cm.)
Signed lower left: C. W.
Signed lower right: Cady Wells
Inscribed verso: #199/Ground Swell
Gift of Mason B. Wells   1983.25

Edwin Whitefield (1816–1892)
Born East Lulworth, Dorset, England; died Dedham, Mass. Studied medicine at his family's insistence but turned to art. About 1840, immigrated to U.S. Traveled throughout North America drawing and subsequently printing views of cities. Published several books with his own illustrations of homes and city views. Whitefield divided his time between teaching, land speculation, and traveling to record the changing landscape and urban life.

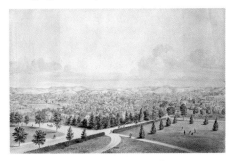

Worcester, Mass., from Union Hill, 1876
Watercolor, ink over graphite on ivory wove paper
25 × 39½ in. (63.5 × 100.3 cm.)
Signed and dated lower left: Sketched from Nature by E. Whitefield 1876
Inscribed lower center: Worcester MASS/ from Union Hill
Anonymous gift   1955.9

William T. Wiley (b. 1937)
Born Bedford, Ind. 1960, B.F.A. and 1962, M.F.A. San Francisco Art Institute. Since 1962, has taught at University of California, Davis, with frequent visiting professorships elsewhere. In mid-1960s, associated with the "Funk" movement. He has cited the influence of the Pacific Northwest Indians, Dada, Giorgio de Chirico, and fellow Californians William Allan and Robert Hudson. Wiley works in a variety of media, frequently including poems, commentary, and word play in his work.

Wiley (continued)
Plate 112
Construct a Vista, 1981
Watercolor, felt-tip marker, graphite on white wove paper
19⅝ × 18¾ in. (50 × 47.2 cm.)
Signed and dated lower left: Wm. T. Wiley/ 1981 ©
Acquired through the National Endowment for the Arts Museum Purchase Plan 1984.133

Douglas Fenn Wilson (b. 1953)
Born Orinda, Calif. 1975, B.A. Dartmouth College. Maintains a studio near San Francisco. Originally influenced by John Singer Sargent and Winslow Homer. His paintings, furniture designs, and sculptures combine both realist images and geometric abstraction.

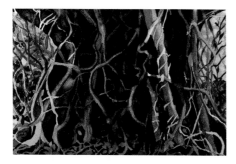

Entangled Banyan, 1975
Watercolor on white wove paper
14¼ × 21⅞ in. (36.1 × 55.5 cm.)
Signed and dated lower left: Douglas Fenn Wilson/1975
Director's Discretionary Fund 1976.124

Charles H. Woodbury (1864–1940)
Born Lynn, Mass.; died Boston. 1886, B.S. in mechanical engineering at M.I.T. 1882–86, attended life classes of Boston Art Club. 1887, began to paint in watercolor. 1890, studied in Paris at Académie Julian. Traveled often to Europe and the West Indies. 1895, taught at Worcester Art Association; 1898–1917 and 1923–39, during summers, at Ogunquit, Me.; 1899–1906 and 1913–14, at Wellesley College. 1900, president of Boston Water Color Club. Also an etcher, lithographer, and illustrator, he is known chiefly as a painter of marine subjects.

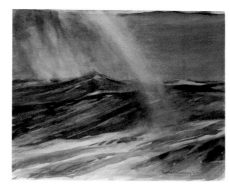

Seascape with Rainbow, 1924
Watercolor on Whatman board
17¼ × 23¼ in. (43.6 × 58.9 cm.)
Signed and dated lower right: Charles H. Woodbury '24
Gift of Edward Kenway 1956.4

Andrew Wyeth (b. 1917)
Born Chadds Ford, Penn. Earliest training from his father, N. C. Wyeth, a painter and illustrator; chiefly self-taught. Frequently visited Maine during childhood. 1937, first one-man show in New York established his reputation as a talented watercolorist, influenced by Winslow Homer. 1939, began to use tempera; first met the Olsons in Cushing, Me., who became important subjects. One of today's most popular realists, Wyeth draws his themes from his immediate surroundings and friends at Chadds Ford and Cushing, his summer home.

Plate 111
The Rope, 1957
Watercolor over graphite on illustration board
20¾ × 12⅝ in. (52.7 × 32.1 cm.)
Signed lower right: Andrew Wyeth
Anonymous promised gift

Mahonri Mackintosh Young (1877–1957)
Born Salt Lake City; died Norwalk, Conn. Studied illustration in Salt Lake City. 1897, studied sculpture with Cyrus Dallin, who had sculpted a monument of Brigham Young, Mahonri's grandfather; 1899, at Art Students League, New York; 1901–3, in Paris. 1903, took up watercolor. 1905, settled in New York. 1913, exhibited in Armory Show. 1916–43, taught at Art Students

League and School of American Sculpture. Young is best known as a realist sculptor.

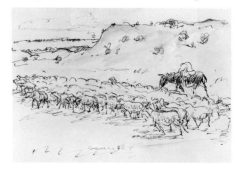

Pony and Rider
Watercolor, brown ink on buff wove paper
5⅞ × 8½ in. (14.8 × 21.6 cm.)
Inscribed bottom center: Granado Oct 8
Museum purchase 1941.12

William Zorach (1889–1966)
Born Eurburick-Kovno, Lithuania; died Bath, Me. 1892, immigrated to U.S. Settled in Cleveland. 1902–12, apprentice to lithographer. 1905–9, studied at Cleveland School of Art; 1909–10, at National Academy of Design, New York; 1910–11, in Paris. Exhibited in 1911 Salon d'Automne and 1913 Armory Show. 1912, married Marguerite Thompson, a painter and textile artist. 1917, began carving wood. 1922, abandoned oil painting. 1929–59, taught sculpture at Art Students League, New York. Primarily a sculptor, Zorach painted watercolor landscapes in his later years.

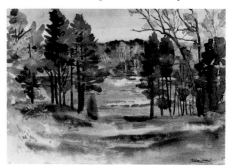

Autumn—Robinhood, Maine, 1960
Watercolor, charcoal on off-white wove paper
15⅜ × 22⅛ in. (39 × 56.3 cm.)
Signed lower right: William Zorach
Gift of the Zorach children in memory of Miriam Pulde 1981.16

Authors and Contributors

Authors of the Essays

Susan E. Strickler, curator of American art at the Worcester Art Museum, has written on a variety of topics in American painting and organized the traveling exhibition that accompanied this publication.

Donelson F. Hoopes, director of the Thomas Cole Foundation in Catskill, New York, has written books on the watercolors of Homer, Sargent, and Eakins as well as the survey *American Watercolor Painting* (New York: Watson-Guptill, 1977).

Judith C. Walsh, paper conservator at the Worcester Art Museum, has worked for museums and private collections since 1977.

Norma Steinberg, who compiled the checklist of this collection, received her M.A. at Tufts University and served as project assistant for this publication.

Contributors to the Entries

CC Carol Clark is adjunct curator of American art at the Sterling and Francine Clark Art Institute and executive fellow of the Maurice and Charles Prendergast Systematic Catalogue Project at Williams College Museum of Art, where she is preparing a catalogue raisonné of the Prendergasts' work.

CT Carol Troyen is associate curator of paintings at the Museum of Fine Arts in Boston. Most recently, she organized the 1987 exhibition *Charles Sheeler: Painter/Photographer* and coauthored the catalogue.

EER Eliza E. Rathbone, associate curator of the Phillips Collection in Washington, D.C., was curator of the 1984 exhibition *Mark Tobey: City Paintings* for the National Gallery of Art, for which she wrote the accompanying catalogue.

GL Gail Levin, curator of the Edward Hopper Collection at the Whitney Museum of American Art from 1978 to 1984, has written several books on the artist.

HAC Helen A. Cooper is curator of American painting and sculpture at the Yale University Art Gallery. In 1986 she organized the most comprehensive exhibition of Winslow Homer's watercolors and wrote the accompanying catalogue.

JLL Judy L. Larson, curator of American art at the High Museum of Art in Atlanta, has written on a variety of aspects of American illustration.

JLY James Leo Yarnall wrote both his master's thesis and Ph.D. dissertation on John La Farge at the University of Chicago and is currently preparing a catalogue raisonné of the artist's work.

KMB Kathleen M. Burnside is currently preparing a catalogue raisonné of Childe Hassam's work with Stuart Feld at Hirshl and Adler Galleries.

NMM Nancy Mowll Mathews, while on sabbatical from Randolph-Macon Woman's College, was a Maurice and Charles Prendergast fellow and curator at the Williams College Museum of Art, where she was preparing a catalogue raisonné of the Prendergasts' work.

PDS Paul D. Schweizer, director of the Munson-Williams-Proctor Institute in Utica, New York, has written widely on nineteenth- and twentieth-century American and British art.

PN Peter Nisbet, assistant curator of the Busch-Reisinger Museum at Harvard University, is a specialist in German and Russian twentieth-century art.

RK Raymond Kass, professor of art at Virginia Polytechnic Institute and State University in Blacksburg, is the author of *Morris Graves: Vision of the Inner Eye*, published for the 1983 exhibition organized by the Phillips Collection, Washington, D.C.

RW Roberta Waddell, formerly curator of prints and drawings at the Worcester Art Museum, currently heads the print department of the New York Public Library.

SCJ Sara C. Junkin wrote her Ph.D. dissertation, ''The Europeanization of Henry Bacon (1839–1912): American Expatriate Painter,'' at Boston University; it is the first in-depth study of this artist.

SES Susan E. Strickler (see above)

TJF Trevor J. Fairbrother, assistant curator of American painting at the Museum of Fine Arts, Boston, wrote his Ph.D. dissertation, ''John Singer Sargent and America,'' at Boston University; it has recently been published by Garland.

WWS Wilford W. Scott, lecturer at the National Gallery of Art, wrote his Ph.D. dissertation, ''The Artistic Vanguard in Philadelphia, 1905–1920,'' at the University of Delaware.

Selected Bibliography

Artists

Henry Bacon

Bacon, Henry. *Parisian Art and Artists.* Boston: James R. Osgood, 1883.

Bacon, Lee. *Our Houseboat on the Nile.* Boston: Houghton Mifflin, 1902.

Catalogue of a Memorial Exhibition of Water Colors of Egypt, Greece, France, Italy, and England, by Henry Bacon. Washington, D.C.: National Gallery of Art, 1931.

Junkin, Sara Caldwell. "The Europeanization of Henry Bacon (1839–1912): American Expatriate Painter." Ph.D. diss., Boston University, 1986.

Frank W. Benson

Downes, William H. "Living American Painters. Part 5: The Spontaneous Gaiety of Frank W. Benson's Work." *Arts and Decoration* 1 (1911): 195–97.

Olney, Susan Faxon. *Two American Impressionists: Frank W. Benson and Edmund C. Tarbell.* Durham, N.H.: University of New Hampshire, 1979.

Ordeman, John T. *Frank W. Benson, Master of the Sporting Print.* Brooklandville, Md.: privately printed, 1983.

Carolyn Brady

Ffrench-Frazier, Nina. "Carolyn Brady." *Art International* 24 (September–October 1980): 183–89.

Singer, Alan D. "Carolyn Brady." *American Artist* 49 (May 1985): 36–41, 93–95.

Charles Burchfield

Baigell, Matthew. *Charles Burchfield.* New York: Watson-Guptill, 1976.

Baur, John I. H. *The Inlander: Life and Work of Charles Burchfield, 1893–1967.* East Brunswick, N.J.: Associated University Presses; London: Cornwall Books, 1982.

Trovato, Joseph S. *Charles Burchfield: Catalogue of Paintings in Public and Private Collections.* Utica, N.Y.: Munson-Williams-Proctor Institute, 1970.

Walter Appleton Clark

Glaenzer, Richard Butler. "Walter Appleton Clark: An Appreciation." *International Studio* 31 (April 1907): xxxiii–xli.

Hambridge, Jay. "Walter Appleton Clark." *Book Buyer* 18 (April 1899): 211–15.

Sargent, David C. *Walter Appleton Clark.* Canton, Conn.: privately printed, 1981.

Jasper F. Cropsey

Bermingham, Peter. *Jasper F. Cropsey, 1823–1900: A Retrospective View of America's Painter of Autumn.* College Park, Md.: University of Maryland, 1968.

Rebora, Carrie. *Jasper F. Cropsey Watercolors.* New York: National Academy of Design, 1985.

Talbot, William S. *Jasper F. Cropsey, 1823–1900.* New York: Garland Publishing, 1977.

Arthur B. Davies

Burroughs, Bryson. Introduction to *Arthur B. Davies Memorial Exhibition.* New York: Metropolitan Museum of Art, 1930.

Czestochowski, Joseph S. *The Works of Arthur B. Davies.* Chicago: University of Chicago Press, 1979.

Gordon, John, and Prior, Harris K. *Arthur B. Davies (1862–1928): A Centennial Exhibition.* Utica, N.Y.: Munson-Williams-Proctor Institute, 1962.

Wright, Brooks. *The Artist and the Unicorn: The Lives of Arthur B. Davies (1862–1928).* Rockland, N.Y.: Historical Society of Rockland County, 1978.

Lyonel Feininger

Campbell, Sara, ed. *The Blue Four: Galka Scheyer Collection.* Pasadena, Calif.: Norton Simon Museum of Art, 1976.

Hess, Hans. *Lyonel Feininger.* New York: Harry N. Abrams, 1961.

Ness, June L., ed. *Lyonel Feininger: Documentary Monographs in Modern Art Series.* New York: Praeger Publishers, 1974.

Morris Graves

Kass, Raymond. *Morris Graves: Vision of the Inner Eye.* Washington, D.C.: Phillips Collection; New York: George Braziller, 1983.

Ross, Nancy Wilson, et al. *Morris Graves: A Retrospective.* Eugene, Ore.: University of Oregon Museum of Art, 1966.

Childe Hassam

Adams, Adeline. *Childe Hassam.* New York: American Academy of Arts and Letters, 1938.

Childe Hassam, 1859–1935. East Hampton, N.Y.: Guild Hall Museum, 1981.

Haskell, Ernest. *Exhibition of a Retrospective Group of Paintings Representative of the Life Work of Childe Hassam, N.A.* Buffalo, N.Y.: Buffalo Fine Arts Academy, Albright Art Gallery, 1929.

Stavitsky, Gail. "Childe Hassam in the Collection of the Museum of Art, Carnegie Institute." *Carnegie Magazine* 6, no. 4 (July–August 1982): 27–39.

Steadman, William E. Introduction to *Childe Hassam, 1859–1935.* Tucson: University of Arizona Museum of Art, 1972.

John William Hill

Ferber, Linda S., and Gerdts, William H. *The New Path: Ruskin and the American Pre-Raphaelites.* Brooklyn, N.Y.: Brooklyn Museum, 1985.

Hill, John Henry, ed. *John William Hill: An Artist's Memorial.* New York: privately printed, 1888.

Koke, Richard J. *American Landscape and Genre Paintings in the New York Historical Society.* 3 vols. Boston: G. K. Hall, 1982.

Winslow Homer

Beam, Philip C. *Winslow Homer Watercolors.* Brunswick, Me.: Bowdoin College Museum of Art, 1983.

Cooke, Hereward Lester. "The Development of Winslow Homer's Water-Color Technique," *Art Quarterly* 24 (Summer 1961): 169–94.

Cooper, Helen A. *Winslow Homer Watercolors.* Washington, D.C.: National Gallery of Art; New Haven, Conn.: Yale University Press, 1986.

Goodrich, Lloyd. *Winslow Homer.* New York: Macmillan, 1945.

Hendricks, Gordon. *The Life and Work of Winslow Homer.* New York: Harry N. Abrams, 1979.

Hoopes, Donelson. *Winslow Homer Watercolors.* New York: Watson-Guptill, 1969.

Edward Hopper

Goodrich, Lloyd. *Edward Hopper.* New York: Whitney Museum of American Art, 1964.

———. *Selections from the Hopper Bequest to the Whitney Museum of American Art.* New York: Whitney Museum of American Art, 1971.

Levin, Gail. *Edward Hopper: The Art and the Artist.* New York: W. W. Norton, 1981.

Earl Horter

d'Harnoncourt, Anne. "Earl Horter." In *Philadelphia: Three Centuries of American Art,* 523–24. Philadelphia: Philadelphia Museum of Art, 1976.

Pitz, Henry C. "Earl Horter: The Man and His Work." *American Artist* 20 (April 1956): 20–26, 66.

Rockwell Kent

Johnson, Fridolf. *Rockwell Kent: An Anthology of His Works.* New York: Alfred A. Knopf, 1982.

Kent, Rockwell. *It's Me O Lord: The Autobiography of Rockwell Kent.* New York: Dodd, Mead, 1955.

Traxel, David. *An American Saga: The Life and Times of Rockwell Kent.* New York: Harper & Row, 1980.

West, Richard V. *"An Enkindled Eye": The Paintings of Rockwell Kent.* Santa Barbara, Calif.: Santa Barbara Museum of Art, 1985.

John La Farge

Weinberg, H. Barbara. *The Decorative Work of John La Farge.* New York: Garland Publishing, 1977.

Yarnall, James L. "The Role of Landscape in the Art of John La Farge." Ph.D. diss., University of Chicago, 1981.

Reginald Marsh

Cohen, Marilyn. *Reginald Marsh's New York: Paintings, Drawings, Prints and Photographs.* New York: Dover Publications, 1984.

Goodrich, Lloyd. *Reginald Marsh.* New York: Harry N. Abrams, 1972.

Laning, Edward. *The Sketchbooks of Reginald Marsh.* Greenwich, Conn.: New York Graphic Society, 1973.

Maurice B. Prendergast

Green, Eleanor. *Maurice Prendergast: Art of Impulse and Color.* College Park, Md.: University of Maryland Art Gallery, 1976.

"Mr. Prendergast's Water Colors and Monotypes at the Macbeth Gallery," *Evening Sun* (New York), March 13, 1900, p. 4.

Owens, Gwendolyn. *Watercolors by Maurice Prendergast from New England Collections.* Williamstown, Mass.: Sterling and Francine Clark Art Institute, 1978.

Rhys, Hedley Howell. *Maurice Prendergast, 1859–1924.* Boston: Museum of Fine Arts, 1960.

Wick, Peter A. "A Critical Note." In *Maurice B. Prendergast Watercolor Sketchbook, 1899* (facsimile edition for the Museum of Fine Arts, Boston). Cambridge, Mass.: Harvard University Press, 1960.

John Singer Sargent

Blaugrund, Annette. " 'Sunshine Recaptured': The Development and Dispersement of Sargent's Watercolors." In Patricia Hills, *John Singer Sargent.* New York: Whitney Museum of American Art and Harry N. Abrams, 1986.

Hoopes, Donelson F. *Sargent Watercolors.* New York: Watson-Guptill, 1970.

Ormond, Richard. *John Singer Sargent: Paintings, Drawings, Watercolors.* New York: Harper & Row, 1970.

Ratcliff, Carter. *John Singer Sargent.* New York: Abbeville Press, 1982.

Stokes, Adrian. "John Singer Sargent, R.A., R.W.S." *Old Water-Colour Society Club Third Annual Volume.* Ed. Randall Davies, F.S.A. (London: Chiswick Press, 1926), pp. 51–65.

Edward Savage

Dickson, Harold E. "The Great Savage." In *John Wesley Jarvis: American Painter, 1780–1840,* 35–57. New York: New-York Historical Society, 1949.

Dresser, Louisa. "Edward Savage, Painter, 1761–1817." *Art in America* 40, no. 4 (Autumn 1952): 157–212.

Hart, Charles Henry. *Edward Savage, Painter and Engraver.* Boston: Massachusetts Historical Society, 1905.

Charles Sheeler

Dochterman, Lillian N. "The Stylistic Development of the Works of Charles Sheeler." Ph.D. diss., State University of Iowa, 1963.

Friedman, Martin. *Charles Sheeler.* New York: Watson-Guptill, 1975.

Friedman, Martin; Hayes, Bartlett; and Millard, Charles. *Charles Sheeler.* Washington, D.C.: National Collection of Fine Arts, Smithsonian Institution, 1968.

Jacob, Mary Jane, and Downs, Linda. *The Rouge: The Image of Industry in the Art of Charles Sheeler and Diego Rivera*. Detroit: Detroit Institute of Arts, 1978.

Troyen, Carol, and Stebbins, Theodore E. *Charles Sheeler: Painter/Photographer*. Boston: Museum of Fine Arts, 1987.

Mark Tobey

Rathbone, Eliza E. *Mark Tobey, City Paintings*. Washington, D.C.: National Gallery of Art, 1984.

Russell, John. *Mark Tobey*. Basel: Editions Beyeler, 1971.

Seitz, William C. *Mark Tobey*. New York: Museum of Modern Art, 1962.

Taylor, Joshua C. *Tribute to Mark Tobey*. Washington, D.C.: National Collection of Fine Arts, Smithsonian Institution, 1974.

William T. Wiley

Beal, Graham, and Perreault, John. *Wiley Territory*. Minneapolis: Walker Art Center, 1979.

Lindberg, Ted. *William T. Wiley*. Vancouver, B.C.: Emily Carr College of Art; New York: Allan Frumkin Gallery, 1982.

Richardson, Brenda. *William T. Wiley*. Berkeley: University Art Museum, 1971.

Stewart, Albert. *William T. Wiley*. Tallahassee: Florida State University, University Fine Arts Galleries, 1981.

Andrew Wyeth

Corn, Wanda. *The Art of Andrew Wyeth*. Greenwich, Conn.: New York Graphic Society, 1973.

Hoving, Thomas. Interview with the artist. In *Two Worlds of Andrew Wyeth: Kuerners and Olsons*. New York: Metropolitan Museum of Art, 1976.

Mongan, Agnes. *Andrew Wyeth: Dry Brush and Pencil Drawings*. Cambridge, Mass.: Fogg Art Museum, Harvard University, 1963.

Wyeth, Betsy. *Christina's World*. Boston: Houghton Mifflin, 1982.

General

Adams, Henry, et al. *American Drawings and Watercolors in the Museum of Art, Carnegie Institute*. Pittsburgh: Carnegie Institute, 1985.

Arthur, John. *Realist Drawings and Watercolors: Contemporary American Works on Paper*. Boston: New York Graphic Society, 1980.

Baker, Kenneth. "New American Watercolour." *Portfolio* 4 (October 1982): 66–75.

Blaugrund, Annette, comp. *American Watercolors, Pastels, Collages: A Complete Illustrated Listing of Works in the Brooklyn Museum's Collection*. Brooklyn: Brooklyn Museum, 1984.

Burroughs, Alan. Introduction to *A History of American Watercolor Painting*. New York: Whitney Museum of American Art, 1942.

Clement, Clara Erskine, and Hutton, Laurence. *Artists of the Nineteenth Century and Their Works*. Boston: Houghton Osgood, 1879.

Cohn, Marjorie B. *Wash and Gouache: A Study of the Development of the Materials of Watercolor*. Cambridge, Mass.: Fogg Art Museum, Harvard University, Center for Conservation and Technical Studies; and Foundation of the American Institute for Conservation, 1977.

Doerner, Max. *The Materials of the Artist and Their Use in Painting, with Notes on the Techniques of the Old Masters*. Translated by Eugen Neuhaus. New York: Harcourt, Brace, 1934.

Drepperd, Carl W. "American Drawing Books." *New York Public Library Bulletin* 49, no. 11 (November 1945): 795–812.

Fabri, Ralph. *History of the American Watercolor Society: The First Hundred Years*. New York: American Watercolor Society, 1969.

Feld, Stuart P. Foreword to *Two Hundred Years of Watercolor Painting in America: An Exhibition Commemorating the Centennial of the American Watercolor Society*. New York: Metropolitan Museum of Art and American Watercolor Society, 1967.

Finch, Christopher. *American Watercolors*. New York: Abbeville Press, 1986.

Foster, Kathleen A. "Makers of the American Watercolor Movement, 1860–1890." Ph.D. diss., Yale University, 1982.

Gallatin, Albert Eugene. *American Water-Colourists*. New York: E. P. Dutton, 1922.

Gardner, Albert Ten Eyck. *A History of Water Color Painting in America*. New York: Reinhold, 1966.

Gervasè, Frank A. "A History of the American Water Color Society, 1866–1950." Manuscript in the possession of the American Watercolor Society, New York.

Hardie, Martin. *Water-colour Painting in Britain*. 3 vols. London: B. T. Batsford; New York: Barnes & Noble, 1966–68.

Hoopes, Donelson F. *American Watercolor Painting*. New York: Watson-Guptill, 1977.

Le Clair, Charles. *The Art of Watercolor Techniques and New Directions*. Englewood Cliffs, N.J.: Prentice-Hall, 1985.

Lee, Sherman E. "A Critical Survey of American Watercolor Painting." Ph.D. diss., Case Western Reserve University, 1941.

Martin, Alvin. *American Realism: Twentieth-Century Drawings and Watercolors from the Glenn C. Janss Collection*. San Francisco: San Francisco Museum of Modern Art; New York: Harry N. Abrams, 1986.

Oresman, Janice C. *Twentieth Century American Watercolor*. Hamilton, N.Y.: Gallery Association of New York State, 1983.

Reynolds, Graham. *A Concise History of Watercolor*. New York: Transatlantic, 1974.

Rossiter, Henry P. Introduction to *American Water Colors and Drawings, 1800–1875 (M. & M. Karolik Collection)*. Boston: Museum of Fine Arts, 1962.

"Selection One: American Watercolors and Drawings from the Museum's Collection." *Bulletin of the Rhode Island School of Design: Museum Notes* 58 (January 1972): 1–75.

Simmons, Linda Crocker. *American Drawings, Watercolors, Pastels, and Collages in the Collection of the Corcoran Gallery of Art*. Washington, D.C.: Corcoran Gallery of Art, 1983.

Stebbins, Theodore E., Jr. *American Master Drawings and Watercolors: A History of Works on Paper from Colonial Times to the Present*. New York: Harper & Row, 1976.

Index

229

231

Photography Credits
All photographs of works in the Worcester Art Museum are by Ron White. The photographers and the sources of additional photographs other than those indicated in the captions are as follows: Bowdoin College Museum of Art, Brunswick, Maine, plate 15; Courtesy Coe Kerr Gallery, New York, plate 48; Isabella Stewart Gardner Museum, Boston, plate 49; R. B. Hoit, plate 85a; New York Public Library, plate 14; Ormond Family, plate 41; Pennsylvania Academy of the Fine Arts Archives, plate 3; private collection, plate 6; Worcester Art Museum archives, plates 4, 5, and 18.

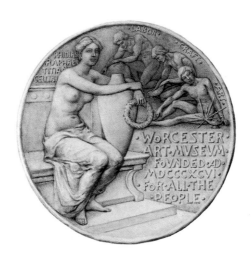